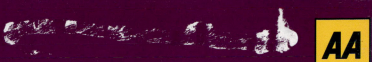

AA

Where to Stay and Eat in Scotland 2012

AA Lifestyle Guides

Please contact:
Advertising Sales Department: advertisingsales@theAA.com
Editorial Department: lifestyleguides@theAA.com
AA Hotel Scheme Enquiries: 01256 844455

AA Media Limited would like to thank the following photographers, companies and picture libraries for their assistance in the preparation of this book. Abbreviations for the picture credits are as follows: (t) top; (b) bottom; (l) left; (r) right; (c) centre; (AA) AA World Travel Library.

Cover photos:
Front cover: (t) Turnberry Resort; (bl) Burt's Hotel; (br) Dalmunzie Castle. Back cover: AA/S Whitehorne

Every effort has been made to trace the copyright holders, and we apologise in advance for any unintentional omissions or errors. We would be pleased to apply any corrections in a following edition of this publication.

Printed and bound by DZS Grafik, d.o.o, Slovenia

This directory is compiled by AA Lifestyle Guides; managed in the Librios Information Management System and generated by the AA establishment database system.

Published by AA Publishing, a trading name of AA Media Limited, whose registered office is Fanum House, Basing View, Basingstoke, Hampshire RG21 4EA.
Registered number 06112600

A CIP catalogue record for this book is available from the British Library

ISBN-13: 978-0-7495-7199-3
A04841

Maps prepared by the
Mapping Services Department of
AA Publishing.

Maps © AA Media Limited 2011.

Contains Ordnance Survey data
© Crown copyright and database right 2011.

Information on National Parks in Scotland provided by Scottish Natural Heritage.

Contents

Welcome to the third edition of Where to Stay and Eat in Scotland.

This book includes all the Scottish establishments currently held in our database. These Hotels, B&Bs, Restaurants and Pubs all belong to our rating schemes (see page 6) or appeared in the 2012 editions of the AA Hotel Guide, AA B&B Guide, AA Restaurant Guide or AA Pub Guide. The guide is arranged in county order, with the Scottish Islands as a section in their own right at the end.

In order to make the guide easier to use, we have in some cases combined our Hotel or B&B guide entry (concerned mostly with describing the establishment's accommodation), with their Restaurant or Pub guide information (concerned chiefly with describing the food).

Throughout the guide you will notice that Star ratings for Hotels and Guest Accommodation, and Rosette awards which are given for food. Although pubs are not rated, they are chosen for having good beer, excellent food, a wonderful location or a combination of all three.

We hope you will find this guide useful when exploring Scotland's many beautiful and historic towns and regions. Scottish hospitality is renowned, and amongst the establishments in this book are some of the best hotels and restaurants in Britain.

Please note: Hotels appear first within a location, in order of star rating. If they have Rosettes for their restaurant (see page 10) then their restaurant details will appear with the Hotel entry. Next in sequence are Restaurants with Rooms, followed by Guest Accommodation (including Rosetted restaurant information if appropriate) then stand-alone Restaurants, and finally Pubs.

If the establishment name appears in italics, this means we did not receive updated information from the establishment for 2012. With restaurants, limited details (usually just opening times) also indicate that we did not receive an update. It is always a good idea to telephone an establishment in advance of your visit to ensure that your expectations will be met.

LOCATION   Map reference

Name of Establishment

★★★★★ ACCOMMODATION TYPE DESIGNATOR

 Cuisine Type **V** 🍷

Strapline giving a brief summary (restaurants only)

☎ telephone number 📠 fax number
Address, including postcode for SatNav
e-mail: emailaddress@establishment.com
web: www.establishment-website.com
dir: Directions to help you reach the establishment, provided by the establishment themselves.

A description of the establishment which will usually include information on the location and area, the type of building, the bedrooms and some of their facilities, the food operation and representative dishes, and anything else that may be relevant.

[Hotel/Guest Accommodation Information]
Rooms Number of bedrooms (1 GF)=1 room on Ground Floor, (1 fmly)=1 family room; **S** Single room price range **D** Double room price range **Facilities** offered by the establishment
Conf Information on conference facilities **Services** such as Lift or Air Con **Parking** number of parking spaces available to guests/customers **Notes** Other information which may be useful

[Restaurant Information]
Chef Name of chef **Owner** Name of owners **Restaurant Times** When restaurant is open during the year, and times it is open during the day **Prices** A guide to meal prices
Wines Number of bottles under £20 and how many available by the glass **Notes** other relevant information including Vegetarian menu **Seats** number of covers **Children** Special facilities for children including own menu

[Pub information]
Open Times that pub is open during the day and during the year **Bar Meals** Serving times for lunch and dinner in the bar, average cost of main course **Restaurant** Serving times for lunch and dinner in the restaurant, average cost of 3 course à la carte
⊕ OWNER/BREWERY ◀ Principal Beers and ⚫ Ciders
🍷 Number of wines available by the glass **Facilities** offered by the establishment

★ Black stars
★ Red stars = AA Inspectors' Choice
★ Yellow stars = Highly Commended
◉ AA Rosettes = AA Award for Food
For full explanation of AA ratings and awards see page 6
V Vegetarian menu
☝ Indicates the use of local and regional produce. More than 50% of the restaurant food ingredients are produced within a 50-mile radius. Suppliers are mentioned by name on the menu.
🍷 NOTABLE WINE LIST Notable wine list (see page 10)
% Inspector's Merit score (see page 7)
Ⓐ Associate Establishments
Ⓤ Star rating not confirmed
☎ Phone number
🖹 Fax number
🛎 A very special breakfast, with an emphasis on freshly prepared local ingredients (Guest accommodation only)
🍽 A very special dinner, with an emphasis on freshly prepared local ingredients (Guest accommodation only)
fmly Number of family rooms available
GF Ground floors rooms available
rms Bedrooms in main building
smoking Number of bedrooms allocated for smokers
pri facs Bedroom with separate private facilities (Restaurant with Rooms & Guest Accommodation only)
S Single room
D Double room (2 people sharing)
* 2011 prices
fr From
incl. bkfst Breakfast included in the price (Hotels only)

TVL Lounge with television
FTV Freeview television
STV Satellite television
Wi-fi Wireless network connection
⊖ Credit cards not accepted
tea/coffee Tea and coffee making facilities
Etr Easter
Air con Air conditioning
🏊 Heated indoor swimming pool
🏊 Outdoor swimming pool
🏊 Heated outdoor swimming pool
🎵 Entertainment
Child facilities Children's facilities (see page 10)
Xmas New Year Special programme for Christmas/New Year
🎾 Tennis court
🏑 Croquet lawn
⛳ Putting green
Conf Conference facilities
Thtr Number of theatre style seats
Class Number of classroom style seats
Board Number of boardroom style seats
🚫 No dogs allowed (guide dogs for the blind and assist dogs should be allowed)
No Children Children cannot be accommodated. If this is followed by a number (e.g. 11 yrs) this means that children under 11 cannot be accommodated.
RS Restricted opening times
Civ Wed Establishment licensed for civil weddings (+ maximum number of guests at ceremony)
LB Special leisure breaks available
Spa Hotel has its own spa
🍷 If this appears by the pub name it means that more than 6 wines by the glass are available
🍺 Principal beers served by the pub
🍶 Principal ciders served by the pub
⊕ Owner or brewery

AA RATINGS EXPLAINED

AA Accommodation Classifications

AA Assessment

In collaboration with VisitBritain, VisitScotland and VisitWales, the AA developed Common Quality Standards for inspecting and rating accommodation. These standards and rating categories are now applied throughout the British Isles.

Any hotel or guest accommodation establishment applying for AA recognition receives an unannounced visit from an AA inspector to check standards. The establishments with full entries in this guide have all paid an annual fee for AA inspection, recognition and rating.

If an establishment changes hands, the new owners must reapply for classification, as standards may change.

AA inspectors pay as a guest for their inspection visit, they do not accept free hospitality of any kind.

HOTELS

★ One Star

Polite, courteous staff providing a relatively informal yet competent style of service, available during the day and evening to receive guests
- At least one designated eating area open to residents for breakfast
- If dinner is offered it should be on at least five days a week, with last orders no earlier than 6.30pm
- Television in bedroom
- Majority of rooms en suite, bath or shower room available at all times

★★ Two Star

As for one star, plus
- At least one restaurant or dining room open to residents for breakfast (and for dinner at least five days a week)
- Last orders for dinner no earlier than 7pm
- En suite or private bath or shower and WC

★★★ Three Star

- Management and staff smartly and professionally presented and usually uniformed
- A dedicated receptionist on duty at peak times
- At least one restaurant or dining room open to residents and non-residents for breakfast and dinner whenever the hotel is open
- Last orders for dinner no earlier than 8pm
- Remote-control television, direct-dial telephone
- En suite bath or shower and WC

★★★★ Four Star

- A formal, professional staffing structure with smartly presented, uniformed staff anticipating and responding to your needs or requests Usually spacious, well-appointed public areas
- Reception staffed 24 hours by well-trained staff
- Express checkout facilities where appropriate
- Porterage available on request
- Night porter available
- At least one restaurant open to residents and non-residents for breakfast and dinner seven days per week, and lunch to be available in a designated eating area
- Last orders for dinner no earlier than 9pm
- En suite bath with fixed overhead shower and WC

★★★★★ Five Star

- Luxurious accommodation and public areas with a range of extra facilities. First time guests shown to their bedroom
- Multilingual service
- Guest accounts well explained and presented
- Porterage offered
- Guests greeted at hotel entrance, full concierge service provided
- At least one restaurant open to residents and non-residents for all meals seven days per week
- Last orders for dinner no earlier than 10pm
- High-quality menu and wine list
- Evening service to turn down the beds. Remote-control television, direct-dial telephone at bedside and desk, a range of luxury toiletries, bath sheets and robes. En suite bathroom incorporating fixed overhead shower and WC

★ Inspectors' Choice

Each year we select the best hotels in each rating. These hotels stand out as the very best in the British Isles, regardless of style.

Merit Score (%)

AA inspectors supplement their hotel reports with an additional quality assessment of everything a hotel provides, including hospitality, based on their findings as a 'mystery guest'. This wider ranging quality assessment results in an overall Merit Score which is shown as a percentage beside the hotel name. When making your selection of hotel accommodation this enables you to see at a glance that a three star hotel with a Merit Score of 79% offers a higher standard overall than one in the same star classification but with a Merit Score of 69%. To gain AA recognition, a hotel must achieve a minimum score of 50%.

Types of hotel

A 'designator' is used to tell you more about the style of establishment. Most hotels choose the Hotel designator; other categories are listed below.

TOWN HOUSE HOTEL A small, individual city or town centre property, which provides a high degree of personal service and privacy

COUNTRY HOUSE HOTEL These are quietly located in a rural area

SMALL HOTEL Has fewer than 20 bedrooms and is owner-managed

METRO HOTEL A hotel in an urban location that does not offer an evening meal

BUDGET HOTEL These are usually purpose built modern properties offering inexpensive accommodation. Often located near motorways and in town or city centres

NB Although AA inspectors do not stay overnight at Budget Hotels they do carry out regular visits to verify standards and procedures.

Guest Accommodation

AA Stars classify guest accommodation at five levels of quality, from one at the simplest, to five offering the highest quality. In order to achieve a one or two Star rating an establishment must meet certain minimum entry requirements, including:
- A cooked breakfast, or substantial continental option is provided.
- The proprietor and/or staff are available for your arrival, departure and at all meal times.
- Once registered, you have access to the establishment at all times unless previously notified.
- All areas of operation meet minimum quality requirements for cleanliness, maintenance and hospitality as well as facilities and the delivery of services.
- A dining room or similar eating area is available unless meals are only served in bedrooms.

Our research shows that quality is very important to visitors. To obtain a higher Star rating, an establishment must provide increased quality standards across all areas, with particular emphasis in four key areas:
- Cleanliness and housekeeping
- Hospitality and service
- Quality and condition of bedrooms, bathrooms and public rooms
- Food quality

There are also particular requirements in order for an establishment to achieve three, four or five Stars, for example:

★★★ Three Stars and above
- access to both sides of all beds for double occupancy
- bathrooms/shower rooms cannot be used by the proprietor
- there is a washbasin in every guest bedroom (either in the bedrooms or the en suite/private facility)

★★★★ Four Stars
- half of bedrooms must be en suite or have private facilities

★★★★★ Five Stars
- all bedrooms must be en suite or have private facilities

Guests can expect to find the following minimum standards at all levels:
- Pleasant and helpful welcome and service, and sound standards of housekeeping and maintenance
- Comfortable accommodation equipped to modern standards
- Bedding and towels changed for each new guest, and at least weekly if the room is taken for a long stay
- Adequate storage, heating, lighting and comfortable seating
- A sufficient hot water supply at reasonable times
- A full cooked breakfast. (If this is not provided, the fact must be advertised and a substantial continental breakfast must be offered)

When an AA inspector has visited a property, and evaluated all the aspects of the accommodation for comfort, facilities, attention to detail and presentation, you can be confident the Star rating will allow you to make the right choice for an enjoyable stay.

★ Highly Commended
Yellow Stars indicate that an establishment is in the top ten percent of its Star rating. Yellow Stars only apply to 3, 4 or 5 Star guest accommodation establishments.

Types of Guest Accommodation

A 'designator' is used to tell you more about the style of establishment.

B&B

A private house run by the owner with accommodation for no more than six paying guests.

GUEST HOUSE

Run on a more commercial basis than a B&B, the accommodation provides for more than six paying guests and there are usually more services; for example staff as well as the owner may provide dinner.

FARMHOUSE

The B&B or guest house accommodation is part of a working farm or smallholding.

INN

The accommodation is provided in a fully licensed establishment. The bar will be open to non-residents and can provide food in the evenings.

RESTAURANT WITH ROOMS

This is a destination restaurant offering overnight accommodation, with dining being the main business and open to non-residents. The restaurant should offer a high standard of food and restaurant service at least five nights a week. A liquor licence is necessary and there is a maximum of 12 bedrooms.

GUEST ACCOMMODATION

Any establishment that meets the minimum entry requirements is eligible for this general category.

Other useful information

- **A** These are establishments that have not been inspected by the AA but which have been inspected by VisitScotland. An establishment marked as "Associate" has paid to belong to either the AA Associate Hotel Scheme or the AA Associate Guest Accommodation Scheme and therefore receives a limited entry in the guide. Descriptions of these establishments can be found on the AA website.*
- **U** A small number of establishments in the guide have this symbol because their Star classification was not confirmed at the time of going to press. This may be due to a change of ownership or because they have only recently joined the AA rating scheme.

* Check the AA website **theAA.com** for current information and ratings

AA ROSETTES & WINE AWARDS

AA Rosette Awards

Out of the many thousands of restaurants in the UK, the AA identifies over 1,900 as the best. The following is an outline of what to expect from restaurants with AA Rosette Awards.

⬤ Excellent local restaurants serving food prepared with care, understanding and skill, using good quality ingredients.

⬤⬤ The best local restaurants, which aim for and achieve higher standards, better consistency and where a greater precision is apparent in the cooking. There will be obvious attention to the selection of quality ingredients.

⬤⬤⬤ Outstanding restaurants that demand recognition well beyond their local area.

⬤⬤⬤⬤ Amongst the very best restaurants in the British Isles, where the cooking demands national recognition.

⬤⬤⬤⬤⬤ The finest restaurants in the British Isles, where the cooking stands comparison with the best in the world.

The AA Wine Awards

The annual AA wine award, sponsored again by T&W Wines, attracted a huge response from our AA recognised restaurants with over 1,000 wine lists submitted for judging. Three national winners were chosen – La Trompette, London, England, Rhubarb – The Restaurant at Prestonfield, Edinburgh, Scotland, and The Bell at Skenfrith, Skenfrith, Wales. The Bell at Skenfrith was selected as the Overall Winner, and a member of their wine team wins an all-expenses-paid trip to Willi Opitz's vineyards at Illmitz in Austria's Burgenland.

All 2,000 or so Rosetted restaurants in last year's guide were invited to submit their wine lists. From these the panel selected a shortlist of 230 establishments throughout Britain. Of these, around 37 appear in this guide, highlighted with the Notable Wine List symbol

NOTABLE WINE LIST

The shortlisted establishments were asked to choose wines from their list (within a budget of £70 per bottle) to accompany a menu designed by Tim Hart, last year's winner, and proprietor of Hambleton Hall, Rutland.

The final judging panel included:–
Simon Numphud, AA Hotel Services Manager, Tim Hart of Hambleton Hall, Trevor Hughes, Managing Director of T&W Wines (our sponsor) and Fiona Sims, an independent wine journalist.

Notable Wine Lists

What makes a wine list notable?
We are looking for high-quality wines, with diversity across grapes and/or countries and style, the best individual growers and vintages.

The list should be well presented, ideally with some helpful notes and, to reflect the demand from diners, a good choice of wines by the glass. What disappoints the judges are spelling errors, wines listed under incorrect regions or styles, split vintages (which are still far too common), lazy purchasing (all wines from a country from just one grower or negociant) and confusing layouts. Sadly, many restaurants still do not pay much attention to wine, resulting in ill considered lists.

To reach the final shortlist, we look for a real passion for wine, which should come across to the customer, a fair pricing policy (depending on the style of the restaurant) an interesting coverage (not necessarily a large list), which might include areas of specialism, perhaps a particular wine area, sherries or larger formats such as magnums.

The AA Wine Awards are sponsored by T&W Wines Ltd,
5 Station Way, Brandon, Suffolk, IP27 0BH
Tel: 01842 814414
email: contact@tw-wines.com
web: www.tw-wines.com

AA WINE AWARD WINNER FOR SCOTLAND 2011-2012

RHUBARB - THE RESTAURANT AT PRESTONFIELD ◉◉
EDINBURGH

Prestonfield House Hotel is a blue-blooded 17th-century mansion kitted out in unapologetically theatrical and decadent style to create a romantic dining destination. In the ambience of a period film set, opulent shades of blood red and burgundy frame linen-clad tables lit seductively with tea lights – all adding up to a serious wow factor. The modern British cooking is equally high-impact, while the wine list is a serious piece of work with a particular emphasis on France and its various regions. Oenophiles with deep pockets will be in wine heaven with plenty of heavyweights to choose from, while those with a little less money to spend will find a good selection of affordable wines (from France and elsewhere in the Old and New Worlds) that are nonetheless excellent quality.

Judges' comments: Clearly a wine list in a different league, with some truly mouth-watering selections. There's good strength and depth throughout the list with great notes – it gives so much information.

AA Awards

Every year the AA presents a range of awards to the finest AA-inspected and rated establishments from England, Scotland, Wales and the Republic of Ireland. See who won the Scottish awards on page 14.

Rooms

Each entry shows the total number of rooms available (this total will include any annexe rooms). All hotel rooms should be en suite, for guest accommodation the number of en suite rooms is shown. The total number may be followed by a breakdown of the type of rooms available, i.e. the number of annexe rooms; number of family rooms (fmly); number of ground-floor rooms (GF); number of rooms available for smokers.

Bedrooms in an annexe or extension are only noted if they are at least equivalent in quality to those in the main building, but facilities and prices may differ. In some establishments all bedrooms are in an annexe or extension.

Prices

Prices are per room per night (and include breakfast in the case of Guest Accommodation) and are provided by the proprietors in good faith. These prices are indications and not firm quotations. * indicates 2011 prices.

Perhaps due to the economic climate at the time we were collecting the data for this guide, fewer establishments than usual were able to tell us their room prices for 2012. Many places have introduced special rates so it is worth looking at theAA.com or their own websites for the latest information.

Payment

As most establishments now accept credit or debit cards we only indicate if a place does not accept any cards for payment. Credit cards may be subject to a surcharge – check when booking if this is how you intend to pay. Not all establishments accept travellers' cheques.

Children

Children's facilities may include baby intercom, baby sitting service, playroom, playground, laundry, drying/ironing facilities, cots, high chairs or special meals. In some places children can sleep in parents' rooms at no extra cost – check when booking.

If 'No children' is indicated, a minimum age may be also given e.g. 'No children 4yrs' would mean no children under 4 years of age would be accepted.

Some establishments, although accepting children, may not have any special facilities for them so it is well worth checking before booking.

Leisure breaks

Some hotels and guest accommodation offer special leisure breaks, and these prices may differ from those quoted in this guide and the availability may vary through the year.

Parking

We indicate the number of parking spaces available for guests. This may include covered parking. Please note that some establishments make a charge to use their car park. We found when producing this guide that the number of spaces quoted for a hotel/guest accommodation and restaurant on the same site may differ. If this was the case, we have quoted the number given by the hotel.

Civil Weddings (Civ Wed)

Indicates that the establishment holds a civil wedding licence, and we indicate the number of guests that can be accommodated at the ceremony.

Conference Facilities

We include three types of meeting layouts – Theatre, Classroom and Boardroom style and include the maximum number of delegates for each. The price shown is the maximum 24-hour rate per delegate. Please note that as arrangements vary between an establishment and a business client, VAT may or may not be included in the price quoted in the guide. We also show if Wi-fi connectivity is available, but please check with the establishment for further details.

Dogs

Although many establishments allow dogs, they may be excluded from some areas of the building and some breeds, particularly those requiring an exceptional licence, may not be acceptable at all.

Under the Disability Discrimination Act 1995 access should be allowed for guide dogs and assistance dogs. Please check the establishment's policy when making your booking.

Entertainment (♫)

This indicates that live entertainment should be available at least once a week all year. Some hotels provide live entertainment only in summer or on special occasions – check when booking.

Map references

Each town is given a map reference – the map page number and a four-figure map reference based on the National Grid.
For example: **MAP 05 SU 48**:
05 refers to the page number of the map section at back of the guide
SU is the National Grid lettered square (representing 100,000sq metres) in which the location will be found
4 is the figure reading across the top or bottom of the map page
8 is the figure reading down at each side of the map page

Restricted service

Some places have restricted service (RS) during quieter months, usually during the winter, and at this time some of the listed facilities will not be available. If your booking is out-of-season, check with the establisment and enquire specifically. Don't forget that in some parts of Scotland the ski season is very busy.

Smoking regulations

If a bedroom has been allocated for smokers, the establishment is obliged to clearly indicate that this is the case. If either the freedom to smoke, or to be in a non-smoking environment is important to you, please check with the establishment when you book.

Spa

For the purposes of this guide the word **Spa** in an entry indicates that the hotel has its own spa which is either managed by themselves or outsourced to an external management company. Facilities will vary but will include a minimum of two treatment rooms. Any specific details are also given, and these are as provided to us by the establishment (i.e. steam room, beauty therapy etc).

HOTEL OF THE YEAR

BLYTHSWOOD SQUARE
★★★★★ ◉◉
GLASGOW (p116)

This new 'boutique' hotel is a restoration of a grand Grade B listed building that dates back to 1823, and was once the headquarters of the Royal Scottish Automobile Club.

The interior has been painstakingly refurbished. Intricate cornices, marble fireplaces, wood panelling and Harris tweed furnishings all combine to create a real sense of luxury. The former grand ballroom is the venue for enjoying award-winning cuisine, and the modern British menu serves up bold contemporary dishes alongside comforting classics.

Hues of purple, grey and beige set the style in the sumptuous bedrooms and suites. For the ultimate stay there's the Penthouse; on its own floor, accessed by a private lift, this stunning suite has a dining area, bar, rooftop terrace and breathtaking views. The hotel's spa features a fantastic Thermal Suite with a whole array of luxurious treatments.

RESTAURANT OF THE YEAR

GORDON'S ◉◉
INVERKEILOR, ANGUS (p33)

Tucked in at one end of the village, the restored Victorian end-terrace house with its unmissable red and blue frontage is home to the Watsons' long-running family business. Parents and son have the practice of hospitality off to a fine art, and with its riot of tartan fabrics, and wealth of pedigree seasonal produce, the place is not shy about celebrating its heritage. Good things flow from Gordon and Garry's kitchen, not least a signature starter dish of whole boned quail with Stornoway black pudding, Puy lentils and thyme blinis. Follow that with olive-crusted baked hake with carrot and courgette 'tagliatelle' in shellfish sauce, or a pairing of Forfar beef fillet and braised ox cheek, sweetly offset with shallot confit and vanilla parsnips in a Pinot Noir jus. If you haven't filled yourself up too much on the excellent home-made breads, a bracing dessert combination such as mango parfait with pineapple compôte and lychee sorbet makes a refreshing end to a memorable meal.

THE CAFÉ ROYAL 🏵
EDINBURGH (p95)

A glorious example of Victorian and Baroque, little has changed at the Café Royal since it moved across the road from its original site in 1863. A stylish Parisian-style building designed by local architect Robert Paterson, entering the Café Royal is like stepping back in time. Elegant stained glass and fine late Victorian plasterwork dominate the building, as do irreplaceable Doulton ceramic murals in the bar and restaurant. The whole building and its interior were listed in 1970 so future generations will enjoy the unique building which still sticks to its early 19th century roots by serving local ales, wine, coffee and fresh oysters in the bar and restaurant. Friendly staff offer relaxed and informal service. Scottish produce dominates the menu, from starters of Stornoway black pudding and apple gratin or Scottish smoked salmon with lemon mayonnaise to main courses of fish stew or haggis and whisky cream pie with chips.

23 MAYFIELD ★★★★★
EDINBURGH (p90)

Ross Birnie has recently overseen a two-year refurbishment of 23 Mayfield, which has turned this Victorian detached house into a relaxing and atmospheric guest house, that combines dark wood panelling, stained glass, old paintings and four-poster beds with modern technology such as radio alarms, LCD TVs, Bose audio gear, and even an Xbox. Ross is an excellent host, and his customer care and hospitality are among the many reasons why people return to 23 Mayfield.

Glen Muick, Cairngorms National Park

CITY OF ABERDEEN

ABERDEEN   Map 5 NJ90

See also **Aberdeen Airport**

Norwood Hall

★★★★ 81% HOTEL

 Modern British

Comforting modern food in a splendid Victorian mansion

☎ 01224 868951 🖷 01224 869868
Garthdee Rd, Cults AB15 9FX
e-mail: info@norwood-hall.co.uk
web: www.norwood-hall.co.uk
dir: Off A90, at 1st rdbt cross Bridge of Dee, left at rdbt onto
Garthdee Rd (B&Q & Sainsburys on left) continue to hotel
sign

Within extensive landscaped grounds just a short drive from
Aberdeen city centre, this imposing Victorian mansion has
retained many of its original features, notably the sweeping
oak staircase, the stained-glass windows and the ornate
fireplaces. Accommodation varies in style from individually
designed bedrooms in the main house to the newest
contemporary bedrooms. The extensive grounds ensure the
hotel is popular as a wedding venue. Attentive, amiable
service sets the right tone in a dining room that is hung with
old tapestries. The food is comforting modern British, along
the lines of ham hock and goose liver terrine, seared halibut
with pak choi, white beans and mussel and brown shrimp
broth, and dark chocolate and orange tart with chocolate oil
and blood orange granita.

Rooms 73 (14 GF) **Facilities** STV FTV Xmas New Year Wi-fi
Conf Class 100 Board 70 Thtr 200 **Services** Lift **Parking** 140
Notes ⊗ Civ Wed 150

Chef Russell R Robertson **Owner** Monument Leisure
Times 12-2.30/6.30-9.45 Closed L Mon-Fri **Prices** Food
prices not confirmed for 2012. Please telephone for details
Wines 43 bottles over £20, 23 bottles under £20, 9 by glass
Notes Vegetarian available, Dress restrictions, Smart casual
Seats 28, Pr/dining room 180 **Children** Portions

Holiday Inn Aberdeen West

★★★★ 76% HOTEL

◉ Italian

Contemporary Italian dining in modern hotel

☎ 01224 270300 🖷 01224 270323
Westhill Dr, Westhill AB32 6TT
e-mail: info@hiaberdeenwest.co.uk
web: www.holidayinn.co.uk
dir: On A944 in Westhill

In a good location at the west side of the city, this modern
hotel caters well for the needs of both business and leisure
guests. The nicely appointed bedrooms and bathrooms have
a contemporary feel. Luigi's is the main restaurant, a smart,
contemporary space, with unclothed tables and friendly
service, offering authentic Italian cooking. The emphasis
here is on quality ingredients treated in a straightforward
way. Start with butternut squash soup, followed by
tagliatelle Portofino – king prawns sautéed in oil with garlic,
chilli and courgette ribbons with a parmesan crisp. Finish
with well-executed lemon tart. The the popular lounge offers
more informal dining, and there is a separate pub operation
with wide-screen TVs showing a range of sporting events.

Rooms 86 (30 fmly) **Facilities** STV FTV Gym Wi-fi
Conf Class 150 Board 80 Thtr 300 **Services** Lift Air con
Parking 90 **Notes** Civ Wed 250

Chef Robert Blair **Owner** EDC Hotels Ltd **Times** 6.30-9.30
Closed Sun **Prices** Fixed D 3 course fr £17.95 Starter £4.50-
£7.95, Main £10.95-£29.95, Dessert £5.25-£8.50 Service
Optional **Wines** 11 bottles over £20, 13 bottles under £20, 8
by glass **Notes** Vegetarian available **Seats** 100, Pr/dining
room 30 **Children** Portions

Mercure Ardoe House Hotel & Spa

★★★★ 74% HOTEL

◉ Modern European

19th-century hotel with 21st-century cooking

☎ 01224 860600 🖷 01224 861283
South Deeside Rd, Blairs AB12 5YP
e-mail: h6626@accor.com
web: www.mercure.com
dir: 4m W of city off B9077

From its elevated position on the banks of the River Dee, this
19th-century baronial-style mansion commands excellent
countryside views. Beautifully decorated, thoughtfully
equipped bedrooms are located in the main house, and in
the more modern extension. Public rooms include a spa and
leisure club, a cosy lounge and cocktail bar and impressive
function facilities. Blairs restaurant is a grand setting with
high wooden hand-carved ceilings, tapestry-clad walls and
striking lighting. To contrast, modern wooden tables are laid
with contemporary crockery and classical music plays in the
background. Good sourcing of ingredients is evident and the
cooking has a decidedly modish sheen. Breast of wood
pigeon, for example, with Cevennes onion tarte Tatin, feta
cheese and grapefruit might precede fillet of Orkney halibut
with pork belly, Ayrshire potatoes, fricassée of razor clams
and samphire. It's creative stuff, continuing with desserts
such as textures of lemon - that's a lemon meringue pie with
a mousse and basil sorbet.

Rooms 109 **Facilities** Spa STV 🎬 ♨ Gym Aerobics studio
Xmas New Year Wi-fi **Conf** Class 200 Board 150 Thtr 600
Services Lift **Parking** 220 **Notes** ⊗ Civ Wed 250

Times 12.30-3.30/6.30-9.30

Copthorne Hotel Aberdeen

★★★★ 73% HOTEL

☎ 01224 630404 📄 01224 640573
122 Huntly St AB10 1SU
e-mail: reservations.aberdeen@millenniumhotels.co.uk
web: www.millenniumhotels.co.uk/aberdeen
dir: West end of city centre, off Union St, up Rose St, hotel
0.25m on right on corner with Huntly St

Situated just outside of the city centre, this hotel offers
friendly, attentive service. The smart bedrooms are well
proportioned and guests will appreciate the added quality of
the Connoisseur rooms. Mac's bar provides a relaxed
atmosphere in which to enjoy a drink or to dine informally,
whilst Poachers Restaurant offers a slightly more formal
dining experience.

Rooms 89 (15 fmly) **S** £55-£300; **D** £55-£300*
Facilities STV FTV New Year Wi-fi **Conf** Class 100 Board 70
Thtr 200 **Services** Lift **Parking** 15 **Notes** LB RS 24-26 Dec
Civ Wed 180

Maryculter House Hotel

★★★★ 71% HOTEL

◉ Traditional Scottish

**Playful modern Scottish cooking at the Knights Templar's
old joint**

☎ 01224 732124 📄 01224 733510
South Deeside Rd, Maryculter AB12 5GB
e-mail: info@maryculterhousehotel.com
web: www.maryculterhousehotel.com
dir: Exit A90 S of Aberdeen onto B9077. Hotel 8m on right,
0.5m beyond Lower Deeside Caravan Park

The early 13th-century house was once a stronghold of the
Knights Templar, as is witnessed by the carved coats-of-
arms that crop up here and there in the stonework. Now a
popular wedding and conference venue, exposed stonework
and open fires feature in the oldest parts. Lunch and
breakfast are taken overlooking the river; bedrooms are
equipped especially with business travellers in mind. The
Priory restaurant looks out on the River Dee, and is the stage
for some lively contemporary cooking that aims for a playful
note, as though in contrast to the stately austerity of the
surroundings. That translates as medallions of monkfish on
a moist sorrel risotto with air-dried pancetta and mint oil,
followed perhaps by tapenade-topped lamb chump with
ratatouille in tomato and oregano jus. The suitably grand
dessert might be rhubarb soufflé, served with a smooth ice
cream flavoured with Glenlivet single malt.

Rooms 40 (1 fmly) (16 GF) **Facilities** STV FTV Fishing Clay
pigeon shooting Archery Xmas New Year Wi-fi

Conf Class 100 Board 50 Thtr 200 **Parking** 150 **Notes** ⊗
Civ Wed 132

Times 7-9 Closed L all week

The Caledonian, Aberdeen

★★★★ 71% HOTEL

☎ 0871 376 9003 📄 0871 376 9103
10-14 Union Ter AB10 1WE
e-mail: aberdeencaledonian@thistle.co.uk
web: www.thistlehotels.com/thecaledonian
dir: Follow signs to city centre & Union St. Turn into Union
Terrace. Hotel on left, parking behind hotel in Diamond St

Centrally located just off Union Street and overlooking Union
Terrace Gardens this traditional hotel offers comfortable and
well-appointed bedrooms, and public areas in keeping with
the age of the building. The upbeat Café Bar Caley serves
informal food, but for a more formal dining experience
there's the Restaurant on the Terrace. A small car park is
available to the rear.

Rooms 83 (5 fmly) **Facilities** FTV Wi-fi **Conf** Class 40
Board 30 Thtr 80 **Services** Lift **Parking** 22 **Notes** ⊗
Civ Wed 40

Malmaison Aberdeen

★★★ 86% HOTEL

◉ Modern British

**Stylish brasserie with theatre kitchen serving modern
Scottish cuisine**

☎ 01224 327370 📄 01224 327371
49-53 Queens Rd AB15 4YP
e-mail: info.aberdeen@malmaison.com
dir: A90, 3rd exit into Queens Rd at 3rd rdbt, hotel on right

Balmoral staff who were once housed here when the Granite
City's outpost of the Malmaison chain was the Queen's
Hotel, may have raised an eyebrow at the sybaritic interiors
that lie beyond the flouncy art nouveau-canopied portal
these days. Bold statement colours and sensual textures
come together in an industrial-chic interior that will strike a
chord with fans of the Mal brand. Popular with business
travellers and as a function venue, the hotel lies east of the
city centre and offers two styles of accommodation, with the
superior rooms being particularly comfortable and well
equipped. In the restaurant, darkwood tables and funky,
modern, royal-blue and damson tartans make for a sexily
sepulchral setting in the cavernous, moodily-lit Brasserie
restaurant; high stools overlook the centrepiece Josper grill,
where bustling chefs turn out fuss-free modern dishes using
top-class Scottish produce. Duck rillettes with celeriac
remoulade gets the ball rolling, followed by yellow-fin tuna
served sizzling pink from the Josper, with broccoli and
almond purée. The operation is certainly up-front about the

importance of wine: you walk through a glassed-in wine tunnel, and on top of the cellar beneath the glass floor on the way to the brasserie.

Rooms 79 (8 fmly) (10 GF) **Facilities** Spa STV FTV Gym Steam room Xmas New Year Wi-fi **Conf** Class 30 Board 20 Thtr 40 **Services** Lift **Parking** 50 **Notes** LB

Chef Mark Taylor **Owner** Malmaison
Times 12-2.30/5.30-10.30 Closed D 25 Dec **Prices** Fixed L 2 course fr £14.95, Fixed D 3 course fr £40, Starter £5.95-£12.25, Main £9.95-£37.50, Dessert £5.95-£8.50, Service added 10% **Wines** 161 bottles over £20, 7 bottles under £20, 13 by glass **Notes** Sunday L, Vegetarian available **Seats** 90, Pr/dining room 30 **Children** Portions, Menu

The Craighaar

★★★ 80% HOTEL

☎ 01224 712275 📠 01224 716362
Waterton Rd, Bucksburn AB21 9HS
e-mail: info@craighaar.co.uk
dir: From A96 (Airport/Inverness) onto A947, hotel signed

Conveniently located for the airport, this welcoming hotel is a popular base for business people and tourists alike. Guests can make use of a quiet library lounge, and enjoy meals in the bar or restaurant. All bedrooms are well equipped, plus there is a wing of duplex suites that provide additional comfort.

Rooms 53 (6 fmly) (16 GF) (6 smoking) **S** £59-£109; **D** £65-£129 (incl. bkfst)* **Facilities** STV FTV Library Wi-fi **Conf** Class 33 Board 30 Thtr 90 Del from £129.50* **Parking** 80 **Notes** LB ⊗ Closed 25-26 Dec Civ Wed 40

The Mariner Hotel

★★★ 79% HOTEL

☎ 01224 588901 📠 01224 571621
349 Great Western Rd AB10 6NW
e-mail: info@themarinerhotel.co.uk
dir: E off Anderson Drive (A90) at Great Western Rd. Hotel on right on corner of Gray St

This well maintained, family operated hotel is located west of the city centre. The smart, spacious bedrooms are well equipped and particularly comfortable, with executive suites available. The public rooms are restricted to the lounge bar, which is food driven, and the Atlantis Restaurant that showcases the region's wide choice of excellent seafood and meats.

Rooms 25 (8 annexe) (4 GF) **S** £55-£100; **D** £85-£130 (incl. bkfst)* **Facilities** FTV New Year Wi-fi **Parking** 51 **Notes** ⊗

Thistle Aberdeen Altens

★★★ 78% HOTEL

☎ 0871 376 9002 📠 0871 376 9102
Souter Head Rd, Altens AB12 3LF
e-mail: aberdeenaltens@thistle.co.uk
web: www.thistle.com/aberdeenaltens
dir: A90 onto A956 signed Aberdeen Harbour. Hotel just off rdbt

Popular with oil industry personnel, this large purpose-built hotel lies in the Altens area, south east of the city. It's worth asking for one of the executive bedrooms that provide excellent space. Guests can eat in the restaurant, brasserie or the bar. Thistle Hotels — AA Hotel Group of the Year 2011-12.

Rooms 216 (96 fmly) (48 GF) **S** £85-£245; **D** £95-£255 (incl. bkfst)* **Facilities** FTV 🏊 Gym Sauna Steam room Solarium Aerobic studio New Year Wi-fi **Conf** Class 144 Board 30 Thtr 400 Del from £165 to £205 **Services** Lift **Parking** 300 **Notes** LB ⊗ Civ Wed 150

Holiday Inn Express Aberdeen City Centre

BUDGET HOTEL

☎ 01224 623500 📠 01224 623523
Chapel St AB10 1SQ
e-mail: info@hieaberdeen.co.uk
web: www.hiexpress.com/exaberdeencc
dir: In west end of city, just off Union Street

A modern hotel ideal for families and business travellers. Fresh and uncomplicated, the spacious rooms include Sky TV, power shower and tea and coffee-making facilities. Continental buffet breakfast is included in the room rate; other meals may be taken at the nearby family pub or restaurant.

Rooms 155 (102 fmly) (30 smoking) **S** £48-£150; **D** £48-£150 (incl. bkfst)* **Conf** Class 18 Board 16 Thtr 35

Holiday Inn Express Aberdeen - Exhibition Centre

BUDGET HOTEL

☎ 01224 706878 📠 01224 823923
Exhibition & Conference Centre, Parkway East, Bridge of Don AB23 8AJ
e-mail: info@hieaberdeenexhibitioncentre.co.uk
Rooms 135 (100 fmly) **Conf** Class 20 Board 24 Thtr 50

Premier Inn Aberdeen Central West

BUDGET HOTEL

☎ 0871 527 8006 ▤ 0871 527 8007
North Anderson Dr AB15 6DW
web: www.premierinn.com
dir: Into Aberdeen from S on A90 follow airport signs. Hotel
1st left after fire station. (NB for Sat Nav use AB15 6TP)

High quality, budget accommodation ideal for both families
and business travellers. Spacious, en suite bedrooms
feature tea and coffee-making facilities, and Freeview TV in
most hotels. Internet access and Wi-fi are available for a
small fee. The adjacent family restaurant features a wide
and varied menu.

Rooms 62 **D** £54-£73*

Premier Inn Aberdeen City Centre

BUDGET HOTEL

☎ 0871 527 8008 ▤ 0871 527 8009
Inverlair House, West North St AB24 5AS
web: www.premierinn.com
dir: A90 onto A9013 into city centre. Take A956 towards King
St, 1st left into Meal Market St

Rooms 162 **D** £55-£75*

Premier Inn Aberdeen North (Murcar)

BUDGET HOTEL

☎ 0871 527 8010 ▤ 0871 527 8011
Ellon Rd, Murcar, Bridge of Don AB23 8BP
web: www.premierinn.com
dir: From city centre take A90 N follow Peterhead signs. At
rdbt 2m after Aberdeen Exhibition & Conference Centre, left
onto B999. Hotel on right

Rooms 40 **D** £53-£70*

Premier Inn Aberdeen South

BUDGET HOTEL

☎ 0871 527 8012 ▤ 0871 527 8013
Mains of Balquharn, Portlethen AB12 4QS
web: www.premierinn.com
dir: From A90 follow Portlethen & Badentoy Park signs. Hotel
on right

Rooms 40 **D** £53-£70*

Premier Inn Aberdeen (Westhill)

BUDGET HOTEL

☎ 0871 527 8004 ▤ 0871 527 8005
Straik Rd, Westhill AB32 6HF
web: www.premierinn.com
dir: On A944 towards Alford, hotel adjacent to Tesco

Rooms 61 **D** £53-£70*

The Jays Guest House

★★★★ GUEST HOUSE

422 King St AB24 3BR
☎ 01224 638295 ▤ 01224 638360
e-mail: alice@jaysguesthouse.co.uk
web: www.jaysguesthouse.co.uk
dir: A90 from S onto Main St & Union St & A92 to King St N

Guests are warmly welcomed to this attractive granite house
on the north side of the city. Maintained in first-class order
throughout, it offers attractive bedrooms, smartly furnished
to appeal to business guests and tourists. Freshly prepared
breakfasts are enjoyed in the carefully appointed dining
room.

Rooms 10 rms (8 en suite) (2 pri facs) (1 GF) S £55-£65; D
£90-£110* **Facilities** STV FTV tea/coffee Cen ht Wi-fi
Parking 9 **Notes** ⊗ No Children 12yrs Closed mid Dec-mid
Jan

Arkaig

★★★ GUEST HOUSE

43 Powis Ter AB25 3PP
☎ 01224 638872 ▤ 01224 622189
e-mail: info@arkaig.co.uk
dir: On A96 at junct with Bedford Rd

A friendly welcome and relaxed atmosphere is assured at
this well-presented guest house, situated on the north side
of the city close to the university and city centre. Bedrooms
vary in size, are attractively decorated, and are all
thoughtfully equipped to appeal to business and leisure
guests. There is a cosy sun lounge with magazines, and an
attractive breakfast room where delicious, freshly cooked
breakfasts are served. Parking is also available.

Rooms 9 rms (7 en suite) (1 fmly) (5 GF) **Facilities** FTV TVL
tea/coffee Direct Dial Cen ht **Parking** 10

The Brandsbutt Stone, with its Ogham inscription, near Inverurie

ABERDEEN CONTINUED

The Silver Darling

 French, Seafood

Fresh seafood dishes with panoramic sea views

☎ 01224 576229
Pocra Quay, North Pier AB11 5DQ
e-mail: silverdarling@hotmail.co.uk
dir: At Aberdeen Harbour entrance

As befits its quayside location at the mouth of Aberdeen harbour, the Silver Darling has a firm focus on the bounty of the sea. The name is a colloquial reference to the herring that were once the mainstay of the local economy, and you can still watch the trawlers come and go from the luminous conservatory-style dining room perched atop a foursquare granite building. The appetite for fish and seafood duly stimulated, a menu of French-accented contemporary treatments proposes starters such as yellowfin tuna carpaccio with tapenade and basil, or a classy meat and fish combo of slow-cooked pork belly with squid a la plancha, pak choi and shiitake mushrooms. Spot-on technique and timing are the hallmarks of elaborate main courses: chorizo-crusted roast monkfish with piperade, deep-fried herb potato gnocchi, and basil and orange dressing, say, or pan-fried black bream with pesto couscous, sweet chilli purée, courgette and aubergine fritters, and roast pine kernel dressing. Desserts are impressive too - chocolate fondant, perhaps, teamed with pistachio ice cream, and chocolate and roast pistachio sauce.

Chef Didier Dejean **Owner** Didier Dejean & Karen Murray
Times 12-1.45/6.30-10 Closed Xmas-New Year, L Sat, D Sun
Prices Fixed L 2 course fr £17.50, Starter fr £9.50, Main fr £22, Dessert fr £8.50, Service added but optional 10%
Wines 51 bottles over £20, 8 by glass **Notes** Vegetarian available **Seats** 50, Pr/dining room 8 **Children** Portions **Parking** On quayside

Old Blackfriars 🍷

52 Castle St AB11 5BB ☎ 01224 581922 ▤ 01224 582153
e-mail: oldblackfriars.aberdeen@belhavenpubs.net
dir: From train station turn right along Guild St then left into Market St, at end turn right onto Union St. Pub on right at end of road

Situated in Aberdeen's historic Castlegate, this traditional split-level city centre pub stands on the site of property owned by Blackfriars Dominican monks, hence the name. Inside you'll find stunning stained glass, plus well kept real ales (nine handpumps) and a large selection of malt whiskies. The pub is also renowned for excellent food and an unobtrusive atmosphere (no background music and no television). The wide ranging menu has all the pub favourites and more – chicken Balmoral, chicken tikka makhani, sweet potato curry and baked lasagne. There is a weekly quiz and live music every Friday.

Open all day all wk Mon-Thu 11am-mdnt (Fri-Sat 11am-1am Sun 11am-11pm) Closed: 25 Dec, 1 Jan **Bar Meals** L served all wk 12-9.30 D served all wk 12-9.30 food served all day **Restaurant** L served all wk 12-9.30 D served all wk 12-9.30 food served all day ⊕ BELHAVEN ◧ Deuchars IPA, Inveralmond, Ossian, Ruddles County, Guest ales. ♀ 9
Facilities Children welcome Children's menu Family room Wi-fi

Thistle Aberdeen Airport

★★★★ 78% HOTEL

☎ 0871 376 9001 ▤ 0871 376 9101
Aberdeen Airport, Argyll Rd AB21 0AF
e-mail: aberdeenairport@thistle.co.uk
web: www.thistle.com/aberdeenairport
dir: Adjacent to Aberdeen Airport

Ideally located at the entrance to the airport this hotel offers ample parking plus a courtesy bus service to the terminal. This is a well presented establishment that benefits from good-sized bedrooms and comfortable public areas. Just Gym offers a good variety of exercise equipment.

Rooms 147 (3 fmly) (74 GF) (18 smoking) **Facilities** FTV Gym Wi-fi **Conf** Class 350 Board 100 Thtr 600 **Parking** 300

Aberdeen Marriott Hotel

★★★★ 76% HOTEL

☎ 01224 770011 ▤ 01224 722347
Overton Circle, Dyce AB21 7AZ
e-mail: reservations.scotland@marriotthotels.com
web: www.aberdeenmarriott.co.uk
dir: Follow A96 to Bucksburn, right at rdbt onto A947. Hotel in 2m at 2nd rdbt

Close to the airport and conveniently located for the business district, this purpose-built hotel is a popular conference venue. The well-proportioned bedrooms come with many thoughtful extras. Public areas include an informal bar and lounge, a split-level restaurant and a leisure centre that can be accessed directly from a number of bedrooms.

Rooms 155 (81 fmly) (61 GF) (10 smoking) **Facilities** STV ⊘ supervised Gym Saunas (male & female) Solarium New Year Wi-fi **Conf** Class 200 Board 60 Thtr 400 **Services** Air con **Parking** 180 **Notes** ⊗ Civ Wed 90

Menzies Dyce Aberdeen Airport

★★★ 78% HOTEL

☎ 01224 723101 📄 01224 773883
Farburn Ter, Dyce AB21 7DW
e-mail: dyce@menzieshotels.co.uk
dir: A96/A947 airport E after 1m turn left at lights. Hotel in 250yds

This hotel is very convenient for air travellers and for those wishing to explore this lovely Highland area. The spacious, well-equipped bedrooms have all the expected up-to-date amenities. The public areas are welcoming and include a contemporary brasserie. Secure parking and Wi-fi are also provided.

Rooms 198 (198 annexe) (3 fmly) (107 GF) (54 smoking)
Facilities STV Xmas New Year Wi-fi **Conf** Class 160
Board 120 Thtr 400 **Parking** 150 **Notes** Civ Wed 220

<table>
<tr><td>**PETERCULTER**</td><td>**Map 5 NJ80**</td></tr>
</table>

Furain

★★★ 🅰 GUEST HOUSE

92 North Deeside Rd AB14 0QN
☎ 01224 732189 📄 01224 739070
e-mail: furain@btinternet.com
dir: 7m W of city centre on A93

Rooms 8 en suite (2 fmly) (3 GF) S £45-£53; D £60-£70
Facilities FTV tea/coffee Cen ht Wi-fi **Parking** 7
Notes Closed Xmas & New Year

<table>
<tr><td>**ABERDEENSHIRE**</td></tr>
</table>

<table>
<tr><td>**BALLATER**</td><td>**Map 5 NO39**</td></tr>
</table>

Darroch Learg

★★★ SMALL HOTEL

◉◉◉ Modern Scottish 🍷 NOTABLE WINE LIST

Stunning Dee Valley views and modern Scottish cooking

☎ 013397 55443 📄 013397 55252
Braemar Rd AB35 5UX
e-mail: enquiries@darrochlearg.co.uk
web: www.darrochlearg.co.uk
dir: On A93, W of Ballater

From its perch on the wooded hillside of Craigendarroch, this Victorian mansion lords it over Ballater and the Dee Valley. If your Gaelic is a bit rusty, the name means 'the oak wood on the sunny hillside', and the house has been in the Franks family for 40 years or so. Inside, tartan upholstery, oak panelling and a lush traditional country-house feel ensure there's no doubting you're in Scotland. Bedrooms, some with four-poster beds, are individually styled, bright and spacious. Modern Scottish cuisine is served in an impeccably smart restaurant, which connects into a luminous conservatory-style space with views over the leafy grounds to the spectacular landscape beyond. Chef David Mutter has been cooking here for a dozen years, so has well-established supply lines to top-grade materials - meat and game from Deeside farms and estates, and spanking fresh fish delivered from Aberdeen and the West Coast. Classical French influences underpin well-conceived menus with a clear seasonal accent. Dinner might begin with a torte of guinea fowl with ceps and foie gras, and sweet chilli jam, or perhaps pan-fried Skye scallops with Orkney black pudding, parsnip purée and five spice sauce to add an exotic dimension. The main event might star loin of Deeside venison, partnered with smoked haunch, turnip confit, Puy lentils, fine beans and goats' cheese, and morel mushroom sauce, while desserts finish along the classic lines of apple and cinnamon Pithiviers with crème anglaise, or lemon tart with berry sauce. Wine buffs take note: the 200-bin cellar is a serious piece of work, and offers great value on high-end bottles thanks to a democratic fixed mark-up policy.

continued

BALLATER CONTINUED

Rooms 12 (1 GF) **S** £120-£195; **D** £190-£320 (incl. bkfst & dinner)* **Facilities** New Year **Conf** Board 12 Thtr 25 Del from £150 to £220* **Parking** 15 **Notes** LB Closed Xmas & Jan (ex New Year)

Chef David Mutter **Owner** The Franks family **Times** 12.30-2/7-9 Closed Xmas, last 3wks Jan, L Mon-Sat **Prices** Fixed L 3 course £24-£25, Fixed D 3 course fr £45, Tasting menu £56, Service included **Wines** 130 bottles over £20, 4 by glass **Notes** Sunday L, Vegetarian available, Dress restrictions, Smart casual **Seats** 48 **Children** Portions, Menu

Loch Kinord

★★★ 78% HOTEL

◉ Modern British ◑

Imaginative Scottish-focused cooking in Royal Deeside hotel

☎ 013398 85229 📄 013398 87007
Ballater Rd, Dinnet AB34 5JY
e-mail: stay@kinord.com
web: www.lochkinord.com
dir: Between Aboyne & Ballater, on A93, in Dinnet

In Royal Deeside, on the A93 between Ballater and Aboyne, this family-run hotel is a solid-looking, stone property dating from Victorian times, well located for leisure and sporting pursuits. Bedrooms are stylish and have smart bathrooms. The restaurant, with upholstered chairs and rugs on the boarded floor, is the setting for some traditional Scottish cooking with occasional international ventures, while the kitchen draws on the wealth of local produce, much of it organic. Start with ham and pea terrine with sauce gribiche, or salmon and crab cake with Thai-style pesto, and go on to noisettes of Hebridean lamb with rosemary jus, or grilled fillet of turbot with salsa verde on crushed new potatoes and broad beans. To finish, choose between the likes of summer pudding or chocolate cheesecake with coffee cream.

Rooms 20 (3 fmly) (4 GF) **Facilities** Pool table Xmas **Conf** Class 30 Board 30 Thtr 40 **Parking** 20 **Notes** Civ Wed 50

Chef Neil Keevill **Owner** Andrew & Jenny Cox **Times** 6.30-9 Closed L all week **Prices** Food prices not confirmed for 2012. Please telephone for details **Wines** 15 bottles over £20, 15 bottles under £20, 4 by glass **Seats** 30 **Children** Portions, Menu

The Green Inn

★★★★ 🏠 RESTAURANT WITH ROOMS

◉◉◉ British, French **V**

Precision cooking bursting with seasonal flavours in a family-run restaurant

9 Victoria Rd AB35 5QQ
☎ **013397 55701**
e-mail: info@green-inn.com
web: www.green-inn.com
dir: In village centre

This old stone house overlooking the eponymous green is these days a restaurant with rooms, run by the O'Halloran family with a good deal of charm and bags of culinary ambition. There are no 21st-century affectations here, simply attention to detail, passion and genuine hospitality. Bedrooms are of a high standard and attractively presented. The décor is smart and traditional, with some deep sofas to sink into in the lounge, and a dining room with rich red walls, well-spaced linen-clad tables and a green tartan carpet. Trevor leads front-of-house with genuine charm and charisma, while son Chris heads the team in the kitchen, ably assisted by his mum, Evelyn. Chris seeks out the very best of local produce and turns out dishes of class and confidence; his training under Raymond Blanc evident in his technical abilities and underlying classical skills. A first-course lasagne of duck confit with wild mushrooms, foie gras and cep foam is a fine-dining dish of luscious textures and flavours, or go for hand-dived Loch Fyne scallops partnered with Parma ham, butternut squash purée and apple vinaigrette. Cod is home-salted and served with roasted tomatoes, chick peas, piquillo peppers and samphire anchovy dressing in a dish that brings a bit of Mediterranean sunshine to proceedings, or there's seared saddle of roe deer with creamed celeriac, wild mushrooms and sweet peppercorn sauce. Everything looks beautiful on the plate. The contemporary flair continues with desserts: chocolate terrine with vodka ice cream and pistachio custard, perhaps.

Rooms 2 en suite **S** £59.50; **D** £79 **Facilities** FTV TVL tea/coffee Dinner available Cen ht Wi-fi **Notes** Closed 1st 2wks Nov, last 2wks Jan No coaches

Chef Chris O'Halloran **Owner** Trevor & Evelyn O'Halloran
Times 7-9 Closed 2 wks Nov, 2 wks Jan, Sun-Mon, L all week
Prices Fixed D 3 course £34.50-£44.50, Service optional
Wines 62 bottles over £20, 3 bottles under £20, 7 by glass
Notes Vegetarian menu, Dress restrictions, Smart casual
Seats 30, Pr/dining room 24 **Parking** On street & car park
nearby

The Auld Kirk

★★★★ RESTAURANT WITH ROOMS

◉◉ Traditional ◔

Ex-village church with modern Scottish dining

Braemar Rd AB35 5RQ
☎ 01339 755762 & 07918 698000 📠 0700 6037 559
e-mail: info@theauldkirk.com
dir: From A93 Braemar, on right just before village centre

When the setting is a stylishly converted Victorian village
church, you know that this one-off restaurant with rooms
will be something out of the ordinary. Original features and
character abound in the well-appointed bedrooms and
bathrooms; and in the Spirit Restaurant high vaulted
ceilings, cathedral windows and ornate chandeliers blend
seamlessly with modern artwork and black leather to provide
an undeniable wow factor. The fine-tuned cooking takes a
modern Scottish approach, delivering emphatic flavours and
some bold thinking in dishes such as home-smoked mallard
teamed with Scottish mature cheddar, grapes, melon and a
salad with lemon and marjoram dressing, followed by local
Aberdeen Angus beef fillet served with a beef, beer and
oyster forcemeat, fondant potato, red cabbage braised with
apricot and onion, sautéed leeks, and neep purée. Finish
with a classic crème brûlée or Scottish cheeses with
oatcakes, and mellow out with the fine array of malts in the
Kirk Bar, where the baptismal font and ancient pew ends
have been imaginatively recycled.

Rooms 7 en suite (1 fmly) S £70-£75; D £110-£140*
Facilities tea/coffee Dinner available Direct Dial Cen ht
Wi-fi **Conf** Max 25 Thtr 25 Class 18 Board 16 **Parking** 7
Notes RS Sun closed No coaches Civ Wed 34

Chef Tony Fuell **Owner** Tony Fuell & Peter Graydon
Times 12-2/6.30-9 Closed Xmas, Mon, L Tue-Sat, D Sun
Prices Fixed D 3 course £36, Service optional **Wines** 27
bottles over £20, 15 bottles under £20, 6 by glass
Notes Sunday L, Vegetarian available **Seats** 26, Pr/dining
room 20 **Children** Portions

Cock & Bull

◉ Modern Scottish ◔

Distinctive country inn with all-day dining

☎ 01358 743249
Ellon Rd, Blairton AB23 8XY
e-mail: info@thecockandbull.co.uk
web: www.thecockandbull.co.uk
dir: 6m N of Aberdeen on A90

In a lovely spot close to the sea, the Cock & Bull is a former
coaching inn and still retains its original character,
complete with cosy nooks and wooden beams. The bar area
is warmed by a cast-iron range and has big sofas and a
hotchpotch of hanging items, from a ship's lifebelt to a
trombone. But it's the food that's gained it a local
reputation. There's artwork by local artists on the walls -
take one home if it takes your fancy (after paying for it of
course). Choose between the conservatory dining area and a
more formal restaurant, but wherever you sit, the all-day
menu embraces lots of modern British crowd-pleasers
supported by some daily specials. Chicken liver parfait
comes with a delicious grape chutney and toasted brioche;
next up, perhaps pork and black pudding burger with apple
compôte and smoked cheddar, or wild mushroom risotto, or
Thai chicken with herb and almond basmati.

Chef Jairon Tarvet **Owner** Rodger Morrison **Times** 10.30-late
Closed 26 Dec, 2 Jan **Prices** Food prices not confirmed for
2012. Please telephone for details **Wines** 13 bottles over
£20, 15 bottles under £20, 7 by glass **Notes** Sunday L,
Vegetarian available, Civ Wed 150 **Seats** 80
Children Portions, Menu **Parking**

Open all day all wk 10am-11.30pm (Sun 12-6.30) Closed:
26-27 Dec, 2-3 Jan **Bar Meals** L served Mon-Sat 10-8.45,
Sun 12-6.30 D served Mon-Sat 10-8.45, Sun 12-6.30 Av
main course £12.95 food served all day **Restaurant** L served
Mon-Sat 10-8.45, Sun 12-6.30 D served Mon-Sat 10-8.45,
Sun 12-6.30 ⊕ FREE HOUSE ◀ Caledonian 80/-, Guinness.
Facilities Children welcome Children's menu Play area Dogs
allowed Garden

Raemoir House Hotel

★★★ 85% COUNTRY HOUSE HOTEL

◉◉ Traditional British

Country house dining

☎ 01330 824884
Raemoir AB31 4ED
e-mail: hotel@raemoir.com

A beautiful country house set in 11 acres of secluded, peaceful grounds, close to Aberdeen and perfectly situated for the whisky and castle trails. There's even a helicopter pad, should you require it. The new owners have been busy refurbishing the property, and the individually styled bedrooms feature modern comforts including Wi-fi access. Cooking is a highlight with delicious meals served in the wood-panelled dining room. Menus feature robust, traditional dishes - you could start with simply presented pigeon breast, black pudding, and juniper jus, followed by beef - perfectly cooked sirloin and braised featherblade with horseradish mash, woodland mushrooms, shallots and merlot jus. To finish, you can't go wrong with treacle tart, caramel ice cream and citrus syrup. Head chef David Littlewood also oversees things at The Milton Restaurant in Crathes (see entry).

Rooms 20 (6 annexe) (2 fmly) **S** fr £125; **D** fr £140 (incl. bkfst) **Facilities** FTV Putt green 🏊 Xmas New Year Wi-fi **Conf** Class 50 Board 40 Thtr 80 **Parking** 20 **Notes** LB Civ Wed 50

Chef David Littlewood **Times Prices** Fixed D 3 course £39.50 **Notes** Sunday L

Best Western Burnett Arms Hotel

★★★ 70% SMALL HOTEL

☎ 01330 824944   📄 01330 825553
25 High St AB31 5TD
e-mail: theburnett@btconnect.com
dir: Town centre on N side of A93

This popular hotel is located in the heart of the town centre and gives easy access to the many attractions of Royal Deeside. Public areas include a choice of eating and

drinking options, with food served in the restaurant, bar and foyer lounge. Bedrooms are thoughtfully equipped and comfortably modern.

Rooms 18 (1 fmly) **Facilities** STV FTV Xmas New Year Wi-fi **Conf** Class 50 Board 50 Thtr 100 **Parking** 23 **Notes** LB Civ Wed 100

Callater Lodge Guest House

★★★★ GUEST HOUSE

9 Glenshee Rd AB35 5YQ
☎ 013397 41275
e-mail: info@hotel-braemar.co.uk
web: www.callaterlodge.co.uk
dir: Next to A93, 300yds S of Braemar centre

Located in the picturesque village of Braemar, this grand Victorian villa is very well presented with stunning views and lots of period features. Bedrooms are attractively decorated with many thoughtful extras. The spacious lounge is inviting and homely. Breakfast is served at individual tables and uses quality local ingredients. The gardens are a very pleasant feature.

Rooms 6 en suite (1 fmly) S fr £40; D fr £78* **Facilities** tea/coffee Cen ht Licensed Wi-fi **Parking** 6 **Notes** ⊗ Closed Xmas

The Milton Restaurant

◉ Traditional British 🍷

Contemporary Scottish dining at the gateway to Royal Deeside

☎ 01330 844566 & 844474
AB31 5QH
e-mail: jay@themilton.co.uk
web: www.themilton.co.uk
dir: On the A93, 15m W of Aberdeen, opposite Crathes Castle

There's always plenty going on here at the gateway to Royal Deeside: whisky and castle trails to explore, art galleries and craft shops to mooch around to your heart's content, and when hunger strikes, the Milton Restaurant offers a smart rustic setting for a well-thought-out menu of modern Scottish ideas. It is an attractive, low-lit space with bare timbers and lots of art on whitewashed walls, plus a light-flooded conservatory extension, and is the scene of many a jazz night, wine tasting session and cookery class. The food has lots of contemporary accents, although there is plenty of familiarity to keep everyone satisfied. To begin, venison loin might be teamed with fondant swede, red onion marmalade and bramble jus, while main courses could embrace everything from roast chump of lamb with pommes noisettes, parsnip purée and barley jus to a herb-crusted turbot fillet with watercress mash and warm tomato fondue.

Chef David Littlewood, Bob Miller **Owner** Neil Rae
Times 9.30am-9.30pm Closed 25 Dec, 1 Jan, D Sun, (Mon-
Tue, Feb-Mar) **Prices** Food prices not confirmed for 2012.
Please telephone for details **Wines** 14 bottles over £20, 17
bottles under £20, 11 by glass **Notes** Sunday L, Vegetarian
available, Civ Wed 60 **Seats** 90 **Children** Portions
Parking 70

HUNTLY   Map 5 NJ53

Gordon Arms Hotel

★★ 65% SMALL HOTEL

☎ 01466 792288 📠 01466 794556
The Square AB54 8AF
e-mail: reception@gordonarms.demon.co.uk
dir: Off A96 (Aberdeen to Inverness road) at Huntly. Hotel
immediately on left after entering town square

This friendly, family-run hotel is located in the town square
and offers a good selection of tasty, well-portioned dishes
served in the bar, and also in the restaurant at weekends or
midweek by appointment. Bedrooms come in a variety of
sizes, but all have a good range of accessories.

Rooms 13 (3 fmly) **Facilities** FTV 🎵 Wi-fi **Conf** Class 80
Board 60 Thtr 160

INVERURIE   Map 5 NJ72

Macdonald Pittodrie House

★★★★ 75% HOTEL

☎ 0870 1942111 & 01467 681744 📠 01467 681648
Chapel of Garioch, Pitcaple AB51 5HS
e-mail: pittodrie@macdonald-hotels.co.uk
web: www.macdonald-hotels.com/pittodrie
dir: From A96 towards Inverness, pass Inverurie under
bridge with lights. Turn left & follow signs

Set in extensive grounds this house dates from the 15th
century and retains many historic features. Public rooms
include a gracious drawing room, restaurant, and a cosy bar
boasting an impressive selection of whiskies. The well-
proportioned bedrooms are found in both the original house
and in the extension that was designed to match the
existing building.

Rooms 27 (3 fmly) **Facilities** STV Clay pigeon shooting Quad
biking Outdoor activities Xmas New Year Wi-fi **Conf** Class 75
Board 50 Thtr 150 **Parking** 200 **Notes** Civ Wed 120

Kintore Arms

★★★★ INN

---

83 High St AB51 3QJ
☎ 01467 621367 📠 01467 625620
e-mail: manager.kintore@ohiml.com
web: www.oxfordhotelsandinns.com
dir: From A96 at rdbt turn signed Inverurie, onto main High
St, on left

Well situated within easy walking distance of the town
centre and benefiting from off-road parking, this traditional
inn has recently undergone a programme of refurbishment.
Good-sized bedrooms are thoughtfully equipped for the
modern traveller. Regular evening entertainment is provided.

Rooms 28 en suite (1 fmly) **Facilities** FTV TVL tea/coffee
Dinner available Cen ht Wi-fi **Conf** Max 150 Thtr 150 Class
75 Board 75 **Parking** 30 **Notes** Civ Wed 150

KILDRUMMY   Map 5 NJ41

Kildrummy Castle Hotel

★★★★ 75% COUNTRY HOUSE HOTEL

☎ 019755 71288 📠 019755 71345
AB33 8RA
e-mail: kildrummy@btconnect.com
web: www.kildrummycastlehotel.co.uk
dir: Off A97 (Huntly to Ballater road)

Set in landscaped gardens and accessed via a tree lined
drive, Kildrummy Castle enjoys a peaceful rural location in
the heart of the beautiful Grampian Highlands, yet is only a
35-minute drive from Aberdeen. The comfortable bedrooms
have fabulous views, often with the ruin of the original
castle as a backdrop. The current owners have
sympathetically restored much of the original features, and
the cosy lounges provide a perfect setting for afternoon tea
or a post dinner drink. Dinner features the best of local
produce, along with an extensive wine list. The relaxed
atmosphere, supported by friendly service, is an obvious
attraction here.

Rooms 16 (2 fmly) **S** £97.50; **D** £134-£217 (incl. bkfst)
Facilities FTV Fishing Xmas New Year Wi-fi **Conf** Board 18
Del from £150 to £185 **Parking** 25 **Notes** LB Closed 3-24 Jan
RS 5-15 Nov

MARYCULTER — Map 5 NO89

Old Mill Inn

South Deeside Rd AB12 5FX ☎ **01224 733212**
📄 **01224 732884**
e-mail: info@oldmillinn.co.uk
dir: 5m W of Aberdeen on B9077

This delightful family-run 200-year-old country inn stands on the edge of the River Dee, five miles from Aberdeen city centre. A former mill house, the 18th-century granite building has been tastefully modernised to include a restaurant where the finest Scottish ingredients feature on the menu: black pudding parcel, seafood chowder, warm salad of monkfish and chicken and ham shank terrine are typical. Food and drink can be enjoyed in the garden in warmer months.

Open all day all wk **Bar Meals** L served all wk 12-2 D served all wk 5.30-9 Av main course £10.50 **Restaurant** L served all wk 12-2 D served all wk 5.30-9 Av 3 course à la carte fr £18.50 ⊕ FREE HOUSE ◖ Caledonian Deuchars IPA, Timothy Taylor Landlord, London Pride. **Facilities** Children welcome Children's menu Children's portions Garden Parking

NETHERLEY — Map 5 NO89

The Lairhillock Inn

AB39 3QS ☎ **01569 730001** 📄 **01569 731175**
e-mail: info@lairhillock.co.uk
dir: From Aberdeen take A90. Right towards Durris on B9077 then left onto B979 to Netherley

Standing alone surrounded by fields in beautiful rural Deeside, the Lairhillock is easily spotted from the B979. Formerly a farmhouse and then a coaching inn, the original building is 17th century and the interior is full of old rustic atmosphere, most notably the fine old bar with its exposed stone, panelling, old settles, and crackling log fires. Here you can quaff Deuchars IPA, Timothy Taylor Landlord or a choice of guest ales. Food is robust and dishes make good use of fresh, quality, local and regional produce such as langoustines from Gourdon, mussels from Shetland, scallops from Orkney, wild boar and venison from the Highlands and salmon from the Dee and Don, not forgetting certified Aberdeen Angus beef. In the bar and conservatory, try the Cullen skink or peat smoked salmon with citrus dressing; followed by seafood pie or braised beef olives with red wine gravy. For a more formal dining option, the atmospheric Crynoch Restaurant menu might offer chicken liver and bacon parfait to start, followed by saddle of venison with a tomato and cannellini bean ragout and thyme jus, or rib-eye steak with wild mushroom sauce.

Open all day all wk Closed: 25-26 Dec, 1-2 Jan **Bar Meals** L served all wk 12-2 booking required D served all wk 6-9.30 booking required **Restaurant** L served Sun 12-2 booking

required D served Tue-Sat 7-9.30 booking required ⊕ FREE HOUSE ◖ Timothy Taylor Landlord, Deuchars IPA, Guest ales. **Facilities** Children welcome Children's menu Children's portions Dogs allowed Garden Parking

NEWBURGH — Map 5 NJ92

The Udny Arms Hotel

★★★ 73% HOTEL

◉◉ Modern British

Traditional inn and great local produce make a winning combination

☎ 01358 789444 📄 01358 789012
Main St AB41 6BL
e-mail: enquiries@udnyarmshotel.com
web: www.udnyarmshotel.com
dir: A90 N, 8m N of Aberdeen turn right to Newburgh (A975), hotel in village centre

Overlooking the picture postcard scenery of the Ythan Estuary and the Newburgh links golf course this hotel offers friendly service in relaxed and comfortable surroundings. Well-equipped and nicely presented bedrooms have flat-screen TVs, while the spacious traditional dining room enjoys a warm and friendly atmosphere and stunning views over Newburgh golf course. Here you'll find the finest Scottish ingredients and some classic French influences, together creating interesting, well executed dishes. Begin with chicken liver and foie gras parfait with toasted brioche and red onion jam, perhaps, and follow that with slow cooked, melt in the mouth pork belly, complimented by the natural sweet flavour of langoustines, and accompanied by cauliflower puree, fondant potato and braised morels. Crème brulee is always a winning dessert – this version comes with excellent shortbread to add a contrasting texture.

Rooms 30 (1 fmly) (4 GF) **S** £57-£70; **D** £67-£89 (incl. bkfst)* **Facilities** STV FTV Fishing Xmas New Year Wi-fi **Conf** Class 50 Board 20 Thtr 80 Del from £90 to £150* **Parking** 40 **Notes** LB Civ Wed 80

Chef Mark Pollock **Times** 6-9 Closed Sun-Mon

Leabaidh an Daimh Bhuidhe, summit tor of Ben Avon in Cairngorms National Park

Map 5 NJ82

Meldrum House Country Hotel & Golf Course

★★★★ 79% COUNTRY HOUSE HOTEL

◉◉ Modern British 🕮

Elegant dining in a splendid country mansion

☎ 01651 872294 📠 01651 872464
AB51 0AE
e-mail: enquiries@meldrumhouse.co.uk
dir: 11m from Aberdeen on A947 (Aberdeen to Banff road)

Set in 350 acres of wooded parkland this imposing mansion has a golf course as its centrepiece. Even if you're not a whizz with a niblick, it's a good place to marinate in the luxury ambience of a turreted baronial pile that has been around in one form or another since the 13th century. Tastefully restored to highlight its original character it provides a peaceful retreat. Bedrooms are massive, and, like the public rooms, transport guests back to a bygone era, and at the same time provide stylish modern amenities including smart bathrooms. In the restaurant, modern Scottish country-house cooking puts local produce firmly on the agenda. A summer dinner kicks off seasonally with crab and beetroot cannelloni, avocado, and gazpacho dressing, then follows with a well-cooked riff on new local lamb, served as belly, loin, spare rib and sweetbread, with pease pudding and noisette potato. Finally, only Valrhona will do for a cherry and chocolate fondant served with cherry ice cream and almond milkshake.

Rooms 22 (13 annexe) (1 fmly) (6 GF) **D** £120-£180 (incl. bkfst)* **Facilities** FTV ⚓ 18 Putt green 🏌 Xmas New Year Wi-fi **Conf** Class 20 Board 30 Thtr 80 **Parking** 70 **Notes** LB Civ Wed 100

Chef Peter Conlin **Owner** Peter Walker **Times** 12-2/6.30-9 **Prices** Starter £6-£12, Main £12-£24, Dessert £5-£8, Service optional **Wines** 46 bottles over £20, 25 bottles under £20, 6 by glass **Notes** Sunday L, Vegetarian available, Dress restrictions, Smart casual **Seats** 40, Pr/dining room 16 **Children** Portions, Menu

The Redgarth

Kirk Brae AB51 0DJ ☎ **01651 872353** 📠 **01651 873763**
e-mail: redgarth1@aol.com
dir: From A947 (Oldmeldrum bypass) follow signs to Golf Club/Pleasure Park. Establishment E of bypass

Built as a house in 1928, this friendly family-run inn has been in the same hands for the past 20 years. It is situated in a small village with an attractive garden that offers magnificent views of Bennachie and the surrounding countryside. Cask-conditioned ales, such as Orkney Scapa and Inveralmond Thrappledouser, and interesting wines are served along with dishes prepared on the premises using fresh local produce. A typical selection might include duo of hot and cold salmon with horseradish mayonnaise, or pork fillet stuffed with black pudding.

Open all wk 11-3 5-11 (Fri-Sat 11-3 5-11.45) Closed: 25-26 Dec, 1-3 Jan **Bar Meals** L served all wk 12-2 D served Sun-Thu 5-9, Fri-Sat 5-9.30 Av main course £9 **Restaurant** L served all wk 12-2 booking required D served Sun-Thu 5-9, Fri-Sat 5-9.30 booking required Av 3 course à la carte fr £20 ⊕ FREE HOUSE ◀ Inveralmond Thrappledouser, Timothy Taylor Landlord, Orkney Scapa & Best, Pivo Estivo. **Facilities** Children welcome Children's menu Children's portions Garden Parking Wi-fi

Map 5 NK14

Buchan Braes Hotel

★★★★ 75% HOTEL

◉ Modern Scottish 🕮

Local produce getting top billing

☎ 01779 871471 📠 01779 871472
Boddam AB42 3AR
e-mail: info@buchanbraes.co.uk
dir: From Aberdeen take A90, follow Peterhead signs. 1st right in Stirling signed Boddam. 50mtrs, 1st right

Formerly the officers mess at RAF Buchan, the building was totally rebuilt to create a modern hotel and restaurant in 2008, and it's an excellent base for exploring the attractions of this wonderful part of Scotland. There is an open-plan lounge for drinks and snacks and the Grill Room has a buzzy vibe, with its fashionably open-to-view kitchen, eye-catching modern chandeliers and black and white seascape pictures. The weekly-changing menu of modern Scottish dishes sets great store by locally-sourced produce, which given the hotel's coastal location means you're in for a seafood treat or two. You might find Boddam crab and green apple salad, quince jelly and celeriac remoulade to start. Following on perhaps with pan-fried mackerel fillet with citrus fruits, hairy tatties and brussel sprouts, or, of course, some meat from the farms around Buchan, cooked simply on the grill. All the bedrooms, including three suites, have 32" flat-screen TVs with satellite channels, king-sized beds and free Wi-fi.

Rooms 47 (1 fmly) (26 GF) **S** £90-£130; **D** £100-£130 (incl. bkfst)* **Facilities** Xmas New Year Wi-fi **Conf** Class 100 Board 130 Thtr 250 Del from £150 to £170* **Services** Lift **Parking** 40 **Notes** ⊗

Chef Gary Christie, Paul McLean, Michael Watt **Owner** Kenneth Watt **Times** 11.45-2.30/6-9.30 **Prices** Fixed L 2 course £12, Fixed D 3 course £25, Starter £4.95-£8.95, Main £14.95-£19.95, Dessert £5.95, Service optional **Wines** 16 bottles over £20, 16 bottles under £20, 7 by glass **Notes** Sunday L, Vegetarian available, Civ Wed 250 **Seats** 70, Pr/dining room 80 **Children** Portions, Menu

Palace

★★★ 81% HOTEL

☎ 01779 474821 🖹 01779 476119
Prince St AB42 1PL
e-mail: info@palacehotel.co.uk
web: www.palacehotel.co.uk
dir: A90 from Aberdeen, follow signs to Peterhead, on entering town turn into Prince St, then right into main car park

This town centre hotel is popular with business travellers and for social events. Bedrooms come in two styles, with the executive rooms being particularly smart and spacious. Public areas include a themed bar, an informal diner reached via a spiral staircase, and a brasserie restaurant and cocktail bar.

Rooms 64 (1 fmly) (14 GF) **S** £70-£85; **D** £80-£95 (incl. bkfst)* **Facilities** Snooker & Pool table ♬ New Year Wi-fi **Conf** Class 100 Board 60 Thtr 250 Del from £120 to £135* **Services** Lift **Parking** 50 **Notes** Civ Wed

---

STONEHAVEN   **Map 5 NO88**

Carron Art Deco Restaurant

◉ Modern British ℮

Art deco stunner with confident, modern Scottish cooking

☎ 01569 760460
20 Cameron St AB39 2HS
e-mail: jacki@cleaverhotels.eclipse.co.uk
dir: From Aberdeen, right at town centre lights, 2nd left onto Ann St, right at road end, 3rd building on right

Built in 1937, at the end of the art deco period, this stylish restaurant was restored to its former glory 10 years ago and is now a smart place to enjoy modern Scottish food. Based on the art deco details of historic liner RMS *Queen Mary*, original features abound, from the unusual glass frontage to the centrepiece Picasso 'mystery mirror' - a 9ft mirror etched with a naked lady, surrounded by thousands of tiny silver mosaic tiles - thought to be a rare piece by the Spanish artist. The food here is no afterthought though. Local ingredients, with a leaning towards seafood, are used in modern dishes with some interesting flavour combinations. Thus seared local scallops come with a smoked trout risotto, pot-roast Aberdeen Angus beef is served with haggis, neeps, a tattie tower and rich Drambuie sauce, and Guinness flavours a cake served with sherry and raisin ice cream.

Chef Robert Cleaver **Owner** Robert Cleaver **Times** 12-2/6-9.30 Closed 24 Dec-10 Jan, Sun-Mon **Prices** Starter £4.25-£7.25, Main £11.50-£21.95, Dessert £5.90-£6.95, Service optional **Wines** 7 bottles over £20, 18 bottles under £20, 5 by glass **Notes** Vegetarian available **Seats** 80, Pr/dining room 30 **Children** Portions, Menu **Parking** Town Square

Tolbooth Restaurant

◉ Modern British, Seafood ℮

Quayside restaurant serving seafood straight off the boats

☎ 01569 762287
Old Pier, Stonehaven Harbour AB39 2JU
e-mail: enquiries@tolbooth-restaurant.co.uk
dir: 15m S of Aberdeen on A90, located in Stonehaven harbour

Few restaurants can beat the Tolbooth when it comes to getting fish and seafood from boat to plate in the quickest possible time. Stonehaven's oldest building has sat on the quayside for 400 years, doing service as the town's lock up and excise house; nowadays the first-floor restaurant goes for a jaunty beachcomber-chic look, with linen-clothed tables on wooden floors, and local artwork on walls of whitewashed rough stone and sky-blue painted tongue-and-groove panelling. A picture window gives fabulous views across the harbour to accompany a menu of spanking fresh seafood, bolstered by blackboard specials. The kitchen knows its way around piscine produce, leaving the raw materials to speak for themselves in starters such as a rich crab soup pointed up with a hit of sherry, or super-fresh sea bass served as a simple céviche, followed, perhaps, by roasted turbot with brown butter and lemon and caper sauce. Unrepentant carnivores are catered for by the likes of crispy duck leg confit with potato and shallot rösti and plum and ginger sauce.

Chef Craig Somers **Owner** J Edward Abbott **Times** 12-4/6-12 Closed 1st 3wks Jan, Sun (Oct-Apr) & Mon **Prices** Fixed L 2 course £13.95, Starter £5-£11.50, Main £14-£23.95, Dessert £6-£8, Service optional, Groups min 10 service 10% **Wines** 24 bottles over £20, 8 bottles under £20, 6 by glass **Notes** Sunday L, Vegetarian available **Seats** 46 **Children** Portions **Parking** Public car park, 100 spaces

The Glenkindie Arms

★★★ INN

◉◉ French, Scottish ✦

Adventurous cooking in a 400-year-old Highland inn

☎ 019756 41288
Glenkindie AB33 8SX
e-mail: iansimpson.glenkindiearms@gmail.com
web: www.theglenkindiearmshotel.com
dir: On A97 between between Alford & Strathdon

A small country pub with friendly staff and great food is always a joy to come across, and this one in the Highlands is a prime specimen. Set in Upper Donsdale, close to Balmoral and the Malt Whisky Trail, and enjoying breathtaking views of the Highlands, this 400-year-old traditional drovers' inn has been spruced-up with style and panache by chef/patron Ian Simpson and Aneta Olechno. Accommodation is provided in brightly decorated and airy rooms, and the bathrooms are thoughtfully equipped. Breakfast is not to be missed, and lunches feature traditional dishes made from the best local produce. The bar setting with its brown leather chairs and open fire makes for a warming ambience in both senses, the bare tables are simply laid, and Ian Simpson's locally-based cooking has real character. Skilled presentation and adventurous combinations are the stock-in-trade, producing perhaps a starter serving of king scallops with pea purée in a well-judged curried velouté, garnished with a smoked bacon crisp, and multi-layered mains such as slow-roast pork belly with greens, black pudding and white truffled mash in a sauce of cider. Finish at the lighter end of the spectrum with a berry jelly enriched with Rioja. The home-made walnut bread should not be missed.

Rooms 3 en suite (1 fmly) S £35-£50; D £70-£100*
Facilities STV FTV tea/coffee Dinner available Cen ht Wi-fi Golf 18 Fishing **Conf** Max 40 Thtr 20 Class 20 Board 30
Parking 25 **Notes** LB ⊗ Closed 3wks Nov RS Jan wknds only

Chef Ian Simpson **Owner** Ian Simpson & Aneta Olechno
Times 12-10 **Prices** Fixed L 2 course £15-£23.50, Fixed D 3 course £27.50, Service optional **Wines** 4 bottles over £20, 15 bottles under £20, 6 by glass **Notes** Only children over 16yrs accepted after 5.30pm, Sunday L, Vegetarian available
Seats 40, Pr/dining room 20 **Children** Portions

Carnoustie Golf Hotel & Spa

★★★★ 73% HOTEL

◉ Traditional British

Fine dining in a championship location

☎ 0844 414 6520 🖷 0844 414 6519
The Links DD7 7JE
e-mail: reservations.carnoustie@ohiml.com
web: www.oxfordhotelsandinns.com
dir: Adjacent to Carnoustie Golf Links

This fine hotel enjoys an enviable location, adjacent to the 1st and 18th green of the famous Championship Course of Carnoustie. All bedrooms are spacious and attractively presented; most overlook the magnificent course and enjoy breathtaking coastal views. The Dalhousie Restaurant allows golfing gastronomes to indulge both their hobbies - watching the action on the fairways through vast windows while dining on straightforward traditional cooking built on top-class local ingredients. It is a clean-cut contemporary space with attentive staff to ensure meals go with a swing, starting perhaps with chicken liver parfait with brioche and chutney - all made in-house - ahead of baked salmon fillet with green-lipped mussels and herb butter sauce, or beef bourguignon with roasted root vegetables and rich red wine jus.

Rooms 85 (11 fmly) **Facilities** Spa STV FTV ⟲ Putt green Gym Xmas New Year Wi-fi **Conf** Class 200 Board 100 Thtr 350 **Services** Lift Air con **Parking** 100 **Notes** ⊗ Civ Wed 325

Times 7-9.30 Closed L all week

INVERKEILOR

Map 5 NO64

RESTAURANT OF THE YEAR FOR SCOTLAND

Gordon's

★★★★ ☎ RESTAURANT WITH ROOMS

◉◉ Modern British ✋

Family-run village restaurant with well-crafted modern cooking

Main St DD11 5RN
☎ 01241 830364 📠 01241 830364
e-mail: gordonsrest@aol.com
dir: Off A92, follow signs for Inverkeilor

Tucked in at one end of the village, the restored Victorian end-terrace house with its unmissable red and blue frontage is home to the Watsons' long-running family business. Parents and son have the practice of hospitality off to a fine art, and with its riot of tartan fabrics, and wealth of pedigree seasonal produce, the place is not shy about celebrating its heritage. Attractive bedrooms are tastefully decorated and thoughtfully equipped; the larger two furnished in pine. Good things flow from Gordon and Garry's kitchen, not least a signature starter dish of whole boned quail with Stornoway black pudding, Puy lentils and thyme blinis. Follow that with olive-crusted baked hake with carrot and courgette 'tagliatelle' in shellfish sauce, or a pairing of Forfar beef fillet and braised ox cheek, sweetly offset with shallot confit and vanilla parsnips in a Pinot Noir jus. A dessert combination such as mango parfait with pineapple compôte and lychee sorbet makes a refreshing change from chocolate and toffee. Don't miss the excellent breads.

Rooms 4 en suite 1 annexe en suite (1 GF) S £60-£75; D £100-£130 **Facilities** FTV Dinner available Cen ht **Parking** 6 **Notes** ⊗ No Children 12yrs Closed 2wks Jan No coaches

Chef Gordon Watson, Garry Watson **Owner** Gordon & Maria Watson **Times** 12-1.45/7-9 Closed 2 wks Jan, Mon, L Sat, D Sun (in Winter) **Prices** Fixed L 3 course £27, Fixed D 4 course £48, Service optional **Wines** 19 bottles over £20, 25 bottles under £20, 3 by glass **Notes** All bookings essential, Sunday L, Vegetarian available, Dress restrictions, Smart casual **Seats** 24, Pr/dining room 8

MONTROSE

Map 5 NO75

Oaklands

★★★ GUEST HOUSE

10 Rossie Island Rd DD10 9NN
☎ 01674 672018 📠 01674 672018
e-mail: oaklands1@btopenworld.com
dir: On A92 at S end of town

A genuine welcome and attentive service are assured at this smart detached house situated on the south side of the

town. Bedrooms come in a variety of sizes and are neatly presented. There is a lounge on the ground floor next to the attractive dining room, where hearty breakfasts are served. Motorcycle guided tours can be arranged for those travelling with their own motorbikes.

Rooms 7 en suite (1 fmly) (1 GF) S £35-£40; D £60-£70* **Facilities** FTV TVL tea/coffee Cen ht Wi-fi **Parking** 8 **Notes** ⊗

ARGYLL & BUTE

APPIN

Map 2 NM94

Pineapple House

★★★★ 🍴 GUEST HOUSE

Duror PA38 4BP
☎ 01631 740557 📠 01631 740557
e-mail: info@pineapplehouse.co.uk
dir: In Duror, off A828. 5m S of A82

Ideally located just south of Glencoe and just north of Appin, this period farmhouse has been lovingly restored and is extremely well presented using a great mix of modern and traditional. Dinners are available on request and use the best local quality produce. Service is friendly and genuine, making it a wonderful base for touring this area of Scotland.

Rooms 6 en suite (1 fmly) S £45; D £75-£95 **Facilities** FTV tea/coffee Dinner available Cen ht Wi-fi **Parking** 10 **Notes** ⊗ No Children 7yrs Closed Oct-25 Mar

ARDUAINE

Map 2 NM71

Loch Melfort

★★★ 83% HOTEL

◉◉ Modern British **V** ✋

First-class ingredients and stunning views

☎ 01852 200233 📠 01852 200214
PA34 4XG
e-mail: reception@lochmelfort.co.uk
web: www.lochmelfort.co.uk
dir: On A816, midway between Oban & Lochgilphead

This family-run Victorian country-house hideaway on the shores of Loch Melfort has fabulous views over Asknish Bay to the islands of Jura, Scarba and Shuna. Accommodation is provided in either the balconied rooms of the Cedar wing or the more traditional rooms in the main hotel. As you might hope, the traditional dining room has widescreen picture windows positioned to take full advantage of the spectacular backdrop to complement its accomplished modern Scottish cooking. The kitchen's approach is focused on local produce with a strong line in locally-caught fish, and fresh vegetables and herbs straight from the garden,

continued

ARDUAINE CONTINUED

which it translates into intelligent daily dinner menus. To start, grilled sea bream fillet might be served with chive risotto, tomato coulis and Cullen skink foam; next, sweet potato and coconut soup with wild mushrooms and truffle oil might intervene before a main course of roast monkfish wrapped in Parma ham with roasted pepper and parmesan tagliatelle and balsamic herb dressing. The meal ends strongly with walnut and apple tarte Tatin with vanilla ice cream. There is also a modern bar and bistro, the Chartroom II, with a relaxed atmosphere making it the place to enjoy all-day drinks and home baking, as well as light lunches and suppers. It has the finest views on the West Coast and serves home-made Scottish fare including plenty of locally landed seafood including fantastic langoustines, scallops, crabs, lobsters and mussels, Highland beef burgers and steak and ale pies. There are also four free moorings from April to October.

Rooms 25 (20 annexe) (2 fmly) (10 GF) **S** £102-£128; **D** £144-£196 (incl. bkfst)* **Facilities** 4 moorings ♫ Xmas New Year Wi-fi **Conf** Class 40 Board 20 Thtr 50 Del from £135* **Parking** 50 **Notes** Closed 4-20 Jan RS Winter Civ Wed 100

Chef David Bell **Owner** Calum & Rachel Ross **Times** 7-9 Closed mid 2 wks Jan, L all week **Prices** Fixed D 4 course fr £41, Service optional **Wines** 25 bottles over £20, 40 bottles under £20, 8 by glass **Notes** Vegetarian menu, Dress restrictions, Smart casual, no jeans **Seats** 60, Pr/dining room 14 **Children** Portions, Menu

BARCALDINE   Map 2 NM94

Barcaldine House

★★★★ GUEST ACCOMMODATION

 British

Classy modern cooking in a high-toned country mansion

PA37 1SG
☎ 01631 720219
e-mail: enquiries@barcaldinehouse.co.uk
web: www.barcaldinehouse.co.uk
dir: Located on A828 (North Argyll), between Oban and Fort William

Originally built in 1709 by Patrick Campbell IV of Barcaldine, this fine country house enjoys a peaceful location on lands that were once part of the extensive estates of the Campbells of Breadalbane. The house has undergone an extensive recent refurbishment, piling on the style in its eight guest rooms, and adding further class to what was already a fairly high-toned operation. Its dining room, which still has its ornate plaster mouldings and original fireplace, also enjoys enchanting views over the gardens. The daily-changing, fixed-price dinner menu of five courses, might offer up on a cold winter's night an opener of foie gras

ballottine with fig chutney and truffled walnut cream, followed by a pickled vegetable salad dressed with toasted seeds and aged sherry, and then a choice of mains - either Highland venison loin with ceps and red cabbage in sauce Grand Veneur, or Mallaig halibut and local shellfish with spinach in brown butter. After a serving of the Scottish heritage pudding, cranachan, there's a choice of either cheeses or a chocolate extravaganza.

Rooms 8 en suite (1 fmly) **Facilities** STV FTV tea/coffee Dinner available Direct Dial Cen ht Licensed Snooker **Conf** Max 24 Thtr 24 Board 24 **Parking** 16 **Notes** Civ Wed 40

Chef Oskars Kalnins **Times** 7-9 **Prices** Food prices not confirmed for 2012. Please telephone for details **Wines** 6 by glass **Notes** Vegetarian available **Seats** 32

CAIRNDOW   Map 2 NN11

Cairndow Stagecoach Inn

★★★ INN

PA26 8BN
☎ 01499 600286 & 600252 📠 01499 600252
e-mail: enq@cairndowinn.com
dir: From N, take either A82 to Tarbet, A83 to Cairndow, or A85 to Palmally, A819 to Inveraray & A83 to Cairndow

A relaxed, friendly atmosphere prevails at this 18th-century inn, overlooking the beautiful Loch Fyne. Bedrooms offer individual decor and thoughtful extras, while the deluxe bedrooms offer more space and luxury. Sample one of many malt whiskies in the friendly bar by the fire, or idle away the time in the loch-side garden watching the oyster-catchers while sipping the local Loch Fyne ales. The menu in the candlelit Stables Restaurant offers sautéed haunch of venison in red wine sauce; salmon from the loch; and home-made mushroom Stroganoff. Meals are also served all day in the bar and lounges.

Rooms 13 en suite 5 annexe en suite (2 fmly) (5 GF) **Facilities** STV FTV tea/coffee Dinner available Direct Dial Cen ht Wi-fi Sauna Solarium **Conf** Max 30 Thtr 30 Class 30 Board 30

Open all day all wk **Bar Meals** L served all wk 12-6 D served all wk 6-9 food served all day **Restaurant** L served all wk 12-6 booking required D served all wk 6-9 booking required food served all day ⊕ FREE HOUSE ◄ Fyne Ales Hurricane Jack, Avalanche, Piper's Gold, Maverick, Jarl. **Facilities** Children welcome Children's menu Children's portions Dogs allowed Garden Parking

CARRADALE Map 2 NR83

Dunvalanree

★★★★ GUEST ACCOMMODATION

◉ Modern British **V**

Superb seafood (and more) in stunning coastal location

Port Righ Bay PA28 6SE
☎ 01583 431226

e-mail: stay@dunvalanree.com
web: www.dunvalanree.com
dir: From centre of Carradale, turn right at x-rds, continue to end of road

This guest accommodation is a genuine family-run enterprise with mum at the stoves and father and daughter welcoming guests in the traditional restaurant. It is a special part of the world out here - a great base for exploring the wild Mull of Kintyre, or you could hop on a ferry to visit the tiny island of Gigha, and back at Dunvalanree there are fabulous views from across the Kilbrannan Sound to the hills of Arran. With just one sitting in the evening, meals have something of a relaxed dinner party ambience. In the kitchen, Alyson turns out simple yet skilfully-prepared Scottish cuisine from the area's fine produce in daily-changing table d'hôte dinner menus that might kick off with locally-smoked haddock tart with leeks and crème fraîche, and follow with Kilbrannon scallops on pea purée with saffron and lemon sauce; fans of local meat might go for roast topside of Ifferdale beef with Yorkshire pudding and pan gravy.

Rooms 5 en suite (1 GF) S £95; D £140-£175* (incl.dinner) **Facilities** tea/coffee Dinner available Cen ht Licensed Wi-fi Golf 9 Fishing **Parking** 8 **Notes** LB Civ Wed

Chef Alyson Milstead **Owner** Alan & Alyson Milstead **Times** 7 Closed L all week **Prices** Fixed D 3 course £22.50, Service optional **Wines** 2 bottles over £20, 11 bottles under £20, 4 by glass **Notes** Vegetarian menu **Seats** 18 **Children** Portions

CLACHAN-SEIL Map 2 NM71

Tigh an Truish Inn

PA34 4QZ ☎ 01852 300242
web: www.tighantruish.co.uk
dir: 12m S of Oban take A816. Onto B844 towards Atlantic Bridge

Popular with tourists and members of the yachting fraternity, the inn's waterfront beer garden is much in demand on summer days, when the tides can be watched as they swirl around the famous Bridge over the Atlantic. The inn's name has quite a tale attached: following the Battle of Culloden in 1746, kilts were outlawed on pain of death. The Seil islanders defied this edict at home but, on excursions to the mainland, they would stop at the Tigh an Truish - the

'house of trousers - to change into the hated trews. These days people pause here for single malts, regularly changing ales from local brewers, and a menu that includes plenty of seafood: salmon and mussels from Argyll producers, and lobster and prawns caught by local fishermen working the Firth of Lorne. Fish-free options include macaroni cheese, chef's beefburger and home-made steak and ale pie. For families, a separate lounge off the main bar is furnished with children's books - another indication of the pub's genuinely warm welcome.

Open all wk 11-11 (Mon-Fri 11-2.30 5-11 Oct-Mar) Closed: 25 Dec & 1 Jan **Bar Meals** L served all wk 12-2 D served all wk 6-8.30 (Apr-Oct) ⊕ FREE HOUSE ◀ Local guest ales, changing regularly. **Facilities** Children welcome Children's menu Children's portions Family room Dogs allowed Garden Parking

CONNEL Map 2 NM93

Falls of Lora Hotel

★★★ 77% HOTEL

☎ 01631 710483 📠 01631 710694
PA37 1PB
e-mail: enquiries@fallsoflora.com
web: www.fallsoflora.com
dir: From Glasgow take A82, A85. Hotel 0.5m past Connel sign (5m before Oban)

Personally run and welcoming, this long-established and thriving holiday hotel enjoys inspiring views over Loch Etive. The spacious ground floor takes in a comfortable, traditional lounge and a cocktail bar with over a hundred whiskies and an open log fire. Guests can eat in the popular, informal bistro, which is open all day. Bedrooms come in a variety of styles, ranging from the cosy standard rooms to high quality luxury rooms.

Rooms 30 (4 fmly) (4 GF) (30 smoking) S £29.50-£69.50; D £55-£151 (incl. bkfst)* **Facilities** FTV Wi-fi Child facilities **Conf** Class 20 Board 15 Thtr 45 **Parking** 40 **Notes** LB Closed mid Dec & Jan

Abandoned croft at Bettyhill, Sutherland

CONNEL CONTINUED

Ards House

★★★★★ 🛏 GUEST HOUSE

PA37 1PT
☎ 01631 710255 & 07703 438341 📠 01631 710857
e-mail: info@ardshouse.com
web: www.ardshouse.com
dir: On A85, 4m N of Oban

This delightful Victorian villa on the approaches to Loch Etive has stunning views over the Firth of Lorne and the Morven Hills beyond. The stylish bedrooms come with added touches such as mineral water and home-made shortbread. There is an inviting drawing room complete with piano, games and books, plus a fire on cooler evenings. The attractive dining room is the setting for delicious breakfasts.

Rooms 4 en suite S £50-£65; D £80-£90* **Facilities** FTV TVL tea/coffee Cen ht Wi-fi **Parking** 12 **Notes** LB ⊗ No Children 10yrs Closed mid Dec-mid Jan

The Oyster Inn

PA37 1PJ ☎ 01631 710666 📠 01631 710042
e-mail: stay@oysterinn.co.uk
dir: Telephone for directions

A comfortable, inviting hotel overlooking the tidal whirlpools and white water of the Falls of Lora, and enjoying glorious views of the mountains of Mull. It was built in the 18th century to serve ferry passengers, but the ferry has long since been superseded by the modern road bridge. Ferryman's Bar in the pub next door was, and still is, known as the Glue Pot. Years ago canny locals knew they could be 'stuck' here between ferries and evade Oban's Sunday licensing laws; additionally, a blacksmith's shop behind the pub melted down horses hooves for glue — the pots hang from the bar ceiling. Food is served all day in the bar and in the evenings in the restaurant. Using locally sourced quality produce, particularly from the sea and lochs, West Coast mussels marinière and ocean pie (smoked haddock, salmon,

mussels, prawns and squid) might appear on the menu. Meaty alternatives may include medallions of Scottish venison fillet with a mild Stornoway black pudding and port and redcurrant jus

Open all day all wk noon-mdnt **Bar Meals** L served all wk 12-6 D served all wk 6-9.30 Av main course £8 food served all day **Restaurant** D served all wk 6-9.30 Av 3 course à la carte fr £27 ⊕ FREE HOUSE ◀ Guinness, John Smith's. **Facilities** Children welcome Children's menu Children's portions Family room Dogs allowed Garden Parking Wi-fi

CRINAN   Map 2 NR79

Crinan Hotel

PA31 8SR ☎ 01546 830261 📠 01546 830292
e-mail: reservations@crinanhotel.com
dir: From M8, at end of bridge take A82, at Tarbert left onto A83. At Inveraray follow Campbeltown signs to Lochgilphead, follow signs for A816 to Oban. 2m, left to Crinan on B841

At the north end of the Crinan Canal which connects Loch Fyne to the Atlantic Ocean, the Crinan is a romantic retreat enjoying fabulous views across the sound of Jura. It's a long-standing place of welcome at the heart of community life in this tiny fishing village. The hotel dates back some 200 years and has been run by owners Nick and Frances Ryan for around 40 of them. Eat in the Crinan Seafood Bar or the Westward Restaurant. The cuisine is firmly based on the freshest of seafood — it's landed daily just 50 metres from the hotel. Starters could include brochettes of Loch Fyne scallops with organic salad leaves and balsamic reduction. For a main course perhaps choose grilled fillet of monkfish with caper lemon butter, or roast rack of Argyll Hill lamb. Boat trips can be arranged to the islands, and there is a classic boats regatta in the summer. Look for the 'secret garden' just behind the hotel.

Open all day all wk 11am-11pm Closed: 25 Dec **Bar Meals** L served all wk 12-2.30 D served all wk 6-8.30 **Restaurant** D served all wk 7-9 booking required ◀ Worthington Bitter, Tennent's Velvet, Guinness, Loch Fyne Ales. **Facilities** Children welcome Children's menu Children's portions Dogs allowed Garden Parking Wi-fi

DUNOON   Map 2 NS17

Selborne

★★ 74% HOTEL

☎ 01369 702761 📠 01369 704032
Clyde St, West Bay PA23 7HU
e-mail: selborne.dunoon@alfatravel.co.uk
dir: From Caledonian MacBrayne pier. Past castle, left into Jane St, right into Clyde St

This holiday hotel is situated overlooking the West Bay and provides unrestricted views of the Clyde Estuary towards the

Isles of Cumbrae. Tour groups are especially well catered for in this good-value establishment, which offers entertainment most nights. Bedrooms are comfortable and many have sea views.

Rooms 98 (6 fmly) (14 GF) **S** £36-£49; **D** £56-£82 (incl. bkfst) **Facilities** FTV Pool table Table tennis 🎵 Xmas New Year **Services** Lift **Parking** 30 **Notes** LB ⊗ Closed Dec-Feb (ex Xmas) RS Nov & Mar

Coylet Inn

Loch Eck PA23 8SG ☎ 01369 840426
e-mail: info@coyletinn.co.uk
dir: N of Dunoon on A815

A blissful hideaway with no television or games machines to disturb the peace, this charming, beautifully refurbished 17th-century coaching inn overlooks the shores of Loch Eck. You may relax and drink your pint of Pipers Gold or Highlander in peace by one of three log fires. Impressive menus are derived from fully traceable produce – from haggis fritters to ham 'n' haddy wi' a drappit egg, there's plenty to choose from. A perfect spot for walking, fishing, cycling or stalking.

Open all day Closed: 3-26 Jan, Mon & Tue (Oct-Mar) **Bar Meals** L served all wk 12-2.30 D served all wk 6-8.30 Av main course £10.95 **Restaurant** L served all wk 12-2.30 D served all wk 6-8.30 ⊕ FREE HOUSE ◀ Highlander, Pipers Gold, Guest ales. **Facilities** Children welcome Children's menu Children's portions Dogs allowed Garden Parking

ERISKA — Map 2 NM94

Isle of Eriska Hotel, Spa & Golf

★★★★★ COUNTRY HOUSE HOTEL

Rosettes not confirmed at time of going to press

Modern British 🍷NOTABLE WINE LIST

Confident cooking at luxurious island retreat

☎ 01631 720371 📄 01631 720531
Eriska, Benderloch, By Oban PA37 1SD
e-mail: office@eriska-hotel.co.uk
dir: Exit A85 at Connel, onto A828, 4m, follow hotel signs from N of Benderloch

There's something magical about an island and Eriska, a 300-acre estate separated from the mainland by an iron bridge, is a place more than capable of ensuring equanimity in body and soul. The wild, natural landscape offers plenty of opportunities for exercise and contemplation, while a golf course is available for those in need of a little healthy competition. The house itself is a Victorian baronial mansion with more than a whiff of castle about it, delivering a top-drawer country-house experience in the form of luxurious bedrooms, a spa, and dining of the highest order. The restaurant is a series of spaces, elegantly proportioned and including a conservatory, with a décor which has a contemporary sheen whilst remaining true to the traditional feel of the building. As we went to press we learned that Robert Macpherson had left the stoves after nigh on 25 years, with a new chef due to be appointed. Dishes from the previous menu included roast Scottish young partridge, for example, with a fine parmesan, thyme and autumn chanterelle tart, is one way to start, preceding a superb piece of roast turbot with cabbage, deliciously plump Loch Linnhe langoustines, mustard cannelloni and vermouth sauce. To finish, griottine cherry tart is served with poached pear and cherry compôte. All the accompanying ancillary bits and pieces - amuse-bouche, breads, petits fours - are first rate, and the front-of-house team are especially worthy of praise.

Rooms 23 (6 fmly) (2 GF) **S** £250-£460; **D** £330-£460 (incl. bkfst)* **Facilities Spa** FTV 🎣 supervised ♪ 9 ⛳ Putt green Fishing 🎣 Gym Squash Sauna Steam room Skeet shooting Nature trails Xmas New Year Wi-fi **Conf** Class 30 Board 30 Thtr 30 **Parking** 40 **Notes** Closed Jan Civ Wed 50

Owner Mr Buchanan-Smith **Times** 7.30-9 Closed Jan **Prices** Fixed D 4 course £44, Service optional **Wines** 236 bottles over £20, 60 bottles under £20, 10 by glass **Notes** Vegetarian available **Seats** 50, Pr/dining room 20 **Children** Portions, Menu

HELENSBURGH — Map 2 NS28

Lethamhill

★★★★★ GUEST ACCOMMODATION

West Dhuhill Dr G84 9AW
☎ 01436 676016 & 07974 798593 📄 01436 676016
e-mail: jane@lethamhill.co.uk
web: www.lethamhill.co.uk
dir: 1m N of pier/town centre. Off A818 onto West Dhuhill Dr. Cross Upper Colquhoun St, then 3rd entrance on right

From the red phone box in the garden to the old typewriters and slot machines inside, this fine house is an Aladdin's cave of unusual collectibles and memorabilia. The house itself offers spacious and comfortable bedrooms with superb bathrooms. The home-cooked breakfasts and delicious baking earn much praise.

Rooms 3 en suite S £65-£70; D £85-£90* **Facilities** FTV tea/coffee Cen ht Wi-fi **Parking** 6 **Notes** LB ⊗

KILCHRENAN
Map 2 NN02

Taychreggan

★★★★ 76% COUNTRY HOUSE HOTEL

◉◉ Modern British **V**

Modern British cooking with sublime loch views

☎ 01866 833211 & 833366 📠 01866 833244
PA35 1HQ
e-mail: info@taychregganhotel.co.uk
dir: W from Crianlarich on A85 to Taynuilt, S for 7m on B845 (single track) to Kilchrenan

This cossetting country-house hotel is a far cry from the simple 17th-century drovers' inn that once put up herders who swam their cattle across Loch Awe. Taychreggan sits in glorious isolation on a peninsula jutting out into the loch; set in 40 acres of wooded grounds with uplifting Highland scenery all around - a view that can be appreciated at leisure from the arched windows of the restaurant. On the food front, the kitchen treads a line between keeping customers happy with old favourites and evolving into more creative French-influenced modern cooking. Four-course dinner sets off with Inverawe smoked haddock flan with red pepper coulis and rocket, follows with a cauliflower velouté with truffle oil, then mains of Gressingham duck breast with Puy lentils, shallot purée, French beans, confit pâté and Madeira jus. An apple crumble soufflé with crème anglaise finishes strongly. The hotel has a smart bar and a choice of quiet lounges with deep, luxurious sofas. Families, and also dogs and their owners, are very welcome.

Rooms 18 (1 fmly) **S** £91-£176; **D** £122-£292 (incl. bkfst) **Facilities** FTV Fishing ✈ Air rifle range Archery Clay pigeon shooting Falconry Mock deer stalk Xmas New Year Wi-fi Child facilities **Conf** Class 15 Board 20 **Parking** 40 **Notes** Closed 3 Jan-9 Feb Civ Wed 70

Chef Colin Cairns **Owner** North American Country Inns **Times** 7-8.45 Closed 3 Jan-9 Feb **Prices** Service optional **Wines** 54 bottles over £20, 16 bottles under £20, 11 by glass **Notes** Fixed 5 course menu £45, Vegetarian menu, Dress restrictions, Smart casual **Seats** 45, Pr/dining room 18 **Children** Portions

The Ardanaiseig

★★★ COUNTRY HOUSE HOTEL

◉◉◉ Modern Scottish **V**

Excellent food in peaceful hotel with stunning views

☎ 01866 833333 📠 01866 833222
by Loch Awe PA35 1HE
e-mail: ardanaiseig@clara.net
web: www.ardanaiseig.com
dir: A85 at Taynuilt onto B845 to Kilchrenan. Left in front of pub (road very narrow) signed 'Ardanaiseig Hotel' & 'No Through Road'. Continue for 3m

The chap who designed this house is also responsible for some of Edinburgh's finest buildings, and it shows: the Victorian (well, it was built in 1834) baronial house of generous proportions has copious soaring chimney stacks, gables, and the requisite tower (albeit a diminutive one). And then there's its position: surrounded by lush gardens, looking out across the waters of Loch Awe to Ben Cruachan. If it sounds like a romantic spot, that's because it most certainly is. Inside it is richly done out with a good deal of style in the traditional manner, so lots of classy antiques and bold, warm colours, with the original features and grand proportions of the rooms giving it a timeless quality. Many fine pieces of furniture are evident in the bedrooms and charming day rooms, which include a drawing room, a library bar and an elegant dining room. The bedrooms are individually designed and include some with four posters, some with loch views and some with access to the garden; standing on its own by the water is the Boat Shed, a delightful one bedroom suite. The dining room is dressed up to the nines, with dark green walls, red carpet, and white linen-clad tables, while the service style is formal but engaging. Gary Goldie has been at the stoves here for more than a decade and has got the kitchen firing on all cylinders. There's a bedrock of classic French technique in his cooking, combined with a good deal of contemporary creativity and a keen eye for buying the best of Scottish produce, with the local waters and the hotel's own kitchen garden the source of many of the ingredients. The fixed-price menu might kick off with a velouté of butternut squash with shaved parmesan and Périgord truffle before the fish course, perhaps Loch Duart salmon, pan-fried and served with a warm potato and beetroot salad. Next up, perhaps best end of lamb with ras el hanout basmati rice risotto, parsley root purée, hazelnuts and apricots, or chargrilled fillet of Aberdeen Angus with Cevenne onion purée, winter vegetable chips and bordelaise syrup. And whichever way you choose to finish - sweetly with the likes of lemon tart with iced yoghurt or a savoury plate of French or Scottish cheese - you're sure to feel a warm glow of satisfaction.

Rooms 18 (4 fmly) (5 GF) **S** £73-£113; **D** £146-£226 (incl. bkfst)* **Facilities** FTV Fishing ✈ Boating Clay pigeon shooting Bikes for hire Xmas New Year Wi-fi **Parking** 20 **Notes** LB Closed 2 Jan-1 Feb Civ Wed 50

Chef Gary Goldie **Owner** Bennie Gray **Times** 12-2/7-9
Closed 2 Jan-10 Feb **Prices** Fixed L 2 course £25, Fixed D 2
course £50, Service optional **Wines** 94 bottles over £20, 4
bottles under £20, 16 by glass **Notes** Gourmet tasting menu
available, Sunday L, Vegetarian menu, Dress restrictions,
Smart casual, no jeans or trainers **Seats** 36
Children Portions, Menu

KILFINAN	Map 2 NR97

Kilfinan Hotel Bar

PA21 2EP ☎ 01700 821201 📄 01700 821205
e-mail: info@kilfinan.com
dir: 8m N of Tighnabruaich on B8000

On the eastern shore of Loch Fyne, set amid spectacular
Highland scenery on a working estate, this hotel has been
welcoming travellers since the 1760s. The bars are cosy with
log fires in winter, and offer a fine selection of malts. There
are two intimate dining rooms, with the Lamont room for
larger parties. Menus change daily and offer the best of
local produce: Loch Fyne langoustines grilled in garlic and
butter; pan seared Loch Fyne scallops with crispy bacon and
sage; or Isle of Bute venison steak. Enjoy the views from the
garden on warmer days.

Open all wk Closed: winter ⊕ FREE HOUSE ◀ McEwens
80/-, Fyne Ales. **Facilities** Children welcome Children's
menu Children's portions Family room Dogs allowed Garden
Parking

LOCHGILPHEAD	Map 2 NR88

Cairnbaan

★★★ 78% HOTEL

◉ British, European

Canal views and local ingredients

☎ 01546 603668 📄 01546 606045
Crinan Canal, Cairnbaan PA31 8SJ
e-mail: info@cairnbaan.com
web: www.cairnbaan.com
dir: 2m N, A816 from Lochgilphead, hotel off B841

The Cairnbaan has been around since 1801, built to serve
the waterborne traffic and fishermen along the newly-opened
Crinan Canal. The old coaching house sits halfway along the
nine-mile waterway connecting Loch Fyne with the Sound of
Jura on the western coast, and is run with easygoing
informality. Bedrooms are thoughtfully equipped, generally
spacious and benefit from stylish decor. Lighter meals are
served from the bistro-style menu in the relaxed atmosphere
of the bar, conservatory lounge, or alfresco. The restaurant
is smartly done out with high-backed leather chairs and
splashes of colourful art, while a split-level layout lets
everyone enjoy the view of 'Britain's most beautiful short
cut'. Given the easy access to splendid piscine produce, the

menu of uncomplicated modern ideas has a strong line in
fish and seafood - perhaps seared scallops with Stornoway
black pudding and pea purée to start, then grilled sea bass
given a Mediterranean touch with a stew of fennel, tomato
and black olives.

Rooms 12 **Facilities** Xmas **Conf** Class 100 Board 80
Thtr 160 **Parking** 53 **Notes** Civ Wed 120

Open all wk 8am-11pm Closed: 25 Dec **Bar Meals** L served
all wk 12-2.30 D served all wk 6-9.30 **Restaurant** L served
all wk 12-2.30 D served all wk 6-9.30 ⊕ FREE HOUSE
◀ Local ales. ♟ 8 **Facilities** Children welcome Children's
menu Children's portions Garden Wi-fi

LUSS	Map 2 NS39

The Lodge on Loch Lomond

★★★★ 76% HOTEL

◉◉ Modern British ᥫ

Idyllic Loch Lomond location for fine dining

☎ 01436 860201 📄 01436 860203
G83 8PA
e-mail: res@loch-lomond.co.uk
web: www.loch-lomond.co.uk
dir: Off A82, follow sign for hotel

The Lodge on Loch Lomond couldn't be more aptly named:
waves lap at its very foundations, and dense pine woods
crowd all around, making the cares of the world seem very
distant. The pine-finished bedrooms enjoy beautiful views of
the loch and are comfortable, spacious and well equipped;
some have en suite saunas and private balconies. There are
spa facilities available in the state-of-the-art health suite.
The fine-dining Colquhoun's restaurant has a fresh
Scotland-meets-Scandinavia décor of pine walls and pillars,
but it is the grandstand views across the celebrated lake
through a wall of full-length windows that really grab the
attention. This unbeatable beachfront position turns into a
little slice of heaven when fine days allow you onto the
decked terrace for open-air dining. The kitchen has an eye
for both comfort and invention in its menu of modern
Scottish dishes, so tangy rhubarb is used to point up a rich
terrine of duck confit, while main courses could see braised
pork belly partnered with black pudding and apple hash

continued

LUSS CONTINUED

brown, parsnip velouté, and cider café au lait. For dessert, blood orange mousse perhaps, served with candied pistachios.

Rooms 47 (17 annexe) (20 fmly) (13 GF) **Facilities** Spa STV FTV 🎣 Fishing Boating Xmas New Year Wi-fi **Conf** Class 80 Board 60 Thtr 150 **Parking** 120 **Notes** Civ Wed 100

Chef Donn Eadie **Owner** Niall Colquhoun **Times** 12-5/6-9.45 **Prices** Food prices not confirmed for 2012. Please telephone for details **Wines** 29 bottles over £20, 20 bottles under £20, 7 by glass **Notes** Sunday L, Vegetarian available **Seats** 100, Pr/dining room 40 **Children** Portions, Menu

The Inn at Inverbeg

 ★★★★ 🏨 🍽 INN

Inverbeg G83 8PD
☎ 01436 860678 📠 01436 860203
e-mail: inverbeg.reception@loch-lomond.co.uk
dir: A82 N of Balloch

Less than half an hour's drive from Glasgow International Airport, and set in glorious scenery with stunning views of Loch Lomond and Ben Lomond, this 18th century inn blends contemporary and rustic styles, making it the perfect stop for visitors exploring the West Highlands. Comfortable, individually styled rooms are split between the inn and, right by the loch, a sumptuous beach house featuring wooden floors, hand-crafted furniture, crisp linen, and a hot tub. Mr C's Fish & Whisky Restaurant/Bar celebrates two things Scotland is famous for: fresh fish and fantastic whisky. Try a starter of smoke house salmon pâté or West Coast steamed mussels, a main of Inverbeg traditional fish supper or home-made fishcakes. Meat dishes include skillet of sirloin with chips and home-made steak pie. Choose from more than 200 malts and real ales, such as Deuchars IPA and Highlander. There is traditional, live folk music every night from April to November.

Rooms 12 en suite 8 annexe en suite (1 fmly) (5 GF) **Facilities** STV FTV TVL tea/coffee Dinner available Cen ht Wi-fi **Parking** 60 **Notes** ⊗ Civ Wed 60

Open all day all wk Mon-Thu & Sun 11-11 (Fri-Sat 11am-mdnt) **Bar Meals** L served all wk 12-9 D served all wk 12-9 Av main course £9.95 food served all day **Restaurant** L

served all wk 12-9 D served all wk 12-9 food served all day ⊕ FREE HOUSE 🍺 Killellan, Highlander, Deuchars IPA. 🍷 30 **Facilities** Children welcome Children's menu Children's portions Wi-fi

Manor House

★★★ 83% HOTEL

◉ Traditional European

Elegant Georgian dower house with quality local produce

☎ 01631 562087 📠 01631 563053
Gallanach Rd PA34 4LS
e-mail: info@manorhouseoban.com
web: www.manorhouseoban.com
dir: Follow MacBrayne Ferries signs, pass ferry entrance for hotel on right

The Duke of Argyll picked the best spot in town for the main residence on his Oban estate. Built in 1780, the Manor House looks clear across Oban Bay to the Isle of Kerrera, while the interior has held on to its authentic Georgian elegance - rich, warming colours on the walls and, in the dining room, oak panelling, tartans and the original cast-iron range. Watch the CalMac ferries in the harbour below as you sip aperitifs in the bar and drawing room, or if fine weather permits, out on the garden terrace. Five-course dinner menus change daily, delivering a European-accented repertoire that might kick off with hot-smoked Argyll salmon with sweet pepper relish and lime vinaigrette, then progress via soup and sorbet to thyme-scented breast of duck with braised red cabbage, and sweet potato and orange glaze. The relaxing public rooms are comfortable and attractive, while most of the well-equipped bedrooms are furnished with period pieces.

Rooms 11 (1 GF) **Facilities** New Year Wi-fi **Parking** 20 **Notes** No children 12yrs Closed 25-26 Dec Civ Wed 30

Chef Patrick Freytag, Shaun Squire **Owner** Mr P L Crane **Times** 12-2.30/6.45-8.45 Closed 25-26 Dec **Prices** Food prices not confirmed for 2012. Please telephone for details **Wines** 23 bottles over £20, 32 bottles under £20, 8 by glass **Notes** Vegetarian available, Dress restrictions, Smart casual **Seats** 34 **Children** Portions

Falls of Lora Hotel

★★★ 77% HOTEL

☎ 01631 710483 📠 01631 710694
PA37 1PB
e-mail: enquiries@fallsoflora.com
web: www.fallsoflora.com

(For full entry see Connel)

Royal

★★★ 75% HOTEL

☎ 01631 563021 📄 01631 562811
Argyll Square PA34 4BE
e-mail: salesroyaloban@strathmorehotels.com
dir: A82 from Glasgow towards Loch Lomond & Crianlarich
then A85 (pass Loch Awe) to Oban

Well situated in the heart of Oban, just minutes from the
ferry terminal and with all the shops on its doorstep, this
hotel really is central. The comfortable and well-presented
bedrooms differ in size, and all public areas are smart.
There is a first-floor restaurant overlooking the town square.

Rooms 91 (5 fmly) **S** £35–£70; **D** £70–£140 (incl. bkfst)*
Facilities 🎵 Xmas New Year Wi-fi **Conf** Class 60 Board 30
Thtr 140 **Services** Lift **Parking** 25 **Notes** Civ Wed 70

The Oban Caledonian Hotel

★★★ 74% HOTEL

☎ 0845 855 9135 📄 01631 562998
Station Square PA34 5RT
e-mail: reservations.caledonian@akkeronhotels.com
web: www.akkeronhotels.com
dir: Opposite ferry & rail terminals

This Victorian hotel, overlooking the bay, has an enviable
location close to the ferry terminal and parking, as well as
Oban's many attractions. Public areas are modern and
stylish and include a smart restaurant, spacious lounges
and an informal dining option in Café Caledonian. Attractive
bedrooms come in a number of different styles and grades,
some with comfortable seating areas, feature bathrooms
and fine sea views.

Rooms 59 (6 fmly) **D** £59–£185* **Facilities** Xmas New Year
Wi-fi **Conf** Class 90 Board 50 Thtr 100 **Services** Lift
Notes Civ Wed 100

The Columba Hotel

★★★ 72% HOTEL

☎ 01631 562183 📄 01631 564683
The Esplanade PA34 5QD
e-mail: columba@mckeverhotels.co.uk
dir: A85 to Oban, at 1st lights turn right

One of Oban's landmarks, this Victorian hotel is located on
the seafront with stunning views out over the Firth of Lorne
to the Isle of Mull. The well-appointed, contemporary
bedrooms offer guests comfortable accommodation. Alba
Restaurant provides a menu of modern Scottish dishes.

Rooms 49 (5 fmly) **Facilities** FTV 🎵 Xmas New Year Wi-fi
Services Lift **Parking** 6 **Notes** LB ⊗

Glenburnie House

★★★★ GUEST HOUSE

The Esplanade PA34 5AQ
☎ **01631 562089** 📄 **01631 562089**
e-mail: graeme.strachan@btinternet.com
dir: On Oban seafront. Follow signs for Ganavan

This impressive seafront Victorian house has been lovingly
restored to a high standard. Bedrooms (including a four-
poster room and a mini-suite) are beautifully decorated and
very well equipped. There is a cosy ground-floor lounge and
an elegant dining room, where hearty traditional breakfasts
are served at individual tables.

Rooms 12 en suite (2 GF) S £55–£60; D £90–£110*
Facilities FTV tea/coffee Cen ht Wi-fi **Parking** 12 **Notes** LB
⊗ No Children 12yrs Closed Dec-Feb

Braeside

★★★★ GUEST HOUSE

Kilmore PA34 4QR
☎ **01631 770243** 📄 **01631 770343**
e-mail: braeside.guesthouse@virgin.net
web: www.braesideguesthouse.net
dir: On A816 5m from Oban

This family-run bungalow stands in gardens overlooking the
spectacular Loch Feochan. Bedrooms, all en suite, are bright
and airy, well equipped and have easy access. The lounge-
dining room has a loch view, a bar with a range of single
malts, wines and a wonderful array of local beers, and offers
a varied choice of tasty home-cooked evening meals and
breakfasts.

Rooms 5 en suite (1 fmly) (5 GF) **Facilities** tea/coffee
Dinner available Cen ht Licensed Wi-fi **Parking** 6 **Notes** LB
⊗ No Children 8yrs

Corriemar House

★★★★ GUEST HOUSE

Corran Esplanade PA34 5AQ
☎ **01631 562476** 📄 **01631 564339**
e-mail: info@corriemarhouse.co.uk
web: www.corriemarhouse.co.uk
dir: A85 to Oban. Down hill in right lane & follow sign for
Ganavan at mini rdbt onto Esplanade

Billy and Sandra Russell have created a stylish haven of
tranquillity at this detached Victorian house close to the
town centre. Bedrooms are furnished with panache, range
from massive to cosy, and even include a suite. Those to the
front of the house have stunning views across Oban Bay to
the Isle of Mull. Expect a substantial breakfast and friendly
attentive service.

Rooms 9 en suite 4 annexe en suite (3 fmly) (1 GF) **Facilities**
tea/coffee Cen ht **Parking** 9 **Notes** ⊗

Lancaster

★★ GUEST ACCOMMODATION

Corran Esplanade PA34 5AD
☎ **01631 562587** 📄 **01631 562587**
e-mail: lancasteroban@btconnect.com
dir: On seafront next to Columba's Cathedral

A family-run establishment on the esplanade that offers
budget accommodation; many bedrooms boast lovely views
out over the bay towards the Isle of Mull. Public areas
include a choice of lounges and bars that also benefit from
the panoramic views. A swimming pool, sauna and jacuzzi
are added benefits.

Rooms 27 rms (24 en suite) (3 fmly) (10 smoking)
Facilities FTV TVL tea/coffee Cen ht Licensed 🐟 Sauna Pool
table Jacuzzi Steam room **Conf** Max 30 Thtr 30 Class 20
Board 12 **Parking** 20 **Notes** LB

Coast

◉◉ Modern

Chic, high street eatery with classy cooking

☎ 01631 569900
104 George St PA34 5NT
e-mail: coastoban@yahoo.co.uk
web: www.coastoban.co.uk
dir: On main street in town centre

Coast is housed in what was once a high street bank and it
retains the impressive original granite façade. Where once
stood bored clerks and plastic screens are bare-wood tables,
autumnal colours on the walls and chairs, plus some raised
tables affording a view onto the main street. On the
seasonal menu much is rightly made of first-class local
produce from sea and land, turned into refined,
contemporary dishes. Crab and spinach risotto, for example,
with chive crème fraîche and parsnip crisps, followed by
roasted partridge with roast potatoes, braised endive, wild
mushrooms, spinach and cocoa nibs. For dessert, dark
chocolate and salted caramel tart with tonka bean ice cream
is a suitably fashionable conclusion.

Chef Richard Fowler **Owner** Richard & Nicola Fowler
Times 12-2/5.30-9.30 Closed 25 Dec, 2 wks Jan, Sun (Nov-
Mar), L Sun **Prices** Fixed L 2 course £12.95, Fixed D 3 course
£15.95, Starter £4.50-£8.95, Main £13.50-£22.95, Dessert
£6.25, Service optional, Groups min 8 service 10% **Wines** 19
bottles over £20, 22 bottles under £20, 5 by glass
Notes Fixed D available early eve, Vegetarian available
Seats 46 **Parking** On street

Kilchurn Castle on Loch Awe

PORT APPIN — Map 2 NM94

Airds Hotel

 ★★★★ SMALL HOTEL

Rosettes not confirmed at time of going to press

Modern British **V** 🍷 NOTABLE WINE LIST

Splendid Argyll views and first-class cooking

☎ 01631 730236 📠 01631 730535
PA38 4DF
e-mail: airds@airds-hotel.com
web: www.airds-hotel.com
dir: From A828 (Oban to Fort William road), turn at Appin signed Port Appin. Hotel 2.5m on left

Airds is a whitewashed 18th-century ferry inn that in a former life put up farmers and livestock on their way to market. In its current incarnation as a sophisticated hotel, it is small and intimate enough to feel homely, but run with consummate professionalism and high standards of service, and furnished in opulent style. Unforgettable views from the dining room sweep across the Sound of Lismore to Loch Linnhe and the Morven Mountains beyond - a jaw-dropping tableau to accompany four-course dinners. The kitchen is a vital part of the show, and we learned of a change of chef just as we went to press. After many years at the Isle of Eriska (see entry) Robert Macpherson has arrived to take charge. Fish and seafood comes fresh from the Oban fleet, and all ingredients are outstanding and chosen for seasonality. Previous menus included dishes such as pan-seared Mull scallops with mushroom, parmesan and herb risotto before citrus-grilled local halibut in a light mussel and pea broth, or a more robust roast fillet of Scotch beef with garden kale, onion marmalade and Pommery mustard sauce. Finish with a classic prune and Armagnac soufflé with crème anglaise. Vegetarians are not sidelined either: they get their own four-course menu. For such a small operation, the wine list punches well above its weight, and politely unstuffy service is the icing on the cake.

Rooms 11 (3 fmly) (2 GF) **D** £260-£460 (incl. bkfst & dinner)* **Facilities** FTV Putt green 🦢 Xmas New Year Wi-fi **Conf** Class 16 Board 16 Thtr 16 **Parking** 20 **Notes** LB RS Nov-Jan Civ Wed 40

Chef Robert Macpherson **Owner** Mr & Mrs S McKivragan **Times** 12-1.45/7.30-9.30 **Prices** Fixed L 3 course £21.95, Fixed D 4 course £53, Tasting menu £70, Service optional **Wines** 225 bottles over £20, 10 bottles under £20, 12 by glass **Notes** Tasting menu D , Gourmet evenings twice weekly, Sunday L, Vegetarian menu, Dress restrictions, Smart casual at D, no jeans/trainers/T-shirts **Seats** 32 **Children** Portions, Menu

Pierhouse

★★★ 80% SMALL HOTEL

🍴 Modern, International

Top-notch fish and seafood with stunning views

☎ 01631 730302 & 730622 📠 01631 730509
PA38 4DE
e-mail: reservations@pierhousehotel.co.uk
web: www.pierhousehotel.co.uk
dir: A828 from Ballachulish to Oban. In Appin right at Port Appin & Lismore ferry sign. After 2.5m left after post office, hotel at end of road

Originally the residence of the Pier Master, with parts of the building dating back to the 19th century, this small family-run hotel is located on the shores of Loch Linnhe with picture-postcard views to the islands of Lismore and Mull. The luminous brasserie-style restaurant sits next to the jetty where the little foot passenger ferry shuttles across the loch to Lismore Island, and peaks spear the skyline beyond. As you might hope in such a glorious location, it is all about fish and seafood here: lobsters and langoustines will have been in the sea a few hours before day boats deliver them at the pier on the doorstep for dinner, while oysters and mussels are hand-picked from the Lismore shellfish beds. There's no point faffing about with produce like that, so the kitchen keeps it all simple: who could resist freshly-landed grilled langoustine with garlic butter to start things off? Main-course monkfish is wrapped in Parma ham and served with crushed new potatoes and tomato salsa, while sticklers for seasonality will appreciate the dates of the hunting season on the menu - maybe roasted venison with fondant potato, buttered kale and meat jus will be on the menu. Lunches in the Ferry bar range from freshly-filled ciabattas and baked potatoes to burgers, pastas and fish dishes. The beautifully appointed, individually designed bedrooms include two with four-poster beds and superb loch views, and three triple family rooms. All have Wi-fi access and include Arran Aromatics toiletries. The hotel has a Finnish sauna, and also offers a range of treatments. Babysitting can be arranged.

Rooms 12 (3 fmly) (6 GF) **Facilities** FTV Aromatherapy Massage Sauna New Year Wi-fi **Conf** Class 20 Board 20 Thtr 20 **Parking** 20 **Notes** LB Closed 25-26 Dec Civ Wed 80

Open all wk 11am-11pm Closed: 25-26 Dec **Bar Meals** L served all wk 12.30-2.30 D served all wk 6.30-9.30 Av main course £10 **Restaurant** L served all wk 12.30-2.30 booking required D served all wk 6.30-9.30 booking required Av 3 course à la carte fr £27.50 ⊕ FREE HOUSE ◀ Calders 80/-, Belhaven Best, Guinness. **Facilities** Children welcome Children's portions Family room Dogs allowed Garden

Rosslea Hall Hotel

★★★ 79% HOTEL

☎ 01436 439955 📄 01436 820897
Ferry Rd G84 8NF
dir: On A814, opposite church

Overlooking the Firth of the Clyde and close to Helensburgh, this imposing mansion is set in its own well tended gardens. Bedrooms and bathrooms are of a good size, well appointed and cater well for the modern traveller. The eating options include the Conservatory Restaurant, overlooking the grounds and the Clyde, which offers dishes cooked with imagination and flair. The hotel is a popular wedding venue.

Rooms 30 (3 fmly) (2 GF) **Facilities** FTV Xmas New Year Wi-fi
Conf Class 60 Board 80 Thtr 150 **Parking** 30 **Notes** ⊗
Civ Wed 110

Creggans Inn

★★★ 80% HOTEL

◉◉ Modern British, French

Locally-sourced cooking on the shore of Loch Fyne

☎ 01369 860279 📄 01369 860637
PA27 8BX
e-mail: info@creggans-inn.co.uk
web: www.creggans-inn.co.uk
dir: A82 from Glasgow, at Tarbet take A83 towards Cairndow, left onto A815 to Strachur

Situated in remote splendour on one of the western inlets of Scotland, and yet not too far from Glasgow, Creggans is a handsomely sized whitewashed inn overlooking Loch Fyne. The MacLellan family run the place like a home from home, where many of the bedrooms are generous in size and enjoy wonderful views of the loch, while comfortable lounges and a daylight-filled dining room offer all the creature comforts, and the kitchen sources from the surrounding waters and hills. Local salmon is hot-smoked and served with potato salad perked up with horseradish and a honey-mustard dressing, while scallops from the loch are briefly sautéed and partnered with ratatouille, ruby chard and fennel. After

a pause for a sorbet, it's on to mains such as slow-braised ox cheek on champ, with caramelised roots in red wine gravy, or roast salmon on Cullen skink risotto in a sauce of Chardonnay butter. Finish with banana parfait, garnished with caramelised banana and toffee sauce. A good range of Scottish ales, including Atlas Latitude and Harviestoun Bitter and Twisted, and some fine malt whiskies are all served at the bar, and there's a formal terraced garden and patio for alfresco summer enjoyment – both make the most of the view.

Rooms 14 (2 fmly) **Facilities** New Year Wi-fi **Parking** 16
Notes Civ Wed 80

Chef Gordon Smilie **Owner** The MacLellan Family **Times** 7-9
Closed 25-26 Dec, L all week **Prices** Fixed D 4 course fr £37,
Starter £4.25-£10.95, Main £11-£19, Dessert £6.50-£7.50,
Service optional **Wines** 32 bottles over £20, 33 bottles under
£20, 6 by glass **Notes** Vegetarian available, Dress
restrictions, Smart casual **Seats** 35 **Children** Portions, Menu

Stonefield Castle

★★★★ 73% HOTEL

◉ Modern British

Plenty of local flavours in an old baronial keep

☎ 01880 820836 📄 01880 820929
PA29 6YJ
e-mail: reservations.stonefieldcastle@ohiml.com
web: www.oxfordhotelsandinns.com
dir: From Glasgow take M8 towards Erskine Bridge onto A82, follow Loch Lomond signs. From Arrochar follow A83 signs through Inveraray & Lochgilphead, hotel on left 2m before Tarbert

continued

TARBERT LOCH FYNE CONTINUED

Stonefield Castle is everything you could ask of a Highland castle hotel. Built in 1837, the turrets and stepped gables of this Victorian Scottish baronial fantasy soar from its perch high on the Kintyre peninsula, lording it over 60 acres of mature woodland and gardens (renowned for their rhododendrons - visit in late spring to see them at their best). Elegant public rooms are a feature, and bedrooms are split between the main house and a purpose-built wing. There is plenty of period grandeur in the restaurant, and the bonus of unforgettable views over Loch Fyne through vast picture windows. The kitchen is committed to local produce, especially the sort that is landed by boat at Tarbert, or shot on local estates, which it deploys in modern dishes with clear classical undertones, as typified by Tarbert langoustines served simply with caper and shallot hollandaise, or crisp duck confit partnered with Anna potatoes, glazed plums, creamed Savoy cabbage and roasting juices. To finish, the Scottish cheeses are particularly fine, while the sweet tooth might prefer apple tarte Tatin with purple basil jam and vanilla ice cream.

Rooms 32 (2 fmly) (10 GF) **Facilities** Xmas New Year Wi-fi **Conf** Class 40 Board 50 Thtr 120 **Services** Lift **Parking** 50 **Notes** Civ Wed 100

Chef Oscar Sinjorgo **Owner** Oxford Hotels & Inns **Times** 12-9 **Prices** Starter £5-£12, Main fr £15, Service optional **Wines** 23 bottles over £20, 38 bottles under £20, 6 by glass **Notes** Vegetarian available, Dress restrictions, Smart casual **Seats** 120, Pr/dining room 40 **Children** Portions, Menu

TAYVALLICH
Map 2 NR78

Tayvallich Inn ♀

PA31 8PL ☎ **01546 870282**
dir: From Lochgilphead take A816 then B841/B8025

The inn stands by a natural harbour at the head of Loch Sween with stunning views over the anchorage, particularly from the outside area of decking, where food and a great selection of real ales can be enjoyed. Not surprisingly given the location, fresh seafood features strongly – the catch is landed from the boats right outside the front door! There's always lobster, crab and langoustine available in the summer and other typical dishes might be line-caught haddock served with chips; fish pie; beef and ale pie; and home-made burgers.

Open all wk all day in summer (closed 3-6 Mon-Fri in winter) Closed: 25-26 Dec, Mon (Nov-Mar) **Bar Meals** L served all wk 12-2.30 D served all wk 6-9 Av main course £9.95 **Restaurant** L served all wk 12-2.30 booking required D served all wk 6-9 booking required Av 3 course à la carte fr £17.95 ⊕ FREE HOUSE ◖ Guinness, Loch Fyne Ales, Belhaven Best, Maverick, Avalanche, Pipers Gold. ♀ 8 **Facilities** Children welcome Children's menu Children's portions Garden Parking

EAST AYRSHIRE

DALRYMPLE
Map 2 NS31

The Kirkton Inn

1 Main St KA6 6DF ☎ **01292 560241**
e-mail: kirkton@cqm.co.uk
dir: 6m SE from centre of Ayr just off A77

In the heart of the village of Dalrymple, this inn was built in 1879 as a coaching inn and has been providing sustenance to travellers ever since; the welcoming atmosphere makes it easy to feel at home. It's a stoutly traditional setting, with open fires and polished brasses. Eat traditional and wholesome dishes in the Coach Room in the oldest part of the building, and perhaps choose chicken and leek pie, or Kirkton burger, followed by hot chocolate fudge cake. Lighter options are soup and sandwiches.

Open all day all wk **Bar Meals** L served all wk 12-2.30 D served all wk 5-8 Av main course £7.50 **Restaurant** L served all wk 12-2.30 D served all wk 5-9 Fixed menu price fr £5.95 Av 3 course à la carte fr £15 ⊕ SCOTTISH & NEWCASTLE ◖ John Smith's, Guinness. **Facilities** Children welcome Children's menu Children's portions Play area Family room Dogs allowed Garden Parking Wi-fi

GATEHEAD
Map 2 NS33

The Cochrane Inn

45 Main Rd KA2 0AP ☎ **01563 570122**
dir: From Glasgow A77 to Kilmarnock, then A759 to Gatehead

There's a friendly, bustling atmosphere inside this traditional ivy-covered village centre pub, which sits just a short drive from the Ayrshire coast. The interior has natural stone walls adorned with gleaming brasses and log fires in winter. The menus combine British and international flavours in hearty, wholesome food. This might translate as salt and pepper squid with jalapeño salsa or smoked duck breast with apple salad, walnuts and orange dressing; then haggis, neeps and tatties; chicken stuffed with cream cheese, chorizo and garlic; or steak and sausage pie.

Open all wk noon-2.30 5.30 onwards (Sun noon-9) **Bar Meals** food served all day **Restaurant** food served all day ⊕ FREE HOUSE ◖ John Smith's. **Facilities** Children welcome Children's menu Children's portions Garden Parking Wi-fi

KILMARNOCK   Map 2 NS43

The Fenwick Hotel

★★★ 82% HOTEL

☎ 01560 600478 📄 01560 600334
Fenwick KA3 6AU
e-mail: info@thefenwickhotel.co.uk
web: www.thefenwickhotel.co.uk
dir: M77 junct 8, B7061 towards Fenwick, follow hotel signs

Benefiting from a great location alongside the M77 and offering easy links to Ayr, Kilmarnock and Glasgow. The spacious bedrooms are thoughtfully equipped; complimentary Wi-fi is available throughout the hotel. The bright restaurant offers both formal and informal dining and there are two bars to choose from.

Rooms 30 (1 fmly) (9 GF) **Facilities** STV Xmas New Year Wi-fi **Conf** Class 280 Board 150 Thtr 280 **Parking** 64 **Notes** Civ Wed 110

Premier Inn Kilmarnock

BUDGET HOTEL

☎ 0871 527 8566 📄 0871 527 8567
Moorfield Roundabout, Annadale KA1 2RS
web: www.premierinn.com
dir: M74 junct 8 signed Kilmarnock (A71). From M77 onto A71 to Irvine. At next rdbt right onto B7064 signed Crosshouse Hospital. Hotel on right

High quality, budget accommodation ideal for both families and business travellers. Spacious, en suite bedrooms feature tea and coffee-making facilities, and Freeview TV in most hotels. Internet access and Wi-fi are available for a small fee. The adjacent family restaurant features a wide and varied menu.

Rooms 40 **D** £52-£59*

SORN   Map 2 NS52

The Sorn Inn

★★★★ 🛏 RESTAURANT WITH ROOMS

◉◉ Modern British

Contemporary-styled coaching inn with modern cuisine

35 Main St KA5 6HU
☎ 01290 551305 📄 01290 553470
e-mail: craig@sorninn.com
dir: A70 from S or A76 from N onto B743 to Sorn

The knife and fork logo next to the Sorn Inn's name makes it clear from the off that this reinvented 18th-century coaching inn deep in the Ayrshire countryside has food at the heart of the operation. A smart contemporary interior features chocolate-brown leather chairs on funky tartan carpets, and whether you go for the cosier pubby Chop House or the chic fine-dining restaurant, robustly-flavoured brasserie-style dishes from the modern British repertoire are the kitchen's stock in trade. Produce is judiciously sourced and reflects the seasons. Seared breast of wood pigeon might share a plate with thyme polenta, fricassée of wild mushrooms and truffle foam in a full-on starter, while mains run from 36-day-aged Scotch steaks from the grill, to comforting classics such as pan-fried calves' liver with bubble-and-squeak, onion marmalade and devilled sauce, or a more ambitious assemblage of honey-confit duck leg with orange and green olives, sage crushed potatoes, and braised raisins and red cabbage. The freshly decorated bedrooms have comfortable beds and good facilities.

Rooms 4 en suite (1 fmly) S £35-£50; D £50-£90 **Facilities** tea/coffee Dinner available Direct Dial Cen ht Wi-fi Fishing **Parking** 9 **Notes** Closed 2wks Jan RS Mon Closed

Chef Craig Grant **Owner** The Grant Partnership **Times** 12-2.30/6-9 Closed 2 wks Jan, Mon **Prices** Fixed L 3 course £13.95, Starter £3.50-£6, Main £10-£19.50, Dessert £4.50-£6, Service optional, Groups min 8 service 10% **Wines** 49 bottles over £20, 15 bottles under £20, 13 by glass **Notes** Sunday L, Vegetarian available **Seats** 42 **Children** Portions, Menu

NORTH AYRSHIRE

DALRY   Map 2 NS24

Braidwoods

◉◉ Modern Scottish

Creative flair from a talented husband-and-wife-team

☎ 01294 833544
Drumastle Mill Cottage KA24 4LN
e-mail: keithbraidwood@btconnect.com
dir: 1m from Dalry on Saltcoats road

When an operation is run by a husband-and-wife-team who are both talented and passionate chefs with impressive CVs, you know you're in for a gastronomic experience way beyond what the rustic miller's cottage setting might suggest. Two dining areas work a cheerful mix of dark beams and exposed stone overlaid with a fresh modern décor of jaunty cream and blue-striped fabrics and stylish high-backed metal chairs, and a relaxed ambience ensures there's no standing on ceremony. The Braidwoods start out on the eminently sound footing of getting the basics right, which means hauling in local ingredients of the highest order and translating them painstakingly into top-quality modern Scottish dishes of intense flavour and clarity. Dinner might

continued

DALRY CONTINUED

start with roast loin of rabbit stuffed with mushrooms and wrapped in Parma ham on braised Puy lentils, then move on to a grilled fillet of wild sea bass with braised fennel and langoustine jus, and wind up proceedings with a truffle terrine of dark, milk and white chocolate with Grand Marnier sauce.

Times 12-1.45/7-9 Closed 25-26 Dec, 1st 3 wks Jan, 1st 2 wks Sep, Mon, L Tue (Sun Etr-Sep), D Sun

IRVINE	Map 2 NS33

Menzies Irvine

★★★★ 76% HOTEL

☎ 01294 274272 📠 01294 277287
46 Annick Rd KA11 4LD
e-mail: irvine@menzieshotels.co.uk
web: www.menzieshotels.co.uk
dir: From A78 at Warrix Interchange follow Irvine Central signs. At rdbt 2nd exit (town centre). At next rdbt right onto A71/Kilmarnock. Hotel 100mtrs on left

Situated on the edge of Irvine with good transportation links (including Prestwick Airport just seven miles away), this is a well-presented hotel that has an extremely friendly team with good customer care awareness. After major refurbishment the decor is contemporary throughout, and there is a brasserie-style restaurant, cocktail bar and spacious lounge.

Rooms 128 (14 fmly) (64 GF) **Facilities** STV Fishing Xmas New Year Wi-fi **Conf** Class 140 Board 100 Thtr 280 **Parking** 220 **Notes** Civ Wed 200

LARGS	Map 2 NS25

Willowbank Hotel

★★★ 75% HOTEL

☎ 01475 672311 & 675435 📠 01475 689027
96 Greenock Rd KA30 8PG
e-mail: iaincsmith@btconnect.com
dir: On A78

A relaxed, friendly atmosphere prevails at this well maintained hotel where hanging baskets are a feature in summer months. The nicely decorated bedrooms are, in general, spacious and offer comfortable modern appointments. The public areas include a large, well-stocked bar, a lounge and a dining room.

Rooms 30 (4 fmly) **S** £70-£100; **D** £80-£140 (incl. bkfst) **Facilities** STV 🎵 Xmas New Year **Conf** Class 100 Board 40 Thtr 200 Del from £100 to £140 **Parking** 40 **Notes** LB

South Whittlieburn Farm

★★★★ 🛏 BED AND BREAKFAST

Brisbane Glen KA30 8SN
☎ 01475 675881 📠 01475 675080
e-mail: largsbandb@southwhittlieburnfarm.freeserve.co.uk
dir: 2m NE of Largs off A78 signed Brisbane Glen, after Vikingar centre

This comfortable and welcoming farmhouse is on a working sheep farm surrounded by gently rolling countryside. The attractive bedrooms are well equipped with all having DVD and video players. There is a spacious ground-floor lounge, and a bright airy dining room where delicious breakfasts are served.

Rooms 3 en suite (1 fmly) S £37.50-£40; D £60-£65* **Facilities** STV FTV TVL tea/coffee Cen ht Golf 18 **Parking** 10 **Notes** LB ⊗ RS Xmas ⊗

SOUTH AYRSHIRE	
AYR	Map 2 NS32

The Western House Hotel

★★★★ 82% HOTEL

◎◎◎ Traditional British

Traditionally-based cooking within the grounds of Ayr racecourse

☎ 0870 055 5510 📠 01292 294990
2 Whitletts Rd KA8 0HA
e-mail: info@westernhousehotel.co.uk
dir: From Glasgow M77 then A77 towards Ayr. At Whitletts rdbt take A719 towards town centre

This impressive hotel is located in its own attractive gardens on the edge of Ayr racecourse. Bedrooms in the main house are superbly appointed, and the courtyard rooms offer much comfort too. Nicely appointed day rooms include the light and airy restaurant with views across the course. As the hotel is just a short canter away from Ayr racecourse, it would seem rather churlish if Western House failed to acknowledge the equestrian theme in its Jockey Club restaurant. Accordingly, there are old black-and-white racing photos set against walls half-panelled in oak in a clean-cut contemporary setting of unclothed wooden tables and black leather high-backed chairs. The kitchen sends out a broad swathe of traditional and modern dishes influenced by the French classics, and built on a solid foundation of fine Scottish ingredients. Dill-coated salmon ballottine with citrus crème fraîche to start perhaps, followed by a three-bone rack of Ayrshire lamb with baked ratatouille, or loin of venison with fondant potato and blackcurrant compôte. To finish, there might be Bramley apple spring rolls with Calvados ice cream.

Rooms 49 (39 annexe) (39 fmly) (16 GF) **Facilities** STV Xmas New Year Wi-fi **Conf** Class 300 Board 50 Thtr 1200 **Del** from £110 to £180* **Services** Lift **Parking** 250 **Notes**  Civ Wed 200

Times 12-2/7-9.30

Fairfield House

★★★★ 79% HOTEL

◉◉ Traditional British 🍃

Wide-ranging menus in a seafront hotel

☎ 01292 267461 📠 01292 261456
12 Fairfield Rd KA7 2AR
e-mail: reservations@fairfieldhotel.co.uk
dir: From A77 towards Ayr South (A30). Follow town centre signs, down Miller Rd, left, then right into Fairfield Rd

Situated in a leafy cul-de-sac close to the esplanade, this hotel enjoys stunning seascapes towards to the Isle of Arran. Bedrooms are in either modern or classical styles, the latter featuring impressive bathrooms. At the heart of the hotel is Martin's Bar and Grill, a large, airy space with spotlights in the high corniced ceiling and well-spaced tables. Choose something from the grill - a steak, or a substantial mixed platter - or go for roast loin of venison with a mushroom jus, or grilled fillet of cod with pea purée, rösti and spinach. Local game pitches up in season, with pheasant breast as a starter with Toulouse sausage and brandied crab apples, and wild mallard as a main course in blackberry sauce with confit root vegetables and fondant potato. For pudding, sample an unusual version of a Scottish classic: bramble cranachan in filo pastry horns.

Rooms 44 (4 annexe) (3 fmly) (9 GF) **S** £79-£150; **D** £89-£160 (incl. bkfst)* **Facilities** FTV 🏊 supervised Gym Fitness room Sauna Steam room Xmas New Year Wi-fi **Conf** Class 80 Board 40 Thtr 120 Del from £130* **Services** Lift **Parking** 50 **Notes** LB ⊗ Civ Wed 150

Owner G Martin **Times** 11am-9.30pm **Prices** Starter £4.95-£7.95, Main £12.45-£26.95, Dessert £4.95-£7.95, Service optional **Wines** 34 bottles over £20, 16 bottles under £20, 6 by glass **Notes** Sunday L, Vegetarian available **Seats** 80, Pr/dining room 12 **Children** Portions, Menu

Enterkine Country House

★★★★ 76% COUNTRY HOUSE HOTEL

◉◉ Modern British **V**

Mix-and-match contemporary cooking in an elegant 1930s country house

☎ 01292 520580 📠 01292 521582
Annbank KA6 5AL
e-mail: mail@enterkine.com
dir: 5m E of Ayr on B743

Enterkine was built in the 1930s in a gently countryfied version of the then prevalent art deco style. It was snapped up by the grandson of one of the founders of the P&O shipping line, and retains much of the feel of that last gasp of high-living elegance that preceded wartime austerity, retaining many original features, notably some splendid bathroom suites. A tree-lined avenue guides you to the door, and its principal restaurant, Browne's, is windowed on three sides to capitalise on views of the surrounding Ayr Valley. Contemporary menus deliver a locally-based version of today's mix-and-match approach, producing pressed suckling pig persillade with langoustines, pickled vegetables and apple purée, and thought-provoking mains such as sea bass with chorizo jam and sauce barigoule. A grand offering of Scottish cheeses maybe served with a range of garnishes, from white truffle honey to membrillo, or you might conclude with the unashamed richness of Valrhona chocolate fondant teamed with salted caramel ice cream. The well-proportioned bedrooms are furnished and equipped to high standards, and many have lovely countryside views.

Rooms 14 (8 annexe) (6 fmly) (5 GF) **S** £60-£100; **D** £80-£120 (incl. bkfst)* **Facilities** FTV Xmas New Year Wi-fi **Conf** Class 140 Board 140 Thtr 200 **Parking** 40 **Notes** LB Civ Wed 70

Chef Paul Moffat **Owner** Mr Browne **Times** 12-2/7-9 **Prices** Fixed L 2 course fr £17.50, Fixed D 3 course £30-£40, Starter £7.95-£11.50, Main £10.95-£24.50, Dessert £6.50-£8.50, Service optional **Wines** 59 bottles over £20, 4 by glass **Notes** Tasting menu available, Sunday L, Vegetarian menu, Dress restrictions, Smart casual **Seats** 40, Pr/dining room 14 **Children** Portions, Menu

Express by Holiday Inn Ayr

BUDGET HOTEL

☎ 01292 272300 📠 01292 272315
Wheatpark Place KA8 9RT
e-mail: info@hiexpressayr.com
web: www.hiexpress.co.uk

A modern hotel ideal for families and business travellers. Fresh and uncomplicated, the spacious rooms include Sky TV, power shower and tea and coffee-making facilities.

continued

Continental buffet breakfast is included in the room rate; other meals may be taken at the nearby family pub or restaurant.

Rooms 84 (44 fmly) (3 GF) **S** £49–£120; **D** £49–£120 (incl. bkfst)* **Conf** Class 12 Board 12 Thtr 23

Premier Inn Ayr/Prestwick Airport

BUDGET HOTEL

☎ 0871 527 8038   📄 0871 527 8039
Kilmarnock Rd, Monkton KA9 2RJ
web: www.premierinn.com
dir: At Dutch House Rdbt (at junct of A77 & A78) at Monkton

High quality, budget accommodation ideal for both families and business travellers. Spacious, en suite bedrooms feature tea and coffee-making facilities, and Freeview TV in most hotels. Internet access and Wi-fi are available for a small fee. The adjacent family restaurant features a wide and varied menu.

Rooms 64 **D** £55–£60*

26 The Crescent

★★★★★ GUEST HOUSE

26 Bellevue Crescent KA7 2DR
☎ 01292 287329   📄 01292 201003
e-mail: enquiries@26crescent.co.uk
web: www.26crescent.co.uk
dir: Leave A79 onto rdbt, 3rd exit onto King St. Left onto Bellevue Crescent

Located in a quiet residential area of Ayr, close to the seafront, town centre and race course, this guest house offers a traditional warm welcome with well appointed and comfortable bedrooms. Bathrooms are of a high standard, as is the hearty breakfast served on individual tables in the charming dining room. Joyce and Michael Brennan were finalists in this year's Friendliest Landlady of the Year award (2011-12).

Rooms 5 en suite S £45–£50; D £55–£80* **Facilities** FTV tea/coffee Cen ht Wi-fi **Notes** LB ⊗

Daviot House

★★★★ GUEST HOUSE

12 Queens Ter KA7 1DU
☎ 01292 269678
e-mail: daviothouse@hotmail.com
web: www.daviothouse.com
dir: Off A719 onto Wellington Sq & Bath Place, turn right

This well-maintained Victorian house stands in a peaceful location close to the beach and town centre. Bedrooms are modern in style and well equipped. Hearty breakfasts are served in the dining room. Daviot House is a member of Golf South Ayrshire - a golf booking service for local municipal courses, so let your hosts know if you'd like a round booked.

Rooms 6 rms (5 en suite) (1 pri facs) (1 fmly) (1 GF) S £25–£40; D £46–£65* **Facilities** FTV tea/coffee Cen ht Wi-fi **Notes** LB ⊗

BALLANTRAE   Map 2 NX08

Glenapp Castle

★★★★★ COUNTRY HOUSE HOTEL

◉◉◉ Modern British **V** 🍷 NOTABLE WINE LIST 🍽️

Scottish castle setting for imaginative cooking

☎ 01465 831212   📄 01465 831000
KA26 0NZ
e-mail: enquiries@glenappcastle.com
web: www.glenappcastle.com
dir: S through Ballantrae, cross bridge over River Stinchar, 1st right, hotel in 1m

Originally built for a coal merchant in 1870, Glenapp Castle is a fine example of Scottish baronial architecture. Restored from virtual dereliction 10 years ago, it is now a wonderfully luxurious country-house hotel set in 36 acres of woodland and tended gardens on the striking Ayrshire coast. Breathtaking views of Arran and Ailsa Craig rock add to the romantic allure of the place and friendly, professional staff - headed up by hands-on owners Graham and Fay Cowan - ensure everything goes swimmingly. Impeccably furnished bedrooms are graced with antiques and period pieces, and include two master rooms and a ground-floor family suite. The dining room has rich red tones set against wood panelling with lots of antiques and atmospheric oil paintings. Booking for dinner is mandatory, such is the popularity of the imaginatively crafted French-rooted six-course menu, with choices for the main and pudding courses only. Expect accomplished, confident modern Scottish cooking, using produce both locally sourced and from the hotel's garden. Baked potato bouillon with Isle of Mull cheddar gnocchi is a first course of real refinement and technique. For the fish course there might be fillet of Dover sole with Ayrshire epicure potatoes, peas and baby wood sorrel; next up an eye-catching main course of breast of

Goosnargh duck with soya roast leeks, coriander and duck scratchings. A slow and steady pace is required as the fine selection of pre-dessert (garden rhubarb crumble soufflé with pink rhubarb sorbet perhaps) and local cheeses are unmissable. Work up an appetite or walk off dinner with an amble around the wonderful gardens taking in the azalea lake and walled vegetable gardens with restored greenhouses.

Rooms 17 (2 fmly) (7 GF) **S** £265-£450; **D** £415-£620 (incl. bkfst & dinner)* **Facilities** STV FTV 🌊 ⛲ New Year Wi-fi **Conf** Class 12 Board 17 Thtr 17 Del from £295 to £500* **Services** Lift **Parking** 20 **Notes** LB Closed Jan-mid Mar & Xmas wk Civ Wed 40

Chef Adam Stokes **Owner** Graham & Fay Cowan
Times 12.30-2/7-10 Closed 2 Jan-25 Mar, Xmas
Prices Fixed L 3 course fr £37.50, Service optional
Wines 200 bottles over £20, 9 by glass **Notes** Fixed D 6 course £60, Gourmet D £60, Sunday L, Vegetarian menu, Civ Wed 40 **Seats** 34, Pr/dining room 20 **Children** Portions, Menu **Parking** 20

Balkissock Lodge

★★★★ 🏠 ☕ GUEST ACCOMMODATION

Balkissock KA26 0LP
☎ **01465 831537**
e-mail: howard.balkissock@btinternet.com
dir: S through Ballantrae (A77) over river, 1st left at campsite sign. Right at T-junct, 1.5m

A warm and genuine welcome awaits after a scenic drive. Set in the rolling South Ayrshire countryside, surrounded by wonderful gardens, Balkissock Lodge is a perfect getaway. The owners show great hospitality and customer care in a very comfortable and well-appointed property.

Rooms 3 en suite (1 fmly) (2 GF) **Facilities** STV TVL tea/coffee Dinner available Cen ht **Parking** 3 **Notes** ⊗ No Children

Parkstone

★★★ 77% HOTEL

☎ 01292 477286 📠 01292 477671
Esplanade KA9 1QN
e-mail: info@parkstonehotel.co.uk
web: www.parkstonehotel.co.uk
dir: From Main St (A79) W to seafront, hotel in 600yds

Situated on the seafront in a quiet residential area only one mile from Prestwick Airport, this family-run hotel caters for business visitors as well as golfers. Bedrooms come in a variety of sizes; all are furnished in a smart, contemporary style. The attractive, modern look of the bar and restaurant is matched by an equally up-to-date menu.

Rooms 30 (2 fmly) (7 GF) **S** £59-£79; **D** £84-£92 (incl. bkfst)* **Facilities** FTV Xmas New Year Wi-fi **Conf** Thtr 100 **Parking** 34 **Notes** LB ⊗ Civ Wed 100

Wheatsheaf Inn

Main St KA1 5QB ☎ **01563 830307** 📠 01563 830307
dir: In Symington, off A77 between Ayr & Kilmarnock

Martin and Marnie Thompson have run this charming 17th-century former coaching inn close to Royal Troon Golf Course for over 25 years. Log fires burn in every room and the work of local artists adorns the walls. Seafood dominates the menu, perhaps sea bass with tomato, basil and balsamic, while meaty options may include lamb shank with redcurrant and mint jus, and braised beef olive with a rich ale gravy. Leave room for cranachan – whipped cream and oats with raspberries soaked in honey and whisky.

Open all day all wk 11-11 (Fri-Sat 11am-mdnt) Closed: 25 Dec, 1 Jan **Bar Meals** L served all wk all day D served all wk all day **Restaurant** L served all wk 12-2 D served all wk 5-9 ⊕ FREE HOUSE 🍺 Belhaven Best, Old Speckled Hen, Guinness. **Facilities** Children welcome Children's menu Children's portions Garden Parking

Lochgreen House Hotel

★★★★ COUNTRY HOUSE HOTEL

◉◉◉ Modern Scottish

Modern Scottish cooking in a stunningly restored manor house

☎ 01292 313343 📠 01292 318661
Monktonhill Rd, Southwood KA10 7EN
e-mail: lochgreen@costley-hotels.co.uk
web: www.costley-hotels.co.uk
dir: From A77 follow Prestwick Airport signs. 0.5m before airport take B749 to Troon. Hotel 1m on left

Standing in 30 acres of woodlands and immaculate gardens parallel to the famous Royal Troon golf course, Lochgreen House on the Ayrshire coast is a lovely mansion house restored to its former glory over 20 years ago, and graced by tasteful extensions which have created stunning public rooms and spacious, comfortable and elegantly furnished bedrooms. Popular for weddings and events, whatever you're in town for you won't lack for something to do around these parts, and the elegant Tapestry restaurant awaits for a leisurely lunch or a restorative dinner. Lit by three crystal chandeliers, the restaurant overlooks the fountain and gardens at the front of the house. The kitchen team is justly proud of Ayrshire produce and what isn't on the doorstep is no less judiciously sourced, and the creative modern cooking

continued

TROON CONTINUED

has a decidedly Scottish flavour. Dig into the light crumbed bread freshly baked in-house before excellent Troon Bay scallops with green olive and peperonata risotto and smoked anchovy butter. Next up, trio of lamb brings forth roast cutlet, caramelised sweetbreads and home-made lamb, leek and mustard sausage (beautifully presented with good depth of flavour), or go for pan-seared fillet of Loch Duart salmon with mushroom and tarragon cannelloni. Banana gets a full-on five ways treatment - pudding, pie, consommé, pannacotta and ice cream - and if you've still got room, the petits fours are pretty fine too.

Rooms 38 (7 annexe) (17 GF) **Facilities** STV Beauty treatments Xmas New Year Wi-fi **Conf** Class 50 Board 50 Thtr 70 **Services** Lift **Parking** 50 **Notes** ⊗ Civ Wed 140

Chef Lesley McQuiston **Owner** Mr W Costley **Times** 12-2/7-10 **Prices** Fixed L 2 course £17.95, Fixed D 4 course £39.50, Service optional **Wines** 98 bottles over £20, 12 bottles under £20, 10 by glass **Notes** Sunday L, Vegetarian available, Dress restrictions, Smart casual **Seats** 80, Pr/dining room 40 **Children** Portions, Menu

Barceló Troon Marine Hotel

  ★★★★ 78% HOTEL

⊛⊛ Modern British

Modern Scottish cooking with golfing and coastal views

☎ 01292 314444 📠 01292 316922
Crosbie Rd KA10 6HE
e-mail: marine@barcelo-hotels.co.uk
web: www.barcelo-hotels.co.uk
dir: A77, A78, A79 onto B749. Hotel on left after golf course

A favourite with conference and leisure guests, this hotel offers attractively appointed bedrooms and public areas. The Fairways restaurant at this coastal hotel has the best of both worlds: hawkeye views of the 18th hole on the Royal Troon course, and sweeping vistas of the coastline and the Isle of Arran for the less golfoholic. There's plenty of diversion going on in the culinary department too, where a fixed-price menu of modern Scottish cooking is full of aromatic surprises and delights. Crisp-cooked mackerel on a salad of orange and sundried tomato with caramelised fennel might give way to Gressingham duck breast with spiced apple chutney, gnocchi and five spice sauce, before roast plums seasoned with star anise and cinnamon, served with honey and yoghurt ice cream, closes the show.

Rooms 89 **Facilities** Spa STV supervised Gym Squash Steam room Beauty room Xmas New Year Wi-fi **Conf** Class 100 Board 40 Thtr 200 **Services** Lift **Parking** 200 **Notes** ⊗ Civ Wed 100

Chef Kevin McGillivray **Owner** Barcelo Hotels **Times** 7-9.30 Closed L all week **Prices** Fixed D 3 course fr £34.95, Service optional **Wines** 67 bottles over £20, 10 bottles under £20 **Notes** Vegetarian available, Dress restrictions, Smart casual **Seats** 120, Pr/dining room 50 **Children** Portions, Menu

MacCallums of Troon

◉ Seafood

Uncomplicated seafood on the quayside

☎ 01292 319339
The Harbour KA10 6DH

Right on Troon's harbour, MacCallums is a simply decorated place, with exposed bricks, a high-raftered ceiling, bench-like seating and plain wooden chairs, and a maritime theme with lots of memorabilia of the America's Cup. The freshest of fresh seafood is the business, from moules marinière to whole sea bass with a lemon, caper and toasted almond butter. Monkfish is given the tempura treatment and served with basmati rice and Thai coconut cream, but searing, grilling and baking are the usual cooking methods: langoustines with garlic butter, followed by bream fillets with cabbage and boulangère potatoes, or ham-wrapped pollock with cauliflower purée and garlic mash.

Chef Philip Burgess **Owner** John & James MacCallums **Times** 12-2.30/6.30-9.30 Closed Xmas, New Year, Mon, Sun **Prices** Starter £4.85-£9.95, Main £10.95-£27.50, Dessert £4.85-£5.85, Service optional, Groups min 12 service 10% **Wines** 9 bottles over £20, 17 bottles under £20, 4 by glass **Notes** Sunday L **Seats** 43 **Children** Portions **Parking** 12

Robert Burns, High Street, Dumfries

TURNBERRY — Map 2 NS20

Turnberry Resort, Scotland

★★★★★ HOTEL

◉◉ British, French

Classical dining (with flambéing) at renowned coastal golf resort

☎ 01655 331000 📄 01655 331706
KA26 9LT
e-mail: turnberry@luxurycollection.com
web: www.luxurycollection.com/turnberry
dir: From Glasgow take A77/M77 S towards Stranraer, 2m past Kirkoswald follow signs for A719/Turnberry. Hotel 500mtrs on right

Golfing doesn't get any more serious than this. Turnberry regularly plays host to the Open Championships, and what a splendid location it is, on the wild Ayrshire coast with the hulk of Ailsa Craig in the background. The hotel itself is a long white building with a red-tiled roof, and facilities include the excellent Colin Montgomerie Golf Academy, a luxurious spa, and a host of outdoor pursuits. Some superbly modern rooms together with more traditional elegant bedrooms and suites are located in the main hotel, while adjacent lodges provide spacious, well-equipped accommodation. The public areas are stunning. The Ailsa Lounge is very welcoming, and there is the fine-dining James Miller room and chef's table (see entry below) in addition to the elegant 1906 restaurant at the heart of the hotel. Surveying the pitching and putting below from panoramically sweeping windows, 1906 isn't above a little tableside flambé theatre as the occasion demands, and the bedrock of the operation is impeccable regional produce treated with respect and old-school classicism. The preamble might be excellent Kilbrannan scallops with apple and celery shoots in walnut dressing, ahead of salmon Mercedes (herb-crusted, served with braised baby leeks in champagne velouté), or chicken marengo with forest mushrooms, langoustine mousse and a quail's egg. If the pyromaniac urge overwhelms you, get them to set fire to some Grand Marnier for the crêpe Suzette, or else opt for the less attention-grabbing, but still indulgent, Amaretto semi-fredo with praline and cherry sorbet.

Rooms 207 (89 annexe) (2 fmly) (12 GF) **Facilities Spa** STV 🔁 supervised ⌇ 36 Putt green Fishing Gym Leisure club

Outdoor activity centre Colin Montgomerie Golf Academy New Year Wi-fi **Conf** Class 145 Board 80 Thtr 300 **Services** Lift **Parking** 200 **Notes** Closed 25 Dec Civ Wed 220

Chef Justin Galea **Times** 7.06-10 **Prices** Starter £8-£18, Main £18-£42, Dessert £7-£11, Service optional **Wines** 100+ bottles over £20, 26 by glass **Notes** Vegetarian available, Dress restrictions, Smart casual **Seats** 160, Pr/dining room 10 **Children** Portions, Menu

The James Miller Room

◉◉ Modern 🍃

Imaginative cooking in famous golfing hotel

☎ 01655 331000
Turnberry Resort, Scotland KA26 9LT
e-mail: turnberry@luxurycollection.com
dir: From Glasgow take A77/M77 S towards Stranraer, 2m past Kirkoswald, follow signs for A719/Turnberry. Hotel 500mtrs on right

Golf fans will find plenty to excite at the world-famous Turnberry Resort, and not only when it comes to playing their favourite game. This luxurious hotel on the stunning Ayrshire coast offers its guests a choice of high quality dining experiences, and one of them is the chic and stylish James Miller Room. Sitting adjacent to the 1906 Restaurant (see entry), the James Miller Room provides an intimate and elegant setting for some serious fine dining. The space is a successful blend of period features (high ceilings, cornicing and grand fireplace) and contemporary furnishings (deep red chairs and darkwood), while the cooking is broadly modern European and centred around superb, locally-sourced ingredients, prepared with flair and a good deal of skill. Torchon of foie gras with candied apple, gingerbread and cider bubbles is an inventive first course, while Clash Farm pork is superbly cooked and comes with dived scallops and noodles. Chocolate cremosa with frangelico jelly, candied hazelnuts and blood orange sorbet ends things on a high.

Chef Justin Galea **Times** 7.06-9.30 Closed Sun-Mon **Prices** Fixed D 4 course £65, Service optional **Wines** 100+ bottles over £20, 26 by glass **Seats** 14, Pr/dining room 10 **Parking**

Malin Court

★★★ 83% HOTEL

☎ 01655 331457 📄 01655 331072
KA26 9PB
e-mail: info@malincourt.co.uk
web: www.malincourt.co.uk
dir: On A74 to Ayr then A719 to Turnberry & Maidens

Forming part of the Malin Court Residential and Nursing Home Complex, this friendly and comfortable hotel enjoys delightful views over the Firth of Clyde and Turnberry golf courses. Standard and executive rooms are available; all are well equipped. Public areas are plentiful, with the restaurant serving high teas, dinners and light lunches.

Rooms 18 (9 fmly) **Facilities** STV Putt green Wi-fi
Conf Class 60 Board 30 Thtr 200 **Services** Lift **Parking** 110
Notes ⊗ RS Oct-Mar Civ Wed 80

CLACKMANNANSHIRE

DOLLAR   Map 3 NS99

Castle Campbell Hotel

11 Bridge St FK14 7DE ☎ 01259 742519 📄 **01259 743742**
e-mail: bookings@castle-campbell.co.uk
dir: A91 (Stirling to St Andrews road). In Dollar centre by bridge overlooking clock tower

Handy for Dollar Glen's spectacular gorges, this 19th-century coaching inn offers a real taste of Scotland. Built in 1821, pictures on the walls date back to that period. Recognised as a Whisky Ambassador, the hotel has over 50 malts; local ale is always on tap and the wine list runs to several pages. Prime Scottish produce features on the menus, with options ranging from fish and chips in the bar to seared rack of lamb with red wine and rosemary in the restaurant. Change of hands.

Open all wk ⊕ FREE HOUSE ◀ Harviestoun Bitter & Twisted, Deuchars IPA (guest), McEwans 70/-. **Facilities** Children welcome Children's menu Children's portions Dogs allowed Parking

DUMFRIES & GALLOWAY

ANNAN   Map 3 NY16

Del Amitri Restaurant

◉ Modern European 🍃

- -

Relaxed contemporary dining

☎ 01461 201999
95a High St DG12 6DJ
e-mail: enquiries@del-amitri.co.uk
web: www.del-amitri.co.uk
dir: Located above the Café Royal

No, the eponymous 1990s Glaswegian pop group are not the inspiration behind the name of this stylish first-floor restaurant on Annan high street: the name is derived from the ancient Greek meaning 'new life'. It is a good-looking, clean cut space decorated in tones of chocolate and plum, with dark brown, high-backed leather seats at smartly-dressed tables. Nothing ever happens to ruffle the relaxed ambience - there's no rush, the table is yours for the evening, so settle in and don't go home too soon. There is solid technique and a French accent underlying the modern Scottish dishes, starting with a pressed mosaic of confit belly pork and smoked ham hock served with carrot remoulade and port wine dressing. Next up, salmon is baked under a haggis crust and teamed with Parmentier potatoes, buttered kale and roast swede. Pastry skills are strong in a finale of dark chocolate and orange tart pointed up with a compôte of kumquat and chilli.

Chef Martin Avey **Owner** Martin & Lisa Avey
Times 12-2/6-10 Closed Mon, L Tue-Sat, D Sun (Nov-May)
Prices Fixed L 2 course £13.95, Starter £4.60-£7.50, Main £12.50-£15.10, Dessert £4.80-£6.75, Service optional
Wines 9 bottles over £20, 21 bottles under £20, 8 by glass
Notes Cinema supper offer, Sunday L, Vegetarian available, Air con **Seats** 45 **Children** Portions **Parking** On street, car park

AUCHENCAIRN — Map 3 NX75

Balcary Bay Hotel

★★★ 86% HOTEL

◉◉ Modern European

Modern country-house cooking on the Solway coast

☎ 01556 640217 & 640311 📠 01556 640272
Shore Rd DG7 1QZ
e-mail: reservations@balcary-bay-hotel.co.uk
web: www.balcary-bay-hotel.co.uk
dir: On A711 between Dalbeattie & Kirkcudbright, hotel 2m
from village

The splendid sparkling-white hotel on the Solway coast has
something for everyone, location-wise. It faces wild, history-
soaked Hestan Isle, once a smuggler's redoubt, while the
hills of the Lake District can be glimpsed somewhere beyond
too. And the Solway coast itself is a majestic environment in
which to wander and unwind. The larger bedrooms enjoy
stunning views over the bay, while others overlook the
gardens, and the comfortable public areas invite relaxation.
Restaurant tables by the windows get snapped up fast, it
should be noted, but it's an agreeable dining room anyway,
with quality linen and fresh flowers in abundance, and a
fixed-price menu of sound country-house cooking. Modern
classics mix with less familiar items such as potato and
leek parfait with soused carrots, glazed goats' cheese and
curry oil to start. After a soup or sorbet, main courses are
well-constructed to offer comfort and flavour, as in fillet of
sea bream with smoked haddock brandade and tomato
nage, or partridge breasts on rösti with creamed Savoy
cabbage in a game jus. Pudding could be ginger parkin with
apple purée, and there is also an array of great Scottish
cheeses with home-made chutney.

Rooms 20 (1 fmly) (3 GF) **S** £65-£75; **D** £134-£164 (incl.
bkfst)* **Facilities** FTV **Parking** 50 **Notes** LB Closed 1st Sun
Dec-last Fri in Jan

Chef Craig McWilliam **Owner** Graeme A Lamb & family
Times 12-2/6.45-7.30 Closed Dec-Jan **Prices** Fixed L 2
course £29.75, Fixed D 2 course £40.75, Service optional
Wines 85 bottles over £20, 15 bottles under £20, 12 by glass
Notes Sunday L, Vegetarian available, Dress restrictions,
Smart casual **Seats** 55 **Children** Portions **Parking**

CASTLE DOUGLAS — Map 3 NX76

Craigadam

★★★★ 🏠 🍴 GUEST HOUSE

Craigadam DG7 3HU
☎ 01556 650233 & 650100 📠 01556 650233
e-mail: inquiry@craigadam.com
web: www.craigadam.com
dir: From Castle Douglas E on A75 to Crocketford. In
Crocketford turn left on A712 for 2m. House on hill

Set on a farm, this elegant country house offers gracious
living in a relaxed environment. The large bedrooms, most
set around a courtyard, are strikingly individual in style.
Public areas include a billiard room with comprehensive
honesty bar, and the panelled dining room which features a
magnificent 15-seater table, the setting for Celia Pickup's
delightful meals.

Rooms 10 en suite (2 fmly) (7 GF) S £60-£94; D £94-£110*
Facilities FTV TVL tea/coffee Dinner available Cen ht
Licensed Wi-fi 🎣 Fishing Snooker Private fishing & shooting
Conf Max 22 **Parking** 12 **Notes** LB Closed Xmas & New Year
Civ Wed 150

West Barmoffity Farmhouse (NX785705)

★★★★ FARMHOUSE

DG7 3HL
☎ 01556 650631   Ms J Wilson
e-mail: jeniffer.wilson@sky.com
dir: A75 to Springholm, follow signs for Kirkpatrick Durham.
Straight ahead at x-rds, after 20yds turn right, follow farm
track 0.5m, on left

Located on a working farm in rolling countryside, this is an
ideal base for touring, and is within easy reach of Castle
Douglas. The bedrooms are spacious and well presented,
plus there is a comfortable lounge and dining room where
home-cooked dinner and hearty breakfasts are served.

Rooms 2 en suite (1 fmly) S £30-£35; D £60-£70*
Facilities FTV TVL tea/coffee Dinner available Cen ht
Parking 4 **Notes** LB 🐾 170 acres beef/sheep

DUMFRIES — Map 3 NX97

See also **Kirkbean**

Cairndale Hotel & Leisure Club

★★★ 80% HOTEL

☎ 01387 254111 📠 01387 240288
English St DG1 2DF
e-mail: sales@cairndalehotel.co.uk
web: www.cairndalehotel.co.uk
dir: From S on M6 take A75 to Dumfries, left at 1st rdbt,
cross rail bridge to lights, hotel 1st building on left

Within walking distance of the town centre, this hotel provides a wide range of amenities, including leisure facilities and an impressive conference and entertainment centre. Bedrooms range from stylish suites to cosy singles. There's a choice of eating options in the evening. The Reivers Restaurant is smartly modern with food to match.

Rooms 91 (22 fmly) (5 GF) **S** £59-£89; **D** £79-£159 (incl. bkfst) **Facilities** ⊛ supervised Gym Steam room Sauna ♫ Xmas New Year Wi-fi **Conf** Class 150 Board 50 Thtr 300 Del from £79 to £119* **Services** Lift **Parking** 100 **Notes** LB Civ Wed 200

Best Western Station Hotel

★★★ 79% HOTEL

☎ 01387 254316 📠 01387 250388
49 Lovers Walk DG1 1LT
e-mail: info@stationhotel.co.uk
web: www.stationhoteldumfries.co.uk
dir: A75, follow signs to town centre, hotel opposite railway station

This friendly hotel built in the Victorian era offers stylish, well-equipped bedrooms that feature satellite TVs and free Wi-fi; three rooms have four-poster beds and spa baths. The Courtyard restaurant creates an informal atmosphere where, each evening, guests can enjoy a popular range of dishes; in addition good-value meals are served at lunchtime in either the lounge bar or on the patio in warmer weather. There is a delightful small garden to relax in.

Rooms 32 **Facilities** Use of local gym Xmas New Year Wi-fi **Conf** Class 35 Board 30 Thtr 60 **Services** Lift **Parking** 34 **Notes** Civ Wed 50

Premier Inn Dumfries

BUDGET HOTEL

☎ 0871 527 8316 📠 0871 527 8317
Annan Rd, Collin DG1 3JX
web: www.premierinn.com
dir: At rdbt junct of Euroroute bypass (A75) & A780

High quality, budget accommodation ideal for both families and business travellers. Spacious, en suite bedrooms feature tea and coffee-making facilities, and Freeview TV in most hotels. Internet access and Wi-fi are available for a small fee. The adjacent family restaurant features a wide and varied menu.

Rooms 40 **D** £62*

Wallamhill House

★★★★ BED AND BREAKFAST

Kirkton DG1 1SL
☎ 01387 248249
e-mail: wallamhill@aol.com
dir: 3m N of Dumfries. Off A701 signed Kirkton, 1.5m on right

Wallamhill House is set in well-tended gardens, in a delightful rural area three miles from Dumfries. Bedrooms are spacious and extremely well equipped. There is a peaceful drawing room, and a mini health club with sauna, steam shower and gym equipment.

Rooms 3 en suite (1 fmly) **Facilities** FTV TVL tea/coffee Cen ht Wi-fi ⌣ Sauna Gym Steam room **Parking** 6 **Notes** ⊗

Rivendell

★★★★ GUEST HOUSE

105 Edinburgh Rd DG1 1JX
☎ 01387 252251 📠 01387 263084
e-mail: info@rivendellbnb.co.uk
web: www.rivendellbnb.co.uk
dir: On A701 Edinburgh Rd, 400yds S of A75 junct

Situated just north of the town and close to the bypass, this lovely 1920s house, standing in extensive landscaped gardens, has been restored to reflect the period style of the property. Bedrooms are thoughtfully equipped, many are spacious and all offer modern facilities. Traditional breakfasts are served in the elegant dining room.

Rooms 6 en suite (2 fmly) (1 GF) S £35-£45; D £60* **Facilities** FTV tea/coffee Cen ht Wi-fi **Parking** 12 **Notes** LB ⊗

Southpark House

★★★★ GUEST ACCOMMODATION

Quarry Rd, Locharbriggs DG1 1QR
☎ 01387 711188 & 0800 970 1588 📠 01387 711155
e-mail: info@southparkhouse.co.uk
web: www.southparkhouse.co.uk
dir: 3.5m NE of Dumfries. Off A701 in Locharbriggs onto Quarry Rd, last house on left

With a peaceful location commanding stunning views, this well-maintained property offers comfortable, attractive and well-equipped bedrooms. The communal lounge has a log fire on colder evenings, and fax and e-mail facilities are available. Friendly proprietor Ewan Maxwell personally oversees the hearty Scottish breakfasts served in the conservatory breakfast room.

Rooms 4 en suite (1 fmly) S £29.99-£49.99; D £49.99-£69.99* **Facilities** STV FTV TVL tea/coffee Cen ht Wi-fi ch fac 2 acres of garden **Parking** 13 **Notes** LB ⊗

GATEHOUSE OF FLEET — Map 2 NX55

Cally Palace

★★★★ 76% COUNTRY HOUSE HOTEL

🍴 Traditional

Formal dining on the Solway coast

☎ 01557 814341   📄 01557 814522
Cally Dr DG7 2DL
e-mail: info@callypalace.co.uk
web: www.callypalace.co.uk
dir: From M6 & A74, signed A75 Dumfries then Stranraer. At Gatehouse-of-Fleet right onto B727, left at Cally

Looking over the Galloway hills, this Georgian country manor in 150 acres of parkland on the Solway coast bills itself as a golf hotel, but you don't have to set off with the clubs to enjoy a stay here. Bedrooms are spacious and well equipped, while public rooms retain a quiet elegance. There's a full complement of leisure facilities, and with 600 acres of the Fleet Oak Woods bordering the estate, plus hiking and biking trails crisscrossing the area, no excuses will be accepted for coming to the table without a keen appetite. The interior exudes opulence from top to toe, while the feeling of a bygone age extends to the formalities in force in the restaurant - that means jacket and tie, please, gentlemen - where a pianist tinkles away in the background. The kitchen deals in updated classics from the country-house idiom - chicken ballottine with toasted hazelnut and truffle dressing to start things off, followed by pan-fried local venison with parsnip purée, fondant potato, green beans and rosemary jus. Classy sweet comfort awaits at the end in the form of dark bitter chocolate marquise with caramel sauce.

Rooms 55 (7 fmly) **Facilities** STV FTV 🎣 ⚓ 18 ⛳ Putt green Fishing 💪 Gym Table tennis Practice fairway Xmas New Year Wi-fi **Conf** Class 40 Board 25 Thtr 40 **Services** Lift **Parking** 100 **Notes** ⊗ Closed Jan-early Feb

Times 12-1/6.45-9 Closed 3 Jan-early Feb

GRETNA (WITH GRETNA GREEN) — Map 3 NY36

Smiths at Gretna Green

★★★★ 73% HOTEL

🍴 Modern British

Sound modish cooking in smart, contemporary setting

☎ 01461 337007   📄 01461 336000
Gretna Green DG16 5EA
e-mail: info@smithsgretnagreen.com
web: www.smithsgretnagreen.com
dir: From M74 junct 22 follow signs to Old Blacksmith's Shop. Hotel opposite

Just off the motorway linking England and Scotland and next to the Old Blacksmith's Shop - made famous for being the place for runaway couples to get married - Smiths brings a bit of 21st-century swagger to the historic location. It's a modern building done out in the boutique manner - bedrooms offer a spacious environment, complete with flat-screen TVs, DVD players and broadband. Family rooms feature a separate children's area with bunk beds, each with its own TV. Three suites and a penthouse apartment are also available, and impressive conference and banqueting facilities are provided. The restaurant that puts locally-sourced food at the heart of its culinary goings-on. There's a recently added conservatory and private dining room in conjunction with the bar brasserie, complete with its leather tiled walls, darkwood tables and spotlights. The owners come from the local farming community - hence that passion for local, seasonal produce - and you can expect the likes of lamb kebab with crushed green pea pattie, mint and apple, and tomato chutney to start, following on with pan-fried grey mullet with tomato risotto and wild mushrooms. Puds extend to hazelnut cake with clotted cream ice cream and pistachio cream.

Rooms 50 (8 fmly) **Facilities** STV FTV New Year Wi-fi **Conf** Class 100 Board 40 Thtr 250 **Services** Lift Air con **Parking** 115 **Notes** Civ Wed 150

Chef Sumit Chakrabarty **Owner** Alasdair Houston **Times** 12-9.30 Closed 25 Dec **Prices** Food prices not confirmed for 2012. Please telephone for details **Notes** Sunday L, Vegetarian available **Seats** 60, Pr/dining room 18 **Children** Portions, Menu

The Gables Hotel

★★★ 75% HOTEL

☎ 01461 338300   📄 01461 338626
1 Annan Rd DG16 5DQ
e-mail: reservations@gables-hotel-gretna.co.uk
dir: M74 S or M6/M74 N follow signs for Gretna. At rdbt at Gretna Gateway take exit onto Annan Rd, hotel 200yds on right

This Grade II listed hotel is located close to the Gretna Gateway and is ideally located to explore both Galloway and the Border City of Carlisle. Bedrooms offer comfortable and well-appointed accommodation. The main restaurant offers a carte menu with a range of freshly prepared dishes, whilst Saddlers bar provides light snacks and meals.

Rooms 31 (5 fmly) (10 GF) **S** £79-£84; **D** £110-£115 (incl. bkfst)* **Facilities** FTV Xmas New Year Wi-fi **Conf** Class 60 Board 48 Thtr 100 Del from £99 to £119* **Parking** 60 **Notes** LB ⊗ Civ Wed 100

Garden House

★★★ 75% HOTEL

☎ 01461 337621 📄 01461 337692
Sarkfoot Rd DG16 5EP
e-mail: info@gardenhouse.co.uk
web: www.gardenhouse.co.uk
dir: Just off M6 junct 45

This purpose-built modern hotel lies on the edge of the village. With a focus on weddings its landscaped gardens provide an ideal setting, while inside corridor walls are adorned with photographs portraying that 'special day'. Accommodation is well presented including bedrooms that overlook the Japanese water gardens.

Rooms 38 (11 fmly) (14 GF) **Facilities** 🛀 supervised 🎵
Xmas New Year **Conf** Class 80 Board 40 Thtr 150
Services Lift **Parking** 105 **Notes** ⊗ Civ Wed 150

Barrasgate

★★★★ GUEST ACCOMMODATION

Millhill DG16 5HU
☎ 01461 337577 & 07711 661938 📄 01461 337577
e-mail: info@barrasgate.co.uk
web: www.barrasgate.co.uk
dir: From N: A74 (M) junct 22 signed Gretna Green/Longtown. At 2nd rdbt right, signed Longtown. Approx 1.5m, establishment on right. From S: M6 junct 45 (A74(M) junct 24) take A6071 signed Gretna/Longtown. Approx 1m turn 2nd left, signed Gretna Green/Springfield. Establishment 1st left

This detached house lies in attractive gardens in a rural setting near Gretna, the Blacksmith Centre and motorway links. Bedrooms are well presented and equipped; some have recently been refurbished with good results. Hearty breakfasts featuring local produce are taken in an attractive dining room, overlooking the gardens.

Rooms 5 en suite (2 fmly) (1 GF) **Facilities** FTV tea/coffee Cen ht Wi-fi **Parking** 10 **Notes** Closed Jan-Feb

Surrone House

★★★ GUEST ACCOMMODATION

Annan Rd DG16 5DL
☎ 01461 338341 📄 01461 338341
e-mail: enquiries@surronehouse.co.uk
web: www.surronehouse.co.uk
dir: In town centre on B721

Guests are assured of a warm welcome at this well-maintained guest accommodation set in attractive gardens well back from the road. Bedrooms are sensibly furnished and include a delightful honeymoon suite. Dinner, drinks and light refreshments are available.

Rooms 7 en suite (3 fmly) (2 GF) S fr £40; D fr £70*
Facilities FTV TVL tea/coffee Dinner available Cen ht Licensed Wi-fi **Parking** 10 **Notes** ⊗

GRETNA SERVICE AREA (A74(M))   Map 3 NY36

Days Inn Gretna Green - M74

BUDGET HOTEL

☎ 01461 337566 📄 01461 337823
Welcome Break Service Area DG16 5HQ
e-mail: gretna.hotel@welcomebreak.co.uk
web: www.welcomebreak.co.uk
dir: Between junct 21/22 on M74 - accessible from both N'bound & S'bound carriageway

This modern building offers accommodation in smart, spacious and well-equipped bedrooms suitable for families and business travellers, and all with en suite bathrooms. Continental breakfast is available and other refreshments may be taken at the nearby family restaurant.

Rooms 64 (54 fmly) (64 GF) **S** £39.95-£59.95;
D £49.95-£69.95

ISLE OF WHITHORN   Map 2 NX43

The Steam Packet Inn ♟

Harbour Row DG8 8LL ☎ 01988 500334 📄 01988 500627
e-mail: steampacketinn@btconnect.com
dir: From Newton Stewart take A714, then A746 to Whithorn, then Isle of Whithorn

This lively quayside pub stands in a picturesque village at the tip of the Machars peninsula. Personally run by the Scoular family for over 20 years, it is the perfect place to escape from the pressures of modern living. Sit in one of the comfortable bars, undisturbed by television, fruit machines or piped music, and enjoy one of the real ales, a malt whisky from the great selection, or a glass of wine. Glance out of the picture windows and watch the fishermen at work, then look to the menu for a chance to sample the fruits of their labours. Extensive seafood choices - perhaps a kettle of mussels cooked in a cream and white wine sauce, isle-landed monkfish tail or fillet of bream - are supported by the likes of haggis-stuffed mushroom; and braised Galloway lamb shank.

Open all wk 11am-11pm (Sun noon-11) Closed: 25 Dec, winter Tue-Thu 2.30-6 **Bar Meals** L served all wk 12-2 D served all wk 6.30-9 **Restaurant** L served all wk 12-2 D served all wk 6.30-9 ⊕ FREE HOUSE ⊄ Timothy Taylor Landlord, Guest ales. ♟ 12 **Facilities** Children welcome Children's menu Children's portions Dogs allowed Garden Parking

KIRKBEAN · Map 3 NX95

Cavens

 ★★★ COUNTRY HOUSE HOTEL

◉ British, French

Locally-sourced food in a tranquil Galloway setting

☎ 01387 880234 📄 01387 880467
DG2 8AA
e-mail: enquiries@cavens.com
web: www.cavens.com
dir: Enter Kirkbean on A710, hotel signed

A family-run manor-house hotel not far from Dumfries, and Galloway Forest Park, Cavens sits in six acres of beautifully manicured grounds. The proprietors spared no effort when they renovated the house, and the interiors have been designed to soothe, with gentle pinks and greens predominating in the lounge and views of the garden from the dining room. Locally-sourced ingredients supply the daily-changing menu, and the cooking style follows sound culinary logic. A summer dinner might begin with pigeon breast sautéed in port, followed by either wild Solway salmon with dill tartare sauce, or Galloway beef sirloin with red onion marmalade. Round things off with the likes of pannacotta or chocolate pot, or with a serving of fine regional cheeses from the Loch Arthur estate. Bedrooms are delightfully individual and very comfortably equipped; choose from the Country rooms or the more spacious Estate rooms.

Rooms 6 (2 fmly) (1 GF) **S** £80-£130; **D** £80-£180 (incl. bkfst)* **Facilities** FTV 🦶 Shooting Fishing Horseriding New Year Wi-fi **Conf** Class 20 Board 20 Thtr 20 **Parking** 20 **Notes** LB Closed Jan Civ Wed 100

Chef A Fordyce **Owner** A Fordyce **Times** 7-8.30 Closed Dec-1 Mar, L all week **Prices** Food prices not confirmed for 2012. Please telephone for details **Wines** 20 bottles over £20, 7 bottles under £20, 2 by glass **Notes** Vegetarian available, Dress restrictions, Smart casual **Seats** 16, Pr/dining room 20

KIRKCUDBRIGHT · Map 2 NX65

Arden House Hotel

★★ 75% HOTEL

☎ 01557 330544 📄 01557 330742
Tongland Rd DG6 4UU
dir: Exit A57, 4m W of Castle Douglas onto A711. Follow Kirkcudbright signs, over Telford Bridge. Hotel 400mtrs on left

Set well back from the main road in extensive grounds on the northeast side of town, this spotlessly maintained hotel offers attractive bedrooms, a lounge bar and adjoining conservatory serving a range of popular dishes, which are also available in the dining room. It boasts an impressive function suite in its grounds.

Rooms 9 (7 fmly) (5 smoking) **S** £60; **D** £80 (incl. bkfst)* **Conf** Class 175 Thtr 175 **Parking** 70

Selkirk Arms Hotel 🍷

Old High St DG6 4JG ☎ 01557 330402 📄 01557 331639
e-mail: reception@selkirkarmshotel.co.uk
dir: M74 & M6 to A75, halfway between Dumfries & Stranraer on A75

On one of his Galloway tours Robert Burns reputedly stopped at this privately owned hotel and wrote the *Selkirk Grace*. The hotel's *Selkirk Grace* ale was produced in conjunction with Sulwath Brewers to celebrate the fact. The public rooms include two bars, and a great choice of dishes is offered in The Bistro or more intimate Artistas Restaurant, including local specialities like scallops, fish and chips and Galloway beef steaks.

Open all day all wk **Bar Meals** L served all wk 12-2 D served all wk 6-9 Av main course £10.50 **Restaurant** L served Sun 12-2 booking required D served all wk 7-9 booking required Fixed menu price fr £26 Av 3 course à la carte fr £29 🍺 Youngers Tartan, John Smith's Bitter, Criffel, Timothy Taylor Landlord, The Selkirk Grace. 🍷 8 **Facilities** Children welcome Children's menu Children's portions Dogs allowed Garden Parking

LANGHOLM · Map 3 NY38

Glengarth Guest Rooms

★★★★ GUEST ACCOMMODATION

Maxwell Rd DG13 0DX
☎ 01387 380777 & 07802 771137
e-mail: info@glengarthguestrooms.co.uk
web: www.glengarthguestrooms.co.uk
dir: M6 junct 44 onto A7, in Langholm 500yds past Co-op

Glengarth Guest Rooms is located in a quiet residential area in the Borders town of Langholm. Strong hospitality and customer care is provided. Bedrooms and en suites are well appointed, comfortable and cater well for the needs of the guest. Quality breakfast is served in the lounge/dining room using locally sourced produce.

Rooms 2 en suite (2 GF) **S** £40; **D** £60* **Facilities** STV tea/coffee Cen ht Wi-fi Golf 9 Fishing **Parking** 1 **Notes** LB ⊗ No Children 🅿

Moffat Water, Dumfries & Galloway

LOCKERBIE
Map 3 NY18

Dryfesdale Country House

★★★★ 73% HOTEL

☎ 01576 202427 📠 01576 204187
Dryfebridge DG11 2SF
e-mail: reception@dryfesdalehotel.co.uk
web: www.dryfesdalehotel.co.uk
dir: From M74 junct 17 follow Lockerbie North signs, 3rd left
at 1st rdbt, 1st exit left at 2nd rdbt, hotel 200yds on left

Conveniently situated for the M74, yet discreetly screened
from it, this friendly hotel provides attentive service.
Bedrooms, some with access to patio areas, vary in size and
style; all offer good levels of comfort and are well equipped.
Creative, good value dinners make use of local produce and
are served in the airy restaurant that overlooks the
manicured gardens and rolling countryside.

Rooms 29 (5 fmly) (20 GF) **S** £65-£89; **D** £99-£129*
Facilities STV FTV Putt green ⛳ Clay pigeon shooting
Fishing ♫ Xmas New Year Wi-fi **Conf** Class 100 Board 100
Thtr 150 Del from £99 to £129* **Parking** 60
Notes Civ Wed 150

Kings Arms Hotel

★★ 78% HOTEL

☎ 01576 202410 📠 01576 202410
High St DG11 2JL
e-mail: reception@kingsarmshotel.co.uk
web: www.kingsarmshotel.co.uk
dir: A74(M), 0.5m into town centre, hotel opposite town hall

Dating from the 17th century this former inn lies in the town
centre. Now a family-run hotel, it provides attractive well-
equipped bedrooms with Wi-fi access. At lunch a menu
ranging from snacks to full meals is served in both the cosy
bars and the restaurant at dinner.

Rooms 13 (2 fmly) **S** £50; **D** £83 (incl. bkfst) **Facilities** FTV
Xmas New Year Wi-fi **Conf** Class 40 Board 30 Thtr 80
Parking 8

Ravenshill House

★★ 74% HOTEL

☎ 01576 202882
12 Dumfries Rd DG11 2EF
e-mail: aaenquiries@ravenshillhotellockerbie.co.uk
web: www.ravenshillhotellockerbie.co.uk
dir: From A74(M) Lockerbie junct onto A709. Hotel 0.5m on
right

Set in spacious gardens on the fringe of the town, this
friendly, family-run hotel offers cheerful service and good
value, home-cooked meals. Bedrooms are generally spacious
and comfortably equipped, including a two-room unit ideal
for families.

Rooms 8 (2 fmly) **S** £40-£65; **D** £78-£85 (incl. bkfst)*
Facilities FTV Wi-fi **Conf** Class 20 Board 12 Thtr 30
Parking 35 **Notes** LB Closed 1-3 Jan

Blackyett Mains

★★★★ 🏠 BED AND BREAKFAST

DG11 3ND
☎ 01461 500750
e-mail: mail@blackyettmains.co.uk
web: www.blackyettmains.co.uk
dir: M74 junct 21 towards Kirkpatrick Fleming, B6357 to
Annan. At Hollee turn right to Irvington after 0.5m, left to
Blackyett Mains. 1st on left

Set in the rolling Dumfriesshire countryside but just 5
minutes from the M74, Blackyett Mains is a converted
farmhouse with many original features along with wonderful
wooden floors. Bedrooms and en suites are generous in size
and very well appointed. Award-winning breakfasts use
locally sourced produce, and a large garden is available for
guests to enjoy.

Rooms 3 rms (2 en suite) (1 pri facs) (1 GF) S £45-£55; D
£60-£75* **Facilities** FTV TVL tea/coffee Dinner available
Cen ht Wi-fi **Parking** 3 **Notes** LB ⊗

MOFFAT — Map 3 NT00

Annandale Arms Hotel

★★★ 78% HOTEL

◉ Modern Scottish ♨

250-year-old inn serving well-cooked local produce

☎ 01683 220013 🖹 01683 221395
High St DG10 9HF
e-mail: reception@annandalearmshotel.co.uk
web: www.annandalearmshotel.co.uk
dir: M74 junct 15/A701. Hotel on west side of central square that forms High St

The Annandale Arms is a template for what a proper inn should be (it used to be a matter of pride that the ostlers here could change the horses of a coach and four in less than a minute, in which time the driver would down a pint of ale). It has been woven into the fabric of Moffat life for 250 years, and is still a real pub with an easygoing welcome in the oak-panelled bar. Travellers can take advantage of well-appointed, modern bedrooms and bathrooms, located away from the hustle and bustle of the high street; loyal locals come for the excellent ales and malts, and food that is also worth more than a passing glance, served at bare darkwood tables and imperial purple velvet seats in a good-looking contemporary venue. The cooking doesn't stray too far from the straight and narrow, using meat, game and fish sourced from north of the border in clear-cut dishes given a modern spin to keep things interesting. Seared West Coast scallops with lardons of smoked bacon, horseradish cream and parmesan crisps is a suitably up-to-date way to start, and if you fancy a good old steak, a chargrilled sirloin of Scotch beef with brandy and pepper cream sauce, onion rings, mushrooms and grilled tomatoes should hit the spot.

Rooms 16 (2 fmly) (5 GF) (5 smoking) **S** £70; **D** £110 (incl. bkfst) **Facilities** FTV New Year Wi-fi **Conf** Class 40 Board 40 Thtr 60 Del from £120 **Parking** 20 **Notes** LB Closed 25-26 Dec

Chef Margaret Tweedie **Owner** Mr & Mrs Tweedie
Times 12-2/6-8.45 Closed 25-26 Dec **Prices** Fixed D 3 course £30, Starter £3.50-£8.50, Main £7.50-£17.50, Dessert £4.50, Service optional **Wines** 23 bottles over £20, 18 bottles under £20, 4 by glass **Notes** Vegetarian available, Civ Wed 40 **Seats** 30, Pr/dining room 50 **Children** Portions, Menu

Well View

★★★★★ GUEST ACCOMMODATION

◉◉ Modern European **V** ♨

Country-house cooking in Dumfries & Galloway

Ballplay Rd DG10 9JU
☎ 01683 220184
e-mail: johnwellview@aol.com
dir: From Moffat on A708 towards Selkirk, 0.5m, left onto Ballplay Rd. Well View 300mtrs on right

An attractive country house, Well View is a Dumfriesshire haven of pastoral tranquillity, set in an elevated position with outstanding views. Floral fabrics, simply laid tables and views of the garden add to the restfulness of the dining room, where Janet Schuckardt offers a fixed-price deal at lunch and dinner, based on fine Scottish ingredients. Canapés and a glass of Glühwein make an unexpected start to an evening, and are the prelude to a four-course drill that might open with smoked trout mousse wrapped in smoked salmon with beetroot and dill dressing, move on to local beef fillet wrapped in Parma ham with porcini, sauced with red wine, then Scottish cheeses not wrapped in anything, and concluding with a dessert trio that could take in cranberry and orange steamed pudding with crème anglaise, chocolate and mango tart and lemon posset.

Rooms 3 en suite S £55-£80; D £75-£115 **Facilities** tea/coffee Dinner available Cen ht **Conf** Max 8 Board 8 **Parking** 4 **Notes** LB

Chef Janet & Lina Schuckardt **Owner** Janet & John Schuckardt **Times** 12.30-7.30 **Prices** Fixed L 2 course £9.50-£12.50, Fixed D 4 course £35, Service included **Notes** Sunday L, Vegetarian menu, Dress restrictions, Smart dress **Seats** 10, Pr/dining room 10 **Children** Portions

Bridge House

★★★★ GUEST HOUSE

Well Rd DG10 9JT
☎ 01683 220558 🖹 01683 220558
e-mail: info@bridgehousemoffat.co.uk
dir: Off A708 The Holm onto Burnside & Well Rd, house 0.5m on left

A fine Victorian property, Bridge House lies in attractive gardens in a quiet residential area on the outskirts of the town. The atmosphere is very friendly and relaxed. The chef-proprietor provides interesting dinners (by arrangement) featuring local produce. The cosy guest lounge is the ideal venue for pre-dinner drinks.

Rooms 7 en suite (1 fmly) S £55; D £70-£95* **Facilities** FTV tea/coffee Dinner available Cen ht Licensed **Parking** 7 **Notes** LB ⊗ No Children 2yrs Closed Xmas & New Year

Hartfell House & The Limetree Restaurant

★★★★ GUEST HOUSE

◉ Modern British ♨

Skilful cooking based on local ingredients

Hartfell Crescent DG10 9AL
☎ 01683 220153
e-mail: enquiries@hartfellhouse.co.uk
web: www.hartfellhouse.co.uk
dir: Off High St at war memorial onto Well St & Old Well Rd.
Hartfell Crescent on right

Dating from around 1850, Hartfell House is a substantial
building of local stone, set high above town with lovely
countryside views. The beautifully maintained bedrooms
offer high quality and comfort. The Limetree restaurant is a
large, bright room with an oak floor, shutters and well-
spaced tables covered with linen against a backdrop of local
artwork on the walls. Cooking is a blend of modern and
traditional, with some Scottish and more global influences
at work; Cajun-spiced tomato and black bean soup,
perhaps, then roast loin of organic mutton with haggis and
bacon, rosemary sauce and boulangère potatoes, or fillet of
Solway salmon with tarragon sauce and braised fennel and
leeks. A choice of Scottish cheeses with chutney is an
appropriate way to end, or go for home-made ice cream.

Rooms 7 en suite (2 fmly) (1 GF) S £35-£40; D £60-£70*
Facilities FTV tea/coffee Dinner available Cen ht Licensed
Wi-fi Golf 18 **Parking** 6 **Notes** LB ⊗ Closed Xmas

Chef Matt Seddon **Owner** Robert & Mhairi Ash
Times 12.30-2.30/6.30-9 Closed Xmas, Mon, L Tue-Sat, D
Sun **Prices** Fixed L 2 course £19.50, Fixed D 3 course
£27.50, Service optional, Groups min 6 service 10%
Wines 12 bottles over £20, 12 bottles under £20, 5 by glass
Notes Sunday L, Vegetarian available **Seats** 26
Children Portions

Limetree House

★★★★ GUEST ACCOMMODATION

Eastgate DG10 9AE
☎ 01683 220001
e-mail: info@limetreehouse.co.uk
web: www.limetreehouse.co.uk
dir: Off High St onto Well St, left onto Eastgate, house
100yds on left

A warm welcome is assured at this well-maintained guest
accommodation, quietly situated behind the main high
street. Recognisable by its colourful flower baskets in
season, it provides an inviting lounge and a bright cheerful
breakfast room. Bedrooms are smartly furnished and include
a large family room.

Rooms 6 en suite (1 fmly) (1 GF) S £40-£45; D £60-£80*
Facilities FTV TVL tea/coffee Cen ht Wi-fi Golf 18 **Parking** 3
Notes LB No Children 5yrs RS Xmas & New Year

No 29 Well Street

★★★★ BED AND BREAKFAST

29 Well St DG10 9DP
☎ 01683 221905
e-mail: mcleancamm1956@btinternet.com
dir: M74 junct 15 follow signs to High St, Well St on right

Located in the heart of Moffat just minutes drive from the
rolling countryside of the Scottish Borders, this is a very
comfortable and well presented property offering high
standards of hospitality and service. Bedrooms are well
appointed with many useful extras provided as standard.
Breakfast is hearty with local produce used to good effect.

Rooms 3 en suite (2 GF) S £30-£40; D £50-£60
Facilities FTV tea/coffee Cen ht Wi-fi **Parking** 1 **Notes** ⊗ No
Children 10yrs Closed 24-26 & 31 Dec, 1 Jan

The Balmoral

★★★ INN

High St DG10 9DL
☎ 01683 220288 📠 01683 220451
web: www.thebalmoralhotel-moffat.co.uk
dir: 0.5m from A/M74 junct 15, halfway up High St on right

The Balmoral is situated in the centre of the town with free
parking in the town square, and a friendly welcome is
guaranteed. Bar meals are available all day until 9.30pm.
Bedrooms are very comfortably equipped with thoughtful
extras. Moffat is a former spa town and is within easy reach
of many major tourist attractions.

Rooms 16 en suite (2 fmly) **Facilities** tea/coffee Dinner
available Cen ht **Notes** ⊗

Barnhill Springs Country Guest House

★★ GUEST ACCOMMODATION

DG10 9QS
☎ 01683 220580
e-mail: barnhillsprings@yahoo.co.uk
dir: A74(M) junct 15, A701 towards Moffat. Barnhill Rd 50yds on right

This former farmhouse is in a quiet, rural location south of the town and within easy reach of the M74. Bedrooms are well proportioned; and have private bathrooms. There is a comfortable lounge and separate dining room. Barnhill Spring continues to welcome pets.

Rooms 5 rms (5 pri facs) (1 fmly) (1 GF) S £35-£36; D £70-£72 **Facilities** TVL tea/coffee Dinner available Cen ht **Parking** 10 **Notes** LB

Brodies

◉ Traditional

Well-crafted modern cooking in Moffat centre

☎ 01683 222869
Holm St DG10 9EB
e-mail: whatscooking@brodiesofmoffat.co.uk

Just off Moffat's high street, Brodies is a bright and breezy contemporary operation with a spacious bar for pre-dinner drinks, and a restaurant done out in a clean cut modern style - pale grey leather banquettes and funky striped chairs at tables dressed with smart white runners. The kitchen's output stands out from the crowd, not least because it sources the lion's share of its supplies from the local Dumfries and Galloway region, and brings them together with thought and imagination. Smoked chicken timbale with an orange and Moffat honey dressing gets a spring meal off to a flying start, while main-course roast rump of lamb might be glazed with lemon and thyme marmalade and served with dauphinoise potatoes; vegetarians are well-catered for here - perhaps an open tart of spinach and Dunsyre Blue with pesto dressing. Finish with tiramisù torte with Amaretto crème anglaise.

Times 10-11

Black Bull Hotel

Churchgate DG10 9EG ☎ 01683 220206 ▤ 01683 220483
e-mail: hotel@blackbullmoffat.co.uk
dir: Telephone for directions

This historic pub was the headquarters of Graham of Claverhouse during the 17th-century Scottish rebellion, and was frequented by Robert Burns around 1790. The Railway Bar, in former stables across the courtyard, houses a collection of railway memorabilia and traditional pub games. Food is served in the lounge, Burns Room or restaurant. Dishes include Black Bull sizzlers (steak, chicken fillets, gammon) served on a cast iron platter; the daily roast, and deep-fried breaded haddock fillet. Recent change of hands.

Open all day all wk 11-11 (Thu-Sat 11am-mdnt Sun 12-11) ⊕ FREE HOUSE ◖ McEwans, John Smith's.
Facilities Children welcome Children's menu Children's portions Dogs allowed Garden Parking

NEW GALLOWAY Map 3 NX67

Cross Keys Hotel ☗

High St DG7 3RN ☎ 01644 420494 ▤ 01644 701071
e-mail: enquiries@thecrosskeys-newgalloway.co.uk
dir: At N end of Loch Ken, 10m from Castle Douglas on A712

This 17th-century former coaching inn sits in a stunning location at the top of Loch Ken and on the edge of Galloway Forest Park, a superb area for walking, fishing, birdwatching, golf, watersports, painting and photography. Part of the hotel was once the police station and in the beamed period bar the food is served in restored, stone-walled cells. The à la carte restaurant offers hearty food with a Scottish accent, such as home-made Galloway steak pie, fish in cider batter, and minted shoulder of lamb. Real ales are a speciality, and there's a good choice of malts in the whisky bar.

Open 6-11.30 Closed: Sun & Mon eve winter **Bar Meals** D served all wk 6.30-8.30 **Restaurant** D served all wk 6.30-8.30 ⊕ FREE HOUSE ◖ Houston, Sulwarth, Guest ales ♺ Stowford Press. ☗ 9 **Facilities** Children's menu Dogs allowed Garden Wi-fi

NEWTON STEWART Map 2 NX46

Kirroughtree House

★★★ COUNTRY HOUSE HOTEL

◉◉ Modern British

Historic Scottish mansion serving up fine Scottish produce

☎ 01671 402141 ▤ 01671 402425
Minnigaff DG8 6AN
e-mail: info@kirroughtreehouse.co.uk
web: www.kirroughtreehouse.co.uk
dir: A75 onto A712, hotel entrance 300yds on left

There's no greater provenance for a Scottish country mansion than having a connection with Robert Burns, and the great poet visited this house many times in the late 1700s, even reciting his poems whilst seated on the winding staircase. On the edge of Galloway Forest Park, it's a splendid baronial-style building on a grand scale, with soaring ceilings, acres of wood panelling, antiques and plush carpets. Well-proportioned, individually styled bedrooms include some suites and mini-suites and many rooms enjoy fine views. Service is very friendly and attentive.

continued

The dining room is a traditional and formal space, with smartly set tables and a menu that is based on good Scottish produce. To start there might be a puff pastry case filled with wild mushrooms in a creamy sauce, or seared king scallops with lemon risotto and asparagus cream. Next up, a soup (cream of white onion perhaps) followed by pan-fried Galloway venison with château potatoes, parsnip purée, green beans and port jus, finishing with raspberry pannacotta or the excellent selection of Scottish cheeses.

Rooms 17 **S** £80-£120; **D** £120-£260 (incl. bkfst)*
Facilities FTV 9-hole pitch & putt Xmas New Year Wi-fi
Conf Class 20 Board 20 Thtr 30 **Services** Lift **Parking** 50
Notes LB No children 10yrs Closed 2 Jan-mid Feb

Chef Matthew McWhir **Owner** Mr D McMillan
Times 12-1.30/7-9 Closed 2 Jan-mid Feb **Prices** Fixed D 4 course £35, Starter £3.50-£6.25, Main £12.75-£18.50, Dessert £4.25-£6, Service optional **Wines** 78 bottles over £20, 9 bottles under £20, 5 by glass **Notes** Sunday L, Vegetarian available, Dress restrictions, Smart casual **Seats** 45

The Bruce Hotel

★★★ 73% HOTEL

☎ 01671 402294 📠 01671 402294
88 Queen St DG8 6JL
e-mail: mail@the-bruce-hotel.com
web: www.the-bruce-hotel.com
dir: Exit A75 at Newton Stewart rdbt towards town. Hotel 800mtrs on right

Named after the Scottish patriot Robert the Bruce, this welcoming hotel is just a short distance from the A75. One of the well-appointed bedrooms features a four-poster bed, and popular family suites contain separate bedrooms for children. Public areas include a traditional lounge, a formal restaurant and a lounge bar, both offering a good choice of dishes.

Rooms 20 (3 fmly) **S** £50-£70; **D** £60-£90 (incl. bkfst)
Facilities FTV New Year Wi-fi **Conf** Class 50 Board 14
Thtr 100 Del from £75 to £105 **Parking** 14 **Notes** LB

Creebridge House Hotel

Minnigaff DG8 6NP ☎ 01671 402121 📠 01671 403258
e-mail: info@creebridge.co.uk
dir: From A75 into Newton Stewart, turn right over river bridge, hotel 200yds on left

A listed building dating from 1760, this family-run, country house hotel stands in three acres of tranquil gardens and woodland at the foot of Kirroughtree forest. Taking its name from the River Cree, the hotel used to be the Earl of Galloway's shooting lodge and the grounds part of his estate. The bar and brasserie offer malt whiskies and real ales, including Deuchars. For lunch or candlelit dinner in the restaurant, the well-filled menu offers plenty of dishes with Scottish credentials, such as grilled locally made haggis with melted Cheddar and rich whisky cream sauce; pan-fried haunch of Highland venison; Galloway wholetail scampi; and West Coast prawn and salmon penne pasta. Home-made desserts include pear and almond tart with custard, and lemon posset with shortbread. If you're an outdoor sort, this is the place to be as there is fishing, golf, cycling, horse riding walking and deer stalking.

Open all wk noon-2 6-11.30 (Fri-Sat noon-2 6-1am) Closed: 1st 3wks Jan **Bar Meals** L served all wk noon-2 D served all wk 6-9 **Restaurant** L served all wk noon-2 D served all wk 6-9 FREE HOUSE Deuchars, Guinness, Guest ales. **Facilities** Children welcome Dogs allowed Garden Parking

The Galloway Arms Hotel

54-58 Victoria St DG8 6DB ☎ 01671 402653
📠 01671 401202
e-mail: info@gallowayarmshotel.com
web: www.gallowayarmshotel.com
dir: In town centre, opposite clock

Founded 260 years ago by 6th Earl of Galloway, the hotel acted as the focus for developing the 'planted' market town of Newton Stewart, first established in the 1650's. On the banks of the River Cree, the town is well sited to explore Galloway Forest or the Machars of Whithorn, working up an appetite for traditional Scottish dishes such as chicken, leek and Highland crowdie or the prosaically-named Bonnie Prince Charlie's Balls (deep-fried haggis in Drambuie-based sauce), accompanied by a dram from the most extensive selection of malts in Galloway.

Open all day all wk 11am-mdnt (Fri-Sat 11am-1am) **Bar Meals** L served all wk 12-2 D served all wk 6-9 **Restaurant** D served all wk 6-9 FREE HOUSE Belhaven Best, Guinness, Caledonian Deuchars IPA, 70/- Shilling. 11 **Facilities** Children welcome Children's menu Children's portions Dogs allowed Garden Parking

PORTPATRICK   Map 2 NW95

Knockinaam Lodge

★★★ HOTEL

⊚⊚⊚ Modern Scottish **V** 🍷NOTABLE WINE LIST

Classically-based cooking on the isolated Galloway coast

☎ 01776 810471   📄 01776 810435
DG9 9AD
e-mail: reservations@knockinaamlodge.com
web: www.knockinaamlodge.com
dir: From A77 or A75 follow signs to Portpatrick. Through Lochans. After 2m left at signs for hotel

No tour of Dumfries & Galloway would be complete without a stay at this haven of tranquillity and relaxation. The Lodge looks rather lost - gloriously so, you might think - at its perch on the wild Galloway coast. Approached along a single-track road, it exerts a powerful attraction to those in need of a retreat, especially when it turns out that it has its own private bit of beach, quite as if it were a Caribbean getaway. Inside is all period style, with tapestry curtains, well-upholstered seating and a warmly inviting feel. There are just ten suites - each individually designed and all with flat-screen TVs. Adjust your settings: Knockinaam works to its own beguilingly sedate pace, not least for the set menus, which change every day. Dinner is a four-course affair, perhaps beginning in spring with a perfectly judged grilled fillet of cod in featherlight dill hollandaise, a flawless exercise in balance. That may be followed by seared Skye scallops with a complex supporting cast of orange, fennel and beetroot, the citrus perhaps a little too dominant. Speyside Angus beef is a favoured main, slow-roasted and classically presented with a crisp potato rösti, shallot purée and a resonant port-based jus. The final course is the only moment at which you'll need to take on the responsibility of choice. Will it be British and French cheeses with walnut bread, or something like a pistachio soufflé with warm chocolate sauce, airily light but packing a great big punch of flavour? A serious wine list includes a decent choice by the glass.

Rooms 10 (1 fmly) **Facilities** FTV Fishing 🎣 Shooting Walking Sea fishing Clay pigeon shooting Xmas New Year Wi-fi **Conf** Class 10 Board 16 Thtr 30 **Parking** 20 **Notes** Civ Wed 40

Chef Anthony Pierce **Owner** David & Sian Ibbotson **Times** 12.30-2/7-9 **Prices** Service optional **Wines** 335 bottles over £20, 18 bottles under £20, 9 by glass **Notes** Fixed L 4 course £40, D 5 course £58, Sunday L, Vegetarian menu, Dress restrictions, No jeans **Seats** 32, Pr/ dining room 18 **Children** Menu

POWFOOT   Map 3 NY16

Powfoot Golf Hotel

★★★ 78% HOTEL

☎ 01461 700254 & 207580 📄 01461 700288
Links Av DG12 5PN
e-mail: reception@thepowfootgolfhotel.co.uk
dir: A75 onto B721, through Annan. B724, approx 3m, left onto unclassified road

This hotel has well presented and comfortable modern bedrooms, many of which overlook the championship golf course. Public areas have panoramic views onto the Solway Firth and the Lakeland hills beyond. The service is friendly and relaxed, and quality food is served in a choice of locations.

Rooms 24 (9 fmly) (5 GF) **Facilities** STV FTV Putt green Xmas New Year Wi-fi **Conf** Class 80 Board 80 Thtr 80 **Parking** 30 **Notes** ⊗ Civ Wed 100

SANDHEAD   Map 2 NX04

Tigh Na Mara Hotel

Main St DG9 9JF ☎ 01776 830210   📄 01776 830432
e-mail: tighnamara@btconnect.com
dir: A75 from Dumfries towards Stranraer. Left onto B7084 to Sandhead. Hotel in village centre

A family-run village hotel at the western end of the Gulf Stream-washed Sands of Luce, with an extensive menu of dishes created from top quality local ingredients. Stornoway black pudding accompanies duo of pheasant and pigeon; roast rib of Galloway beef shares its plate with Yorkshire pudding; and the seafood in the pancakes comes from Scotland's West Coast waters. Relax in the beer garden, comfortable lounge or beside the fire in the public bar. By the way, Tigh na Mara means 'house by the sea'.

Open all day all wk **Bar Meals** L served all wk 12-2.30 D served all wk 6-9 **Restaurant** L served all wk 12-2.30 D served all wk 6-9 booking required Fixed menu price fr £10.95 🌐 BELHAVEN ◀ Belhaven Best, Morland Old Speckled Hen. **Facilities** Children welcome Children's menu Children's portions Family room Dogs allowed Garden Parking Wi-fi

SANQUHAR — Map 3 NS70

Blackaddie House Hotel

★★★ 79% COUNTRY HOUSE HOTEL

◉◉ Modern British 🍷

Vibrant modern cooking in a stone-built manse

☎ 01659 502700
Blackaddie Rd DG4 6JJ
e-mail: ian@blackaddiehotel.co.uk
web: www.blackaddiehotel.co.uk
dir: Exit A76 just N of Sanquhar at Burnside Service Station. Take private road to hotel 300mtrs on right

The stone-built 16th-century house, which was once the manse to St Bride's church nearby, stands on a bank of the River Nith, in an appealingly tranquil setting. The bedrooms and suites, including family accommodation, are all well presented and comfortable with many useful extras provided as standard. Guests making their way to the breakfast room may have an encounter with the resident ghost, but we are assured she does nothing more than flounce by a little disdainfully. A simply but smartly furnished small dining room with light walls makes a civilised space for the proprietor's vibrant modern cooking. Start with John Dory fillet on lemon and thyme risotto with shrimp salad, before moving on to an ensemble of outdoor-reared rose veal, comprised of the sautéed loin, a tongue salad and kidney ragoût on white bean cassoulet, or perhaps a salmon variations plate, with seared salmon on purple potato crush, a salmon sausage and céviche. The serial approach continues into desserts, where the versatility of cinnamon is explored via doughnuts, a pistachio croquant with banana cream, coffee and cinnamon milk, and more.

Rooms 9 (3 annexe) (2 fmly) (3 GF) **Facilities** Xmas New Year Wi-fi **Conf** Class 12 Board 16 Thtr 20 **Parking** 20 **Notes** Civ Wed 24

Chef Ian McAndrew **Owner** Ian McAndrew **Times** 12-2/6.30-9 **Prices** Fixed L 2 course £15-£21, Starter £5.75-£12.50, Main £15-£28, Dessert £9.75-£10.50, Service optional **Wines** 61 bottles over £20, 3 bottles under £20, 10 by glass **Notes** Sunday L, Vegetarian available **Seats** 20, Pr/dining room 20 **Children** Portions, Menu

STRANRAER — Map 2 NX06

Corsewall Lighthouse Hotel

★★★ 80% HOTEL

◉ Modern Scottish **V**

To the lighthouse for local produce and charming hospitality

☎ 01776 853220 📠 01776 854231
Corsewall Point, Kirkcolm DG9 0QG
e-mail: lighthousehotel@btinternet.com
web: www.lighthousehotel.co.uk
dir: A718 from Stranraer to Kirkcolm (approx 8m). Follow hotel signs for 4m

Looking for something completely different? Set on the rugged Atlantic shoreline, this charming, fully-functioning lighthouse dating back to 1815 now houses a comfortable if intimate hotel and restaurant. Bedrooms come in a variety of sizes, some reached by a spiral staircase, and like the public areas, are cosy and atmospheric. The cottage suites in the grounds offer greater space. In the restaurant, bare-wood tables and linen napkins add to the romantic feel in the restaurant and informal service is in-keeping with it all. It goes without saying that the view across the Mull of Kintyre is stunning but generous portions using locally-sourced ingredients mean it's not just about the novelty of eating somewhere this unique. The five-course fine-dining menu might take in chicken liver pâté, then guinea fowl and venison sausage in a rowanberry and port wine game stock reduction, finishing off with a lemon and mango cheesecake.

Rooms 11 (5 annexe) (4 fmly) (2 GF) (3 smoking) **Facilities** FTV Xmas New Year Wi-fi **Conf** Thtr 20 **Parking** 20 **Notes** ⊗ Civ Wed 28

Chef Andrew Downie **Owner** Gordon, Kay & Pamela Ward **Times** 12-1.45/7-8.45 **Prices** Fixed L 2 course £15.95-£28.50, Starter £7.75, Main £16.95-£21.70, Dessert £7.25, Service optional **Wines** 30 bottles over £20, 13 bottles under £20, 4 by glass **Notes** Fixed D 5 course £35-£39.75, Sunday L, Vegetarian menu, Dress restrictions, Smart casual **Seats** 28 **Children** Portions, Menu

THORNHILL — Map 3 NX89

Gillbank House

★★★★★ GUEST ACCOMMODATION

8 East Morton St DG3 5LZ
☎ 01848 330597 📠 01848 331713
e-mail: hanne@gillbank.co.uk
web: www.gillbank.co.uk
dir: In town centre off A76

Gillbank House was originally built for a wealthy Edinburgh merchant. Convenient for the many outdoor pursuits in this area, such as fishing and golfing, this delightful house offers comfortable and spacious bedrooms and smart shower rooms en suite. Breakfast is served at individual tables in the bright, airy dining room, which is next to the comfortable lounge.

Rooms 6 en suite (2 GF) S £50; D £75* **Facilities** tea/coffee Cen ht Wi-fi Golf 18 **Parking** 8 **Notes** ⊗ No Children 8yrs

EAST DUNBARTONSHIRE

MILNGAVIE — Map 2 NS57

Premier Inn Glasgow (Milngavie)

BUDGET HOTEL

☎ 0871 527 8428 📄 0871 527 8429
103 Main St G62 6JQ
web: www.premierinn.com
dir: M8 junct 16, follow Milngavie (A879) signs. Approx. 5m. Pass Murray Park Training Ground. Left at lights. Hotel on A81adjacent to West Highland Gate Beefeater

High quality, budget accommodation ideal for both families and business travellers. Spacious, en suite bedrooms feature tea and coffee-making facilities, and Freeview TV in most hotels. Internet access and Wi-fi are available for a small fee. The adjacent family restaurant features a wide and varied menu.

Rooms 60 **D** £52-£60*

WEST DUNBARTONSHIRE

BALLOCH — Map 2 NS38

Cameron House on Loch Lomond

★★★★★ 85% HOTEL

 British

A popular grill on the shore of Loch Lomond

☎ 01389 755565 📄 01389 759522
G83 8QZ
e-mail: reservations@cameronhouse.co.uk
web: www.devere.co.uk
dir: M8 (W) junct 30 for Erskine Bridge. A82 for Crianlarich. 14m, at rdbt signed Luss, hotel on right

Enjoying an idyllic location on the banks of Loch Lomond in over 100 acres of wooded parkland, this stylish hotel offers an excellent range of leisure facilities. These include two golf courses, a world-class spa and a host of indoor and outdoor sporting activities. A choice of restaurants and bars cater for all tastes and include the fine dining Martin Wishart at Loch Lomond (see entry below). Bedrooms are stylish, well equipped and many boast wonderful loch views. The Scottish-themed Cameron Grill is notable for its low lighting, open-to-view kitchen and mural depicting various carousing chaps from long-gone clan days, is just one eating option here (see entry, Martin Wishart, for one of the

others). Naturally enough the grill's the thing, with steaks a strength. Grilled veal chop, of excellent quality, has been an estimable alternative, served with Madeira sauce, caramelised apple and diced pepper and onion, and might follow chicken liver parfait within a ring of bramble chutney and, around that, a jelly of orange liqueur. Crème brûlée flavoured with heather honey and served with lavender honeycomb brings a good Scottish scent to a classic.

Rooms 96 (9 fmly) **Facilities** ⊛ ♨ 9 ♨ Fishing ♨ Gym Squash Outdoor sports Motor boat on Loch Lomond Hairdresser Xmas **Conf** Class 80 Board 80 Thtr 300 **Services** Lift **Parking** 200 **Notes** ⊗ Civ Wed 200

Times 5.30-9.30 Closed L all week

Martin Wishart at Loch Lomond

⚛⚛⚛ Modern French V 🍷 NOTABLE WINE LIST 🍷

The very best Scottish produce in the hands of a talented kitchen team

☎ 01389 722504
Cameron House on Loch Lomond G83 8QZ
e-mail: info@mwlochlomond.co.uk
dir: From A82, follow signs for Loch Lomond. Restaurant 1m after Stoneymullan rdbt on right

Scottish culinary superstar Martin Wishart's first venture outside his eponymous Leith restaurant HQ (see entry) has been a key address on the foodie itinerary north of the border since it opened in 2009. The stately castellated mansion of Cameron House is a suitably five-star setting for the expansion of Brand Wishart, and one that must have held an irresistible appeal for him to return as head honcho after having worked there previously. The loch-side restaurant looking over the bonnie, bonnie banks of Loch Lomond is a sybaritic setting worthy of a glossy interiors magazine: tones of coffee and cream blend with a tartan carpet reminiscent of a heather-filled glen, and a highly-polished front-of-house team makes sure everything happens at the right pace. Leith is still the centre of operations, so don't expect Wishart to be at the stoves: the man charged with interpreting the boss's contemporary take on French classics is head chef Stewart Boyles, who keeps faith with the house style of hyper-precise, refined modern cooking. He likes to paint a pretty picture on the plate, and delivers assured

continued

BALLOCH CONTINUED

flavours; underpinnning it all are spanking fresh, conscientiously-sourced materials - perhaps Shetland mussels as the foundation of a mouclade and langoustines starter, pointed up with curry and saffron velouté. Next up, roast John Dory and bone marrow might appear in a full-throttle pairing, backed up with wild mushrooms, cocotte potatoes and truffle jus, or roast loin of Borders roe deer could share a plate with goats' cheese gnocchi, braised gem lettuce and sauce grand veneur.

Chef Stewart Boyles **Owner** Martin Wishart
Times 12-2.30/6.30-10 Closed 25-26 Dec, 1 Jan, Mon-Tue, L Wed-Fri **Prices** Fixed L 3 course £25, Tasting menu £70, Service added but optional 10% **Wines** 190 bottles over £20, 12 by glass **Notes** ALC menu £65, Tasting menu 6 course, Sunday L, Vegetarian menu, Dress restrictions, Smart casual **Seats** 40 **Children** Portions **Parking** 150

The Waterhouse Inn

★★★★ INN

34 Balloch Rd G83 8LE
☎ 01389 752120 📄 01389 752125
e-mail: info@waterhouseinn.co.uk
web: www.waterhouseinn.co.uk

The Waterhouse Inn is located on the high street of Balloch close to the park and the mouth of Loch Lomond. Bedrooms are well equipped and spacious, with modern bright bathrooms. The Inn is welcoming and friendly, with a café that serves home-cooked food throughout the day, and is a perfect base for touring Loch Lomond and the Trossachs National Park.

Rooms 7 en suite (2 fmly) **Facilities** STV FTV TVL tea/coffee Dinner available Cen ht Wi-fi **Notes** ⊗

Sunnyside

★★★ BED AND BREAKFAST

35 Main St G83 9JX
☎ 01389 750282 & 07717 397548
e-mail: enquiries@sunnysidebb.co.uk
dir: From A82 take A811 then A813 for 1m, over mini-rdbt 150mtrs on left

Set in its own grounds well back from the road by Loch Lomond, Sunnyside is an attractive, traditional detached house, parts of which date back to the 1830s. Bedrooms are attractively decorated and provide comfortable modern accommodation. Free Wi-fi is also available. The dining room is located on the ground floor, and is an appropriate setting for hearty Scottish breakfasts.

Rooms 6 en suite (2 fmly) (1 GF) S £32-£38; D £54-£65* **Facilities** FTV tea/coffee Dinner available Cen ht Wi-fi **Parking** 8

Beardmore Hotel

★★★★ 77% HOTEL

 Modern British

Modern and traditional mix on the banks of the Clyde

☎ 0141 951 6000 📄 0141 951 6018
Beardmore St G81 4SA
e-mail: info@beardmore.scot.nhs.uk
dir: M8 junct 19, follow signs for Clydeside Expressway to Glasgow road, then A814 (Dumbarton road), then follow Clydebank Business Park signs. Hotel on left

About 10 miles from Glasgow airport, on the banks of the Clyde, the Beardmore is a purpose-built modern hotel and conference centre with a range of dining options, including a bar menu with outdoor piazza and fine-dining restaurant. In the latter, a mix of modern Scottish and French modes is overlaid with traditional elements, with some commitment to local produce. Start with smoked mackerel on sweet potato and watercress purée, and follow either classically with chicken chasseur and fondant potato, or roast loin and braised shoulder of lamb with caramelised shallots, pea shoots and little breaded onion rings. Dessert might include a milk chocolate and peanut butter mousse with caramelised banana and peanut brittle. The lounge bar offers a more extensive choice of lighter dishes. The leisure facilities include a 15-metre swimming pool, sauna and steam room.

Rooms 166 **Facilities** STV 🖈 supervised Gym Sauna Steam room Whirlpool Xmas New Year Wi-fi **Conf** Class 84 Board 27 Thtr 240 **Services** Lift Air con **Parking** 300 **Notes** ⊗ Civ Wed 170

Chef Iain Ramsay **Owner** NHS **Times** 6.30-10 Closed Sun, L all week **Prices** Starter £5.25-£9.25, Main £10.75-£25, Dessert £6.35-£8.50, Service included **Wines** 18 bottles over £20, 12 bottles under £20, 12 by glass **Notes** Sunday L, Vegetarian available, Air con **Seats** 36, Pr/dining room 200 **Children** Menu

Premier Inn Dumbarton

BUDGET HOTEL

☎ 0871 527 9274 📄 0871 527 9275
Lomondgate Dr G82 2QU
web: www.premierinn.com
dir: From Glasgow follow A82 towards Crainlarich, right at Lomondgate rdbt onto A813, hotel on right. From N: A82 towards Glasgow, left at Lomondgate rdbt onto A813, hotel on right

High quality, budget accommodation ideal for both families and business travellers. Spacious, en suite bedrooms feature tea and coffee-making facilities, and Freeview TV in most hotels. Internet access and Wi-fi are available for a small fee. The adjacent family restaurant features a wide and varied menu.

Rooms 60 **D** £55-£59*

CITY OF DUNDEE

BROUGHTY FERRY   Map 3 NO43

The Royal Arch Bar ♟

285 Brook St DD5 2DS ☎ 01382 779741 ▤ **01382 739174**
dir: 3m from Dundee. 0.5 min from Broughty Ferry rail station

Handy for the Tay-side esplanade and sandy beach at Broughty Ferry, the pub's striking, tile-hung exterior hides a superb art deco lounge (note the stools, table legs and vivid stained glass) off a fine Victorian panelled, turned-wood bar. Its name derives from the Masonic Arch, its logo from a now-demolished monument to Queen Victoria. At this popular community local, sup Carnoustie-brewed beers and chow on robust pub food (maybe haddock Kiev); the pavement café here is busy in good weather.

Open all day all wk **Bar Meals** L served Mon-Fri 12-2.15, Sat-Sun 12-5 booking required D served all wk 5-7.30 booking required Av main course £7 ⊕ FREE HOUSE ◀ McEwans 80/-, Belhaven Best, Caledonian Deuchars IPA, Angus Mashie Niblick Cask. ♟ 30 **Facilities** Children welcome Children's portions Family room Dogs allowed Garden Beer festival Wi-fi

DUNDEE   Map 3 NO43

Apex City Quay Hotel & Spa

★★★★ 77% HOTEL

☎ 0845 365 0000 & 01382 202404 ▤ 01382 201401
1 West Victoria Dock Rd DD1 3JP
e-mail: dundee.reservations@apexhotels.co.uk
web: www.apexhotels.co.uk
dir: A85/Riverside Drive to Discovery Quay. Exit rdbt for City Quay

This stylish, purpose-built hotel occupies an enviable position at the heart of Dundee's regenerated quayside area. Bedrooms, including a number of smart suites, feature the very latest in design. Warm hospitality and professional service are an integral part of the hotel's appeal. Open-plan public areas with panoramic windows and contemporary food options complete the package.

Rooms 151 (17 fmly) **Facilities** Spa FTV ✹ Gym Steam room Sauna Xmas New Year Wi-fi **Conf** Class 180 Board 120 Thtr 375 **Services** Lift Air con **Parking** 150 **Notes** ⊗ Civ Wed 300

The Landmark Hotel

★★★★ 74% HOTEL

◉ British, European

Contemporary setting for modish and trad food

☎ 01382 641122 ▤ 01382 631201
Kingsway West DD2 5JT
e-mail: sales@thelandmarkdundee.co.uk
web: www.thelandmarkdundee.co.uk
dir: From A90 (Kingsway) at rdbt junct with A85, follow hotel signs

Just a short drive from Dundee, the Landmark is a modern hotel with a leisure club, luxurious bedrooms and a crowd-pleasing restaurant. The Garden Room restaurant is housed in a conservatory overlooking the hotel grounds. Well-spaced tables and subdued lighting in the evening set the mood for a menu of two halves: creative Scottish cuisine alongside more straightforward comfort dishes (think spaghetti carbonara and garlic bread) covers all the bases. Dig into seared breast of wood pigeon with apple and pearl barley risotto, followed by a perfectly cooked grilled fillet of halibut with a macadamia nut crust, celeriac and parsnip dauphinoise and green pea velouté. Finish with a superb dark chocolate delice and white chocolate sorbet.

Rooms 95 (11 fmly) (45 GF) **Facilities** STV FTV ✹ supervised Gym Sauna Steam room Xmas New Year Wi-fi **Conf** Class 50 Board 45 Thtr 100 **Parking** 140 **Notes** ⊗ Civ Wed 100

Chef Graham Riley **Owner** BDL Management **Times** 12-2/6.30-9.30 Closed L Mon-Sat **Prices** Starter £5-£9, Main £12-£22, Dessert £5-£7, Service optional **Wines** 30 bottles over £20, 10 bottles under £20, 12 by glass **Notes** Sunday L, Vegetarian available, Dress restrictions, Smart casual, **Seats** 100, Pr/dining room 50 **Children**Portions, Menu

Holiday Inn Express Dundee

BUDGET HOTEL

☎ 01382 314330 ▤ 01382 314343
Dock St DD1 3DR
e-mail: dm1@hiexpressdundee.com
dir: Telephone for directions

A modern hotel ideal for families and business travellers. Fresh and uncomplicated, the spacious rooms include Sky TV, power shower and tea and coffee-making facilities. Continental buffet breakfast is included in the room rate; other meals may be taken at the nearby family pub or restaurant.

Rooms 95 (49 fmly) **Conf** Class 25 Board 25 Thtr 30

DUNDEE CONTINUED

Premier Inn Dundee Centre

BUDGET HOTEL

☎ 0871 527 8320 📠 0871 527 8321
Discovery Quay, Riverside Dr DD1 4XA
web: www.premierinn.com
dir: Follow signs for Discovery Quay, hotel on waterfront

High quality, budget accommodation ideal for both families and business travellers. Spacious, en suite bedrooms feature tea and coffee-making facilities, and Freeview TV in most hotels. Internet access and Wi-fi are available for a small fee. The adjacent family restaurant features a wide and varied menu.

Rooms 40 **D** £65-£70*

Premier Inn Dundee East

BUDGET HOTEL

☎ 0871 527 8322 📠 0871 527 8323
115-117 Lawers Dr, Panmurefield Village, Broughty Ferry DD5 3UP
web: www.premierinn.com
dir: From N: A92 (Dundee & Arbroath). Hotel 1.5m after Sainsbury's. From S: A90. At end of dual carriageway follow Dundee to Arbroath signs

Rooms 60 **D** £49-£55*

Premier Inn Dundee (Monifieth)

BUDGET HOTEL

☎ 0871 527 8318 📠 0871 527 8319
Ethiebeaton Park, Arbroath Rd, Monifieth DD5 4HB
web: www.premierinn.com
dir: From A90 (Kingsway Rd) follow Carnoustie/Arbroath (A92) signs

Rooms 40 **D** £49-£55*

Premier Inn Dundee North

BUDGET HOTEL

☎ 0871 527 8324 📠 0871 527 8325
Camperdown Leisure Park, Dayton Dr, Kingsway DD2 3SQ
web: www.premierinn.com
dir: 2m N of city centre on A90 at junct with A923, adjacent to cinema. At entrance to Camperdown Country Park

Rooms 78 **D** £49-£55*

Premier Inn Dundee West

BUDGET HOTEL

☎ 0871 527 8326 📠 0871 527 8327
Kingsway West DD2 5JU
web: www.premierinn.com
dir: On A90 towards Aberdeen adjacent to Technology Park rdbt

Rooms 64 **D** £49-£58*

Speedwell Bar ▼

165-167 Perth Rd DD2 1AS ☎ 01382 667783
dir: From A92 (Tay Bridge), A991 signed Perth/A85/Coupar Angus/A923. At Riverside rdbt 3rd exit (A991). At lights left into Nethergate signed Parking/South Tay St. Forward into Perth Rd. Pass university. Bar on right

This fine example of an unspoiled Edwardian bar is worth visiting for its interior alone; all the fitments in the bar and sitting rooms are beautifully crafted mahogany – gantry, drink shelves, dado panelling and fireplace. The same family owned it for 90 years, until the present landlord's father bought it in 1995. As well as the cask-conditioned ales, 157 whiskies and imported bottles are offered. A kitchen would be good, but since the pub is listed this is impossible. This community pub is home to several clubs and has live Scottish music from time to time on a Tuesday.

Open all day all wk 🌐 FREE HOUSE ◀ McEwans, Belhaven Best, Caledonian, Deuchars IPA. ▼ 18 **Facilities** Dogs allowed Wi-fi **Notes** ♨

CITY OF EDINBURGH

EDINBURGH	Map 3 NT27

See also Livingston, West Lothian

Balmoral

★★★★★ HOTEL

 Modern Scottish **V** 🍷 NOTABLE WINE LIST

Highly refined haute cuisine at the heart of the Scottish capital

☎ 0131 556 2414 📠 0131 557 3747
1 Princes St EH2 2EQ
e-mail: reservations.balmoral@roccofortecollection.com
e-mail: numberone@roccofortecollection.com
web: www.roccofortecollection.com
dir: Follow city centre signs. Hotel at E end of Princes St, adjacent to Waverley Station

The Balmoral is Edinburgh's most prestigious hotel, a classic of the Edwardian railway age in the city's most coveted Princes Street postcode. Bedrooms and suites are stylishly furnished and decorated, all boasting a thoughtful range of extras and impressive marble bathrooms. Hotel amenities include a Roman-style health spa, extensive function facilities, a choice of bars and two very different dining options - Hadrians (see entry below) is a bustling, informal brasserie, while the flagship Number One restaurant was designed by Olga Polizzi to exude class, which it does in spades, thanks to the deep lustre of onyx-red lacquered walls, golden velvet banquettes, ankle-deep carpets, and tables separated by oceans of space. The confident and well-established kitchen remains under the charge of Jeff Bland, who continues to chart a classically-French course, with modern re-workings in dishes based on pedigree Scottish produce. A typical starter might see a roulade of foie gras sharing a plate with endives, fig and grape vinaigrette, and smoked almonds, or there might be plump West Coast scallops, teamed with celeriac purée, pig's cheek, pak choi, peanuts and lime jus. Fish is always a good bet: monkfish with langoustine, chive gnocchi, leeks, and saffron sauce, for example, while meaty options could offer Borders venison with braised lentils, Jerusalem artichoke, beetroot and pickled walnuts. The same luxurious vein runs through to desserts such as chocolate chiboust with pineapple and cardamom purée and lime sorbet.

Rooms 188 (22 fmly) (15 smoking) **S** £325-£2100; **D** £395-£2100 **Facilities** Spa STV ⊗ Gym ♫ Xmas New Year Wi-fi **Conf** Class 180 Board 60 Thtr 350 **Services** Lift Air con **Parking** 100 **Notes** ⊗ Civ Wed 120

Chef Jeff Bland, Craig Sandle **Owner** Rocco Forte Collection **Times** 6.30-10 Closed 1st 2 wks Jan, L all week **Prices** Fixed D 3 course fr £62, Tasting menu £69, Service optional, Groups min 6 service 10% **Wines** 350 bottles over £20, 8 by glass **Notes** Tasting menu 8 course, Vegetarian menu, Dress restrictions, Smart casual preferred, Civ Wed 60 **Seats** 50, Pr/dining room 50 **Children** Portions

AA WINE AWARD WINNER FOR SCOTLAND

Prestonfield

★★★★★ TOWN HOUSE HOTEL

⊚⊚ Traditional British ▮NOTABLE WINE LIST

Opulent surroundings for high-impact cooking

☎ 0131 225 7800 Rhubarb 0131 225 1333 🖷 0131 220 4392
Priestfield Rd EH16 5UT
e-mail: reservations@prestonfield.com
web: www.prestonfield.com
web: www.rhubarb-restaurant.com
dir: A7 towards Cameron Toll. 200mtrs beyond Royal Commonwealth Pool, into Priestfield Rd

Prestonfield House Hotel is a blue-blooded 17th-century mansion, kitted out in unapologetically theatrical and decadent style to create deeply comfortable and dramatically furnished bedrooms and a romantic dining destination. Facilities and services are up-to-the-minute,

and carefully prepared meals are served in the award-winning Rhubarb restaurant. Why rhubarb? Back in 1746, erstwhile owner Sir Alexander Dick introduced the eponymous Asian vegetable to Scotland when it was an exotic rarity on the table. In the ambience of a period film set, opulent shades of blood red and burgundy frame linen-clad tables lit seductively with tea lights - it all adds up to a serious wow factor, and the cooking does not sit in the shadow of the décor. You might start dinner with Isle of Mull crab, honey-roast ham ribs, toasted hazelnuts and mango salsa, and progress to chorizo-crumbed cod fillet with brandade, cauliflower purée and black olives. For pudding, stick with the theme and go for rhubarb crumble and custard with candied ginger ice cream.

Rooms 23 (6 GF) **D** £295-£365 (incl. bkfst)* **Facilities** STV FTV ♨ 18 Putt green 🚲 Free bike hire Xmas New Year Wi-fi **Conf** Class 500 Board 40 Thtr 700 **Services** Lift **Parking** 250 **Notes** Civ Wed 350

Chef John McMahon **Owner** James Thomson OBE **Times** 12-2/6.30-10 **Prices** Fixed L 2 course £16.95, Fixed D 3 course £30, Starter £12-£17.50, Main £19-£35, Dessert £6.50-£8.95, Service optional, Groups min 8 service 10% **Wines** 500+ bottles over £20, 12 by glass **Notes** Theatre D 2 course £16.95, Sunday L, Vegetarian available **Seats** 90, Pr/dining room 500 **Children** Portions

Hadrian's

⊚ Modern Scottish

Classy brasserie in landmark hotel

☎ 0131 557 5000 & 557 2414
The Balmoral Hotel, 1 Princes St EH2 2EQ
e-mail: hadrians.balmoral@roccofortecollection.com
web: www.thebalmoralhotel.com/dining/hadrians
dir: Follow city centre signs. Hotel at E end of Princes St, adjacent to Waverley Station

Offering admirable support to its glamourous and ambitious fine-dining sibling also in the landmark Balmoral Hotel (see entry above), Hadrian's is a valuable address in the city in its own right. The art-deco styling, with walnut floors and shades of unshouty lime, make for a distinctly chic setting, and the elegantly turned out staff set the right tone for its European-accented menu. Start with a classic foie gras parfait served with toasted brioche and grape chutney, followed by grilled fillet of cod with a mustard velouté or fillet of Blairgowrie beef with Lyonnaise onions and red wine béarnaise. To finish, go for warm apple tart with caramel sauce and Chantilly cream, and note there's an imaginative children's menu on offer, too.

Chef Jeff Bland **Owner** Rocco Forte Collection **Times** 12-2.30/6.30-10.30 **Prices** Fixed L 2 course £16, Fixed D 3 course £25.45, Starter £7-£10, Main £13.50-£27.50, Dessert £6.95, Service optional, Groups min 8 service 10% **Wines** 42 bottles over £20, 8 by glass

EDINBURGH CONTINUED

Notes Sunday L, Vegetarian available, Dress restrictions, Smart casual, Civ Wed 60 **Seats** 100, Pr/dining room 26 **Children** Portions, Menu **Parking** 40

Hotel Missoni Edinburgh

★★★★★ 84% HOTEL

☎ 0131 220 6666 📄 0131 226 6660
1 George IV Bridge EH1 1AD
e-mail: info.edinburgh@hotelmissoni.com
dir: At corner of Royal Mile & George IV Bridge

Located on the corner of the George IV Bridge and the Royal Mile in the heart of the old town, this hotel's design is strikingly different. Bold use of black and white and vivid colours together with strong patterns creates a stunning impression. Stylish bedrooms, some with great city views, have iPod/AV hook-up, Wi-fi, coffee machines, and bathrooms with walk-in showers as standard. The buzzing cocktail bar and Cucina Missoni, for modern Italian cuisine, attract locals and residents alike.

Rooms 136 **D** £140-£300 (incl. bkfst)* **Facilities** Spa STV FTV Gym Xmas New Year Wi-fi **Conf** Class 24 Board 24 Thtr 63 **Services** Lift Air con **Parking** 13

The Howard

★★★★★ 83% TOWN HOUSE HOTEL

◉ Modern Scottish

Modern Scottish cooking in a debonair Georgian hotel

☎ 0131 537 3500 📄 0131 557 6515
34 Great King St EH3 6QH
e-mail: reserve@thehoward.com
web: www.thehoward.com
dir: E on Queen St, 2nd left, Dundas St. Through 3 lights, right, hotel on left

The Howard was created in the 1960s from three late-Georgian townhouses to form a debonair hotel in Edinburgh's New Town. Furnished in period style, it's a smart and stylish place, with sumptuous bedrooms in a variety of styles, including spacious suites, well-equipped bathrooms and a host of thoughtful touches. Ornate chandeliers and lavish drapes adorn the drawing room,

while the Atholl dining room contains unique hand-painted 19th century murals. Attentive, well-drilled staff serve a menu of modern Scottish food that gently updates Scottish classics, perhaps skirlie potatoes with rump of Pentland lamb, or can be as modish as scallops with roast pork belly, mushy peas and lemon foam, followed by accurately grilled Gigha halibut with steamed greens, a fairly shy chorizo mash and citrus oil. Finish with a selection of cheeses from Mellis, or a praline crème brûlée with hazelnut biscotti and pineapple granité.

Rooms 18

Times 12-2/6-9.30

The Scotsman

★★★★★ 82% TOWN HOUSE HOTEL

◉ Modern British, Scottish

Unique brasserie setting for Scotland's native produce

☎ 0131 556 5565 📄 0131 652 3652
20 North Bridge EH1 1YT
e-mail: reservations@thescotsmanhotelgroup.co.uk
e-mail: northbridge@tshg.co.uk
web: www.thescotsmanhotel.co.uk
dir: A8 to city centre, left onto Charlotte St. Right into Queen St, right at rdbt onto Leith St. Straight on, left onto North Bridge, hotel on right

Formerly the headquarters of The Scotsman newspaper, this grand baronial property has been stunningly converted into a 21st-century boutique hotel, its design combining sheet glass and girders with original walnut panelling, stained-glass windows and a marble staircase. The classical elegance of the public areas blends seamlessly with the contemporary bedrooms and their state-of-the-art technology, and the superbly equipped leisure club includes a stainless steel swimming pool and large gym. The North Bridge Brasserie, once the reception hall, brings contemporary style to Victorian architecture. The menus showcase Scotland's abundant larder, so seasonality is to the fore, with a kitchen at home with what it describes as modern Scottish cuisine. This translates into Loch Fyne crab with a matching jelly, and Ayrshire wild boar stovie cake with garlic purée and a fried quail's egg. Among many steaks and grills may be poached Shetland sea trout with sorrel mayonnaise, and flank of lamb with sweetbreads, black pudding and mint hollandaise, with sticky toffee pudding among desserts.

Rooms 69 (4 GF) **Facilities** Spa STV 🏊 supervised Gym Beauty treatments Xmas New Year Wi-fi **Conf** Class 50 Board 40 Thtr 100 **Services** Lift **Notes** ⊗ Civ Wed 70

Times 12-2.30/6-10.30

Sheraton Grand Hotel & Spa

★★★★★ 78% HOTEL

☎ 0131 229 9131 📄 0131 228 4510
1 Festival Square EH3 9SR
e-mail: grandedinburgh.sheraton@sheraton.com
dir: Follow City Centre signs (A8). Through Shandwick Place,
right at lights into Lothian Rd. Right at next lights. Hotel on
left at next lights

This modern hotel boasts one of the best spas in Scotland -
the external top floor hydro pool is definitely worth a look
whilst the thermal suite provides a unique venue for serious
relaxation. The spacious bedrooms are available in a variety
of styles, and the suites prove very popular. There is a wide
range of eating options including Santini's, which has a
loyal local following, and One Spa Café for light meals and
snacks.

Rooms 269 **S** £120-£265; **D** £120-£285* **Facilities Spa** STV
FTV ⚡ ⚡ Gym Indoor/outdoor hydropool Kinesis studio
Thermal suite Fitness studio 🎵 Xmas New Year Wi-fi
Conf Class 350 Board 120 Thtr 485 Del from £255 to £340*
Services Lift Air con **Parking** 122 **Notes** LB ⊗ Civ Wed 485

Norton House

★★★★ HOTEL

◉◉◉ Modern British, French

Virtuoso cooking just outside the capital

☎ 0131 333 1275 📄 0131 333 5305
Ingliston EH28 8LX
e-mail: nortonhouse@handpicked.co.uk
web: www.handpicked.co.uk
dir: Off A8, 5m W of city centre

This extended Victorian mansion, set in 55 acres of
parkland, is peacefully situated just outside the city and is
convenient for the airport. The original building dates from
1840, and it was bought nearly 40 years later by John Usher
of the Scottish brewing family. Today both the contemporary
bedrooms and the very spacious, traditional ones have an
impressive range of accessories including large flat-screen
satellite TVs, DVD/CD players and free high speed internet
access; executive rooms have more facilities, of course,
including MP3 connection and 'tilevision' TVs at the end of
the baths. Public areas take in a choice of lounges as well
as dining options, with a popular brasserie and Ushers
Restaurant, where Scotland's best produce is skilfully and
imaginatively treated. West Coast scallops are seared and
accompanied by truffled gnocchi, morels and artichokes,
and Borders roe deer comes with Savoy cabbage, Jerusalem
artichoke, nuts and juniper. The kitchen is clearly in touch
with what appeals to modern palates, serving seared foie
gras with rhubarb and gingerbread, and woodcock with
beetroot, apple and onions, and Puy lentils. Dishes can be
vividly flavoured without being overly complicated: lasagne
made with langoustines, pork cheeks, chocolate and white
truffle, say, or a main course of pan-fried John Dory, its
timing of pinpoint accuracy, with wild leeks, morels, white
asparagus and nettles. Like the rest, pudding descriptions
sound straightforward but mask the skill that goes into their
making, choices typically including rhubarb crumble soufflé
with matching sorbet, or rich chocolate tart with Jaffa ice
cream and orange sponge.

Rooms 83 (10 fmly) (20 GF) **Facilities Spa** STV ⚡ Gym
Archery Laser Clay shooting Quad biking Xmas New Year
Wi-fi **Conf** Class 100 Board 60 Thtr 300 Del from £149 to
£239* **Services** Lift **Parking** 200 **Notes** ⊗ Civ Wed 140

Chef Graeme Shaw, Glen Bilins **Owner** Hand Picked Hotels
Times 7-9.30 Closed 26 Dec, 1 Jan, Sun-Tue, L all week
Prices Starter £7-£9, Main £17-£24, Dessert £6.50-£8.95,
Service optional **Wines** 168 bottles over £20, 12 by glass
Notes Vegetarian available **Seats** 22, Pr/dining room 40
Children Portions

Channings

★★★★ TOWN HOUSE HOTEL

◉ Modern British

Quirky Edinburgh hotel with neighbourhood bistro eating

☎ 0131 315 2226 📄 0131 332 9631
15 South Learmonth Gardens EH4 1EZ
e-mail: reserve@channings.co.uk
e-mail: food@channings.co.uk
web: www.channings.co.uk
dir: From A90 & Forth Road Bridge, follow signs for city
centre

Just minutes from the city centre, this elegant town house
occupies five Edwardian terraced houses. One of the
properties was the home of Sir Ernest Shackleton at the time
he was Secretary of the Royal Scottish Geographical Society;
top floor bedrooms are named after him and his fellow
explorers. Channings offers a polished boutique hotel
experience on all fronts: from the moment you enter, the
whole place exudes a relaxed, unstuffy quirkiness. The
attractive and individually designed bedrooms have a hi-
tech spec for business guests, while the wood-panelled
basement restaurant has a classy vibe, since it is a well-
frequented neighbourhood bistro as well as a hotel dining
room. The kitchen takes an intelligent, fuss-free modern
approach that might send out celeriac soup with lemon oil
and crispy monkfish cheek, ahead of pan-fried fillet of black
bream with braised fennel sautéed ratte potatoes and
lobster oil. To finish, there may be hot chocolate fondant
with espresso ice cream.

continued

Rooms 41 (4 GF) **S** £85-£145; **D** £120-£240 (incl. bkfst)*
Facilities STV FTV 🎵 Xmas New Year Wi-fi **Conf** Class 40
Board 30 Thtr 60 Del from £125 to £185* **Services** Lift
Notes ⊗

Chef Karen Higgins **Owner** Rakesh Kapour
Times 11.30-10/6-10 **Prices** Food prices not confirmed for
2012. Please telephone for details **Wines** 27 bottles over
£20, 12 bottles under £20, 7 by glass **Notes** Sunday L,
Vegetarian available **Seats** 40, Pr/dining room 30
Children Portions **Parking** On street

Marriott Dalmahoy Hotel & Country Club

★★★★ 81% HOTEL

🌺 Modern, Traditional

Georgian manor serving up a genuine Scottish flavour

☎ 0131 333 1845   📠 0131 333 1433
Kirknewton EH27 8EB
e-mail: mhrs.edigs.frontdesk@marriotthotels.com
web: www.marriottdalmahoy.co.uk
dir: A720 (Edinburgh City Bypass) onto A71 towards
Livingston, hotel on left in 2m

The rolling Pentland Hills and beautifully kept parkland
provide a stunning setting for this imposing Georgian
mansion. With two championship golf courses and a health
and beauty club, there is plenty here to occupy guests.
Bedrooms are spacious and most have fine views, while
public rooms offer a choice of formal and informal drinking
and dining options that include the Pentland restaurant,
named after the hills which provide the spectacular
backdrop. Scottish ingredients rightly take centre stage in
the likes of haggis spring roll with red cabbage and plum
sauce dressing, followed by hot-smoked salmon with Mull
cheddar potato cake, poached egg and grain mustard sauce.
Drambuie crème brûlée and shortbread biscuit or a Scottish
cheeseboard brings proceedings to a satisfying close.

Rooms 215 (172 annexe) (59 fmly) (6 smoking)
Facilities Spa STV ⊛ ♨ 36 ⛳ Putt green Gym Health &
beauty treatments Steam room Dance studio Driving range
Golf lessons Xmas New Year Wi-fi **Conf** Class 200 Board 120
Thtr 300 **Services** Lift Air con **Parking** 350 **Notes** ⊗
Civ Wed 250

Chef Alan Matthew **Owner** Marriott Hotels Ltd **Times** 7-10
Closed L all week **Prices** Starter £6.50-£9.50, Main £19.50-
£32, Dessert £6.50-£8, Service optional **Wines** 21 bottles
over £20, 7 bottles under £20, 11 by glass **Notes** Vegetarian
available, Dress restrictions, Smart casual **Seats** 120, Pr/
dining room 16 **Children** Portions, Menu

Hotel du Vin Edinburgh

★★★★ 80% TOWN HOUSE HOTEL

🌺 European **V** 🍷 NOTABLE WINE LIST

Brasserie dishes with the HdV stamp

☎ 0131 247 4900   📠 0131 247 4901
11 Bristo Place EH1 1EZ
dir: M8 junct 1, A720 (signed Kilmarnock/W Calder/
Edinburgh W). Right at fork, follow A720 signs, merge onto
A720. Take exit signed A703. At rdbt take A702/Biggar Rd.
3.5m. Right into Lauriston Pl which becomes Forrest Rd.
Right at Bedlam Theatre. Hotel on right

If the edifice of HdV's Edinburgh branch looks a little
forbidding, that's because it started life as a mental health
facility, in the days when 'hospital' would have been too
dignified a description. In these more hospitable days, it
offers very stylish and comfortable accommodation; all
bedrooms display the Hotel du Vin trademark facilities - air
conditioning, free Wi-fi, plasma TVs, monsoon showers and
Egyptian cotton linen to name but a few. There's a whisky
snug on the premises, not to mention a cigar bothy for
aficionados of the weed, and La Roche tasting room where
wines from around the world can be appreciated. Then of
course there is the up-to-date brasserie cooking that the
group specialises in everywhere from Royal Tunbridge Wells
to the Scottish capital. Expect Isle of Mull cheese soufflé, a
fishy version of cassoulet with smoked haddock, or merguez
sausage with mint tabbouleh and chick pea stew.

Rooms 47 **S** £125-£495; **D** £125-£495* **Facilities** STV Wi-fi
Services Lift Air con

Chef Matt Powell **Owner** Hotel du Vin & Malmaison
Times 12-2.30/5.30-10.30 Closed D 25 Dec **Prices** Food
prices not confirmed for 2012. Please telephone for details
Wines 600 bottles over £20, 5 bottles under £20, 12 by glass
Notes Sunday L, Vegetarian menu **Seats** 82, Pr/dining room
26 **Children** Portions

Forth Road Bridge, South Queensferry

Edinburgh Marriott Hotel

★★★★ 80% HOTEL

☎ 0131 334 9191 📄 0131 316 4507
111 Glasgow Rd EH12 8NF
e-mail: edinburgh@marriotthotels.com
web: www.edinburghmarriott.co.uk
dir: M8 junct 1 for Gogar, at rdbt turn right for city centre, hotel on right

This smart, modern hotel is located on the city's western edge which is convenient for the bypass, airport, showground and business park. Public areas include an attractive marbled foyer, extensive conference facilities and a restaurant serving a range of international dishes. The air-conditioned bedrooms are spacious and equipped with a range of extras.

Rooms 245 (76 fmly) (64 GF) (6 smoking) **Facilities** Spa STV FTV ⚡ Gym Steam room Sauna Massage & beauty treatment room Hairdresser Xmas New Year Wi-fi **Conf** Class 120 Board 50 Thtr 250 Del from £130 to £200* **Services** Lift Air con **Parking** 300 **Notes** ⊗ Civ Wed 80

Apex International Hotel

★★★★ 79% HOTEL

◉◉ Modern Scottish

Accomplished cooking and magnificent castle views

☎ 0845 365 0000 & 0131 300 3456 📄 0131 220 5345
31/35 Grassmarket EH1 2HS
e-mail: edinburgh.reservations@apexhotels.co.uk
e-mail: heights@apexhotels.co.uk
web: www.apexhotels.co.uk
dir: Into Lothian Rd at west end of Princes St, 1st left into King Stables Rd, leads into Grassmarket

Entering the contemporary boutique-style Apex International Hotel at ground level from the city's historic Grassmarket area, there's nothing to give away its best secret: up on the fifth floor, a full-length wall of windows in the Heights Restaurant opens onto some of the best views in town of Edinburgh Castle. Textures of wood and marble, glass and chrome make for setting of stripped-out modern minimalism, while the kitchen delivers some well-tuned and original cooking with a sound appreciation of the importance of top-notch seasonal Scottish ingredients. Flavours are deep, and textures clearly defined in a labour-intensive deconstructed venison pot au feu starter, the perfectly-timed meat served in a glass with shredded Savoy cabbage, venison jus jelly, and juniper vinaigrette, and in a main course where braised Ayrshire pork belly goes perfectly with spiced apples, black pudding, crackling, and cider foam. The good ideas keep coming all the way to an assiette of apples: sticky toffee apple, apple pie ice cream, and a

Granny Smith crème brûlée. The hotel also boasts a versatile business and conference centre, and also a leisure and fitness facility with a stainless steel ozone pool. Bedrooms are contemporary in style and very well equipped.

Rooms 169 (99 fmly) **Facilities** FTV ⚡ Gym Tropicarium Xmas New Year Wi-fi **Conf** Class 80 Board 40 Thtr 200 **Services** Lift **Parking** 60 **Notes** ⊗ Civ Wed 200

Chef John Newton **Owner** Norman Springford **Times** 6-9.30 Closed L all week **Prices** Starter £5.25-£10.95, Main £13.50-£21.95, Dessert £5.25-£5.50, Service optional **Wines** 14 bottles over £20, 8 bottles under £20, 14 by glass **Notes** Scottish tasting menu 5 course, Vegetarian available **Seats** 85, Pr/dining room 120 **Children** Portions, Menu

George Hotel Edinburgh

★★★★ 79% HOTEL

☎ 0131 225 1251 📄 0131 226 5644
19-21 George St EH2 2PB
e-mail: enquiries.thegeorge@principal-hayley.com
web: www.principal-hayley.com/thegeorge
dir: In city centre

A long-established hotel, the George enjoys a city centre location. The splendid public areas have many original features such as intricate plasterwork, a marble-floored foyer and chandeliers. The Tempus Bar offers menus that feature a wide range of dishes to suit most tastes. The elegant, modern bedrooms come in a mix of sizes and styles; the upper ones having fine city views.

Rooms 249 (20 fmly) (4 GF) **Facilities** STV Xmas New Year Wi-fi **Conf** Class 120 Board 50 Thtr 300 **Services** Lift **Notes** ⊗ Civ Wed 300

Apex City Hotel

★★★★ 77% HOTEL

◉ Modern Scottish

Stylish modern hotel with contemporary flavour

☎ 0845 365 0000 & 0131 243 3456 📄 0131 225 6346
61 Grassmarket EH1 2JF
e-mail: edinburgh.reservations@apexhotels.co.uk
web: www.apexhotels.co.uk
dir: Into Lothian Rd at west end of Princes St, 1st left into King Stables Rd. Leads into Grassmarket

The Apex City Hotel cuts a dash with its contemporary good looks; the end-of-terrace building has been given a make-over that brings it up to speed with contemporary tastes without looking out of place in the historic Grassmarket. The design-led bedrooms are fresh and contemporary and each has artwork by Richard Demarco. Residents can use the spa at a sister hotel, Apex International, nearby. The Agua restaurant has a suitably minimalist look with a fashionable sheen - sleek black-leather chairs, colours from the natural palette, and slate place mats on bare wooden tables. Fish is a strong suit - sea bass with borlotti bean and chorizo casserole, for example, or a seafood platter from the crustacean menu - but there is also the likes of game terrine with five spice pear chutney and toasted brioche, and Scotch lamb faggot and rump served with confit garlic and parsley fondue.

Rooms 119 (10 smoking) **Facilities** FTV Complimentary use of leisure facilities at Apex International Hotel Xmas New Year Wi-fi **Conf** Class 30 Board 34 Thtr 70 **Services** Lift **Notes** ⊗ Civ Wed 60

Chef Fraser Brash **Owner** Norman Springford **Times** 12-2.30/3-9.30 Closed Xmas **Prices** Fixed L 3 course £19.95, Fixed D 3 course £19.95, Starter £5.50-£10.50, Main £14-£22.50, Dessert £5.95-£6.50, Service optional **Wines** 5 bottles over £20, 8 bottles under £20, 12 by glass **Notes** Sunday L, Vegetarian available **Seats** 70, Pr/dining room 60 **Children** Portions, Menu **Parking** On street & NCP

Novotel Edinburgh Park

★★★★ 77% HOTEL

☎ 0131 446 5600 🖹 0131 446 5610
15 Lochside Av EH12 9DJ
e-mail: h6515@accor.com
dir: Near Hermiston Gate shopping area

Located just off the city by-pass and within minutes of the airport, this modern hotel offers bedrooms that are spacious and comfortable. The public areas include the open-plan lobby, bar and a restaurant where some tables have their own TVs.

Rooms 170 (130 fmly) **Facilities** 🏊 Gym Wi-fi **Conf** Class 60 Board 40 Thtr 150 Del from £135 to £165* **Services** Lift **Parking** 96 **Notes** Civ Wed 90

Radisson Blu Hotel Edinburgh

★★★★ 77% HOTEL

☎ 0131 557 9797 & 557 6523 🖹 0131 557 8789
80 High St, The Royal Mile EH1 1TH
e-mail: sales.edinburgh@radissonblu.com
web: www.radissonblu.com/hotel-edinburgh
dir: On Royal Mile

Centrally located in the heart of the old town on the Royal Mile, the spacious and comfortable bedrooms cater well for both leisure and corporate guests. The staff provide very attentive service. Leisure facilities, parking and complimentary Wi-fi are all assets at this hotel.

Rooms 238 (5 fmly) **Facilities** STV FTV 🏊 supervised Gym Saunas Wi-fi **Conf** Class 105 Board 52 Thtr 240 **Services** Lift Air con **Parking** 131 **Notes** ⊗ Civ Wed 180

The Royal Terrace

★★★★ 76% HOTEL

🍴 Modern British

Smart Georgian townhouse with good brasserie cooking

☎ 0131 557 3222 🖹 0131 557 5334
18 Royal Ter EH7 5AQ
e-mail: sales@royalterracehotel.co.uk
web: www.royalterracehotel.co.uk
dir: A8 to city centre, follow one-way system, left into Charlotte Sq. At end right into Queens St. Left at rdbt. At next island right into London Rd, right into Blenheim Place leading to Royal Terrace

Within one of those impressive Georgian townhouses the city has in abundance, The Royal Terrace Hotel is on a quiet street close to the teeming central attractions. Its traditional features have been brought up to date with all mod cons, making it a hit for wedding parties, whilst the health club can be appreciated by all. Although most rooms afford lovely views, the top floor rooms provide excellent panoramas over the city to the Firth of Forth; for something unusual book an Ambassador Suite with a glass bathroom. The Terrace brasserie has lovely views of the landscaped gardens - and note you can eat outside in the warmer months. Good local produce turns up in unfussy dishes such as smoked haddock risotto with parmesan and herb crostini, followed by rump of lamb from the grill, served with ratatouille and creamed mashed potatoes. Roasted apple crumble with mint crème fraîche is a fine finish to meal.

Rooms 107 (13 fmly) (7 GF) **Facilities** 🏊 Gym Steam room Sauna Aromatherapy shower Xmas New Year Wi-fi **Conf** Class 40 Board 40 Thtr 100 **Services** Lift **Notes** ⊗ Civ Wed 80

Chef Gregor Karmierczak **Owner** Liam Walshe **Times** 5-9.30 **Prices** Starter £4.95-£8.95, Main £16.95-£23, Dessert £4.95-£8.95 **Wines** 50 bottles over £20, 6 bottles under £20, 10 by glass **Notes** Pre-theatre menu 2 course 5-7pm, Vegetarian available **Seats** 40, Pr/dining room 24 **Parking** On street (charged)

Apex Waterloo Place Hotel

★★★★ 76% HOTEL

☎ 0845 365 0000 & 0131 523 1819 🖺 0871 221 1432
23 - 27 Waterloo Place EH1 3BH
e-mail: edinburgh.reservations@apexhotels.co.uk
dir: At E end of Princes St. Telephone for detailed directions

This stunning hotel provides a state-of-the-art experience with slick interior design. Bedrooms, many with city views, are well appointed for both the business and leisure guest; stunning duplex suites provide extra space, surround-sound TV systems and luxurious feature bathrooms. The restaurant provides an appealing menu both at dinner and breakfast. There is also a well-equipped fitness centre and indoor pool. The hotel has direct, pedestrian access to Edinburgh's Waverley Station.

Rooms 187 (5 fmly) (15 GF) **Facilities** FTV ⓩ Gym Sauna Steam rooms Xmas New Year Wi-fi **Conf** Class 70 Board 40 Thtr 150 **Services** Lift Air con **Notes** ⊗ Civ Wed 80

Macdonald Holyrood

★★★★ 76% HOTEL

☎ 0870 1942106 🖺 0131 550 4545
Holyrood Rd EH8 8AU
e-mail: general.holyrood@macdonald-hotels.co.uk
web: www.macdonaldhotels.co.uk/holyrood
dir: Parallel to Royal Mile, near Holyrood Palace & Dynamic Earth

Situated just a short walk from Holyrood Palace, this impressive hotel lies next to the Scottish Parliament building. Air-conditioned bedrooms are comfortably furnished, whilst the Club floor boasts a private lounge. Full business services complement the extensive conference suites.

Rooms 156 (16 fmly) (13 GF) **Facilities** Spa STV ⓩ Gym Beauty treatment rooms Sauna Steam room Library ♫ Xmas New Year Wi-fi **Conf** Class 100 Board 80 Thtr 200 **Services** Lift Air con **Parking** 38 **Notes** LB Civ Wed 100

Novotel Edinburgh Centre

★★★★ 76% HOTEL

☎ 0131 656 3500 🖺 0131 656 3510
Lauriston Place, Lady Lawson St EH3 9DE
e-mail: H3271@accor.com
web: www.novotel.com
dir: From Edinburgh Castle right onto George IV Bridge from Royal Mile. Follow to junct, then right into Lauriston Place. Hotel 700mtrs on right

This modern hotel is located in the centre of the city, close to Edinburgh Castle. Smart and stylish public areas include a cosmopolitan bar, brasserie-style restaurant and indoor leisure facilities. The air-conditioned bedrooms feature a comprehensive range of extras and bathrooms with baths and separate shower cabinets.

Rooms 180 (146 fmly) **Facilities** STV ⓩ Gym Sauna Steam room Xmas Wi-fi **Conf** Class 50 Board 32 Thtr 80 **Services** Lift Air con **Parking** 15

Holiday Inn Edinburgh

★★★★ 75% HOTEL

☎ 0871 942 9026 🖺 0131 334 9237
Corstorphine Rd EH12 6UA
e-mail: edinburghhi@ihg.com
web: www.holidayinn.co.uk
dir: On A8, adjacent to Edinburgh Zoo

A modern hotel situated three miles west of Edinburgh and near Edinburgh Business Park. The hotel enjoys panoramic views of the Pentland Hills and makes a good base for visiting the attractions of the city. Bedrooms include family and executive rooms. The eating options are Traders Restaurant or Sampans Oriental Restaurant, as well as a café and bar. The Spirit Health and Fitness Club has a gym, swimming pool, sauna, spa and beauty treatments. There is also a conference centre.

Rooms 303 (76 fmly) (41 smoking) **Facilities** Spa STV FTV ⓩ supervised Gym New Year Wi-fi **Conf** Class 60 Board 45 Thtr 120 Del from £99 to £185* **Services** Lift Air con **Parking** 105 **Notes** ⊗ Civ Wed 80

Barceló Carlton Hotel

★★★★ 74% HOTEL

☎ 0131 472 3000 🖺 0131 556 2691
North Bridge EH1 1SD
e-mail: carlton@barcelo-hotels.co.uk
web: www.barcelo-hotels.co.uk
dir: On North Bridge which links Princes St to The Royal Mile

The Carlton occupies a city centre location just off the Royal Mile. Inside, it is modern and stylish in design, with an impressive open-plan reception/lobby, spacious first-floor lounge, bar and restaurant, plus a basement leisure club. Bedrooms, many air-conditioned, are generally spacious, with an excellent range of accessories.

Rooms 189 (20 fmly) **Facilities** STV ⓩ supervised Gym Squash Table tennis Dance studio Exercise classes Treatment rooms Crèche ♫ Xmas New Year Wi-fi **Conf** Class 110 Board 60 Thtr 220 **Services** Lift **Notes** Civ Wed 160

The King James, Edinburgh

★★★★ 74% HOTEL

☎ 0871 376 9016 📄 0871 376 9116
107 Leith St EH1 3SW
e-mail: edinburgh@thistle.co.uk
web: www.thistlehotels.com/edinburgh
dir: M8/M9 onto A8 signed city centre. Hotel at end of
Princes St adjacent to St James shopping centre

This purpose-built hotel adjoins one of Edinburgh's premier
shopping malls at the east end of Princes Street. The
friendly team of staff are keen to please whilst stylish, well-
equipped bedrooms provide excellent levels of comfort and
good facilities. Public areas include a spacious restaurant,
popular bar and an elegant lobby lounge. Thistle Hotels – AA
Hotel Group of the Year 2011-12.

Rooms 143 (12 fmly) **Facilities** STV FTV Xmas New Year
Wi-fi **Conf** Class 160 Board 50 Thtr 250 **Services** Lift
Parking 18 **Notes** LB ⊗

The Roxburghe Hotel

★★★★ 74% HOTEL

☎ 0844 879 9063 & 0131 240 5500 📄 0131 240 5555
38 Charlotte Square EH2 4HQ
e-mail: general.roxburghe@macdonald-hotels.co.uk
web: www.macdonaldhotels.co.uk/roxburghe
dir: On corner of Charlotte Sq & George St

This long-established hotel lies in the heart of the city
overlooking Charlotte Square Gardens. Public areas are
inviting and include relaxing lounges, a choice of bars (in
the evening) and an inner concourse that looks onto a small
lawned area. Smart bedrooms come in both classic and
contemporary styles. There is a secure underground car park.

Rooms 199 (3 fmly) **S** £90-£240; **D** £95-£320*
Facilities Spa STV FTV ⟳ Gym Dance studio Sauna Steam
room Xmas New Year Wi-fi **Conf** Class 160 Board 50
Thtr 300 **Services** Lift Air con **Parking** 20 **Notes** LB ⊗
Civ Wed 280

Malmaison Edinburgh

★★★ 86% HOTEL

◉ British, French ☺

Waterfront hotel serving up refined brasserie classics

☎ 0131 468 5000 📄 0131 468 5002
One Tower Place, Leith EH6 7DB
e-mail: edinburgh@malmaison.com
web: www.malmaison.com
dir: A900 from city centre towards Leith, at end of Leith
Walk, through 3 sets of lights, left into Tower St. Hotel on
right at end of road

The first of the Malmaison boutique brand, Edinburgh's Mal
is in a renovated seamen's mission on the Forth in the old
part of Leith. It's a perfect spot as the dockyards have been
overhauled to house restaurants and bars aplenty so there's
a buzzy vibe about the place. Bedrooms are comprehensively
equipped with CD players, mini-bars and loads of individual
touches. Ask for one of the stunning superior rooms for a
really memorable stay. The brasserie is a dark, masculine
space with dark brown seating and ornate ironwork, deep
red walls, bold artwork, unclothed tables and candles, and
overlooks the Port of Leith (there's outdoor eating on the
cards when the weather allows). East Lothian ingredients
turn up in trademark brasserie classics served in generous
portions; Welch's smoked haddock and wild leek tart to start
perhaps, before venison and heather ale pie with buttered
romaine, or pork noisette with Armagnac and prunes. Save
room for rhubarb tartlet with honeycomb crust and
vanilla crème fraîche.

Rooms 100 (18 fmly) **Facilities** STV Gym Xmas New Year
Wi-fi **Conf** Class 30 Board 40 Thtr 55 **Services** Lift
Parking 50

Chef Colin Manson **Owner** Malmaison Hotels Ltd
Times 12-2.30/6-10.30 Closed D 25 Dec **Prices** Fixed L 2
course £15, Fixed D 3 course £25.95, Starter £4.95-£6.95,
Main £9.50-£22.50, Dessert £5.95-£8.50, Service added but
optional 10% **Wines** 94 bottles over £20, 6 bottles under
£20, 18 by glass **Notes** Sunday L, Vegetarian available, Civ
Wed 100 **Seats** 60, Pr/dining room 60 **Children** Portions,
Menu

Apex European Hotel

★★★ 83% HOTEL

☎ 0845 365 0000 & 0131 474 3456 📄 0131 474 3400
90 Haymarket Ter EH12 5LQ
e-mail: edinburgh.reservations@apexhotels.co.uk
web: www.apexhotels.co.uk
dir: A8 to city centre, 100m from Haymarket Railway Station

Lying just west of the city centre, close to Haymarket Station
and handy for the Conference Centre, this modern hotel is
popular with business travellers. Smart, stylish bedrooms
offer an excellent range of facilities and have been designed
with work requirements in mind. Public areas include Metro,
an informal bistro. Service is friendly and pro-active.

Rooms 66 (3 GF) (8 smoking) **Facilities** FTV New Year Wi-fi
Conf Class 30 Board 36 Thtr 80 **Services** Lift **Parking** 10
Notes ⊗ Closed 24-27 Dec

Dalhousie Castle and Aqueous Spa

★★★ 82% HOTEL

 Modern European

Creative cuisine in a truly unique setting

☎ 01875 820153 📄 01875 821936
Bonnyrigg EH19 3JB
e-mail: info@dalhousiecastle.co.uk
web: www.dalhousiecastle.co.uk
dir: A7 S from Edinburgh through Lasswade/Newtongrange,
right at Shell Garage (B704), hotel 0.5m from junct

A popular wedding venue, this imposing 15th century castle
sits amid acres of lawns and parkland on the banks of the
Esk, and even has a falconry. Bedrooms offer a mix of styles
and sizes, including richly decorated themed rooms named
after various historical figures. As for the Dungeon
restaurant - what's in a name? Quite a lot when the
dungeon in question is the real deal: a barrel-vaulted
chamber beneath the medieval castle This sort of venue is
clearly popular for special occasion dining, so while you're in
the blow-out frame of mind, take in a spot of pampering in
the swish hydro-spa before enjoying the atmosphere at
dinner. Expect suits of armour, an arsenal of battleaxes and
broadswords, and romantic candlelight. Happily this is not a
kitchen that sits back and lets the setting bring in the
punters: the French classics are a clear influence, and
materials are both luxurious and of excellent quality, but it
is the spirit of bold creativity that brings it all together with
great impact. Braised oxtail and foie gras terrine is pointed
up with a shallot salad with truffle oil, ahead of wild boar,
served as roast saddle with raspberry jus, and a casserole
with pommes mousseline and roast salsify.

Rooms 36 (7 annexe) (3 fmly) **Facilities** Spa FTV Fishing
Falconry Clay pigeon shooting Archery Laserday Xmas New
Year Wi-fi **Conf** Class 60 Board 45 Thtr 120 **Parking** 110
Notes Civ Wed 100

Chef Francois Graud **Owner** von Essen Hotels **Times** 7-10
Closed L all week **Prices** Service optional **Wines** 100 bottles
over £20, 23 bottles under £20, 15 by glass **Notes** Fixed D 5
course £49.50, Vegetarian available **Seats** 45, Pr/dining
room 100 **Children** Portions

Best Western Braid Hills Hotel

★★★ 82% HOTEL

☎ 0131 447 8888 & 446 3003 📄 0131 452 8477
134 Braid Rd EH10 6JD
e-mail: bookings@braidhillshotel.co.uk
web: www.braidhillshotel.co.uk
dir: 2.5m S A702, opposite Braid Burn Park

From its elevated position on the south side, this long-
established hotel enjoys splendid panoramic views of the
city and castle. Bedrooms are smart, stylish and well
equipped. The public areas are comfortable and inviting,
and guests can dine in either the restaurant or popular
bistro/bar.

Rooms 67 (14 fmly) (14 GF) **S** £60-£130; **D** £70-£195 (incl.
bkfst)* **Facilities** STV FTV Xmas New Year Wi-fi
Conf Class 50 Board 30 Thtr 100 Del from £130 to £160*
Parking 38 **Notes** LB ⊗ Civ Wed 100

Old Waverley

★★★ 81% HOTEL

☎ 0131 556 4648 📄 0131 557 6316
43 Princes St EH2 2BY
e-mail: reservations@oldwaverley.co.uk
web: www.oldwaverley.co.uk
dir: In city centre, opposite Scott Monument, Waverley
Station & Jenners

Occupying a commanding position opposite Sir Walter
Scott's famous monument on Princes Street, this hotel lies
right in the heart of the city close to the station. The
comfortable public rooms are all on first-floor level and
along with front-facing bedrooms enjoy the fine views.

Rooms 85 (5 fmly) **Facilities** Leisure facilities at sister hotel
Wi-fi **Services** Lift **Notes** ⊗

The Point Hotel, Edinburgh

★★★ 80% HOTEL

☎ 0131 221 5555 📄 0131 221 9929
34 Bread St EH3 9AF
e-mail: enquiries@pointhoteledinburgh.co.uk
dir: A71 to Haymarket Station. Straight on at junct & right
on Torphichen St, left onto Morrison St, straight on to Bread
St, hotel on right

Built in 1892 as a Co-op which once employed Sean Connery
as a milkman, the hotel has won many awards for its design
and presentation. Bedrooms are spacious and cater well for
the needs of the modern guest. Open-plan public areas are
enhanced with coloured lighting and an array of artwork. The
Point Restaurant offers imaginative dishes. The Glass Box
Penthouse conference room affords fantastic views of the
city.

Rooms 139 **Facilities** FTV Wi-fi **Conf** Class 60 Board 40 Thtr 120 Del from £130 to £160* **Services** Lift **Notes** ⊗ Civ Wed 90

Best Western Kings Manor

★★★ 79% HOTEL

☎ 0131 669 0444 & 468 8003 ▤ 0131 669 6650
100 Milton Road East EH15 2NP
e-mail: reservations@kingsmanor.com
web: www.kingsmanor.com
dir: A720 E to Old Craighall junct, left into city, right at A1/A199 junct, hotel 400mtrs on right

Lying on the eastern side of the city and convenient for the by-pass, this hotel is popular with business guests, tour groups and for conferences. It boasts a fine leisure complex and a bright modern mistro, which complements the quality, creative cooking in the main restaurant.

Rooms 95 (8 fmly) (13 GF) **S** £60-£125; **D** £70-£180
Facilities Spa STV FTV ⊗ ⤵ Gym Health & beauty salon Steam room Sauna Wi-fi **Conf** Class 80 Board 60 Thtr 160 Del from £98 to £168* **Services** Lift **Parking** 130 **Notes** LB Civ Wed 100

Holiday Inn Edinburgh West

★★★ 75% HOTEL

☎ 0871 942 9025 ▤ 0131 332 3408
107 Queensferry Rd EH4 3HL
e-mail: reservations-edinburghcitywest@ihg.com
web: www.holidayinn.co.uk
dir: On A90 approx 1m from city centre

Situated on the north-west side of the city, close to Murrayfield Stadium and just five miles from the airport, this purpose-built hotel has a bright contemporary look. The colourful, modern bedrooms are well equipped and three specifications are available - with two double beds; with a double bed and sofa; or with a double bed and separate lounge. Some have great views of the city too. There is limited free parking.

Rooms 101 **Facilities** STV New Year Wi-fi **Conf** Class 60 Board 50 Thtr 140 Del from £79 to £265* **Services** Lift Air con **Parking** 80 **Notes** ⊗ Civ Wed 120

Express by Holiday Inn Edinburgh Waterfront

BUDGET HOTEL

☎ 0131 555 4422 ▤ 0131 555 4646
Britannia Way, Ocean Dr, Leith EH6 6JJ
e-mail: info@hiex-edinburgh.com
web: www.hiexpress.com/exedinburghwat
dir: Follow signs for Royal Yacht Britannia. Hotel just before Britannia on right

A modern hotel ideal for families and business travellers. Fresh and uncomplicated, the spacious rooms include Sky TV, power shower and tea and coffee-making facilities. Continental buffet breakfast is included in the room rate; other meals may be taken at the nearby family pub or restaurant.

Rooms 145 (36 fmly) **Conf** Class 15 Board 18 Thtr 35

Holiday Inn Express Edinburgh City Centre

BUDGET HOTEL

☎ 0131 558 2300 ▤ 0131 558 2323
Picardy Place EH1 3JT
e-mail: info@hieedinburgh.co.uk
web: www.hiexpress.com/edinburghctyct
dir: Follow signs to city centre & Greenside NCP. Hotel near E end of Princes St

A modern hotel ideal for families and business travellers. Fresh and uncomplicated, the spacious rooms include Sky TV, power shower and tea and coffee-making facilities. Continental buffet breakfast is included in the room rate; other meals may be taken at the nearby family pub or restaurant.

Rooms 161 (53 fmly) (27 GF) (13 smoking) **D** £69-£299 (incl. bkfst)* **Conf** Class 8 Board 18 Thtr 20

Holiday Inn Express Edinburgh Royal Mile

BUDGET HOTEL

☎ 0131 524 8400 ▤ 0131 524 8401
South Grays Close, Cowgate EH1 1NA
e-mail: info@hiexpressedinburgh.co.uk
web: www.hiexpressedinburgh.co.uk
Rooms 78 (50 fmly) (10 GF) **S** £39.99-£299.99; **D** £39.99-£299.99 (incl. bkfst)* **Conf** Class 20 Board 20 Thtr 40

Ibis Edinburgh Centre

BUDGET HOTEL

☎ 0131 240 7000 ▤ 0131 240 7007
6 Hunter Square, (off The Royal Mile) EH1 1QW
e-mail: H2039@accor.com
web: www.ibishotel.com
dir: M8/M9/A1 over North Bridge (A7) & High St, take 1st right off South Bridge, into Hunter Sq

Modern, budget hotel offering comfortable accommodation in bright and practical bedrooms. Breakfast is self-service and dinner is available in the restaurant.

Rooms 99 (2 GF)

Premier Inn Edinburgh Airport (Newbridge)

BUDGET HOTEL

☎ 0871 527 9284 📄 0871 527 9285
2A Kirkliston Rd, Newbridge EH28 8SL
web: www.premierinn.com
dir: M9 junct 1, A89 signed Broxburn. At lights turn right, then 2nd right

High quality, budget accommodation ideal for both families and business travellers. Spacious, en suite bedrooms feature tea and coffee-making facilities, and Freeview TV in most hotels. Internet access and Wi-fi are available for a small fee. The adjacent family restaurant features a wide and varied menu.

Rooms 119 **D** £54*

Premier Inn Edinburgh City Centre (Haymarket)

BUDGET HOTEL

☎ 0871 527 8368 📄 0871 527 8369
1 Morrison Link EH3 8DN
web: www.premierinn.com
dir: Adjcent to Edinburgh International Conference Centre
Rooms 281 **D** £74*

Premier Inn Edinburgh City Lauriston Place

BUDGET HOTEL

☎ 0871 527 8366 📄 0871 527 8367
82 Lauriston Place, Lady Lawson St EH3 9DG
web: www.premierinn.com
dir: A8 onto A702 (Lothian Rd). Left into Lauriston Place. Hotel on left
Rooms 112 **D** £74*

Premier Inn Edinburgh East

BUDGET HOTEL

☎ 0871 527 8370 📄 0871 527 8371
228 Willowbrae Rd EH8 7NG
web: www.premierinn.com
dir: M8 junct 1, A720 S for 12m, then A1. At Asda rdbt turn left. In 2m, hotel on left before Esso garage
Rooms 39 **D** £62-£65*

Premier Inn Edinburgh (Inveresk)

BUDGET HOTEL

☎ 0871 527 8358 📄 0871 527 8359
Carberry Rd, Inveresk, Musselburgh EH21 8PT
web: www.premierinn.com
dir: From A1 follow Dalkeith (A6094) signs. At rdbt turn right, hotel 300yds on right
Rooms 40 **D** £62-£65*

Premier Inn Edinburgh (Leith)

BUDGET HOTEL

☎ 0871 527 8360 📄 0871 527 8361
51-53 Newhaven Place, Leith EH6 4TX
web: www.premierinn.com
dir: From A1 follow coast road through Leith. Pass Ocean Terminal, straight ahead at mini-rdbt, 2nd exit signed Harry Ramsden's car park
Rooms 60 **D** £65*

Premier Inn Edinburgh (Newcraighall)

BUDGET HOTEL

☎ 0871 527 8362 📄 0871 527 8363
91 Newcraighall Rd, Newcraighall EH21 8RX
web: www.premierinn.com
dir: At junct of A1 & A6095 towards Musselburgh
Rooms 42 **D** £62-£65*

Elmview

★★★★★ 🛏 GUEST ACCOMMODATION

15 Glengyle Ter EH3 9LN
☎ 0131 228 1973
e-mail: nici@elmview.co.uk
web: www.elmview.co.uk
dir: 0.5m S of city centre. Off A702 Leven St onto Valleyfield St, one-way to Glengyle Ter

Elmview offers stylish accommodation on the lower ground level of a fine Victorian terrace house. The bedrooms and smart bathrooms are comfortable and extremely well equipped, with thoughtful extras such as safes, and fridges with fresh milk and water. Breakfasts are excellent and are served at a large, elegantly appointed table in the charming dining room.

Rooms 3 en suite (3 GF) S £70-£105; D £90-£130*
Facilities FTV tea/coffee Direct Dial Cen ht Wi-fi **Notes** ⊗ No Children 15yrs Closed Dec-Feb

Kew House

★★★★★ GUEST ACCOMMODATION

1 Kew Ter, Murrayfield EH12 5JE
☎ 0131 313 0700 📄 0131 313 0747
e-mail: info@kewhouse.com
web: www.kewhouse.com
dir: 1m W of city centre A8

Forming part of a listed Victorian terrace, Kew House lies within walking distance of the city centre, and is convenient for Murrayfield Stadium and tourist attractions. Meticulously maintained throughout, it offers attractive bedrooms in a variety of sizes, all thoughtfully equipped to suit business and leisure guests. There is a comfortable lounge offering a supper and snack menu. Internet access is also available.

Rooms 6 en suite (1 fmly) (2 GF) S £79-£96; D £94-£194*
Facilities FTV tea/coffee Direct Dial Cen ht Wi-fi **Parking** 6
Notes LB ⊗ Closed approx 5-23 Jan

21212

★★★★★ RESTAURANT WITH ROOMS

◉◉◉ Modern French 🍷 NOTABLE WINE LIST

Bold and dynamic cooking from unique talent

3 Royal Ter EH7 5AB
☎ 0131 523 1030 & 0845 222 1212 📄 0131 553 1038
e-mail: reservations@21212restaurant.co.uk
dir: Calton Hill, city centre

Paul Kitching is not a 'celebrity chef', his name does not trip off the tongue like Heston and Gordon, there are no TV programmes bearing his name, no appearances on panel shows under his belt - you'll find him in the kitchen at 21212. He is at the sharp end of culinary thinking, with a reputation for creative, surprising, exciting and sometimes perplexing food. There is never a dull moment with Mr Kitching. It all takes place in a fabulous Edinburgh townhouse, done out with a good deal of panache and a soupcon of flamboyance - there are four cool bedrooms (numbered 1, 2, 12 and 21), a splendid drawing room on the first floor with views through large Georgian windows across the Royal Terrace gardens to the Firth of Forth, private dining and a restaurant which manages to be both comfortable and chic and suitably bold and avant-garde. Through patterned-glass partitions in the restaurant you can see the chefs at work. Now for the explanation of the menu format, which reveals the logic behind the name: there are a total of five courses (you can have two to five depending on your appetite and budget) - '2' choices of first course, '1' choice of soup or intermediary dish, '2' choices of main dishes, '1' cheese course, '2' choices of dessert. Simple...21212. With his sound classical training and experience behind him, Kitching plays with flavour and texture, confounds expectations and delivers food that is both delightful to eat and constantly surprising. Risotto de-luxe is a creamy gruyère version with a whole lot more going on - white asparagus, for example, plus mortadella, smoked bacon, celery, peanuts and a kidney bean garlic cream sauce (along with a few other things). Cauliflower espuma with split peas and confit mushroom might be the '1' between starter and main courses, followed by 'Fish & Extra Carbs', which is slow-baked pink sea trout with young globe artichokes, confit of leeks, crumpets, saffron pancakes and wild mushroom omelette. It is best, perhaps, not to pay too much attention to the dish descriptions, simply put yourself in the hands of the chef and go with the flow. The service, directed by the ever-present Katie O'Brien, is suitably charming. And you can be sure that the coffee is served in a paper cup for a very good reason.

Rooms 4 en suite D £175-£325* **Facilities** STV FTV Dinner available Cen ht Wi-fi **Notes** ⊗ No Children 5yrs Closed 1wk Jan RS Sun & Mon closed No coaches

Chef Paul Kitching **Owner** P Kitching, K O'Brien, J Revle
Times 12-1.45/6.30-9.30 Closed 2 wks Jan, Sun-Mon
Prices Food prices not confirmed for 2012. Please telephone for details **Wines** 8 by glass **Notes** Fixed L 4/5 course £36/£46, 5 course D £67, Vegetarian available **Seats** 36, Pr/ dining room 10 **Parking** On street

The Witchery by the Castle

★★★★★ 🍴 RESTAURANT WITH ROOMS

🌀 Traditional Scottish 🍷 NOTABLE WINE LIST

Traditional Scottish dishes in handsome rooms near the Castle

352 Castlehill, The Royal Mile EH1 2NF
☎ 0131 225 5613 📄 0131 220 4392
e-mail: mail@thewitchery.com
web: www.thewitchery.com
dir: Top of Royal Mile at gates of Edinburgh Castle

One of the most strikingly handsome restaurants in the capital, the Witchery is to be found near the top of the mound where Edinburgh Castle is perched. A 16th-century merchant's house, it offers just two luxurious and theatrically decorated suites, known as the Inner Sanctum and the Old Rectory, located above the restaurant and reached via a winding stone staircase. Filled with antiques, opulently draped beds, large roll-top baths and a plethora of memorabilia, this ancient and exciting establishment is often described as one of the country's most romantic destinations. There are two dining rooms - the tapestry-hung Witchery itself and the lighter Secret Garden, an enclosed courtyard with magnificent views over the Royal Mile. Interpretations of many of Scotland's traditional dishes are showcased on the menu, together with much regional produce, so expect the likes of dressed Mull crab with fennel salad in cider dressing, or haggis with neeps and tatties, to start, followed by hot-smoked Loch Duart salmon in butter sauce, or Cairngorm venison loin with squash purée and chocolate oil. Finish with the refreshing passionfruit and mascarpone trifle with pistachio biscotti.

Rooms 3 en suite 5 annexe en suite (1 GF) **Facilities** STV FTV tea/coffee Dinner available Direct Dial Cen ht **Notes** ⊗ No Children 12yrs Closed 25-26 Dec No coaches

Chef Douglas Roberts **Owner** James Thomson OBE
Times 12-4/5-11.30 Closed 25-26 Dec **Prices** Fixed L 2 course £15.95, Fixed D 3 course £30, Starter £8-£17, Main £15-£35, Dessert £7-£9, Service optional, Groups min 8 service 10% **Wines** 700+ bottles over £20, 20 bottles under £20, 14 by glass **Notes** Theatre supper 2 course £15.95, Sunday L, Vegetarian available **Seats** 120, Pr/dining room 70

23 Mayfield

★★★★★ 🏠 GUEST ACCOMMODATION

23 Mayfield Gardens EH9 2BX
☎ 0131 667 5806 📄 0131 667 6833
e-mail: info@23mayfield.co.uk
web: www.23mayfield.co.uk
dir: A720 bypass S, follow city centre signs. Left at Craigmillar Park, 0.5m on right

23 Mayfield is well located en route into Edinburgh with the added benefit of off-road parking. The spacious accommodation has retained many of its original period features. Breakfast is a real delight, with the very best local produce used to give guests a great start to their day. 23 Mayfield is the AA's Guest Accommodation of the Year for Scotland (2011-2012).

Rooms 9 en suite (2 fmly) (2 GF) S £75-£110; D £90-£170 **Facilities** FTV tea/coffee Cen ht Wi-fi Bike hire **Parking** 10 **Notes** LB ⊗

Bonnington Guest House

★★★★ GUEST HOUSE

202 Ferry Rd EH6 4NW
☎ 0131 554 7610
e-mail: booking@thebonningtonguesthouse.com
web: www.thebonningtonguesthouse.com
dir: On A902, near corner of Ferry Rd & Newhaven Rd

This delightful Georgian house offers individually furnished bedrooms on two floors, that retain many of their original features. Family rooms are also available. A substantial freshly prepared breakfast is served in the refurbished dining room. Off-street parking is an added bonus.

Rooms 7 rms (5 en suite) (2 pri facs) (4 fmly) (1 GF) **Facilities** FTV tea/coffee Cen ht Wi-fi **Parking** 9 **Notes** ⊗

Fraoch House

★★★★ ⌂ GUEST ACCOMMODATION

66 Pilrig St EH6 5AS
☎ 0131 554 1353
e-mail: info@fraochhouse.com
dir: 1m from Princes St

Situated within walking distance of the city centre and convenient for many attractions, Fraoch House, which dates from the 1900s, has been appointed to offer well-equipped and thoughtfully furnished bedrooms. Delicious, freshly cooked breakfasts are served in the charming dining room on the ground floor.

Rooms 9 rms (7 en suite) (2 pri facs) (1 fmly) (1 GF)
Facilities FTV tea/coffee Cen ht Wi-fi Free use of DVDs and CDs & internet access **Notes** ⊗

Southside

★★★★ ⌂ GUEST HOUSE

8 Newington Rd EH9 1QS
☎ 0131 668 4422   🖷 0131 667 7771
e-mail: info@southsideguesthouse.co.uk
web: www.southsideguesthouse.co.uk
dir: E end of Princes St onto North Bridge to Royal Mile, continue S, 0.5m, house on right

Situated within easy reach of the city centre and convenient for the major attractions, Southside is an elegant sandstone house. Bedrooms are individually styled, comfortable and thoughtfully equipped. Traditional, freshly cooked Scottish breakfasts are served at individual tables in the smart ground-floor dining room.

Rooms 8 en suite (2 fmly) (1 GF) S £68-£85; D £90-£180
Facilities FTV tea/coffee Direct Dial Cen ht Licensed Wi-fi
Notes LB ⊗ No Children 10yrs

Allison House

★★★★ GUEST ACCOMMODATION

17 Mayfield Gardens EH9 2AX
☎ 0131 667 8049   🖷 0131 667 5001
e-mail: info@allisonhousehotel.com
web: www.allisonhousehotel.com

Part of a Victorian terrace, Allison House offers modern comforts in a splendid building. It's convenient for the city centre, theatres, tourist attractions, and the main bus route. The attractive bedrooms are generally spacious and very well equipped. Breakfast is served at individual tables in the ground-floor dining room. Off-road parking is available.

Rooms 11 rms (10 en suite) (1 pri facs) (1 fmly) (2 GF) (2 smoking) **Facilities** tea/coffee Direct Dial Cen ht Wi-fi
Parking 6 **Notes** ⊗

Ashlyn Guest House

★★★★ GUEST HOUSE

42 Inverleith Row EH3 5PY
☎ 0131 552 2954
e-mail: info@ashlynguesthouse.com
web: www.ashlynguesthouse.com
dir: Adjacent to Edinburgh Botanic Gardens, then follow signs for North Edinburgh & Botanics

The Ashlyn Guest House is a warm and friendly Georgian home, ideally located to take advantage of Edinburgh's attractions. The city centre is within walking distance and the Royal Botanical Gardens are minutes away. Bedrooms are all individually decorated and furnished to a high standard. A generous and hearty breakfast gives a great start to the day.

Rooms 8 rms (4 en suite) (2 pri facs) (1 fmly) (1 GF) S £35-£40; D £70-£90* **Facilities** FTV TVL tea/coffee Cen ht Wi-fi **Notes** ⊗ No Children 7yrs Closed 23-28 Dec

The Edinburgh Lodge

★★★★ GUEST HOUSE

6 Hampton Ter, West Coates EH12 5JD
☎ 0131 337 3682   🖷 0131 313 1700
e-mail: info@thelodgehotel.co.uk
dir: On A8, 0.75m W of Princes St

Situated at the west end of Edinburgh, benefiting from off-road parking this well presented property offers comfortable bedrooms with many thoughtful extras, including complimentary Wi-fi. A well-cooked breakfast is served on individual tables which overlook the well maintained gardens.

Rooms 12 en suite (2 fmly) (4 GF) **Facilities** STV TVL tea/coffee Direct Dial Cen ht Licensed Wi-fi **Conf** Max 16 **Parking** 8 **Notes** ⊗

Heriott Park

★★★★ GUEST HOUSE

256 Ferry Rd, Goldenacre EH5 3AN
☎ 0131 552 3456
e-mail: reservations@heriottpark.co.uk
web: www.heriottpark.co.uk
dir: 1.5m N of city centre on A902

A conversion of two adjoining properties, which retain many original features. Heriott Park is on the north side of the city and has lovely panoramic views of the Edinburgh skyline, including the castle and Arthur's Seat. The attractive bedrooms are well equipped and have excellent en suite bathrooms.

Rooms 15 en suite (7 fmly) (1 GF) S £40-£80; D £60-£110*
Facilities FTV tea/coffee Cen ht Wi-fi **Notes** ⊗

International Guest House

★★★★ GUEST HOUSE

37 Mayfield Gardens EH9 2BX
☎ 0131 667 2511 & 0845 241 7551 ▤ 0131 667 1112
e-mail: intergh1@yahoo.co.uk
web: www.accommodation-edinburgh.com
dir: On A701 1.5m S of Princes St

Guests are assured of a warm and friendly welcome at this attractive Victorian terraced house, situated to the south of the city centre. The smartly presented bedrooms are thoughtfully decorated, comfortably furnished and well equipped. Hearty Scottish breakfasts are served at individual tables in the traditionally styled dining room, which boasts a beautiful ornate ceiling.

Rooms 9 en suite (3 fmly) (1 GF) S £40–£80; D £70–£140
Facilities FTV tea/coffee Direct Dial Cen ht Wi-fi **Parking** 3
Notes LB ⊗

Kingsway Guest House

★★★★ GUEST HOUSE

5 East Mayfield EH9 1SD
☎ 0131 667 5029
e-mail: room@edinburgh-guesthouse.com
web: www.edinburgh-guesthouse.com
dir: A701 to city centre, after 4m road name changes to Mayfield Gdns. Turn right at lights onto East Mayfield

Well situated for the city centre and with off-road parking, this well presented Victorian building maintains a number of original features, and genuine and warm hospitality is assured. All the bedrooms are comfortable, and the quality Scottish breakfasts make an excellent start to the day

Rooms 7 rms (6 en suite) (1 pri facs) (2 fmly) S £40–£60; D £60–£100 **Facilities** FTV tea/coffee Cen ht Wi-fi Golf 18 **Parking** 4 **Notes** ⊗

Sherwood

★★★★ GUEST HOUSE

42 Minto St EH9 2BR
☎ 0131 667 1200 ▤ 0131 667 2344
e-mail: enquiries@sherwood-edinburgh.com
web: www.sherwood-edinburgh.com
dir: On A701, S of city centre

Lying on the south side of the city, this guest house is immaculately maintained and attractively presented throughout. Bedrooms vary in size, the smaller ones being thoughtfully appointed to make the best use of space. All include iron and ironing board, and several come with a fridge and microwave. Continental breakfast is served in the elegant dining room.

Rooms 6 rms (5 en suite) (1 pri facs) (2 fmly) (1 GF) S £40–£75; D £55–£90* **Facilities** FTV tea/coffee Cen ht Wi-fi **Parking** 3 **Notes** LB ⊗ Closed 20-29 Dec & 5 Jan-2 Mar

Gildun

★★★★ ▲ GUEST HOUSE

9 Spence St EH16 5AG
☎ 0131 667 1368 ▤ 0131 668 4989
e-mail: gildun.edin@btinternet.com
dir: A720 city bypass to Sheriffhall rdbt onto A7 for 4m to Cameron Toll rdbt. Under rail bridge follow A7 sign onto Dalkeith Rd. Spence St 4th left opp church

Rooms 8 rms (7 en suite) (1 pri facs) (5 fmly) (2 GF) S £30–£68; D £60–£134* **Facilities** FTV tea/coffee Cen ht Wi-fi **Parking** 4 **Notes** LB

Arden Guest House

★★★ GUEST HOUSE

126 Old Dalkeith Rd EH16 4SD
☎ 0131 664 3985 ▤ 0131 621 0866
e-mail: ardenguesthouse@btinternet.com
dir: 2m SE of city centre near Craigmillar Castle. On A7, 200yds W of hospital

Arden Guest House is well situated on the south-east side of the city, close to the hospital, and benefits from off-road parking. Many thoughtful extras are provided as standard, including Wi-fi. Attentive and friendly service enhances the guest experience.

Rooms 8 en suite (2 fmly) (3 GF) S £30–£45; D £50–£90* **Facilities** STV tea/coffee Cen ht Wi-fi **Parking** 8 **Notes** Closed 22-27 Dec

Arthur's Seat, overlooking Edinburgh

EDINBURGH CONTINUED

Averon City Centre Guest House

★★★ GUEST HOUSE

44 Gilmore Place EH3 9NQ
☎ 0131 229 9932
e-mail: info@averon.co.uk
web: www.averon.co.uk
dir: From W end of Princes St onto A702, right at Kings Theatre

Situated within walking distance of the west end of the city and close to the Kings Theatre, Mrs Iliazova's guest house offers comfortable good value accommodation, with a secure car park to the rear.

Rooms 10 rms (6 en suite) (1 pri facs) (3 fmly) (5 GF) S £28-£44; D £48-£90 **Facilities** tea/coffee Cen ht **Parking** 19 **Notes** ⊗

Elder York Guest House

★★★ GUEST HOUSE

38 Elder St EH1 3DX
☎ 0131 556 1926 📠 0131 624 7140
e-mail: reception@elderyork.co.uk
web: www.elderyork.co.uk
dir: Close to Princes St, next to bus station

Centrally located just minutes from the bus station, Harvey Nichols and the St James Shopping Centre. Accommodation is situated up flights of stairs but all bedrooms are well appointed with many thoughtful extras including Wi-fi. Quality breakfast is served on individual tables overlooking Queen Street.

Rooms 13 rms (10 en suite) (1 fmly) **Facilities** FTV tea/coffee Cen ht Wi-fi **Notes** ⊗

Ardbrae House B&B

★★★ Ⓐ BED AND BREAKFAST

85 Drum Brae South, Corstorphine EH12 8TD
☎ 0131 467 5787
e-mail: info@ardbrae.com
dir: From W enter Edinburgh on A8. At PC World/Drum Brae rdbt turn left, up hill, on left, adjacent to speed camera

Rooms 3 en suite (3 GF) S £35-£60; D £50-£80
Facilities FTV tea/coffee Cen ht Wi-fi ch fac **Parking** 5
Notes LB ⊗ Closed 24-28 Dec

Classic House

★★★ Ⓐ GUEST HOUSE

50 Mayfield Rd EH9 2NH
☎ 0131 667 5847 📠 0131 662 1016
e-mail: info@classicguesthouse.co.uk
web: www.classichouse.demon.co.uk
dir: From bypass follow signs for A701 city centre. At Liberton Brae, keep left, 0.5m on left

Rooms 7 rms (6 en suite) (1 pri facs) (2 fmly) S £35-£60; D £50-£90* **Facilities** TVL Cen ht **Notes** LB ⊗

Ravensdown Guest House

★★★ Ⓐ GUEST HOUSE

248 Ferry Rd EH5 3AN
☎ 0131 552 5438
e-mail: david@ravensdownhouse.com
web: www.ravensdownhouse.com
dir: N of city centre, close to Royal Botanic Gardens, A902 Goldenacre

Rooms 7 en suite (5 fmly) (1 GF) S £50-£115; D £80-£125
Facilities FTV tea/coffee Cen ht Wi-fi **Parking** 2 **Notes** LB ⊗

Café Royal

◉ Modern Scottish

Grandly opulent drinking and eating in the heart of the city

☎ 0131 556 1884
19 West Register St EH2 2AA
e-mail: info@caferoyal.org.uk
dir: Just off Princes St, close to Waverley Station

The fabulously Baroque-style Café Royal opened on this site in 1863 (it used to be elsewhere in the city, originally opening in 1826) and is extravagantly done out with acres of panelled walls, stained glass, ornately decorated ceilings, and Doulton ceramic murals. The whole building and its interior were listed in 1970 so future generations will enjoy the unique building which still sticks to its early 19th century roots by serving local ales, wine, coffee and fresh oysters in the bar and restaurant. There's a popular bar and a separate restaurant with its own entrance via a revolving door. The bar deals in hand-pumped beers and food such as sandwiches, fresh oysters and haggis and whisky cream pie (served with chips, of course), while in the restaurant the tables are spruced up with white linen cloths and the menu goes up a gear. Start with hickory-smoked duck or Scottish smoked salmon served straight-up with a lemon mayonnaise, before the likes of a seafood platter (also available next door in the bar), grilled mullet with ratatouille, or a steak from the chargrill with Arran mustard butter.

Times 12-2.30/5-9.30

Open all day all wk **Bar Meals** Av main course £9 food served all day **Restaurant** L served all wk 12-2.30 booking required D served all wk 5-9.30 booking required Av 3 course à la carte fr £30 ⊕ PUNCH PUB CO ◧ Deuchars IPA, Kelburn Ca'Canny & Goldihops, Harviestoun Bitter & Twisted. ♟ 10
Facilities Children welcome Children's portions

Castle Terrace Restaurant

◉◉◉ Scottish, French **V**

Refined, intelligent cooking near the castle
☎ 0131 229 1222
33-35 Castle Ter EH1 2EL
e-mail: info@castleterracerestaurant.com

Chef-patron Dominic Jack - a friend and erstwhile colleague of Tom Kitchin (see entry, The Kitchin) - has opened Castle Terrace in conjunction with his old mucker. The two restaurants bear a resemblance when it comes to their chic interiors (natural shades recalling heather-filled glens, rich fabrics, cool lighting, and an all-round fine-dining sheen) and in the food, which follows the 'from nature to plate philosophy'. Jack is his own man though and has proved his worth at some pretty top-notch places in France, and here he serves up classy modish dishes using top quality Scottish produce. Excellent breads and canapés demonstrate the skill in the kitchen, while first-course crispy pan-fried ox tongue with bresaola and quail's egg has its accompanying celeriac soup deftly poured by the waiter. Main-course brings forth Shetland skate, helpfully removed from the bone before making its entrance with a minestrone of root vegetables, coriander, ginger and crab consommé (once again decanted at the table), and for dessert, a superb pithivier of Mouneyrac apples looks a picture on the plate and is just as good to eat. A very welcome addition to the Edinburgh dining scene.

Chef Dominic Jack **Owner** Dominic Jack **Times** 12-2/6.30-10 Closed Xmas, New Year (subject to change), Sun-Mon **Prices** Fixed L 3 course £20-£37.50, Tasting menu £60-£100, Service optional, Groups min 8 service 10% **Wines** 250+ bottles over £20, 14 by glass **Notes** ALC Fixed L/D 3 course £35-£53, Tasting menu 6 course, Vegetarian menu, Dress restrictions, Smart casual **Seats** 52, Pr/dining room 16 **Children** Portions **Parking** NCP, on street

Chop Chop

◉ Chinese

Popular northern Chinese cooking in Haymarket
☎ 0131 221 1155
248 Morrison St EH3 3DT
e-mail: info@chop-chop.co.uk
dir: From Haymarket Station, restaurant 150 yds up Morrison St

Jian Wang's popular Chinese restaurant in the Haymarket district began by specialising in the steamed dumplings (jiaozi) of her native region of northeastern China. It has gradually expanded to provide a more broadly based Chinese operation, though with the centre of gravity still in the north. Fixed-price banquets are an abidingly successful way of testing the repertoire. Otherwise, choose from main dishes

continued

EDINBURGH CONTINUED

like Northern hotpot (pork, aubergine, potatoes, beans and Chinese leaves), fried tilapia, or crispy chicken dressed in soy, rice vinegar and sugar, accompanied by smaller dishes such as barbecued lamb with cumin seed, or glass noodle salad dressed in garlic, chilli, mustard and coriander. It's all top value, and is served with attentiveness and charm.

Times 12-2/5.30-10 Closed Mon, L Sat-Sun

La Favorita

Modern Italian, Mediterranean

Authentic wood-fired oven pizzas in a funky modern Italian

☎ 0131 554 2430 & 555 5564
325-331 Leith Walk EH6 8SA
e-mail: info@la-favorita.com
dir: On A900 from Edinburgh to South Leith

When you have a craving for the authentic thin, crispy pizzas you only ever find on holiday in Italy, head for La Favorita, where two spanking new wood-fired ovens have replaced the original workhorse that had been producing the goods since 1970. But, exemplary as they are, it's not all about pizza here, and although a pizza Pugliese with tomato, mozzarella, Burrata cheese, Parma ham and basil might sound tempting, it would be a shame to overlook the rest of the wide-ranging repertoire of modern regional Italian dishes. You might start with a perfectly sticky risotto imperiale, made with fish stock and Italian sparkling wine, and brimming with prawns, langoustine and smoked salmon to provide a fishy hit, then go for pesce spada in crosta di basilico - a swordfish steak crusted with breadcrumbs and herb and basil pesto, served with capers, spinach and pine nuts. All in all, an operation that hits the spot with high-class produce, done right, and served in a buzzy modern setting by amiable Italian staff.

Chef Japeck Splawski **Owner** Tony Crolla **Times** 12-11 Closed 25 Dec-1 Jan **Prices** Fixed L 2 course £9.70-£14.90, Fixed D 3 course £22-£26, Starter £3-£6.75, Main £7.25-£20.45, Dessert £2.95-£5.45, Service added but optional 10%, Groups min 10 service 10% **Wines** 15 bottles over £20, 25 bottles under £20, 7 by glass **Notes** Sunday L, Vegetarian available **Seats** 120, Pr/dining room 30 **Children** Portions, Menu **Parking** On street

La Garrigue

French, Mediterranean

Charming French bistro in the heart of Edinburgh

☎ 0131 557 3032
31 Jeffrey St EH1 1DH
e-mail: reservations@lagarrigue.co.uk
web: www.lagarrigue.co.uk
dir: Halfway along Royal Mile towards Holyrood Palace, turn left at lights into Jeffrey St

This bustling bistro is situated in the heart of the Old Town, although when you enter it does feel somewhat like you've stumbled into a little corner of old France. Indeed, the restaurant is named after a pretty stretch of land in the Languedoc region - a place influential to the culinary approach here. The Modern, rustic interior is fitted out with plain wooden tables and chairs hand-made by artist and woodcarver Tim Stead. Expect a locally-sourced produce on a menu chock full of hearty French dishes executed with finesse. Begin with smoked ham shank terrine served with a mustard dressing that does a fine job of counter-pointing any richness, follow on with Toulouse sausage with grapes, apples and parsley potatoes, and to finish, a traditional baked cheesecake with Pastis cream and a drizzle of raspberry coulis.

Chef Jean Michel Gauffre **Owner** Jean Michel Gauffre **Times** 12-3/6.30-10.30 Closed 26-27 Dec, 1-2 Jan, Sun **Prices** Fixed L 2 course fr £13.50, Fixed D 3 course fr £30, Service added but optional 10% **Wines** 24 bottles over £20, 10 bottles under £20, 11 by glass **Notes** Vegetarian available **Seats** 48, Pr/dining room 11 **Children** Portions **Parking** On street, NCP

Harvey Nichols Forth Floor Restaurant

Modern, International **NOTABLE WINE LIST**

City views and modern Scottish cooking

☎ 0131 524 8350 & 524 8388
30-34 St Andrew Square EH2 2AD
e-mail: forthfloor.reservations@harveynichols.com
web: www.harveynichols.com
dir: Located on St Andrew Square at the east end of George Street, 2 min walk from Princes Street

Its position on the store's top floor and its floor-to-ceiling glazing mean that the Forth Floor restaurant has unparalleled views over the city and - you've guessed - the Forth. The open-plan layout, contemporary in design and décor, takes in the food hall and brasserie as well as the restaurant, where the kitchen creates modish menus by matching up-to-the-minute flavours with classical technique. The Scottish Market Menu may open with home-cured duck with a salad of apples and fennel, and go on to pan-fried calves' liver with snails, shallot confit and potato purée, while the carte has the same vitality: Tarbert scallops with carrot and aniseed purée, glazed carrots and coconut 'air', then braised shin of beef with spicy aubergine purée, roast vegetables, a truffled potato crisp and garlic confit. Saffron-poached pears with honey cream and lemony sweet pastry is a flavourful way to finish.

Chef Stuart Muir **Owner** Harvey Nichols **Times** 12-3/6-10 Closed 25 Dec, 1 Jan, D Sun-Mon, 24 & 26 Dec, 2 Jan **Prices** Fixed L 2 course £22.50-£29.50, Starter £7-£12, Main £18-£24, Dessert £6-£8, Service added but optional 10% **Wines** 300 bottles over £20, 2 bottles under £20, 12 by glass **Notes** Tasting menu 7 course, Vegetarian available, Air con **Seats** 65 **Children** Portions, Menu **Parking** 20

Iggs

 Spanish

Enterprising modern Spanish cooking in the city centre

☎ 0131 557 8184
15-19 Jeffrey St EH1 1DR
e-mail: info@iggs.co.uk
web: www.iggs.co.uk
dir: In heart of Old Town, 0.5m from castle, just off Royal Mile

The eponymous Igg is not that superannuated old rocker in the insurance ads, but the enterprising Iggy Campos, whose restaurante Español opened in the Scottish capital as long ago as 1989. The repertoire has never stopped evolving in that time, but still offers modern Spanish cooking based on a mix of imported ingredients and pedigree Scottish produce. Seared scallops and braised pork belly make a classic modern pairing, appearing with chestnut purée and hazelnut dressing, while a seafood-themed main might bring together grilled cod with sautéed squid, wild garlic and a coral jus. Bellota pig cheeks and Buccleuch beef crop up among meats, and meals end perhaps with traditional almond tart and vanilla ice cream.

Chef Graham Scott **Owner** Mr I Campos
Times 12-2.30/6-10.30 Closed Sun **Prices** Food prices not confirmed for 2012. Please telephone for details **Wines** 80 bottles over £20, 20 bottles under £20, 18 by glass **Notes** Sunday L, Vegetarian available **Seats** 80, Pr/dining room 40 **Children** Portions **Parking** On street, NCP

The Indian Cavalry Club

 Indian

The West End's Indian star

☎ 0131 220 0138
22 Coates Crescent EH3 7AF
e-mail: shahid@indiancavalryclub.co.uk
dir: Few mins walk from Haymarket Railway Station & the west end of Princes St

What makes this restaurant stand out from the crowd is its pan-Indian cooking and commitment to using good quality fresh ingredients in a fine-dining environment. Quality prints and objets d'art decorate the four small dining rooms, while service is formal, the staff more than happy to advise on the menu. It's not a case of one central sauce pot fits all curries here, instead flavours are distinct and consistently good. Start perhaps with sev puri (tamarind and garlic based stuffing in crispy and crunchy dough) or perhaps 'our famous' Indo Thai seafood soup, before Kathmandu lamb with split lentils, cinnamon and lime juice.

Chef Muktar Miah, M D Qayum **Owner** Shahid Chowdhury **Times** 12-4/5.30-11.30 **Prices** Food prices not confirmed for 2012. Please telephone for details **Wines** 15 bottles over £20, 16 bottles under £20, 2 by glass **Notes** Vegetarian available **Seats** 120, Pr/dining room 50 **Parking** On street

The Kitchin

Scottish, French

Nature-to-plate cooking of a very high order in fashionable Leith

☎ 0131 555 1755
78 Commercial Quay, Leith EH6 6LX
e-mail: info@thekitchin.com
dir: In Leith opposite Scottish Executive building

An old whisky distillery in Leith seems an appropriate place for a chef passionate about Scottish ingredients to open his first restaurant. Driven by the mantra 'from nature to plate', Tom Kitchin and his wife Michaela have breathed new life into the old building and put it once again at the forefront of Scottish dynamism. There can surely be no greater advocate of fabulous Scottish produce than Tom, and when he brings his acute cooking skills to bear, tutored in French classicism from some of the best around, great things happen. The old building has scrubbed up very well indeed and now looks the part of a high-end dining establishment, but without any airs or graces; the colours chosen are from nature's palette, indeed reminiscent of a heather-filled glen, tables are left bare to expose the rich walnut tones, the kitchen is open to view behind a glass screen, and there's a palpable sense that you're at the centre of Scottish culinary goings on. The front-of-house team, largely French and thoroughly clued-up, imbue a sense of confidence. The best way to

continued

EDINBURGH CONTINUED

ensure things are done how you want is to do them yourself and thus shellfish arrive in the kitchen alive, all the butchery and filleting is done in-house, and every supplier is a valued cog in the chain. Seasonality, seasonality, seasonality - that is the name of the game. There's a good value set-lunch menu, a taster (Tom's Land and Sea Surprise), plus a carte that is bursting with appealing combinations and seasonal flavours. The spring menu brings forth a ragoût of sea kale from Essie Farm with seared hand-dived Orkney scallops, or razor clams (spoots they call them in these parts) from Arisaig with diced vegetables, chorizo and lemon confit. For main course, red mullet is seared and comes with bouillabaisse sauce and rouille, while saddle of Burnside Farm rabbit is stuffed with spinach and foie gras, served up with its crispy leg and seared lettuce. The clever combinations, spot-on timings, and technical flair are evident right to the end: Moss House Farm rhubarb, for example, in a tart with crème fraîche, perfectly partnered with a rhubarb sorbet, or mini chocolate soufflé with chocolate ice cream and blood orange marmalade.

Chef Tom Kitchin **Owner** Tom & Michaela Kitchin **Times** 12.15-3/6.45-10 Closed Xmas, New Year, 1st 2wks Jan, Sun-Mon **Prices** Fixed L 3 course £25, Fixed D 3 course £56-£62, Tasting menu £70, Starter £17-£18, Main £30-£33, Dessert £9-£10.50, Service optional, Groups min 8 service 10% **Wines** 239 bottles over £20, 21 by glass **Notes** Tasting menu 6 course, Vegetarian available **Seats** 50 **Children** Portions **Parking** On site parking eve. Parking nearby daytime

Locanda de Gusti

◉◉ Italian

Red-hot, straightforward Italian cooking

☎ 0131 558 9581
7-11 East London St EH7 4BN
e-mail: info@locandadegusti.com
dir: Corner of Broughton & East London St, 5 min walk from the Playhouse

A contemporary city-centre Italian, Locanda de Gusti is the real deal and speaks with a strong Neapolitan accent. The décor comes with a fashionable, pared-back minimal feel of terracotta floors, whitewashed brick walls splashed with vibrant artworks and unclothed darkwood tables. The kitchen deals in authentic southern Italian cooking with a strong helping of Neapolitan style and verve. The modern approach keeps things simple using prime Scottish ingredients, with fish and seafood at its bedrock. Thus seafood is simply sautéed in olive oil - clams, mussels, prawns, langoustine, scallops, pepped up with white wine, chilli and parsley - while black ink spaghetti might come mixed with calamari, fresh vine tomatoes and fresh basil. You can almost smell the Med.

Chef Rosario Sartore **Owner** Rosario Sartore, Mario Gagliardini **Times** 12-2.30/5-11 Closed 2nd 2 wks Jul, Mon, L Sun **Prices** Fixed L 2 course £11.95, Tasting menu £24.95-£29.50, Starter £6.95-£9.95, Main £11.95-£20.95, Dessert £4.50-£5.50, Service optional **Wines** 80% bottles over £20, 20% bottles under £20, 7 by glass **Notes** Fixed L 2 course available until 6.30pm & Tue-Sat until 4pm, Vegetarian available **Seats** 60, Pr/dining room 30 **Children** Portions **Parking** On street

Plumed Horse

◉◉◉ Modern European ⬤ NOTABLE WINE LIST

Confident, creative cooking in Georgian Leith

☎ 0131 554 5556 & 05601 123266
50-54 Henderson St, Leith EH6 6DE
e-mail: plumedhorse@aol.com
web: www.plumedhorse.co.uk
dir: From city centre N on Leith Walk, left into Great Junction St & 1st right into Henderson St. Restaurant 200mtrs on right

It may look humble enough from the outside, on an unassuming Georgian street in Leith, but once across the threshold it is clear that there is nothing ordinary about Tony Borthwick's gaff. The restaurant has a mature, calm, and confident demeanour, with warm colours on the walls, period plasterwork, high class fixtures and fittings, and a regularly-changing array of bold modern artworks on display; it has fine dining written all over it, and that's exactly what comes out of the kitchen. High quality produce is central to everything here, with the well developed supply lines bringing in Scottish produce of the highest order, and the food is best described as modern European, with classical technique to the fore and bags of contemporary finesse. There are four choices at each course at dinner, or a tasting menu (with matching wines) if you want to put the kitchen through its paces. A first course hot and cold wood pigeon with plum and fig jam, thyme brioche and sauce Cumberland gets things off to a flying start, or there might be a foie gras soufflé with foie gras 'nugget', Gewürztraminer jelly and golden raisins. Next up could be main-course 'casserole' of free-range Scottish rose veal with accompanying sautéed kidney and sweetbreads, or roast fillet of monkfish with Alsace bacon, smoked eel, capers, sauce vierge and green ham sauce. The verve and vigour continues to the very end: chocolate and blood orange trifle, perhaps, served with a blood orange sorbet.

Chef Tony Borthwick **Owner** The Company of The Plumed Horse Ltd **Times** 12-3.30/7-11.30 Closed Xmas, New Year, 2 wks Summer, I wk Etr, Sun-Mon **Prices** Fixed L 3 course £26, Fixed D 3 course £55, Tasting menu £65, Service optional **Wines** 290 bottles over £20, 16 by glass **Notes** ALC menu 3 course £55, Taster menu 8 course **Seats** 40 **Parking** On street

Restaurant Martin Wishart

@@@@ Modern French **V** 🍷 NOTABLE WINE LIST

Reference-point Scottish address for outstanding contemporary food

☎ 0131 553 3557
54 The Shore, Leith EH6 6RA
e-mail: info@martin-wishart.co.uk
dir: The Shore is off the A199

In the years since he opened in Leith in 1999, Martin Wishart has certainly spread his wings. There is now a restaurant on Loch Lomond, Cameron House (see entry), as well as a cookery school. It's been a career of travel too, taking in stints in the United States, Australia and around Europe, but it is to here, the self-named restaurant on the approach road into the Leith redevelopment area, that the compass needle inevitably returns. This place has been able to lay serious claim for some years now to being not just Edinburgh's but Scotland's finest, an accolade that sits pleasantly at odds

with its un-ostentatiousness. The décor is defiantly muted in its beige and wood surfaces. It's run with consummate professionalism though, with the kind of service approach that doesn't believe in intruding extraneously, but is fully clued-up as to what the kitchen is about. And what it's about is a style of localised Scottish food inflected with modern French technique, built around combinations of ingredients that are capable of inducing those moments of serendipity that an entire generation of UK practitioners is currently striving for, but which few achieve with this degree of precision. It's perhaps too easy to say it's worth splashing out on one of the six-course tasting menus, but these are the kinds of dishes that make you want to try as many of them as possible. An opener might be Kilbannan langoustines with parsnip and white chocolate in melted smoked butter, or Loch Ryan native oysters, the traditional sharpening accompaniments to which are recast here as green apple and sauerkraut, with some Aquitaine caviar for good measure. Main courses go up a gear for combinations that deepen the intensity of impeccable principal materials, whether Puy lentils, apple, beetroot and black pudding sauce with a roast loin and blood-enriched civet of mountain hare, or a voguish pairing of squab pigeon and foie gras, served with a celeriac and potato galette on truffle cream. And then just when you could be forgiven for expecting something avant-garde like a Jerusalem artichoke for pudding, desserts veer towards a more classical line, with pistachio soufflé, tarte Tatin with vanilla ice cream, or an assiette of the all important rhubarb, presented in the variegated guises of madeleine, cannelloni, macaroon and sorbet. The picture is completed by a formidably fine wine list that encompasses an excellent choice by the glass, opening with an Austrian Grüner Veltliner and a Chilean Carmenère.

Chef Martin Wishart, Joe Taggart **Owner** Martin Wishart **Times** 12-2/6.30-10 Closed 25-26 Dec, 1 Jan, 2 wks Jan, Sun-Mon **Prices** Fixed L 3 course £28.50, Fixed D 3 course £65, Tasting menu £60-£65, Service optional, Groups min 6 service 10% **Wines** 200+ bottles over £20, 14 by glass **Notes** Vegetarian menu, Dress restrictions, Smart casual **Seats** 50, Pr/dining room 10 **Children** Portions **Parking** On street

Santini Restaurant

 Italian

Authentic Italian flavours in a stylish bistro and restaurant

☎ 0131 221 7788 & 229 9131
Sheraton Grand Hotel & Spa, 8 Conference Square EH3 8AN
e-mail: info@santiniedinburgh.co.uk
dir: From west end of Princes St, turn onto Lothian Rd. 1st right at lights onto West Approach Rd.1st left to the Sheraton Grand Hotel & Spa, restaurant on right

Part of the glossy Sheraton Grand complex in the heart of Edinburgh, Santini is a vibrant contemporary-styled Italian. There's a buzzy cocktail bar to linger in and people watch before progressing through to either the bistro, where you could perch at a high black leather bar stool, or the restaurant, which is a masterpiece of cool Italian design in glass, chrome and neutral shades. The menu takes its inspiration from an eclectic spread of the Italian regions, and pulls together top-drawer Scottish produce with specialist stuff brought in from Italy for total authenticity. Prawns in filo pastry with tomato and basil sauce is an eye-catching starter, ahead of a textbook tender osso buco - braised veal shank with tomatoes and herbs and saffron risotto - or perhaps chargrilled tuna with Sicilian caponata vegetables. The restaurant is now also open for breakfast.

Chef Malcolm Webster, Ray Wong **Owner** Sheraton Grand Hotel & Spa **Times** 12-2.30/6-10.30 Closed 27 Dec-8 Jan **Prices** Fixed L 2 course £10, Fixed D 3 course £19, Starter £4-£15, Main £8-£28, Dessert £5-£7, Service added but optional 10% **Wines** 51 bottles over £20, 3 bottles under £20, 7 by glass **Notes** Vegetarian available, Dress restrictions, Smart casual **Seats** 100 **Children** Portions, Menu **Parking** 50

Stac Polly

 Modern Scottish

Scottish cuisine in fashionable city centre venues

☎ 0131 556 2231
29-33 Dublin St EH3 6NL
e-mail: bookings@stacpolly.com
dir: On corner of Albany St & Dublin St

Stac Polly has been a stalwart of the Edinburgh eating scene for over two decades, growing into a mini-chain of three city centre venues in St Mary's Street, Grindlay Street and Dublin Street. Each has its own identity, but all share the same formula of kitting out characterful buildings in appealing contemporary style. The Dublin Street branch occupies a basement labyrinth of rough stone-walled cellars beneath a 200-year-old building. The kitchen injects plenty of Scottish authenticity into its output, turning out good robust flavours; baked filo pastry parcels of haggis with sweet plum and red wine sauce are a signature starter, while mains might be as delicate as poached lemon sole with fondant potato, spring greens, asparagus and lime and saffron cream sauce, or as hearty as baked pork fillet stuffed with apple and Stornaway black pudding, new potatoes, red onions and cider jus.

Chef Andre Stanislas **Owner** Roger Coulthard **Times** 12-2/6-10 Closed L Sat-Sun **Prices** Fixed L 2 course £12.95, Starter £6.95-£8.25, Main £17.95-£23.95, Dessert £6.75, Service added but optional 10% **Wines** 40+ bottles over £20, 12 bottles under £20, 8 by glass **Notes** Pre-theatre menu 2 course £18, 3 course £23, Vegetarian available **Seats** 100, Pr/dining room 54 **Children** Portions **Parking** On street - after 6.30pm

The Stockbridge Restaurant

 Modern European

Bold cooking in a boldly designed basement room

☎ 0131 226 6766
54 Saint Stephen St EH3 5AL
e-mail: jane@thestockbridgerestaurant.com
web: www.thestockbridgerestaurant.com
dir: From A90 towards city centre, left Craigleith Rd B900, 2nd exit at rdbt B900, straight on to Kerr St, turn left onto Saint Stephen St

Named after the chic district of Edinburgh in which it's located, the Stockbridge occupies the basement of a Georgian house, reached down a flight of steps with fairylights twined about the wrought-iron railing. If you've wearied of understated monochrome, your senses will be restored by the room that awaits, where large modern still lifes and framed mirrors hang on the black-painted brick walls, and the brooding lighting level creates an intimate atmosphere. The surroundings encourage you to expect out of the ordinary cooking, and the kitchen by and large obliges, with multi-layered dishes designed to make bold statements. Start with seared scallops, parmesan-flaked crab risotto and avocado ice cream, before going on perhaps with a trio of duck preparations - breast, confit and foie gras - with a potato gâteau, wild mushrooms and Madeira sauce. Desserts go more trad, with a plum and nut crumble and praline ice cream bringing up the rear.

Chef Jason Gallagher **Owner** Jason Gallagher & Jane Walker **Times** 12.30-2.30/7-9.30 Closed 1st 2 wks Jan after New

Year, Mon, L Tue-Fri **Prices** Fixed L 2 course £14.95, Fixed D 3 course £23.95, Starter £4.95-£11.95, Main £12.95-£21.95, Dessert £4.95-£7.95, Service optional, Groups min 6 service 10% **Wines** 34 bottles over £20, 19 bottles under £20, 5 by glass **Notes** Pre-theatre menu available in Aug, Vegetarian available **Seats** 40 **Children** Portions **Parking** On street

Tower Restaurant & Terrace

 Modern British NOTABLE WINE LIST

Views of the Edinburgh skyline and creative cooking

☎ 0131 225 3003
National Museum of Scotland, Chambers St EH1 1JF
e-mail: reservations@tower-restaurant.com
web: www.tower-restaurant.com
dir: Above Museum of Scotland building at corner of George IV Bridge & Chambers St, on level 5

Lesser restaurants might sit back and trade on the splendid views across Edinburgh's cityscape, but the Tower Restaurant turns out inventive cooking good enough to distract diners from the castle and spires that spike the skyline. The lofty eyrie atop the roof of the 20th-century Museum of Scotland is a jaw-dropping setting, which the lucky or hardy can soak up from the alfresco terrace, but indoors is more likely to be on the cards; it's a chic contemporary space that works textures of aluminium and velvet, and rich shades of purple and red. Scottish produce stars on an eclectic modern output that might kick off with Isle of Mull crab with spicy prawn toast and sesame dressing, before rack of Scotch lamb with spiced faggot, sprout colcannon and cranberry compôte. Finish with warm baklava, spiced brandy and mixed peel ice cream.

Times 12-11.30 Closed 25-26 Dec

The Vintners Rooms

 Mediterranean, Italian NOTABLE WINE LIST

Atmospheric surroundings for Mediterranean cooking

☎ 0131 554 6767
The Vaults, 87A Giles St, Leith EH6 6BZ
e-mail: info@vintnersrooms.com
dir: At end of Leith Walk, left into Great Junction St, right into Henderson St. Restaurant in old warehouse on right

The Vintners Rooms occupy the ground floor of vaults used since the 15th century as a wine and whisky warehouse (over 1,000 of the latter on offer in the bar). Given the age of the place, expect beams in a low ceiling, whitewashed walls hung with rugs and 18th-century plasterwork, plus the contemporary additions of subdued lighting and correctly set tables. Southern Europe is the food's focus, and a meal could start off simply enough with Aberdeen Angus carpaccio with truffle oil and parmesan shavings, or a plate of smoked salmon with a blini and caviar. Home-made pasta with a variety of sauces could be an option, or

perhaps pan-seared sea bream fillet with braised fennel and creamed potatoes, with rib-eye steak with mushrooms, spinach and Lyonnaise potatoes for traditionalists. Tarragon-flavoured ice cream with a poached pear is an intriguing way to end.

Chef David Spanner **Owner** Lonico Ltd **Times** 12-2/7-10 Closed 24 Dec-6 Jan, Sun-Mon **Prices** Fixed L 2 course £19.50, Starter £6.50-£13.50, Main £23.50-£28.50, Dessert £6-£8.50, Service added but optional 10%, Groups min 5 service 10% **Wines** 160 bottles over £20, 12 bottles under £20, 6 by glass **Notes** Vegetarian available **Seats** 64, Pr/dining room 34 **Children** Portions **Parking** 4

Bennets Bar 🍷

8 Leven St EH3 9LG ☎ **0131 229 5143**
e-mail: bennetsbar@hotmail.co.uk
dir: Next to Kings Theatre. Please phone for more detailed directions

Bennets is a listed property dating from 1839 with hand-painted tiles and murals on the walls, original stained glass windows, intricate wood carving on bar fitments and brass beer taps. It's a friendly pub, popular with performers from the adjacent Kings Theatre. The traditional bar has some contemporary twists and serves real ales, over 120 malt whiskies and a decent selection of wines. The home-made food, at a reasonable price, ranges from toasties, burgers and salads to stovies, steak pie, and Scottish fare. There's also a daily roast and traditional puddings. Coffee and tea are served all day.

Open all day all wk 11am-1am Closed: 25 Dec **Bar Meals** L served Mon-Sat 12-2, Sun 11-8 D served Mon-Sat 5-8.30, Sun 11-8 Av main course £7.55 **Restaurant** L served Mon-Sat 12-2 D served Mon-Sat 5-8.30 🍺 IONA PUB
🍺 Caledonian Deuchars IPA, Guinness, Caledonian 80/-.
🍷 10 **Facilities** Children welcome Children's menu Children's portions Family room Wi-fi

The Bow Bar

80 The West Bow EH1 2HH ☎ **0131 226 7667**
dir: Telephone for directions

This free house in the heart of Edinburgh's old town reflects the history and traditions of the area. Tables are from decommissioned railway carriages, and a gantry reclaimed from an old church is used to house around 200 malt whiskies. Eight real ales from micro-breweries across the UK, along with some keg beers, are dispensed from antique Aitken founts driven by air pressure. Such is the focus on liquid refreshment that bar snacks are the only solids served. Conversation is highly prized too – there are no gaming machines or music to detract from the agreeable ambience.

continued

EDINBURGH CONTINUED

Open all day all wk Closed: 25-26 Dec, 1-2 Jan **Bar Meals** L served Mon-Sat 12-2 ⊕ FREE HOUSE ◑ Deuchars IPA, Stewarts 80/-, Timothy Taylor Landlord, Harviestoun Bitter & Twisted, Atlas Latitude, Trade Winds, Stewarts Pentland IPA Ö Stowford Press, Thistly Cross. **Facilities** Dogs allowed Beer festival Wi-fi

Doric Tavern

15-16 Market St EH1 1DE ☎ 0131 225 1084
e-mail: info@the-doric.com
dir: In city centre opp Waverly Station & Edinburgh Dungeons

Built in the 17th-century, The Doric claims to be Edinburgh's oldest gastro-pub. It became a pub in the mid-1800s and takes its name from a language that used to be spoken in north-east Scotland, mainly in Aberdeenshire. Conveniently located for Waverley Station, the pub is just a short walk from Princes Street and Edinburgh Castle. Public rooms include a refurbished ground-floor bar, and a wine bar and bistro upstairs. In these pleasantly informal surroundings, a wide choice of fresh, locally sourced food is prepared by the chefs on site. While sipping a pint of Deuchars IPA or Edinburgh Pale Ale, you can nibble on traditional Cullen skink or slow roasted barbecue ribs. Starter options include steamed Scottish mussels, smoked salmon or deep-fried Brie with cranberry and orange jelly. Main dishes range from linguine with fresh clams sautéed with garlic, chilli and white wine to roast lamb rump served on a garlic and rosemary mash with butternut squash, plum tomato stuffed with ratatouille. Haggis, neeps and tatties covered with a whisky jus will also satisfy traditionalists.

Open all day all wk 11.30am-mdnt (Thu-Sat 11.30am-1am) Closed: 25-26 Dec, 1 Jan **Bar Meals** Av main course £13 food served all day **Restaurant** Fixed menu price fr £12 Av 3 course à la carte fr £22 food served all day ⊕ FREE HOUSE ◑ Deuchars IPA, Guinness, Stewarts 80/, Edinburgh Gold, Edinburgh Pale Ale. **Facilities** Children welcome Children's portions Family room

The Shore Bar & Restaurant ▼

3 Shore, Leith EH6 6QW ☎ 0131 553 5080
📄 0131 553 5080
e-mail: info@theshore.biz
dir: Telephone for directions

Part of this historic pub was a 17th-century lighthouse and, as befits its location beside the Port of Leith, it has a fine reputation for fish and seafood. Both restaurant and bar serve food all day from noon, with the carte changing as and when fresh produce arrives. Typical of the snacks are smoked mackerel pâté, and ham hash cake with free-range poached egg and hollandaise. For a main course expect the likes of the Shore Bar's fish pie, or pork belly with snail scampi and boulangère potatoes.

Open all wk noon-1am (Sun 12.30pm-1am) Closed: 25-26 Dec, 1 Jan **Bar Meals** L served all wk 12-6 booking required D served all wk 6-10.30 booking required Av main course £15 **Restaurant** L served all wk 12-6 booking required D served all wk 6-10.30 booking required Av 3 course à la carte fr £25 ⊕ FREE HOUSE ◑ Belhaven 80/-, Deuchars IPA, Guinness. ▼ 14 **Facilities** Children welcome Dogs allowed

RATHO	Map 3 NT17

The Bridge Inn ▼

27 Baird Rd EH28 8RA ☎ 0131 333 1320
e-mail: info@bridgeinn.com
dir: From Newbridge at B7030 junct, follow signs for Ratho and Edinburgh Canal Centre

Just to the west of Edinburgh, this canal-side inn makes the most of its idyllic waterside location, catering for boaters, cyclists and ramblers using this popular waterway and basing two floating restaurants on renovated barges which ply the canal most weekends, a diverting trip on the tree-lined Edinburgh and Glasgow Union Canal first opened in 1820. The waterside beer garden is a popular summertime venue, where a grand selection of beers from Scotland's burgeoning micro-brewery sector is the order of the day. Inside, the Pop Inn or a brand new bar attract locals to regular quiz nights, whilst the bistro restaurant, with its equally strong commitment to Scottish produce, may include on the menu pork from the inn's own herd of saddleback pigs. Starters cover pan-seared pigeon breast and breaded Camembert, whilst mains include courgette and blue cheese fritters with chickpea salsa.

Open all day all wk 11-11 (Fri-Sat 11am-mdnt) Closed: 25-26 Dec, 2 Jan **Bar Meals** L served Mon-Fri 12-3, Sat 12-9, Sun 12.30-8.30 D served Mon-Fri 5.30-9, Sat 12-9, Sun 12-30-8.30 Av main course £9.95 **Restaurant** L served Mon-Fri 12-3, Sat 12-9, Sun 12.30-8.30 booking required D served Mon-Fri 5.30-9, Sat 12-9, Sun 12.30-8.30 booking required Fixed menu price fr £17.95 Av 3 course à la carte fr £17.95 ⊕ FREE HOUSE ◑ Belhaven, Deuchars IPA, Guest ales Ö Aspall. ▼ 21 **Facilities** Children welcome Children's menu Children's portions Dogs allowed Garden Beer festival Parking Wi-fi

SOUTH QUEENSFERRY — Map 3 NT17

Premier Inn Edinburgh (South Queensferry)

BUDGET HOTEL

☎ 0871 527 8364 📠 0871 527 8365
Builyeon Rd EH30 9YJ
web: www.premierinn.com
dir: M8 junct 2 follow M9 Stirling signs, exit at junct 1a take A8000 towards Forth Road Bridge, at 3rd rdbt 2nd exit into Builyeon Rd (NB do not go onto Forth Road Bridge)

High quality, budget accommodation ideal for both families and business travellers. Spacious, en suite bedrooms feature tea and coffee-making facilities, and Freeview TV in most hotels. Internet access and Wi-fi are available for a small fee. The adjacent family restaurant features a wide and varied menu.

Rooms 70 **D** £60-£63*

FALKIRK

BANKNOCK — Map 3 NS77

Glenskirlie House and Castle

 Modern British

Inventive Scottish cuisine in a castle setting

☎ 01324 840201
Kilsyth Rd FK4 1UF
e-mail: macaloneys@glenskirliehouse.com
web: www.glenskirliehouse.com
dir: Follow A803 signed Kilsyth/Bonnybridge, at T-junct turn right. Hotel 1m on right

In a luxurious setting of landscaped gardens and parkland and next to the impressive castle, this Edwardian country-house turned boutique hotel serves up creative modern Scottish cuisine. There are two dining options: the Castle Grill or the fine-dining restaurant. In the latter, a rather clever layout allows for an intimate atmosphere while plush fabrics and well-dressed tables impart an air of luxury (which continues when you take a look at the ingredients on the menu). Top-quality seasonal ingredients are paired off in effective combinations; smoked crayfish and chervil ravioli, for example, with a shellfish consommé and warm micro herbs, or a main-course roast breast of duck with smoked tattie scone, cep risotto, parsip purée and ginger sauce. Pudding arrives courtesy of the charmingly retro-style dessert trolley.

Times 12-2/6-9.30 Closed 26-27 Dec, 1-4 Jan, D Mon

FALKIRK — Map 3 NS88

Premier Inn Falkirk Central

BUDGET HOTEL

☎ 0871 527 8388 📠 0871 527 8389
Main St, Camelon FK1 4DS
web: www.premierinn.com
dir: From Falkirk A803 signed Glasgow. At mini-rdbt right, continue on A803. At Rosebank rdbt 2nd exit signed Glasgow & Stirling

High quality, budget accommodation ideal for both families and business travellers. Spacious, en suite bedrooms feature tea and coffee-making facilities, and Freeview TV in most hotels. Internet access and Wi-fi are available for a small fee. The adjacent family restaurant features a wide and varied menu.

Rooms 31 **D** £59*

Premier Inn Falkirk (Larbert)

BUDGET HOTEL

☎ 0871 527 8390 📠 0871 527 8391
Glenbervie Business Park, Bellsdyke Rd, Larbert FK5 4EG
web: www.premierinn.com
dir: Just off A88. Approx 1m from M876 junct 2
Rooms 60 **D** £52-£58*

GRANGEMOUTH — Map 3 NS98

The Grange Manor

★★★★ 76% HOTEL

☎ 01324 474836 📠 01324 665861
Glensburgh FK3 8XJ
e-mail: info@grangemanor.co.uk
web: www.grangemanor.co.uk
dir: E: M9 junct 6, hotel 200mtrs to right. W: M9 junct 5, A905 for 2m

Located south of town and close to the M9, this stylish hotel, popular with business and corporate clientele, benefits from hands-on family ownership. It offers spacious, high quality accommodation with superb bathrooms. Public areas include a comfortable foyer area, a lounge bar and a smart restaurant. Wallace's bar and restaurant is adjacent to the main house in the converted stables. Staff throughout are very friendly.

Rooms 36 (30 annexe) (6 fmly) (15 GF) **S** £68-£148; **D** £68-£148 **Facilities** STV FTV New Year Wi-fi **Conf** Class 68 Board 40 Thtr 120 Del from £115 to £145 **Services** Lift **Parking** 154 **Notes** ⊗ Civ Wed 120

POLMONT — Map 3 NS97

Macdonald Inchyra Grange

★★★★ 72% HOTEL

☎ 01324 711911 📄 01324 716134
Grange Rd FK2 0YB
e-mail: inchyra@macdonald-hotels.co.uk
web: www.macdonaldhotels.co.uk
dir: Just beyond BP Social Club on Grange Rd

Ideally placed for the M9 and Grangemouth terminal, this former manor house has been tastefully extended. It provides extensive conference facilities and a choice of eating options: the relaxed atmosphere of the Café Crema or the Opus 504 Restaurant, which provides a more formal dining experience. Bedrooms are comfortable and mostly spacious.

Rooms 98 (6 annexe) (35 fmly) (33 GF) **Facilities** Spa STV
🏃 ⛵ Gym Steam room Sauna New Year **Conf** Class 300
Board 80 Thtr 750 **Services** Lift **Parking** 500
Notes Civ Wed 450

Premier Inn Falkirk East

BUDGET HOTEL

☎ 0871 527 8392 📄 0871 527 8393
Beancross Rd FK2 0YS
web: www.premierinn.com
dir: M9 junct 5, Polmont A9 signs. Hotel on left

High quality, budget accommodation ideal for both families and business travellers. Spacious, en suite bedrooms feature tea and coffee-making facilities, and Freeview TV in most hotels. Internet access and Wi-fi are available for a small fee. The adjacent family restaurant features a wide and varied menu.

Rooms 40 **D** £52-£58*

FIFE

ABERDOUR — Map 3 NT18

Woodside

★★★ Ⓐ HOTEL

☎ 01383 860328 📄 01383 860920
High St KY3 0SW
e-mail: reception@thewoodsidehotel.co.uk
web: www.thewoodsidehotel.co.uk
dir: M90 junct 1, E on A291 for 5m, hotel on left on entering village

Rooms 20 (3 fmly) **Facilities** FTV Wi-fi **Conf** Class 80 Thtr 60
Del from £110 to £120 **Parking** 22 **Notes** ⊗ Closed 25 Dec
& 1 Jan

ANSTRUTHER — Map 3 NO50

The Spindrift

★★★★ 🏠 ⬭ GUEST HOUSE

Pittenweem Rd KY10 3DT
☎ 01333 310573 📄 01333 310573
e-mail: info@thespindrift.co.uk
web: www.thespindrift.co.uk
dir: Enter town from W on A917, 1st building on left

This immaculate Victorian villa stands on the western edge of the village. The attractive bedrooms offer a wide range of extra touches; the Captain's Room, a replica of a wood-panelled cabin, is a particular feature. The inviting lounge has an honesty bar, while imaginative breakfasts, and enjoyable home-cooked meals by arrangement, are served in the cheerful dining room.

Rooms 8 rms (7 en suite) (1 pri facs) (2 fmly) S £40-£80; D
£66-£80 **Facilities** FTV TVL tea/coffee Dinner available
Direct Dial Cen ht Licensed Wi-fi Golf 18 **Parking** 12
Notes LB No Children 10yrs Closed Xmas-late Jan

Bannet Stane in the Lomond Hills

The Waterfront

★★★★ 🏠 🍽 RESTAURANT WITH ROOMS

18-20 Shore St KY10 3EA
☎ **01333 312200** 📄 **01333 312288**
e-mail: chris@anstruther-waterfront.co.uk
dir: Off A917 opposite marina

Situated overlooking the harbour, The Waterfront offers spacious, stylish, contemporary accommodation, with bedrooms located in lovingly restored buildings in a courtyard behind the restaurant. There is a comfortable lounge with a smartly fitted kitchen and dining room, and laundry facilities are available in the granary. Dinner and breakfast are served in the attractive restaurant that offers a comprehensive menu featuring the best of local produce.

Rooms 8 annexe en suite (3 fmly) (1 GF) **Facilities** STV TVL tea/coffee Dinner available Cen ht **Notes** ⊗

The Cellar

◉◉◉ Seafood

Romantic old smokery turned classy seafood restaurant

☎ 01333 310378
24 East Green KY10 3AA
dir: Behind Scottish Fisheries Museum

Ducking behind the Scottish Fisheries Museum on the harbour front and wandering through a pretty cobbled courtyard will take you into the safe and welcoming hands of owners Peter and Susan Jukes. The 17th-century house that is home to The Cellar has lots of period charm - low ceilings, original beams, an open fire, bare-stone walls, and some of the unclothed darkwood tables even have cast iron bases made from old sewing machines. Given its proximity to the harbour, and the fact it used to be a cooperage and smokery back in the day, it is fitting that seafood is the star of the show nowadays. Chef-proprietor Peter has been cooking here for nearly 30 years so knows what works best - namely clean and simple flavours from the supremely fresh seafood and fish. The weekly-changing menu might be supplemented with a robustly flavoured amuse-bouche of smoked haddock in a pastry basket topped with bacon and cream sauce, plus excellent freshly baked bread with good quality butter. Start, perhaps, with Cellar's fish soup - a crayfish bisque with a little cream and gruyère, before grilled fillet of prime North Sea halibut - the fish cooked perfectly - or a warm salad of John Dory with scallops and mussels in a herb and garlic butter, plus tomatoes and a subtle kick of chilli. Finish with iced hazelnut praline parfait with fruits and Cassis sauce before settling down to coffee and home-made whisky chocolates.

Chef Peter Jukes **Owner** Susan & Peter Jukes
Times 12.30-1.30/6.30-9.30 Closed Xmas, Sun (also Mon

winter), L Mon-Tue **Prices** Fixed L 2 course £19.50, Fixed D 3 course fr £37.50, Service optional **Wines** 300 bottles over £20, 20 bottles under £20, 5 by glass **Seats** 38
Children Portions **Parking** On street

The Dreel Tavern

16 High Street West KY10 3DL ☎ 01333 310727
📄 **01333 310577**
e-mail: thedreeltavern@btconnect.com
dir: From Anstruther centre take A917 towards Pittenweem

Complete with a local legend concerning an amorous encounter between James V and a local gypsy woman, the welcoming 17th-century Dreel Tavern has plenty of atmosphere. Its oak beams, open fire and stone walls retain much of the distant past, while home-cooked food and cask-conditioned ales are served to hungry visitors of the present. Peaceful gardens overlook Dreel Burn.

Open all day all wk 11am-mdnt (Sun 12.30-mdnt)
🌐 SCOTTISH & NEWCASTLE 🍺 Deuchars IPA, 2 guest ales.
Facilities Children welcome Family room Dogs allowed Garden Parking

---

BURNTISLAND — Map 3 NT28

Kingswood

★★★ 75% HOTEL

☎ 01592 872329 📄 01592 873123
Kinghorn Rd KY3 9LL
e-mail: enquiries@kingswoodhotel.co.uk
web: www.kingswoodhotel.co.uk
dir: A921 (coast road) at Burntisland, right at rdbt, left at T-junct, at bottom of hill to Kinghorn Rd, hotel 0.5m on left

Lying east of the town, this hotel has views across the Firth of Forth to Edinburgh. Public rooms feature a range of cosy sitting areas, and a spacious and attractive restaurant serving good value meals. There is also a good-size function room and multi-purpose conservatory. Bedrooms include two family suites and front-facing rooms with balconies.

Rooms 13 (3 fmly) (1 GF) **S** £59-£69; **D** £60-£115 (incl. bkfst)* **Facilities** FTV New Year Wi-fi **Conf** Class 20 Board 40 Thtr 150 **Parking** 50 **Notes** LB ⊗ Closed 26 Dec & 1 Jan Civ Wed 120

Burntisland Sands Hotel

Lochies Rd KY3 9JX ☎ **01592 872230** 📄 **01592 872230**
e-mail: mail@burntislandsands.co.uk
dir: Towards Kirkcaldy, Burntisland on A921. Hotel on right before Kinghorn

Once a highly regarded girls' boarding school, this small, family-run hotel stands just 50 yards from an award-winning sandy beach. Visitors can expect reasonably priced breakfasts, snacks, lunches and evening meals, including internationally themed evenings. Typical choices range from Mexican-style chicken to haggis, neeps and tatties. Relax and enjoy a drink in the bar and lounge area or in the courtyard.

Open all day all wk **Bar Meals** L served Mon-Fri 12-2.30, Sat-Sun all day booking required D served Mon-Fri 5-8.30 booking required Av main course £8.20 **Restaurant** L served Mon-Fri 12-2.30, Sat-Sun all day booking required D served Mon-Fri 5-8.30 booking required Fixed menu price fr £22 Av 3 course à la carte fr £26 ⊕ FREE HOUSE ◼ Scottish Courage ales, Guinness, Guest ales. **Facilities** Children welcome Children's menu Children's portions Play area Dogs allowed Garden Parking Wi-fi

---

CRAIL Map 3 NO60

Balcomie Links Hotel

★★ 75% SMALL HOTEL

☎ 01333 450237 📄 01333 450540
Balcomie Rd KY10 3TN
e-mail: mikekadir@balcomie.co.uk
web: www.balcomie.co.uk
dir: A917 into Crail to village shops, right into Market Gate, becomes Balcomie Rd, hotel on left

Especially popular with visiting golfers, this family-run hotel on the east side of the village represents good value for money and has a relaxing atmosphere. Bedrooms come in a variety of sizes and styles and offer all the expected amenities. Food is served from midday in the attractive lounge bar, and also in the bright cheerful dining room in the evening.

Rooms 14 (3 fmly) **S** £59-£69; **D** £79-£89 (incl. bkfst)
Facilities FTV Games room Xmas New Year Wi-fi **Parking** 20
Notes LB ⊗ Closed Jan-Feb Civ Wed 45

CUPAR Map 3 NO31

Ostlers Close Restaurant

◉◉ Modern British **V** ◖

Local stalwart serving unfussy, full-flavoured food

☎ 01334 655574
Bonnygate KY15 4BU
dir: In small lane off main street, A91

After three decades in their cosy restaurant hidden away down a skinny alley off Cupar's high street, Jimmy and Amanda Graham could consider themselves well and truly entrenched into the local dining scene. Ostlers Close was once the kitchen and scullery of the local 17th-century Temperance Hotel, but any thoughts of abstinence are long banished from an operation that is passionate about

sourcing the finest ingredients; well-established supply lines to local producers provide the lion's share, while fruit, veg and herbs travel straight from garden to kitchen, and wild mushrooms are foraged seasonally from the woods. The kitchen has no place for grandstanding or chasing the latest gastro trends, relying instead on intuitive, fuss-free combinations turbo-charged with powerful stocks, reductions and olive oil rather than dairy-based sauces. Pot-roasted breast of wood pigeon served in a herb potato scone with pork belly confit opens in typically forthright fashion, then main course might bring roast saddle of venison with red cabbage and roast celeriac pointed up with juniper-flavoured game sauce.

Chef James Graham **Owner** James & Amanda Graham **Times** 12.15-1.30/7-9.30 Closed 25-26 Dec, 1-2 Jan, 2 wks Oct, 2 wks Apr, Sun-Mon, L Tue-Fri **Prices** Fixed D 3 course £27, Starter £5.95-£12.50, Main £13-£22.50, Dessert £6.75-£7.75, Service optional **Wines** 60 bottles over £20, 31 bottles under £20, 6 by glass **Notes** Fixed D 3 course only available Tue-Fri Nov-May, Vegetarian menu **Seats** 26 **Children** Portions **Parking** On street, public car park

---

DUNFERMLINE Map 3 NT08

Pitbauchlie House

★★★ 79% HOTEL

☎ 01383 722282 📄 01383 620738
Aberdour Rd KY11 4PB
e-mail: info@pitbauchlie.com
web: www.pitbauchlie.com
dir: M90 junct 2, A823, then B916. Hotel 0.5m on right

Situated in three acres of wooded grounds this hotel is just a mile south of the town and has a striking modern interior. The bedrooms are well equipped, and the deluxe rooms have 32-inch LCD satellite TVs and CD micro systems; there is one bedroom designed for less able guests. The eating options include Harvey's Conservatory bistro and Restaurant 47 where Scottish and French influenced cuisine is offered.

Rooms 50 (3 fmly) (19 GF) **Facilities** STV FTV Gym Wi-fi
Conf Class 80 Board 60 Thtr 150 **Parking** 80
Notes Civ Wed 150

King Malcolm

★★★ 73% HOTEL

☎ 01383 722611 📄 01383 730865
Queensferry Rd KY11 8DS
e-mail: info@kingmalcolm-hotel-dunfermline.com
web: www.peelhotels.com
dir: On A823, S of town

Located to the south of the city, this purpose-built hotel remains popular with business clientele and is convenient

continued

DUNFERMLINE CONTINUED

for access to both Edinburgh and Fife. Public rooms include a smart foyer lounge and a conservatory bar, as well as a restaurant. Bedrooms, although not large, are well laid out and well equipped.

Rooms 48 (2 fmly) (24 GF) **Facilities** ♬ Xmas New Year Wi-fi **Conf** Class 60 Board 50 Thtr 150 **Parking** 60 **Notes** Civ Wed 120

Holiday Inn Express Dunfermline

BUDGET HOTEL

☎ 01383 748220 📄 01383 748221
Lauder College, Halbeath KY11 8DY
e-mail: info@hiexpressdunfermline.co.uk
web: www.hiexpress.com/dunfermline
dir: M9 junct 7 signed A994/A907, 3rd exit Lynebank rdbt or M90 junct 3, 2nd exit for A907, next rdbt 3rd exit, next rdbt 1st exit

A modern hotel ideal for families and business travellers. Fresh and uncomplicated, the spacious rooms include Sky TV, power shower and tea and coffee-making facilities. Continental buffet breakfast is included in the room rate; other meals may be taken at the nearby family pub or restaurant.

Rooms 82 **Conf** Class 8 Board 16 Thtr 25

Premier Inn Dunfermline

BUDGET HOTEL

☎ 0871 527 8328 📄 0871 527 8329
4-12 Whimbrel Place, Fife Leisure Park KY11 8EX
web: www.premierinn.com
dir: M90 junct 3 (Forth Road Bridge exit) 1st left at lights signed Duloch Park. 1st left into Fife Leisure Park

High quality, budget accommodation ideal for both families and business travellers. Spacious, en suite bedrooms feature tea and coffee-making facilities, and Freeview TV in most hotels. Internet access and Wi-fi are available for a small fee. The adjacent family restaurant features a wide and varied menu.

Rooms 40 **D** £52-£58*

Sangsters

◉◉ Modern British

Modern cooking in relaxed surroundings

☎ 01333 331001
51 High St KY9 1BZ
e-mail: bruce@sangsters.co.uk
dir: From St Andrews on A917 take B9131 to Anstruther, right at rdbt onto A917 to Elie. (11m from St Andrews)

Sangsters might have the unassuming look of a small seaside village restaurant, but chef-patron Bruce Sangster raises the operation to the level of a dining destination with his pedigree cooking. On the supply side, the 'local is best' mantra means Scottish materials are key; crab from Kyle of Lochalsh, Ross-shire diver scallops, Glen Isla venison - it is all hauled in and brought together in precisely-crafted cooking that takes a sure-footed modern line, and with just 28 covers to cater for, the kitchen stays clearly focused. Wife Jackie keeps everything ticking along at just the right pace in the intimate dining room, where local art adds splashes of colour to a light and uncluttered décor. Expect dishes that sparkle with imagination and flair - Thai fishcakes with spiced tomato jam and an orange and cardamom reduction, say, followed by seared medallions of monkfish with a stew of butter beans, basil and tomato, and red pepper essence. Desserts shine too, in the form, perhaps, of Valrhona chocolate torte served with poached pear, hot fudge sauce and orange yoghurt ice cream.

Times 12.30-1.30/7-9.30 Closed 25-26 Dec, early Jan, mid Feb/Oct, mid Nov, Mon, L Tue & Sat, D Sun

The Ship Inn

The Toft KY9 1DT ☎ 01333 330246 📄 01333 330864
e-mail: info@ship-elie.com
dir: Follow A915 & A917 to Elie. From High Street follow signs to Watersport Centre & The Toft

A pub since 1838, this lively free house sits right on the waterfront at Elie Bay. It has been run by the enthusiastic Philip family for over 20 years. The cricket team plays regular fixtures on the beach, live music is regularly staged, and a full programme of charity and celebratory events runs throughout the year, including a barbecue on New Year's Day. The best of local produce features on the concise menu which offers the likes of deep-fried haddock in beer batter, and baguettes of chicken mayonnaise and spicy chorizo sausage.

Open all wk Closed: 25 Dec ⊕ FREE HOUSE ◀ Caledonian Deuchars IPA, Belhaven Best, Caledonian 80/-, Tartan Special. **Facilities** Children welcome Children's menu Children's portions Play area Family room Dogs allowed Garden

GLENROTHES
Map 3 NO20

Express by Holiday Inn Glenrothes

BUDGET HOTEL

☎ 01592 745509 🖹 01592 743377
Leslie Roundabout, Leslie Rd KY6 3EP
e-mail: ebhi-glenrothes@btconnect.com
web: www.hiexpress.com/glenrothes
dir: M90 junct 2A, onto A911 for Leslie. Through 4 rdbts, hotel on left

A modern hotel ideal for families and business travellers. Fresh and uncomplicated, the spacious rooms include Sky TV, power shower and tea and coffee-making facilities. Continental buffet breakfast is included in the room rate; other meals may be taken at the nearby family pub or restaurant.

Rooms 49 (40 fmly) (21 GF) **Conf** Class 16 Board 16 Thtr 30

Premier Inn Glenrothes

BUDGET HOTEL

☎ 0871 527 8454 🖹 0871 527 8455
Beaufort Dr, Bankhead Roundabout KY7 4UJ
web: www.premierinn.com
dir: M90 junct 2a N'bound, A92 to Glenrothes. At 2nd rbt (Bankhead) take 3rd exit. Hotel on left

High quality, budget accommodation ideal for both families and business travellers. Spacious, en suite bedrooms feature tea and coffee-making facilities, and Freeview TV in most hotels. Internet access and Wi-fi are available for a small fee. The adjacent family restaurant features a wide and varied menu.

Rooms 41 **D** £50-£57*

INVERKEITHING
Map 3 NT18

The Roods

★★★★ BED AND BREAKFAST

16 Bannerman Av KY11 1NG
☎ 01383 415049 🖹 01383 415049
e-mail: isobelmarley@hotmail.com
web: www.the-roods.co.uk
dir: N of town centre off B981(Church St/Chapel Place)

This charming house stands in secluded, well-tended gardens close to the station. Bedrooms are individually styled and have state-of-the-art bathrooms. There is an inviting lounge, and breakfast is served at individual tables in an attractive conservatory.

Rooms 2 en suite (2 GF) S fr £35; D £70-£80* **Facilities** FTV TVL tea/coffee Direct Dial Cen ht Wi-fi **Parking** 4 **Notes** LB
⊗

KINCARDINE
Map 3 NS98

Premier Inn Falkirk North

BUDGET HOTEL

☎ 0871 527 8394 🖹 0871 527 8395
Bowtrees Roundabout, Houghs of Airth FK2 8PJ
web: www.premierinn.com
dir: From N: M9 junct 7 (or from S: M876) towards Kincardine Bridge. On rdbt at end of slip road

High quality, budget accommodation ideal for both families and business travellers. Spacious, en suite bedrooms feature tea and coffee-making facilities, and Freeview TV in most hotels. Internet access and Wi-fi are available for a small fee. The adjacent family restaurant features a wide and varied menu.

Rooms 40 **D** £52-£58*

The Unicorn

15 Excise St FK10 4LN ☎ 01259 739129
e-mail: info@theunicorn.co.uk
dir: Exit M9 junct 7 towards Kincardine Bridge. Cross bridge, bear left. 1st left, then sharp left at rdbt

This 17th-century pub-restaurant in the heart of the historic port of Kincardine used to be a coaching inn. And it was where, in 1842, Sir James Dewar, inventor of the vacuum flask, was born. There is a comfortable lounge bar, a grillroom, and a more formal dining room upstairs. Leather sofas and modern decor blend in well with the older parts of the building; relax and enjoy a pint of Old Engine Oil by the open fire in the bar.

Open noon-2.30 5.30-mdnt (Sun 12.30-mdnt) Closed: 3rd wk Jul, Mon ⊕ FREE HOUSE 🛢 Bitter & Twisted, Schiehavillion, Old Engine Oil. **Facilities** Children welcome Children's menu Children's portions Parking

KIRKCALDY — Map 3 NT29

Dean Park

 ★★★ 78% HOTEL

☎ 01592 261635 📠 01592 261371
Chapel Level KY2 6QW
e-mail: reception@deanparkhotel.co.uk
dir: Signed from A92 (Kirkcaldy West junct

Popular with both business and leisure guests, this hotel has extensive conference and meeting facilities. Executive bedrooms are spacious and comfortable, and all are well equipped with modern decor and amenities. Twelve direct access, chalet-style rooms are set in the grounds and equipped to the same specification as main bedrooms. Public areas include a choice of bars and a restaurant.

Rooms 34 (2 fmly) (5 GF) (12 smoking) **Facilities** STV FTV Wi-fi **Conf** Class 125 Board 54 Thtr 250 **Services** Lift **Parking** 250 **Notes** ⊗ Civ Wed 200

LEUCHARS — Map 3 NO42

Hillpark House

★★★★ GUEST HOUSE

96 Main St KY16 0HF
☎ 01334 839280 📠 01334 839051
e-mail: enquiries@hillparkhouse.com
web: www.hillparkhouse.com
dir: Leaving Leuchars for St Michaels, house last on right

Lying peacefully on the edge of the village, Hillpark House is an impressive Edwardian home offering comfortable, well-appointed and equipped bedrooms. There is an inviting lounge, a conservatory and a peaceful dining room.

Rooms 5 rms (3 en suite) (1 pri facs) (1 fmly) S £38-£45; D £76-£90 **Facilities** TVL tea/coffee Cen ht Wi-fi Golf **Parking** 6 **Notes** ⊗

MARKINCH — Map 3 NO20

Balbirnie House

★★★★ COUNTRY HOUSE HOTEL

 ◉◉ Modern British

Modern country-house cooking in listed Georgian mansion

☎ 01592 610066 📠 01592 610529
Balbirnie Park KY7 6NE
e-mail: info@balbirnie.co.uk
web: www.balbirnie.co.uk
dir: Off A92 onto B9130, entrance 0.5m on left

The perfect venue for a business trip, wedding or romantic break, Balbirnie, surrounded by over 400 acres of undulating scenery and a golf course, was built in 1777 as a private residence and bears the graceful proportions and columns associated with mansions of that period. It's still privately owned, run nowadays as a luxury country-house hotel, with the sort of décor, furnishings and staff expected in such an operation. Delightful public rooms include a choice of inviting lounges, and accommodation features splendid well-proportioned bedrooms, with the best overlooking the gardens. But even the smaller standard rooms include little touches such as sherry, shortbread, fudge and mineral water. There is a choice of eating options - the informal Bistro, or The Orangery restaurant, sumptuously decorated in shades of copper, chocolate and silver, with floor-to-ceiling lunette windows and a glass roof. Given the nature of the cosseting surroundings and a kitchen using top-end Scottish produce, the menus are appealingly eclectic in tone, starters typically ranging from chicken liver parfait with spiced lentils and orange salad, to home-cured bresaola with olives, tomato salad and a parmesan crisp. Main courses are in similar vein: fillet of Loch Duart salmon with citrus and coriander couscous, calamari and sauce vierge, say, or roast chump of lamb with red wine jus, butter beans and polenta flavoured with garlic and rosemary.

Rooms 30 (9 fmly) (7 GF) **Facilities** STV ⬗ Woodland walks Jogging trails Treatment room Xmas New Year Wi-fi **Conf** Class 100 Board 60 Thtr 220 **Parking** 120 **Notes** LB Civ Wed 200

Chef Mark Lindsey **Owner** The Russell family **Times** 12-2/7-9.30 Closed Mon-Tue **Prices** Fixed D 3 course £35, Service optional **Wines** 56 bottles over £20, 42 bottles under £20, 12 by glass **Notes** Chefs Table, Sunday L, Vegetarian available **Seats** 65, Pr/dining room 216 **Children** Portions, Menu

Town House

★★★★ RESTAURANT WITH ROOMS

1 High St KY7 6DQ
☎ 01592 758459 📠 01592 755039
e-mail: townhousehotel@aol.com
web: www.townhousehotel-fife.co.uk
dir: In town centre opposite railway station

Well situated on the edge of town and close to the railway station, this friendly establishment offers well presented bedrooms with pleasant colour schemes, modern furnishings, and a good range of facilities and extras. The attractive bar-restaurant is popular with locals and serves a choice of good-value dishes.

Rooms 3 en suite (1 fmly) S £50-£65; D £80-£90* **Facilities** FTV tea/coffee Dinner available Cen ht Wi-fi **Notes** ⊗ Closed 25-26 Dec & 1-2 Jan No coaches

PEAT INN	Map 3 NO40

The Peat Inn

★★★★★ RESTAURANT WITH ROOMS

⚜⚜⚜ Modern British 🍷NOTABLE WINE LIST 🍸

Classy cooking using first-class local produce

KY15 5LH
☎ 01334 840206 📠 01334 840530
e-mail: stay@thepeatinn.co.uk
web: www.thepeatinn.co.uk
dir: At junct of B940 & B941, 5m SW of St Andrews

The Peat Inn has long been established as one of Scotland's top dining experiences, and continues to go from strength to strength with Geoffrey and Katherine Smeddle at the reins. Comfort and tranquillity are the hallmarks of a stay at the 18th-century whitewashed inn; an agreeable beamed lounge welcomes with the warmth of a log fire and leads through to a trio of intimate dining rooms done out with unfussy elegance. Geoffrey's cooking certainly stands out from the crowd for all the right reasons: he starts from the ground up, using top-quality seasonal ingredients, and takes provenance seriously - locally-landed fish, for example, travels just 10 miles to the kitchen. Dishes are often multi-layered, but never overwrought, and flavours are clearly delineated so that they work together rather than fight it out on the plate. Home-smoked breast of pigeon might be supported by quince compôte, pearl barley, and prunes poached in Earl Grey, while a main course of wild venison could turn up with salsify gratin, wild garlic, black pudding and grand veneur sauce. It all arrives with great visual impact, ending with desserts such as blood orange bavarois teamed with iced honey mousse, pistachio cake and dark chocolate sorbet.

Rooms 8 annexe en suite (3 fmly) (8 GF) S £150; D £195*

Facilities FTV tea/coffee Dinner available Direct Dial Cen ht Wi-fi **Parking** 24 **Notes** LB ⊗ Closed 25-26 Dec, 2wks Jan RS Sun-Mon Closed No coaches

Chef Geoffrey Smeddle **Owner** Geoffrey & Katherine Smeddle **Times** 12.30-2/7-9.30 Closed 25-26 Dec, 1-14 Jan, Sun-Mon **Prices** Fixed L 3 course £19, Fixed D 3 course £36, Starter £14-£17, Main £22-£27, Dessert £10.50-£11.50, Service optional **Wines** 250 bottles over £20, 3 bottles under £20, 9 by glass **Notes** Tasting menu 6 course, ALC menu D only, Vegetarian available **Seats** 40, Pr/dining room 14

ST ANDREWS	Map 3 NO51

The Old Course Hotel, Golf Resort & Spa

★★★★★ HOTEL

⚜⚜⚜ British V 🍷NOTABLE WINE LIST

High achieving Scottish cooking on the Fife coast

☎ 01334 474371 📠 01334 477668
KY16 9SP
e-mail: reservations@oldcoursehotel.co.uk
dir: M90 junct 8, A91 to St Andrews

A haven for golfers, this internationally renowned hotel sits adjacent to the 17th hole of the championship course. Bedrooms vary in size and style but all provide decadent levels of luxury. Day rooms include intimate lounges, a bright conservatory, a spa and a range of pro golf shops. There's a good choice of places to eat, the Sands Grill specialising in seafood and steaks, and the informal Jigger Inn (see entries below) in addition to the Road Hole Restaurant, which may not be the most romantically named restaurant in the Guide, but sure looks the part. The room enjoys inspiring views of the Fife coastline from full-drop windows - if that doesn't provide distraction enough, turn the other way to see the culinary team at work in the open kitchen. The chefs work to principles of sustainability and traceability to produce a style of modern Scottish cooking that isn't over-sold in any way in the menu descriptions, but looks and tastes fit to compete with the best. You'd think chefs would be running out of things to do to scallops these days, but an opening serving of Oban's finest comes with endive marmalade, carrot purée and liquorice for an array of surprising accompaniments. Reinterpretations of traditional dishes might see a coq au vin made with local farm chicken cropping up, along with velvet-smooth olive oil mash, or there may be Black Isle Scotch beef fillet, slow-roasted and served with a thyme-spiked beetroot jus. A tarte fine of Braeburn apples is a grand finisher, served with caramel sauce and a tart green apple sorbet, or there might be rhubarb soufflé with matching rippled ice cream and posh custard.

Rooms 144 (5 fmly) (3 GF) S £170-£1535; D £200-£1535 (incl. bkfst) **Facilities** Spa STV FTV 🦢 ♿ 18 Putt green Gym Thermal suite 🎵 Xmas New Year Wi-fi **Conf** Class 473 Board 259 Thtr 950 Del from £250 to £1395 **Services** Lift **Parking** 125 **Notes** LB ⊗ Civ Wed 180

Owner Kohler Company **Times** 7-10 Closed Jan, Sun-Mon, L all week **Prices** Starter £9-£12, Main £19-£32, Dessert £8-£12, Service optional **Wines** 400 bottles over £20, 11 by glass **Notes** Tasting menu & vegetarian tasting menu available, Vegetarian menu, Dress restrictions, Smart, no jeans/trainers, collared shirt req **Seats** 70, Pr/dining room 20

Sands Restaurant

 Modern American

Sophisticated décor and accurate, unpretentious cooking

☎ 01334 474371 & 468228
The Old Course Hotel, Golf Resort & Spa KY16 9SP
e-mail: reservations@oldcoursehotel.co.uk
dir: M90 junct 8 then A91 to St Andrews

The Old Course is in an enviable spot overlooking the world-famous golf course and the coast. The Sands Grill presents the hotel's informal (yet suitably stylish) dining option, with lots of black leather, dark wood and service that gets the tone just right. The menu is biased towards steak, sourced from local farms, and seafood, represented perhaps by Orkney mussels with spring onions and Dijon cream. Global influences can be seen in pan-fried prawns with linguine and Arrabbiata sauce or chargrilled tuna steak with salade Niçoise in a citrus dressing, while chocolate pot with coffee foam and biscotti will round things off nicely.

Times 12-2.30/6-10

The Jigger Inn ♟

The Old Course Hotel KY16 9SP ☎ 01334 474371
📄 01334 477688
e-mail: reservations@oldcoursehotel.co.uk
dir: M90 junct 8, A91 to St Andrews

Steeped in history, The Jigger was a stationmaster's lodge in the 1800s on a railway line that disappeared many years ago. Located in the grounds of The Old Course Hotel, its close proximity to the world famous St Andrew's golf course means that it is home to some impressive golfing memorabilia. Don't be surprised if you are sharing the bar with a caddy or a golfing legend fresh from a game. Crackling open-hearth fires, traditional Scottish pub hospitality and plenty of golfing gossip are the backdrop for a selection of Scottish beers, including St Andrew's Best and Jigger Ale. All-day availability is one advantage of a short, simple menu that lists soups, inviting sandwiches and quenelles of haggis, neeps and tatties as starters, and continues with Jigger burger with Mull Cheddar, Ayrshire bacon and fries; shepherd's pie with roasted root vegetables; pork and honey sausages on colcannon mash; and desserts such as apple and pear crumble.

Open all day all wk 11-11 (Sun noon-11) Closed: 25 Dec **Bar Meals** L served all wk 12-9.30 food served all day **Restaurant** D served all wk 12-9.30 booking required 🌐 FREE HOUSE ◖ Guinness, St Andrews Best, Jigger Ale. ♟ 8 **Facilities** Children welcome Garden Parking

Fairmont St Andrews, Scotland

★★★★★ 85% HOTEL

◉◉ Modern European

Extensive golf resort and spa with Mediterranean-tinged cooking

☎ 01334 837000 📄 01334 471115
KY16 8PN
e-mail: standrews.scotland@fairmont.com
dir: Approx 2m from St Andrews on A917 towards Crail

The colossal Fairmont resort at St Andrews sits in 520 acres, including the obligatory golf course, and hosted the G20 summiteers in 2009. Sitting just a few miles from St Andrews, overlooking the rugged Fife coastline the hotel offers spacious bedrooms and bathrooms and an impressive spa and health club. Good standards of service are found throughout. In the vibrantly red Esperante restaurant you'll find dishes that are devised for nutritional balance and are innocent of trans-fats. If that sounds a touch worthy, fear not, for the kitchen here combines good Scottish ingredients with a Mediterranean approach to produce hearty, stimulating dishes. Start robustly with roasted sweetbreads, garnished with a foam of ceps, petit pois and truffle, before venturing on to a generous assemblage of scallops, squid and John Dory, or the speciality seared Barbary duck with roasted figs and champ. Desserts to help you briefly forget your diet include pistachio cake with apple sorbet and chocolate ganache.

Rooms 209 **Facilities** Spa STV FTV 🚫 ⚓ 36 Putt green Gym Xmas New Year Wi-fi **Conf** Class 450 Board 168 Thtr 500 **Services** Lift Air con **Parking** 150 **Notes** Civ Wed 350

Chef Adam Handling **Owner** Apollo European Real Estate **Times** 6.30-10 Closed Seasonal, L all week **Prices** Fixed D 3 course £49.50-£65, Tasting menu £65-£105, Service optional **Wines** 115 bottles over £20, 1 bottles under £20, 6 by glass **Notes** Vegetarian available, Dress restrictions, Semi formal, no denim, trainers or shorts, Air con **Seats** 60, Pr/dining room 80

Rufflets Country House

★★★★ HOTEL

◉◉ British, European ⬥ NOTABLE WINE LIST

Scottish cuisine in friendly country-house hotel

☎ 01334 472594 📄 01334 478703
Strathkinness Low Rd KY16 9TX
e-mail: reservations@rufflets.co.uk
web: www.rufflets.co.uk
dir: 1.5m W on B939

Built in the Roaring Twenties for the widow of a Dundee jute baron, Rufflets is a turreted mansion in 10 acres of fabulous landscaped gardens just a few minutes' drive from the centre of St Andrews. Stylish, spacious bedrooms are individually decorated, and public rooms include a well-stocked bar and a choice of inviting lounges. The Terrace Restaurant has booted out the tweedy fine-dining concept, replacing it with a richly-hued contemporary look, with bold fabrics and vibrant artworks as a setting for flexible, up-to-date menus of inventive Mediterranean-accented modern Scottish dishes. The kitchen takes a creative approach to its output, offering locally-reared lamb and venison, fish and seafood landed nearby, and the bounty of the hotel's own garden in interesting combinations of flavour and texture. You might find a savoury carrot and walnut tarte Tatin with cumin ice cream alongside lobster ravioli with sautéed kale, roast garlic and Pernod foam, while main courses extend to loin of venison Wellington with dauphinoise potatoes, braised red cabbage and blackcurrant jus, or steamed turbot fillet with Anna potatoes, braised leeks and mussel broth. Dessert might play a riff on an apple theme, serving up Calvados bavarois, Braeburn Charlotte and green apple sorbet.

Rooms 24 (5 annexe) (2 fmly) (5 GF) **S** £125-£255; **D** £130-£265 (incl. bkfst)* **Facilities** STV FTV Putt green 🏌 Golf driving net Children's outdoor games Xmas New Year Wi-fi **Conf** Class 60 Board 60 Thtr 200 Del from £175 to £280* **Parking** 50 **Notes** ⊗ Civ Wed 130

Chef Mark Nixon **Owner** Ann Murray-Smith **Times** 12.30-2.30/7-9.30 Closed L Mon-Sat **Prices** Fixed L 3 course £23.50-£27.50, Starter £4.75-£9, Main £15-£35, Dessert £6-£10, Service optional, Groups min 20 service 10% **Wines** 88 bottles over £20, 18 bottles under £20, 9 by glass **Notes** Sunday L, Vegetarian available, Dress restrictions, No shorts **Seats** 80, Pr/dining room 130 **Children** Portions, Menu

Macdonald Rusacks

★★★★ 75% HOTEL

@@ Italian, Scottish

Modern Italian cooking in world-famous golf hotel

☎ 0844 879 9136 & 01334 474321 📄 01334 477896 **Pilmour Links KY16 9JQ**
e-mail: general.rusacks@macdonald-hotels.co.uk
e-mail: info@roccagrill.com
web: www.roccagrill.com
web: www.macdonald-hotels.co.uk
dir: From A91 W, straight on at rdbt into St Andrews. Hotel 220yds on left

For many people, St Andrews means only one thing. This is, and always will be, the home of golf, and the Macdonald Rusacks Hotel sits within putting distance of the 18th hole on the hallowed turf of the Old Course. What's more, front-row balcony seats for the golfing action are available for the cost of a meal in the Rocca restaurant. Relaunched as a contemporary modern Italian bar and grill in 2010, the deal here is splendid Scottish ingredients subjected to Italian-accented contemporary treatments. A spring dinner starts with silky pea soup topped by a red-wine-poached quail's egg and crispy ham, followed by Gressingham duck breast teamed with a duck leg croquette and celeriac fondant; elsewhere, red-blooded slabs of prime Scottish meats are grilled and served with a classic garnish, while those in search of more obviously Italian fare might find linguine of butter-poached Scottish lobster with coriander and chilli among an array of pasta and risotto dishes. Finish with a decadent chocolate ganache with peanut butter ice cream. Bedrooms, though varying in size, are comfortably appointed and well equipped. Classically styled public rooms include an elegant reception lounge a modern restaurant and brasserie bar.

Rooms 70 (1 annexe) **Facilities** STV FTV New Year Wi-fi **Conf** Class 35 Board 20 Thtr 80 Del from £185 to £485* **Services** Lift **Parking** 21 **Notes** Civ Wed 60

Chef Liam McKenna **Owner** Macdonald Hotels/APSP Restaurants Ltd **Times** 12-2.30/6.30-9.30 Closed L Mon-Sat, D Sun (Oct-Mar) **Prices** Fixed D 3 course £20-£35, Starter £4.95-£10.95, Main £10.95-£28, Dessert £6.95-£8.95, Service optional **Wines** 52 bottles over £20, 2 bottles under £20, 10 by glass **Notes** Sunday L, Vegetarian available, Dress restrictions, Smart casual **Seats** 80, Pr/dining room 34 **Children** Portions, Menu

Best Western Scores

★★★ 79% HOTEL

☎ 01334 472451 📄 01334 473947
76 The Scores KY16 9BB
e-mail: reception@scoreshotel.co.uk
web: www.bw-scoreshotel.co.uk
dir: M90 junct 2a, A92 E. Follow Glenrothes signs then St Andrews signs. Straight on at at next 2 rdbts, left into Golf Place, right into The Scores

Enjoying views over St Andrews Bay, this well presented hotel is situated only a short pitch from the first tee of the famous Old Course. Bedrooms are impressively furnished and come in various sizes; many are quite spacious. Smart public areas include Champions Grill offering food all day from breakfast to dinner; Scottish High Teas are served here from 4.30-6.30pm. Alexander's Restaurant opens Thursday, Friday and Saturdays evenings.

Rooms 30 (1 fmly) **S** £87-£206; **D** £128-£295 (incl. bkfst)* **Facilities** FTV Xmas New Year Wi-fi **Conf** Class 60 Board 40 Thtr 180 Del from £142 to £199* **Services** Lift **Parking** 12 **Notes** LB ⊗ Civ Wed 100

Russell Hotel

★★ 81% HOTEL

◉ Scottish, International

Scottish-influenced menus in small townhouse hotel

☎ 01334 473447 📄 01334 478279
26 The Scores KY16 9AS
e-mail: russellhotel@talk21.com
web: www.russellhotelstandrews.co.uk
dir: From A91 left at 2nd rdbt into Golf Place, right in 200yds into The Scores, hotel in 300yds on left

In a Victorian terrace, this small family-run hotel overlooks St Andrews Bay and is just minutes away from the world-famous golf course. Bedrooms are well appointed bedrooms and come in varying sizes; some enjoy fine sea views. The kitchen puts fine Scottish produce to good use on its imaginative menus, served in the intimate, candlelit dining room. Tay salmon is cured with beetroot and accompanied by citrus salad and mustard and lemon crème fraîche, and mixed game goes into a roulade, wrapped in pancetta and served with juniper and plum chutney. Among main courses, expect roast loin of Perthshire lamb with Stornoway black pudding, baby onions and tomato and Glayva jus, and seared fillet of sea bass on crab risotto with shellfish bisque.

Rooms 10 (3 fmly) **Facilities** New Year **Notes** ⊗

Times 12-2/6.30-9.30 Closed Xmas

The Paddock

★★★★★ ≙ GUEST ACCOMMODATION

Sunnyside, Strathkinness KY16 9XP
☎ 01334 850888 📄 01334 850870
e-mail: thepaddock@btinternet.com
web: www.thepadd.co.uk
dir: 3m W from St Andrews off B939. The Paddock signed from village centre

Situated in a peaceful village overlooking rolling countryside, this friendly, family-run guest accommodation offers stylish and very well-equipped bedrooms. Superb fish tanks, one freshwater, the other salt, line the entrance hall and contain beautiful and unusual fish. The lounge-dining room in the conservatory is a lovely setting for the delicious breakfasts.

Rooms 4 en suite (1 fmly) (2 GF) **Facilities** FTV tea/coffee Cen ht Wi-fi **Parking** 8 **Notes** ⊗ No Children 12yrs Closed Nov-Mar

Nethan House

★★★★ GUEST HOUSE

17 Murray Park KY16 9AW
☎ 01334 472104 📄 01334 850870
e-mail: enquiries@nethan-standrews.com
dir: A91 towards St Andrews, over 2nd rdbt onto North St, Murray Park on left before cinema

This large Victorian terrace house is set in the heart of St Andrews; a short walk from the main tourist attractions and the famous golf course. The bright bedrooms are stylish and well appointed. The freshly cooked breakfast is a highlight and is served in the attractive dining room.

Rooms 7 en suite (1 fmly) (1 GF) **Facilities** FTV TVL tea/coffee Cen ht Wi-fi **Notes** ⊗ Closed 24-26 Dec

The Inn at Lathones

★★★★ INN

◉◉ Modern European

Imaginative cooking in a characterful coaching inn

Largoward KY9 1JE
☎ 01334 840494 📄 01334 840694
e-mail: lathones@theinn.co.uk
web: www.theinn.co.uk
dir: 5m S of St Andrews on A915, 0.5m before village of Largoward on left just after hidden dip

In days of yore before the world of golf invaded St Andrews, this stylish, much-extended inn tucked away among the back roads was a simple drovers' inn surrounded by rolling countryside. Nowadays the 400-year-old hostelry is a stylishly updated venue with smart contemporary bedrooms in two separate wings, and it doubles up as an award-winning live music venue, the walls displaying one of the best collections of music memorabilia in the country. Ancient meets modern here and guests can relax in deep sofas and enjoy excellent ales from Orkney Brewery around log-burners. The cosy restaurant has whitewashed walls, bare stone fireplaces and contemporary artworks; tables are smartly laid with crisp linen, but amiable staff keep things ticking over with an easygoing vibe. Divided into categories of 'seafood and pasta', 'roasts and grills', and 'casseroles and slow-cooked dishes', the menu is easy to navigate and offers a trio of choices under each heading - expect top-notch Scottish materials to be put to imaginative use in dishes that rework traditional themes. Start with crab fritters with mango salsa and wasabi mayonnaise, moving on to simple grilled halibut with crayfish butter, or a more hearty chargrilled fillet of Angus beef teamed with an oxtail bridie (that's a sort of Scottish pasty) and slow-cooked boneless short rib. End on a sweet note with an orange blossom crème brûlée with fruit compôte and yoghurt ice cream, or go savoury with a platter of Scottish cheeses.

Rooms 21 annexe en suite (1 fmly) (18 GF) **Facilities** STV TVL tea/coffee Dinner available Direct Dial Cen ht Wi-fi
Conf Max 40 Thtr 40 Class 10 Board 20 **Parking** 35
Notes Closed 26 Dec & 3-16 Jan RS 24 Dec Civ Wed 45

Open all day all wk **Bar Meals** Av main course £10.50 food served all day **Restaurant** L served all wk 12-2.30 D served all wk 6-9.30 Av 3 course à la carte fr £32.95 ⊕ FREE HOUSE ◄ Dark Island, Three Sisters, Belhaven Best. ♟ 11 **Facilities** Children welcome Dogs allowed Garden

Lorimer House

★★★★ ⒶGUEST HOUSE

19 Murray Park KY16 9AW
☎ 01334 476599 📄 01334 476599
e-mail: info@lorimerhouse.com
dir: A91 to St Andrews, left onto Golf Place, right onto The Scores, right onto Murray Park

Rooms 5 en suite (1 GF) D £80-£110* **Facilities** STV FTV TVL tea/coffee Cen ht Wi-fi **Notes** ⊗ No Children 12yrs

Millhouse B&B

★★★★ ⒶBED AND BREAKFAST

2 Cauldside Farm Steading, Strathkinness High Rd KY16 9TY
☎ 01334 850557
e-mail: millhousebandb@yahoo.co.uk
web: www.bandbinstandrews.co.uk
dir: B939 W of St Andrews, right onto Strathkinness High Rd. After 1m, right onto farm track

Rooms 2 en suite D £65-£75* **Facilities** FTV TVL tea/coffee Cen ht Wi-fi **Parking** 3 **Notes** ⊗ No Children 12yrs

Nahm-Jim & the L'Orient Lounge

 Japanese, Thai

Thai and Japanese cuisine in buzzy ambience

☎ 01334 470000 & 474000
60-62 Market St KY16 9NT
e-mail: manager@nahm-jim.co.uk

This family-run Thai and Japanese restaurant in St Andrews has a fanatical local fan base, who were no doubt pleased to see their local darling reach the final of Gordon *Ramsay's Best Restaurant* TV show in 2010. Taking its name from the hot, sour and salty paste of chilli, coriander, garlic, galangal and lime juice used in Thai dishes, Nahm-Jim is a smart venue with whitewashed stone walls, wooden floors and tasteful artefacts to give a nod to its culinary roots. The kitchen deals in authentic Thai cooking using fresh herbs and spices flown in weekly from the markets of Bangkok, as well as hugely popular Japanese bento boxes, sushi and sashimi. Squid kari - crispy squid with lime and fresh chilli - gets the palate's attention, or you could try the signature

Thai-style haggis. Moving on, chilli Thai basil pork and rice with oyster sauce is a well-balanced dish, or turning Japanese, you could go for miso lamb cutlets with spicy papaya salad.

Times 12-5/5-10 Closed 25-26 Dec, 1 Jan

The Seafood Restaurant

◎◎◎ Modern Seafood ⓦNOTABLE WINE LIST

First-rate seafood in a dramatic setting

☎ 01334 479475
The Scores KY16 9AS
e-mail: reservations@theseafoodrestaurant.com
dir: On A917 turn left along Golf Place

A blunt local might call it a glass box on the sea wall, but this sleek, cubist's dream of a building perched above the cold water's of St Andrews Bay has been a bold 21st-century statement in this historic city since 2003. With all that glass everyone gets a view over the West Sands beach (where they filmed that famous slo-mo running scene in *Chariots of Fire*) and the legendary Old Course beyond. And the sea, of course. In the circumstances, anything but fresh, vibrant seafood on the menu wouldn't be cricket (or should that be golf?) and, as revealed by the name of the place, it is duly delivered. They know well enough here that the produce speaks for itself, but that is not to say the food lacks for ideas and a modern touch. From the open-plan kitchen comes all the simplicity of a half-dozen West Coast oysters with shallot vinaigrette and lemon, or go for salad Niçoise with steamed hake and anchovy purée. For main course, sustainable North Sea coley comes with a sage risotto, confit fennel and lemon butter, while the seafood platter is piled high with the freshest of shellfish. There are meat and vegetarian options on the menu. Finish with rhubarb crumble - no humble crumble this, served as it is with mango and dates, papaya curd and milk ice cream. The excellent wine list is worth more than a moment of your time.

Chef Douglas Sillars **Owner** Tim Butler
Times 12-2.30/6.30-10 Closed 25-26 Dec, 1 Jan
Prices Fixed L 2 course £15-£22, Fixed D 3 course £32-£45, Tasting menu £47-£80, Starter £6-£12, Main £10-£23, Dessert £5-£9, Service optional **Wines** 180 bottles over £20, 5 bottles under £20, 12 by glass **Notes** Tasting menu 5 course without/with wine, Sunday L, Vegetarian available **Seats** 60 **Children** Portions **Parking** 50mtrs away

ST MONANS — Map 3 NO50

Craig Millar @ 16 West End

◉◉ Modern Scottish, Seafood · NOTABLE WINE LIST

Top-notch seafood in an old fisherman's cottage

☎ 01333 730327
16 West End KY10 2BX
e-mail: craigmillar@16westend.com
dir: Take A959 from St Andrews to Anstruther, then W on A917 through Pittenweem. In St Monans to harbour then right

Occupying an old fisherman's cottage (it's the cottage that's old, not the fisherman), this restaurant is a sibling to The Seafood Restaurant in St Andrews (see entry), and was rebranded in 2011 under the name of chef-patron Craig Millar. There's an 800-year-old freshwater well with mythical healing powers here, but you may well find the fabulous seafood has equally restorative abilities. Wonderful views across historic St Monan's harbour help too, of course; there's now a seafront dining area fashioned from what used to be the kitchen, plus a lovely outside terrace. The décor doesn't need to compete and keeps it simple with dark Rennie Mackintosh-style chairs and neutral tones. The succinct menu (three options for each course) always offers a meaty option but it's the seafood that's the star attraction here. Fresh fish cooked with a lightness of touch is the name of the game: hot-smoked salmon with savoury lentils and tomato dressing to start, followed by hand-dived scallops with potato gnocchi, Jerusalem artichoke mousse, lemon and thyme jelly, with chocolate fondant and bitter dark chocolate ice cream showing consistency and technical ability to the end.

Chef Craig Millar **Owner** Craig Millar **Times** 12.30-2/6.30-9 Closed 25-26 Dec, 1-2 Jan, Mon-Tue (Sep-Jun) **Prices** Fixed L 2 course £15-£22, Fixed D 3 course £32-£40, Service optional **Wines** All bottles over £20, 6 by glass **Notes** Seasonal opening, please check, open Mar-Oct, Sunday L, Vegetarian available **Seats** 44, Pr/dining room 25 **Children** Portions **Parking** 10

CITY OF GLASGOW

GLASGOW — Map 2 NS56

See also **Clydebank, West Dunbartonshire & Uplawmoor East Renfrewshire**

HOTEL OF THE YEAR FOR SCOTLAND

Blythswood Square

★★★★★ 88% HOTEL

◉◉ Modern British

Contemporary and classic cooking in former automobile headquarters

☎ 0141 248 8888
11 Blythswood Square G2 4AD
e-mail: reserve@blythswoodsquare.com

Built in 1821 and once the headquarters for the Royal Scottish Automobile Club, the building has been carefully restored to its former glory. The bedrooms and bathrooms are sumptuous, and include suites and a penthouse. Take afternoon tea or cocktails in the 35 metre long Salon Lounge or head for the former RSAC ballroom, which the restaurant now occupies. The high ceilings and elaborate cornice work provide a backdrop to well-spaced tables laid with linen cloths and napkins. The modern British menu serves up some bold contemporary dishes alongside comforting classics (indicated as such on the menu). Hand-dived scallops with scallop tripe, basmati crème, vadouvan (a curry spice) and pea shoots kicks things off, before a tender Gressingham duck breast with pastilla of the leg, cumin-roasted carrots, pine nut skordalia and bergamot lemon. There are steaks from the grill, too. An inventive dessert of iced apple and mascarpone mousse, toffee apple porridge, chilled buttermilk and crème fraîche soup is a triumphant finale.

Rooms 100 **S** £105-£195; **D** £140-£245 (incl. bkfst)*

Times 12-2.30/6-10

Kelvingrove Park, Glasgow

Hotel du Vin at One Devonshire Gardens

★★★★ TOWN HOUSE HOTEL

Rosettes not confirmed at time of going to press

French, European 🕭

Modern cooking in an elegant townhouse hotel

☎ 0141 339 2001 📄 0141 337 1663
1 Devonshire Gardens G12 0UX
e-mail: reservations.odg@hotelduvin.com
e-mail: bistro.odg@hotelduvin.com
web: www.hotelduvin.com
dir: M8 junct 17, follow signs for A82, in 1.5m left into
Hyndland Rd, 1st right, right at mini rdbt, right at end

Fashioned from a row of porticoed townhouses on a tree-lined boulevard in the upscale West End of the city, this is undoubtedly HdV's swankiest address. Stunning, individually designed bedrooms and suites have the trademark Egyptian linens and seriously good showers. The place has been a magnet for fine dining through the generations, and fine drinking too, as is evidenced by the whisky bar alone, which is on hand to beguile you with an appetising or digestive dram, according to taste. The multi-part dining room, doggedly styled a Bistro in concordance with the group idiom (but actually a smart, tartan-carpeted, white-napieried setting) has a new chef as we go to print. Entering into the bistro spirit, you could still have a perfectly timed steak and leave it at that, but only the most incurious could fail to be tempted by the more adventurous dishes on show. A dinner might open with foie gras three ways - cured, sautéed and cromesqui - with pistachios and dried fruit chutney, before rolling on with turbot in garlic fondue, served with white asparagus and parmesan crumbs. Main course might tip the nod to bistro style with a pasta dish, cannelloni perhaps, but filled with quail, accompanied by an oyster, salsify and pak choi in a chocolate-tinged sauce. The wine list is the treasure house that comes as standard at the Hotel du Vin but, if you're stumped, the tasting menu comes with optional pre-selected wines.

Rooms 49 (7 GF) **Facilities** Gym Tennis & Squash facilities at nearby club Xmas New Year Wi-fi **Conf** Class 30 Board 30 Thtr 50 **Notes** Civ Wed 70

Chef Darin Campbell **Owner** MWB/Hotel Du Vin
Times 12-2.30/6-10 Closed L Sat **Prices** Fixed L 2 course fr £14.50, Starter £7-£9, Main £16-£29, Dessert £6.50-£9, Service added but optional 10% **Wines** 600 bottles over £20, 12 bottles under £20, 12 by glass **Notes** Sunday L, Vegetarian available, Dress restrictions, Smart casual **Seats** 78, Pr/dining room 70 **Children** Portions **Parking** Nearby

Mint Hotel Glasgow

★★★★ 78% HOTEL

🌹 British, European 🕭

Clydeside views and bistro food

☎ 0141 240 1002 & 227 1026 📄 0141 248 2754
Finnieston Quay G3 8HN
e-mail: glasgow.reservations@minthotel.com
e-mail: glasgow.citycafe@minthotel.com
web: www.minthotel.com
dir: M8 junct 19 follow signs for SECC. Hotel on left 200yds before entrance to SECC

A contemporary hotel sitting alongside the River Clyde and the 'Squinty Bridge' and offering modern, well-equipped bedrooms and bathrooms with many thoughtful extras for guests. The hotel is ideally located for the SECC & Science Centre. With panoramic views across the river, Queens Dock and the Finnieston Crane, the City Café bistro is a chilled-out place to eat and drink. Vibrant artwork on the walls, a mix of banquette and regular seating and informally laid tables set the modish scene inside. There's a terrace too, which fills up fast when the sun is out. Comfort food sits alongside some more modern combinations on the menu, but it all makes the best of local Scottish ingredients. Start perhaps with gin and sloe berry-cured Loch Duart salmon with beetroot jelly, dill and English radish, before roast lamb neck fillet and braised shoulder Shepherd's pie, spring greens and white onion purée. The Garden Dishes vegetarian section adds to the appeal. Puds might include almond pannacotta with banana cake and pistachio ice cream.

Rooms 164 **S** £69-£209; **D** £69-£209 **Facilities** STV FTV Gym Free use of nearby health club Xmas New Year Wi-fi **Conf** Class 36 Board 40 Thtr 60 Del from £120 to £250 **Services** Lift Air con **Parking** 120 **Notes** LB ⊗ Civ Wed 60

Chef Scott MacDonald, Chris Naylor **Owner** Mint Hotel Ltd **Times** 12-2.30/5-10 **Prices** Fixed L 2 course £9.95, Fixed D 3 course £18.95, Starter £4.95-£7.95, Main £10.50-£22.95, Dessert £5.50-£7.95, Service added but optional 10% **Wines** 43 bottles over £20, 7 bottles under £20, 19 by glass **Notes** Pre-theatre menu from 5pm 2 course £16.95, 3 course £21.95, Sunday L, Vegetarian available, Dress restrictions, Smart casual **Seats** 80, Pr/dining room 60 **Children** Portions, Menu

Beardmore Hotel

★★★★ 77% HOTEL

◉ Modern British

Modern and traditional mix on the banks of the Clyde

☎ 0141 951 6000 📄 0141 951 6018
Beardmore St G81 4SA
e-mail: info@beardmore.scot.nhs.uk

(For full entry see Clydebank, West Dunbartonshire)

Menzies Glasgow

★★★★ 77% HOTEL

◉ British, European

☎ 0141 222 2929 & 270 2323 📄 0141 270 2301
27 Washington St G3 8AZ
e-mail: glasgow@menzieshotels.co.uk
web: www.menzieshotels.co.uk
dir: M8 junct 19, follow signs for SECC & Broomielaw. Left at lights

Centrally located, this modern hotel is a short drive from the airport and a short walk from the centre of the city. Bedrooms are generally spacious and boast a range of facilities, including high-speed internet access. Facilities include an impressive indoor leisure facility. Service in the new contemporary-style brasserie restaurant is friendly and attentive with a relaxed atmosphere. Continental and British classics appear alongside more complex combinations on the appealing modern menu. A starter of grilled chorizo, pancetta and poached egg salad might be followed by a hearty main course of grilled Toulouse sausage with parsley mash and grain mustard sauce, or pan-seared trout fillet with asparagus wrapped in Parma ham with cherry confit tomatoes and cream sauce. Desserts like boozy raspberry crème brûlée with lemon shortcake are sure to please.

Rooms 141 (16 fmly) (15 smoking) **Facilities** STV 🏊 supervised Gym Sauna Steam room Hair & beauty salon Xmas New Year Wi-fi **Conf** Class 60 Board 70 Thtr 160 **Services** Lift Air con **Parking** 50 **Notes** Civ Wed 150

Glasgow Marriott Hotel

★★★★ 76% HOTEL

☎ 0141 226 5577 📄 0141 221 9202
500 Argyle St, Anderston G3 8RR
e-mail: cork.regional.reservations@marriott.com
web: www.glasgowmarriott.co.uk
dir: M8 junct 19, turn left at lights, then left into hotel

Conveniently located for all major transport links and the city centre, this hotel benefits from extensive conference and banqueting facilities and a spacious car park. Public areas include an open-plan lounge/bar and a Mediterranean style restaurant. High quality, well-equipped bedrooms benefit from air conditioning and generously sized beds; the suites are particularly comfortable.

Rooms 300 (89 fmly) **Facilities** 🏊 Gym Beautician Poolside steam room Sauna New Year Wi-fi **Conf** Class 300 Board 50 Thtr 800 **Services** Lift Air con **Parking** 180 **Notes** ⊗

Thistle Glasgow

★★★★ 75% HOTEL

☎ 0871 376 9043 📄 0871 376 9143
36 Cambridge St G2 3HN
e-mail: glasgow@thistle.co.uk
web: www.thistle.com/glasgow
dir: In city centre, just off Sauchiehall St

Ideally located within the centre of Glasgow and with ample parking, this hotel is well presented with the lobby area that gives a great impression on arrival. It also benefits from having a well-presented leisure club along with the largest ballroom in Glasgow. Service is friendly and attentive. Thistle Hotels – AA Hotel Group of the Year 2011-12.

Rooms 300 (38 fmly) (1 smoking) **Facilities** STV FTV 🏊 Gym Sauna Steam room New Year Wi-fi **Conf** Class 800 Board 15 Thtr 1000 **Services** Lift Air con **Parking** 216 **Notes** LB ⊗ Civ Wed 720

Millennium Hotel Glasgow

★★★★ 74% HOTEL

☎ 0141 332 6711 📄 0141 332 4264
George Square G2 1DS
e-mail: glasgow.reservations@millenniumhotels.co.uk
web: www.millenniumhotels.co.uk
dir: M8 junct 15 through 4 sets of lights, at 5th left into Hanover St. George Sq directly ahead, hotel on right

Right in the heart of the city, this hotel has pride of place overlooking George Square. Inside, the property has a contemporary air, with a spacious reception concourse and a glass veranda overlooking the square. There is a stylish brasserie and separate lounge bar, and bedrooms come in a variety of sizes.

Rooms 116 (17 fmly) **Facilities** STV New Year Wi-fi **Conf** Class 24 Board 32 Thtr 40 **Services** Lift **Notes** ⊗ Closed 25 Dec Civ Wed 120

Grand Central Hotel

★★★★ 72% HOTEL

☎ 0141 240 3720 📄 0141 240 3701
99 Gordon St G1 3SF
e-mail: grandcentralhotel@principal-hayley.com
dir: M8 junct 19 towards city centre turn left at Hope St.
Hotel 200mtrs on right

This is the place where John Logie Baird transmitted the world's first long-distance television pictures in 1927, and this 'grand old lady' of the Glasgow hotel scene has been completely updated and refurbished throughout to a very good standard. The result is a blend of contemporary, art deco and original Victorian styles. Bedrooms are well equipped and suit business travellers especially. There is Champagne Central, a glamorous bar, the Tempus Bar and Restaurant, and Deli Central (with direct access to the Central Station) which is an eat-in deli and a take-away. Ample meeting facilities are available, and NCP car parks are nearby.

Rooms 186 (13 fmly) **Facilities** ♫ Wi-fi **Conf** Class 350 Board 60 Thtr 500 **Services** Lift **Notes** ⊗ Civ Wed 500

Crowne Plaza Glasgow

★★★★ Ⓐ HOTEL

☎ 0871 942 9091 📄 0141 221 2022
Congress Rd G3 8QT
e-mail: cpglasgow@qmh-hotels.com
web: www.crowneplaza.co.uk
dir: M8 junct 19, follow signs for SECC, hotel adjacent to centre

Rooms 283 (15 fmly) **Facilities** Spa STV ⊛ supervised Gym Beauty salon Xmas New Year Wi-fi **Conf** Class 482 Board 68 Thtr 800 **Services** Lift Air con **Parking** 300 **Notes** ⊗ Civ Wed 120

Malmaison Glasgow

★★★ 82% HOTEL

◉ Modern French, Scottish ♋

Enjoyable informal cooking in the crypt at the Glasgow Mal

☎ 0141 572 1000 📄 0141 572 1002
278 West George St G2 4LL
e-mail: glasgow@malmaison.com
web: www.malmaison.com
dir: From S & E: M8 junct 18 (Charing Cross). From W & N: M8 city centre

The Glasgow Mal, as this boutique chain hotel chummily styles itself, is lodged in a former Greek Episcopal church in the city centre, as you may discern when passing through its grandiose façade. A smart, contemporary establishment offering impressive levels of service and hospitality, withspacious bedrooms that feature a host of modern facilities, such as CD players and mini bars. The Brasserie, situated in the former crypt, is a relaxed, informal venue with a vaulted ceiling, comfortable banquette seating and a dark, earthy colour scheme. The menu offers an enjoyably heterogeneous mix of refined and demotic elements, with the 250g Mal burger showing proudly amid the likes of roast partridge with sumptuously textured bread pudding and tarragon jus. They may be preceded by breadcrumbed salt-cod beignets and tomato confit, or home-smoked duck breast with potted leg and port jelly.

Rooms 72 (4 fmly) (19 GF) **Facilities** STV Gym Cardiovascular equipment New Year Wi-fi **Conf** Board 22 Thtr 30 **Services** Lift **Notes** LB Civ Wed 80

Chef Graham Digweed **Owner** Malmaison Hotels Ltd **Times** 12-2.30/5.30-10.30 **Prices** Fixed L 2 course fr £14.95, Fixed D 3 course fr £24.95, Starter £4.95-£8.50, Main £11.50-£23, Dessert £5.95-£7.95, Service added but optional 10%, Groups min 10 service 10% **Wines** 160 bottles over £20, 20 bottles under £20, 20 by glass **Notes** Pre-theatre menu available, Sunday L, Vegetarian available **Seats** 85, Pr/dining room 22 **Children** Portions, Menu **Parking** Q Park Waterloo St

Uplawmoor Hotel

★★★ 81% HOTEL

◉ Modern Scottish ♋

Modern Scottish cooking in a converted barn

☎ 01505 850565 📄 01505 850689
Neilston Rd G78 4AF
e-mail: info@uplawmoor.co.uk
web: www.uplawmoor.co.uk

(For full entry see Uplawmoor, East Renfrewshire)

Holiday Inn Glasgow City Centre-Theatreland

★★★ 80% HOTEL

🌹 French, Mediterranean

Varied menus within a brasserie-look restaurant

☎ 0141 352 8300   📄 0141 332 7447
161 West Nile St G1 2RL
e-mail: reservations@higlasgow.com
web: www.holidayinn.co.uk
dir: M8 junct 16, follow signs for Royal Concert Hall, hotel opposite

Built on a corner site close to the Theatre Royal Concert Hall and the main shopping areas, this contemporary hotel features well equipped and comfortable bedrooms; suites are available. Staff are friendly and attentive. Despite the Parisian-style brasserie décor, the menu in La Bonne Auberge restaurant here is surprisingly more international than staunchly French. Fish soup there may be, but here it comes with prawn beignets, and another starter may be chicken satay with peanut and coriander dip. Accurate timing and quality ingredients are clear in main courses: tender pork fillet with white bean and chorizo stew, Highland Reserve rib-eye, or baked nut-crusted salmon fillet with sesame dressing and roast vegetables. Puddings are pretty well cosmopolitan too, among them vanilla pannacotta with passionfruit and orange compôte.

Rooms 113 (20 fmly) (10 smoking) **S** £65-£180; **D** £70-£190* **Facilities** STV FTV Wi-fi **Conf** Class 60 Board 60 Thtr 100 Del from £125 to £195* **Services** Lift Air con **Notes** ⊗

Chef Gerry Sharkey **Owner** Chardon Leisure Ltd **Times** 12-2.15/5-10 **Prices** Fixed L 2 course £7.95-£21.95, Fixed D 2 course fr £16.95, Starter £4.95-£7.50, Main £14.95-£25.95, Dessert £4.95-£6.50, Service added but optional 12.5% **Wines** 32 bottles over £20, 15 bottles under £20, 10 by glass **Notes** Pre-theatre menu £16.95 from 5pm, Sunday L **Seats** 90, Pr/dining room 100 **Children** Portions, Menu **Parking** NCP opposite

Novotel Glasgow Centre

★★★ 79% HOTEL

☎ 0141 222 2775   📄 0141 204 5438
181 Pitt St G2 4DT
e-mail: H3136@accor.com
web: www.novotel.com
dir: M8 junct 18 for Charing Cross. Follow to Sauchiehall St. 3rd right

Enjoying a convenient city centre location and with limited parking spaces, this hotel is ideal for both business and leisure travellers. Well-equipped bedrooms are brightly decorated and offer functional design. Modern public areas include a small fitness club and a brasserie serving a range of meals all day.

Rooms 139 (139 fmly) **Facilities** Gym Sauna Steam room Xmas Wi-fi **Conf** Class 20 Board 20 Thtr 40 **Services** Lift Air con **Parking** 19

Best Western Glasgow City Hotel

★★★ 75% TOWN HOUSE HOTEL

☎ 0141 227 2772   📄 0141 227 2774
27 Elmbank St G2 4PB
e-mail: glasgowcity@mckeverhotels.co.uk
dir: M8 junct 18, Charing Cross into Sauchiehall St, 1st right into Elmbank St, pass petrol station, hotel on right

Situated in the heart of the city, this hotel offers spacious and well-equipped accommodation suitable for both families and business guests. Staff are friendly and helpful, and are mindful of the needs of the modern traveller. There is a secure pay car park close to the hotel.

Rooms 52 (4 fmly) (12 GF) **Facilities** FTV Xmas Wi-fi **Notes** ⊗

Argyll Hotel

★★★ 70% HOTEL

☎ 0141 337 3313 📄 0141 337 3283
973 Sauchiehall St G3 7TQ
e-mail: info@argyllhotelglasgow.co.uk
web: www.argyllhotelglasgow.co.uk
dir: M8 junct 18, stay in right lane, to 2nd lights. Right into
Berkley St, right into Elderslie St, 1st left into Sauchiehall St

Enjoying a prime city-centre location this popular hotel is
within easy reach of the main shopping district, the
university and the Scottish Exhibition & Conference Centre.
The bedrooms are attractively presented with a good range
of facilities including flat-screen TVs and free Wi-fi. The
public areas include Sutherlands Restaurant and a cosy
basement bar.

Rooms 38 (8 fmly) (5 GF) **S** £45-£65; **D** £60-£95 (incl.
bkfst)* **Facilities** FTV Wi-fi **Conf** Class 16 Board 20 Thtr 25
Del from £110 to £150* **Services** Lift **Parking** 5 **Notes** ⊗

Campanile Glasgow

BUDGET HOTEL

☎ 0141 287 7700 📄 0141 287 7701
10 Tunnel St G3 8HL
e-mail: glasgow@campanile.com
dir: M8 junct 19, follow signs to SECC. Hotel adjacent to
SECC

This modern building offers accommodation in smart, well-
equipped bedrooms, all with en suite bathrooms.
Refreshments may be taken at the informal bistro.

Rooms 106 (2 fmly) (21 GF) **Conf** Class 60 Board 90
Thtr 150

Holiday Inn Express Glasgow City Centre - Riverside

BUDGET HOTEL

☎ 0141 548 5000 📄 0141 548 5048
122 Stockwell St G1 4LT
e-mail: info@expressglasgow.co.uk
web: www.expressglasgow.co.uk
dir: M8 (E & S) junct 19 SECC, left at end of exit, follow river
under Central Station bridge to Stockwell St

Rooms 128 (79 fmly) (13 smoking) **Conf** Class 16 Board 16
Thtr 30 Del from £85 to £125

Holiday Inn Express, Glasgow Theatreland

BUDGET HOTEL

☎ 0141 331 6800 📄 0141 331 6828
165 West Nile St G1 2RL
e-mail: frontoffice.exp@higlasgow.com
web: www.hiexpressglasgow.co.uk
dir: Follow signs to Royal Concert Hall

A modern hotel ideal for families and business travellers.
Fresh and uncomplicated, the spacious rooms include Sky
TV, power shower and tea and coffee-making facilities.
Continental buffet breakfast is included in the room rate;
other meals may be taken at the nearby family pub or
restaurant.

Rooms 118 (34 fmly) (17 smoking) **S** £49-£139.95;
D £49-£139.95 (incl. bkfst)* **Conf** Board 12 Thtr 20

Ibis Glasgow

BUDGET HOTEL

☎ 0141 225 6000 📄 0141 225 6010
220 West Regent St G2 4DQ
e-mail: H3139@accor-hotels.com
web: www.ibishotel.com

Modern, budget hotel offering comfortable accommodation
in bright and practical bedrooms. Breakfast is self-service
and meals are also available in the café-bar 24 hours.

Rooms 141 **S** £55-£85; **D** £55-£85*

Premier Inn Glasgow (Bearsden)

BUDGET HOTEL

☎ 0871 527 8418 📄 0871527 8419
279 Milngavie Rd G61 3DQ
web: www.premierinn.com
dir: M8 junct 16, A81. Pass Asda on right. Hotel on left,
behind The Burnbrae

High quality, budget accommodation ideal for both families
and business travellers. Spacious, en suite bedrooms
feature tea and coffee-making facilities, and Freeview TV in
most hotels. Internet access and Wi-fi are available for a
small fee. The adjacent family restaurant features a wide
and varied menu.

Rooms 61 **D** £52-£60*

Premier Inn Glasgow (Bellshill)

BUDGET HOTEL

☎ 0871 527 8421 📄 0871 527 8421
New Edinburgh Rd, Bellshill ML4 3PD
web: www.premierinn.com
dir: M74 junct 5, A725. Follow Bellshill A721 signs, bear left.
At rdbt left, follow Tannochside sign. At next rdbt left into
Bellziehill Rd. Hotel on right

Rooms 40 **D** £54-£60*

Premier Inn Glasgow (Cambuslang/M74 Jct 1)

BUDGET HOTEL

☎ 0871 527 8422 📄 0871 527 8423
Cambuslang Investment Park, Off London Rd G32 8YX
web: www.premierinn.com
dir: At end of M74, turn right at rdbt. At 1st lights turn right,
at 2nd lights straight ahead. Hotel on right

Rooms 40 **D** £54-£60*

Premier Inn Glasgow City Centre Argyle St

BUDGET HOTEL

☎ 0871 527 8436 📄 0871 527 8437
377 Argyle St G2 8LL
web: www.premierinn.com
dir: From S: M8 junct 19, at pedestrian lights left into Argyle
St. Hotel 200yds on right

Rooms 121 **D** £59*

Premier Inn Glasgow City Centre (Charing Cross)

BUDGET HOTEL

☎ 0871 527 8438 📄 0871 527 8439
10 Elmbank Gardens G2 4PP
e-mail: glasgow@premierlodge.co.uk
web: www.premierinn.com
dir: Telephone for directions

Rooms 278 **D** £55*

Premier Inn Glasgow City Centre (George Square)

BUDGET HOTEL

☎ 0871 527 8440 📄 0871 527 8441
187 George St G1 1YU
web: www.premierinn.com
dir: M8 junct 15, into Stirling Rd. Right into Cathedral St. At
1st lights left into Montrose St. Hotel after 1st lights

Rooms 239 **D** £65*

Premier Inn Glasgow City Centre South

BUDGET HOTEL

☎ 0871 527 8442 📄 0871 527 8443
80 Ballater St G5 0TW
web: www.premierinn.com
dir: M8 junct 21 follow East Kilbride signs, right onto A8 into
Kingston St. Right into South Portland St, left into Norfolk St,
through Gorbals St into Ballater St

Rooms 114 **D** £60*

Premier Inn Glasgow East

BUDGET HOTEL

☎ 0871 527 8444 📄 0871 527 8445
601 Hamilton Rd, Uddington G71 7SA
web: www.premierinn.com
dir: At entrance to Glasgow Zoo, adjacent to junct 4 of M73
& M74

Rooms 66 **D** £54-£60*

Argyll Guest House

★★★ GUEST ACCOMMODATION

960 Sauchiehall St G3 7TH
☎ 0141 357 5155 📄 0141 337 3283
e-mail: info@argyllguesthouseglasgow.co.uk
web: www.argyllguesthouseglasgow.co.uk
dir: M8 junct 18 right hand lane, at 2nd set of lights turn
right onto Berkley St. Right onto Elderslie St, 1st left onto
Sauchiehall St

This very popular guest accommodation is close to the city
centre, the Scottish Conference and Exhibition centre and
the University. The bedrooms have all been refurbished and
each room is attractively presented, well equipped and
includes features like free Wi-fi. A full hot and cold buffet
breakfast is served at the adjacent Argyll Hotel.

Rooms 20 en suite (5 fmly) (5 GF) **Facilities** FTV tea/coffee
Direct Dial Cen ht Wi-fi **Notes** LB ⊗

Clifton Guest House

★★★ GUEST HOUSE

26-27 Buckingham Ter, Great Western Rd G12 8ED
☎ 0141 334 8080 📠 0141 337 3468
e-mail: kalam@cliftonhotelglasgow.co.uk
web: www.cliftonhotelglasgow.com
dir: 1.25m NW of city centre off A82 (Inverquhomery Rd)

Located north-west of the city centre, the Clifton forms part of an elegant terrace and is ideal for business and leisure. The attractive bedrooms are spacious, and there is an elegant lounge. Hearty breakfasts are served at individual tables in the dining room.

Rooms 23 rms (17 en suite) (6 fmly) (3 GF) Facilities STV TVL tea/coffee Direct Dial Cen ht Parking 8 Notes ⊗

Georgian House

★★★ GUEST HOUSE

29 Buckingham Ter, Great Western Rd G12 8ED
☎ 0141 339 0008 & 07973 971563
e-mail: thegeorgianhouse@yahoo.com
web: www.thegeorgianhousehotel.com
dir: M8 junct 17 towards Dumbarton, through 4 sets of lights & right onto Queen Margaret Dr, then right onto Buckingham Ter

Georgian House offers good value accommodation at the west end of the city in a peaceful tree-lined Victorian terrace near the Botanic Gardens. Bedrooms vary in size and are furnished in modern style. A continental style breakfast is served in the first-floor lounge-dining room.

Rooms 11 rms (10 en suite) (1 pri facs) (4 fmly) (3 GF) S £40-£60; D £70-£110* Facilities FTV tea/coffee Cen ht Wi-fi Parking 6 Notes LB

The Kelvin

★★★ GUEST HOUSE

15 Buckingham Ter, Great Western Rd, Hillhead G12 8EB
☎ 0141 339 7143 📠 0141 339 5215
e-mail: enquiries@kelvinhotel.com
web: www.kelvinhotel.com
dir: M8 junct 17, A82 Kelvinside/Dumbarton, 1m on right before Botanic Gardens

Two substantial Victorian terrace houses on the west side of the city have been combined to create this friendly establishment close to the Botanic Gardens. The attractive bedrooms are comfortably proportioned and well equipped with flat-screen TVs offering an array of channels, and Wi-fi available also. The dining room on the first floor is the setting for breakfasts served at individual tables.

Rooms 21 rms (9 en suite) (4 fmly) (2 GF) (14 smoking) S £30-£48; D £60-£68 Facilities FTV tea/coffee Cen ht Wi-fi Parking 5

Lomond

★★★ GUEST ACCOMMODATION

6 Buckingham Ter, Great Western Rd, Hillhead G12 8EB
☎ 0141 339 2339 📠 0141 339 0477
e-mail: info@lomondhotel.co.uk
web: www.lomondhotel.co.uk
dir: M8 junct 17, A82 Dumbarton, 1m on right before Botanic Gardens

Situated in the west end of the city in a tree-lined Victorian terrace, the Lomond offers well maintained, good value accommodation in a friendly environment. Bedrooms are brightly appointed and suitably equipped for leisure guests. Hearty breakfasts are served at individual tables in the bright ground-floor dining room.

Rooms 17 rms (6 en suite) (5 fmly) (3 GF) Facilities tea/coffee Direct Dial Cen ht

Craigielea House B&B

★★ Ⓐ BED AND BREAKFAST

35 Westercraigs G31 2HY
☎ 0141 554 3446 & 07890 991063
e-mail: craigieleahouse@yahoo.co.uk
dir: 1m E of city centre. M8 junct 15, onto A8, left onto Duke St, pass Tennents Brewery & left onto road after lights onto Craigpark. 3rd on left, then right onto Westercraigs

Rooms 3 rms (1 GF) S £28-£33; D £40-£50* Facilities FTV tea/coffee Cen ht Wi-fi Parking 3 Notes ⊗ No Children 3yrs 🐾

Brian Maule at Chardon d'Or

◉ French V 🍷 NOTABLE WINE LIST

Classical cooking in classy city-centre venue

☎ 0141 248 3801
176 West Regent St G2 4RL
e-mail: info@brianmaule.com
dir: 10 minute walk from Glasgow central station

Brian Maule's city-centre restaurant, close to the financial district, has been serving up refined French-inspired classical food based on superb Scottish produce since 2001. Chardon d'Or is home to a small bar with a range of whiskies, private function rooms, and the restaurant done out in a modish manner with suede and leather banquettes, high-backed chairs, wooden floors, cream walls and glass panels. The chef-patron is hands-on, ensuring everything is as it should be; expect the likes of cauliflower soup with tapenade croûtons, followed by grilled sea bream with braised Savoy cabbage and a caper butter sauce. Tarte Tatin is a suitably Gallic finale.

Chef Brian Maule **Owner** Brian Maule at Chardon d'Or **Times** 12-2/5-10 Closed 25-26 Dec, 1-2 Jan, 1 wk Jan, BHs, Sun, L Sat **Prices** Food prices not confirmed for 2012. Please telephone for details **Wines** 170 bottles over £20, 2 bottles under £20, 9 by glass **Notes** Tasting menu 6 course, Pre-theatre 5-6.30, 3 course set L, Vegetarian menu, Dress restrictions, Smart casual **Seats** 90, Pr/dining room 60 **Children** Portions **Parking** On street (metered)

Gamba

◉ Scottish, Seafood ◔

Vibrant fish and seafood in the West End

☎ 0141 572 0899
225a West George St G2 2ND
e-mail: info@gamba.co.uk
dir: On the corner of West Campbell St & West George St, close to Blythswood Sq

Gamba prides itself on a long-established reputation as the place to head for in Glasgow for all things fishy. The snug venue in the basement of a Georgian townhouse in the trendy West End goes for a clean-cut contemporary style involving terracotta floor tiles, pale wooden tables and plenty of piscine references in its fish-themed artwork - all very warm and simple, and nothing to distract from the business in hand. The kitchen draws on Mediterranean and Asian influences in an eclectic repertoire: starters can be as unadorned as half a dozen Donegal oysters, or as homely as smoked haddock fishcakes with thyme and lemon creamed leeks, but there might also be yellowfin tuna sashimi with wasabi, soy and pickled ginger. Oriental influences continue in a main course of sea bass with king prawns, ginger, spring onions and soy steamed in paper, while fillets of red mullet with chorizo peperonata call to those with a love of Mediterranean warmth.

Chef Derek Marshall **Owner** Mr D Marshall
Times 12-2.30/5-10.30 Closed 25-26 Dec, 1st wk Jan, L Sun **Prices** Fixed L 2 course £16.95, Starter £7.50-£14, Main £13.50-£42, Dessert £5.50-£8.50, Service optional, Groups min 6 service 12.5% **Wines** 60 bottles over £20, 8 bottles under £20, 8 by glass **Notes** Pre-theatre menu, 3 course market menu for 2 incl wine £50, Vegetarian available **Seats** 66 **Parking** On street

Jamie's Italian

◉ Italian

Jamie O's vibrant Italian chain

☎ 0141 404 2690
1 George Square G1 1HL
e-mail: glasgow@jamiesitalian.com
dir: On the corner of Hanover St, opposite the Millennium Hotel

The first of Jamie Oliver's blossoming chain to open north of the border, but doubtless not the last, the Glasgow Jamie's is smack-bang in the middle of the city in what was the GPO building. Through a grand pillared entrance is a vast space with high ceilings, large windows overlooking the square, and shelves stacked high with Italian foodstuffs. It's relaxed, unpretentious and full of energy - just like the man himself. The staff are passionate and hungry to impress. The antipasti boards are great for sharing, serving up excellent artisan cured meats, Italian cheeses and pickles, or start with something as richly comforting as porcini and chestnut mushroom soup. Rabbit ragu pappardelle is a delicious pasta option, while hearty main courses include British feather steak and burger Italiano. For dessert, ice cream comes in numerous tantalising flavours, or go for the creamy pannacotta with seasonal fruit compôte.

Chef Guy Callister **Owner** Jamie Oliver **Times** 12-11 Closed 25-26 Dec **Prices** Starter £3.55-£8.20, Main £9.45-£16.95, Dessert £4.50-£4.95, Service optional **Wines** 11 bottles over £20, 12 bottles under £20, 16 by glass **Notes** Vegetarian available, Air con **Seats** 240 **Children** Portions, Menu **Parking** George Square

La Parmigiana

◉◉ Italian, Mediterranean

Popular Italian eatery in the West End

☎ 0141 334 0686
447 Great Western Rd G12 8HH
e-mail: sgiovanazzi@btclick.com
web: www.laparmigiana.co.uk
dir: Opposite Hillhead underground station

Family-run La Parmigiana, on busy Great Western Road, has been going strong since it opened its doors in 1978, and it's

continued

easy to see why: a comfortable restaurant, with a striking colour scheme of red and cream, dealing in authentic Italian cooking. Pasta is made in-house, seen in perhaps farfalle with Italian sausage, basil and tomatoes, and the kitchen deploys fine Scottish produce, from Minch scallops, simply dressed with lime and olive oil, to fillet of beef in a creamy tarragon sauce. Treatments are not too complicated, resulting in dishes of forthright flavours, evident in veal escalopes with Parma ham, mozzarella and asparagus in a tomato and white wine jus, and in salmon fillet baked in pastry with basil sauce. Finish with gelato misto or strawberry semi-fredo. A set-price pre-theatre menu is served until 7.30.

Chef Peppino Camilli **Owner** Sandro & Stefano Giovanazzi **Times** 12-2.30/5.30-10.30 Closed 25-26 Dec, 1 Jan, Sun **Prices** Fixed L 3 course £15.90-£24.40, Fixed D 3 course £18.25-£26.25, Starter £5.40-£10.90, Main £15.90-£25.65, Dessert £5.90-£6.80, Service optional **Wines** 50 bottles over £20, 7 bottles under £20 **Notes** Pre-theatre 2 course £16.10, 3 course £18.25 5.30-7.30pm, Sunday L, Vegetarian available **Seats** 50 **Children** Portions

Shish Mahal

◉ Modern Indian, European

Long-standing Indian in a quiet part of the city

☎ 0141 339 8256
60-68 Park Rd G4 9JF
e-mail: reservations@shishmahal.co.uk
web: www.shishmahal.co.uk
dir: From M8/A8 take exit towards Dumbarton. On Great Western Rd 1st left into Park Rd

A Glaswegian institution of more than 50 years, Kelvinbridge's Shish Mahal commands a loyal following for its reliable classic Indian cooking. From the big window frontage to its warm, rustic Asian colours, leather seating and clothed tables, there's a modern feel, while informed, friendly service and an extensive repertoire of regional dishes all elevate it above the high-street curry-house norm. Firm favourites, fresh quality produce, accuracy and flavour refinement keep everyone happy. Classics like chicken tikka masala sit alongside rogan josh, or korma (perhaps a Mughlai rendition - prepared with crushed nuts and cream) to Hyderabadi biryani (maybe lamb or king prawn versions).

Roti and naan breads come freshly baked, while to finish, perhaps a chocolate samosa or kulfi (in pistachio or mango flavours).

Chef Mr I Humayun **Owner** Ali A Aslam, Nasim Ahmed **Times** 12-2/5-11 Closed 25 Dec, L Sun **Prices** Food prices not confirmed for 2012. Please telephone for details **Wines** 3 bottles over £20, 13 bottles under £20, 1 by glass **Notes** Fixed L 4 course, Vegetarian available **Seats** 95, Pr/dining room 14 **Children** Portions **Parking** Side street, Underground station car park

Stravaigin

◉◉ Modern International

Popular eatery with a 'think global, eat local' motto

☎ 0141 334 2665
28-30 Gibson St, Kelvinbridge G12 8NX
e-mail: stravaigin@btinternet.com
dir: Next to Glasgow University. 200yds from Kelvinbridge underground

A three-floor operation, with a distinctly contemporary décor, modern art and quirky antiques, Stravaigin never seems to disappoint. The kitchen makes the best use of fresh Scottish ingredients, giving them a modern, international interpretation. West Coast mussels, for example, come with sweet chilli and coriander sauce, and cep and celeriac 'cappuccino' is served with parmesan doughnuts. Pumpkin gratin with tapenade, a ricotta dumpling and Puy lentil cream has been a full-on vegetarian option, sitting alongside a trad haggis, neeps and tatties. Momentum doesn't flag at dessert stage: witness the real triumph of deep-fried coconut rice pudding ice cream with toffee pineapple and mango slaw.

Chef Doug Lindsay **Owner** Colin Clydesdale, Carol Wright **Times** 11-5/5-1am Closed 25 Dec, 1 Jan **Prices** Fixed L 2 course £10-£11.95, Service optional **Wines** 34 bottles over £20, 26 bottles under £20, 22 by glass **Notes** Pre-theatre menu 2 course £13.95, 3 course £15.95, Sunday L, Vegetarian available **Seats** 50, Pr/dining room 50 **Children** Portions, Menu **Parking** On street, car park 100yds

Ubiquitous Chip

 Scottish ⬥ NOTABLE WINE LIST

Ambitious modern Scottish cooking in a choice of rooms

☎ 0141 334 5007
12 Ashton Ln G12 8SJ
e-mail: mail@ubiquitouschip.co.uk
dir: In West End, off Byres Rd. Adjacent to Hillhead underground station

In 2011, the Chip celebrated its 40th anniversary, during which time this old stalwart in the heart of the West End has not failed to move with the times. It's a positive warren of dining venues, including a courtyard and rockery with a mezzanine level above it, a tiled dining room, a skylit brasserie, and three bars - the traditional pub, serving real ales, nearly 30 wines by the glass, more than 150 malt whiskies; the Wee Bar, which is indeed quite 'wee', possibly the wee-est in Scotland; and the Corner Bar, which serves cocktails across a granite slab reclaimed from a mortuary. Large colourful figure murals in what might politely be called the naïve style crop up throughout. At its most ambitious, the food in the restaurant offers a dynamic take on modern Scottish modes, incorporating an opener of grilled monkfish with smoked pancetta, haricots and tempura pea shoots in fennel and almond sauce, followed perhaps by breast of guinea fowl with roasted squash, beetroot purée and prune and Armagnac chutney, and concluding with either top-notch Scottish cheeses, or Hebridean snow egg with carrageen moss, toasted almonds and Grand Marnier.

Open all wk 11am-mdnt Closed: 25 Dec, 1 Jan **Bar Meals** L served all wk 12-11 D served all wk 12-11 Av main course £15 food served all day **Restaurant** L served Mon-Sat 12.30-2.30, Sun 12.30-3.30 booking required D served all wk 5.30-11 booking required Fixed menu price fr £39.95 food served all day ⊕ FREE HOUSE ◀ Deuchars IPA, The Chip 71 Ale. ♟ 29 **Facilities** Children welcome Children's menu Children's portions

Urban Bar and Brasserie

◉ Modern British, French

Modern brasserie food in a former bank building

☎ 0141 248 5636
23/25 St Vincent Place G1 2DT
e-mail: info@urbanbrasserie.co.uk
dir: In city centre between George Sq & Buchanan St

The chic modern brasserie was once one of those palatial banks, as evidenced by its now neoned-up portico entrance. Vivid modern paintings lighten the space, which is given an expansive feel by well-spaced tables and plenty of natural daylight. Some self-assured contemporary cooking brings on the likes of richly textured fish soup with ginger, coriander and prawn dumplings, sea bass with crayfish Caesar salad,

and grilled Barnsley chop with peas, pancetta and mint gravy. A full-on dark chocolate tart served with praline ice cream is the note to end on. The alternatives include a plated selection of British, Irish and French cheeses.

Chef John Gillespie **Owner** Alan Tomkins **Times** noon-10 Closed 25-26 Dec, 1-2 Jan **Prices** Fixed L 2 course fr £16.95, Fixed D 3 course fr £19.95, Starter £6-£12, Main £11-£22, Dessert £6-£7, Service optional, Groups min 6 service 10% **Wines** 40 bottles over £20, 20 bottles under £20, 10 by glass **Notes** Pre-theatre 5-6pm £16.95, Table d'hote £20, both incl wine, Sunday L, Vegetarian available **Seats** 110, Pr/dining room 20 **Children** Portions **Parking** NCP West Nile St

Bon Accord ♟

153 North St G3 7DA ☎ **0141 248 4427**
e-mail: paul.bonaccord@ntlbusiness.com
dir: M8 junct 19 merge onto A804 (North Street) signed Charing Cross

Paul and Thomas McDonagh run this award-winning ale house and malt whisky bar, patronised by tourists from all over the world, their taste buds primed for some of the annual tally of a thousand-plus different beers (perhaps at one of the four beer festivals), the 240-strong malts collection, or over 40 ciders. To line the stomach are all-day breakfasts, baguettes, jacket potatoes, burgers, fish dishes, grills and chicken salad, with Glamorgan sausage and macaroni cheese for vegetarians.

Open all day all wk **Bar Meals** L served all wk 12-8 D served all wk 12-8 Av main course £4.95 food served all day **Restaurant** food served all day ⊕ FREE HOUSE ◀ Over 1000 real ales per year ♙ Over 40 ciders per year. ♟ 11 **Facilities** Children welcome Garden Beer festival

Rab Ha's

83 Hutchieson St G1 1SH ☎ **0141 572 0400**
🖹 **0141 572 0402**
e-mail: management@rabhas.com
dir: Telephone for directions

In the heart of Glasgow's revitalised Merchant City, Rab Ha's takes its name from Robert Hall, a local 19th-century character known as 'The Glasgow Glutton'. This hotel, restaurant and bar blend Victorian character with

continued

GLASGOW CONTINUED

contemporary Scottish decor. Pre-theatre and set menus show extensive use of carefully sourced Scottish produce in starters like poached egg on grilled Stornoway black pudding, and pan-seared Oban scallops, followed by roast saddle of Rannoch Moor venison. Change of hands.

Open all day all wk noon-mdnt (Sun 12.30pm-mdnt) ⊕ FREE HOUSE ◪ Tennent's. **Facilities** Children welcome Children's portions

HIGHLAND

ACHILTIBUIE   Map 4 NC00

The Summer Isles Hotel

⚛⚛ Modern British **V**

Tranquil surroundings, superb sea views and top class Scottish ingredients

☎ 01854 622282
IV26 2YG
e-mail: info@summerisleshotel.co.uk
dir: 10m N of Ullapool. Left off A835 onto single track road. 15m to Achiltibuie. Hotel 100yds after post office on left

It takes effort to get to this hotel, lost among the elemental wilderness of islands and mountains in Scotland's far north west, but once visited the Summer Isles Hotel is never forgotten. Terry and Irina Mackay took the reins in 2008 from the Irvine family, who had run the place for 40 years and have continued with a wise 'if it ain't broke, don't fix it' approach - after all what's not to love about the far-flung location overlooking the Summer Isles and the Hebrides, and the refined but totally unstuffy ambience. The all-year bar at the side of the hotel is open all day, serving fresh ground coffee, snacks, lunch, afternoon tea and evening meals in an informal setting. (Note that the pub restaurant only serves food from April until October.) This is where the local crofters gathered to drink well over a century ago. Today they would probably ask for the list, such is the choice of ales and bottled beers available. Chief among these are the An Teallach Brewery draught ales, but multi-award-winning bottles from the Orkney Brewing Company are well worth trying too. In the restaurant, evenings revolve around five-course dinner menus, and you can expect superb Scottish ingredients since just about everything that turns up on the

plate is either made in-house, home-grown or locally caught. Proceedings might get under way with a filo parcel of monkfish with tamarind sauce and warm oatmeal bread; next, Summer Isles langoustines and spiny lobsters with hollandaise could be followed by roast rib of Aberdeen Angus beef with wild mushrooms and red onions in red wine, then the sweet trolley is wheeled in before superb Scottish cheeses bring down the curtain.

Chef Chris Firth-Bernard **Owner** Terry MacKay
Times 12.30-2/8 Closed mid Oct-Etr **Prices** Fixed L 2 course fr £58, Service included **Wines** 4 by glass **Notes** Fixed D 5 course, Vegetarian menu **Seats** 28 **Children** Portions
Parking 15

Open all wk noon-11 **Bar Meals** L served all wk 12-2.30, soup & snacks till 5 D served all wk 5-8.30 Av main course £13 food served all day **Restaurant** L served Apr-Oct 12.30-2.30 D served Apr-Oct all wk till 8 ⊕ FREE HOUSE ◪ An Teallach, Crofters Pale, Beinn Deorg.
Facilities Children welcome Children's menu Children's portions Garden Wi-fi

ARDELVE   Map 4 NG82

Caberfeidh House

★★★ GUEST HOUSE

IV40 8DY
☎ 01599 555293
e-mail: info@caberfeidh.plus.com
web: www.caberfeidh.plus.com
dir: A87 over Dornie Bridge into Ardelve, 1st left, 100yds on right

Set in a peaceful location overlooking Lochs Alsh and Duich, Caberfeidh House offers good value, comfortable accommodation in relaxed and friendly surroundings. Bedrooms are traditionally furnished and thoughtfully equipped, and there is a cosy lounge with a wide selection of books, games and magazines. Hearty breakfasts are served at individual tables in the dining room. Discount available for stays of two or more nights.

Rooms 5 rms (4 en suite) (1 pri facs) (3 fmly) S £32; D £64
Facilities FTV tea/coffee Cen ht **Parking** 4 **Notes** ⊗ Closed 25-26 Dec

ARISAIG

Map 4 NM68

Cnoc-na-Faire

★★★★ INN

🌹 Modern Scottish

Passionate Scottish cooking atop a hill

Back of Keppoch PH39 4NS
☎ 01687 450249 📠 01687 450249
e-mail: cnocnafaire@googlemail.com
dir: A830 1m past Arisaig, turn left onto B0080, 0.5m on left
into driveway

In an idyllic setting on a small knoll, this croft house turned
intimate inn enjoys marvellous views across white beaches
to the islands of Skye and Rum, and the Keppoch and Morar
hills. Indeed the name is Gaelic for 'hill of vigil'. Inside art
deco rubs shoulders with a bit of Scottish traditionalism.
Modern bedrooms and bathrooms cater well for guests'
needs. The bar is the best spot to enjoy the view, perhaps in
the company of a wee dram. The kitchen makes full use of
the fine produce on its doorstep, particularly the daily catch
from the Mallaig fishermen, to produce good honest,
Scottish-accented food. Arisaig mussels or partan bree
(creamy crab soup) might precede line fish of the day - dab,
perhaps, served with cherry tomatoes and fresh basil.

Rooms 6 en suite **Facilities** STV tea/coffee Dinner available
Cen ht Wi-fi Golf 9 **Conf** Max 20 Thtr 20 Class 16 Board 16
Parking 15 **Notes** Closed 23-27 Dec No coaches Civ Wed 25

Times 12-2/6-9 Closed 23-27 Dec

AVIEMORE

Map 5 NH81

Macdonald Highlands

★★★★ 75% HOTEL

☎ 01479 815100 📠 01479 815101
Aviemore Highland Resort PH22 1PN
e-mail: general@aviemorehighlandresort.com
web: www.aviemorehighlandresort.com
dir: From N: Exit A9 to Aviemore (B970). Right at T-junct,
through village. Right (2nd exit) at 1st rdbt into Macdonald
Aviemore Highland Resort, follow reception signs. From S:
Exit A9 to Aviemore, left at T-junct. Immediately after Esso
garage, turn left into Resort

This hotel is part of the Aviemore Highland Resort which
boasts a wide range of activities including a championship
golf course. The modern, well-equipped bedrooms suit
business, leisure guests and families, and Aspects
Restaurant is the fine dining option. In addition there is a
state-of-the-art gym, spa treatments and a 25-metre pool
with a wave machine and flume.

Rooms 151 (10 fmly) (44 GF) **S** £84-£225; **D** £89-£230 (incl.
bkfst) **Facilities** Spa STV FTV 🏊 supervised ⛳ 18 Putt green

Fishing Gym Steam room Sauna Children's indoor & outdoor
playgrounds Xmas New Year Wi-fi **Conf** Class 610 Board 38
Thtr 1000 Del from £110 to £260 **Services** Lift **Parking** 500
Notes ⊗ Civ Wed 300

Ravenscraig

★★★★ GUEST HOUSE

Grampian Rd PH22 1RP
☎ 01479 810278 📠 01479 810210
e-mail: info@aviemoreonline.com
web: www.aviemoreonline.com
dir: N end of main street, 250yds N of police station

This friendly, family-run guest house is on the north side of
the village, a short walk from local amenities. Bedrooms
vary between the traditionally styled rooms in the main
house and modern spacious rooms in a chalet-style annexe.
There is a relaxing lounge and separate dining room, where
freshly prepared breakfasts are served at individual tables.

Rooms 6 en suite 6 annexe en suite (6 fmly) (6 GF) S
£35-£42; D £70-£84* **Facilities** FTV TVL tea/coffee Cen ht
Wi-fi **Parking** 15 **Notes** ⊗

The Old Bridge Inn

Dalfaber Rd PH22 1PU ☎ 01479 811137
e-mail: sayhello@oldbridgeinn.co.uk
dir: Exit A9 to Aviemore, 1st right to Ski Rd, then 1st left
again 200mtrs

Overlooking the River Spey, this friendly pub is in an area
popular for outdoor pursuits and now with a new landlord.
Drink in the attractive riverside garden or in the relaxing
bars warmed by a roaring log fire. Here malt whiskies
naturally have their place, but not to the exclusion of
excellent real ales. In winter try a warming seasonal cocktail
while perusing the après-ski menu in the comfortable
restaurant. After an active day, a Dalfour brown trout starter
could easily be followed by a Geddes Farm chicken with
braised cabbage and Puy lentils.

Open all day all wk Mon-Thu 11am-mdnt (Fri-Sat 11am-
1am Sun 12.30-mdnt) **Bar Meals** L served Mon-Sat 12-3,
Sun 12.30-3 booking required D served Mon-Thu 6-9, Fri-Sat
6-10 booking required Av main course £13 **Restaurant** L
served Mon-Sat 12-3, Sun 12.30-3 booking required D
served Mon-Sat 12-3, Fri-Sat 6-10 booking required Fixed
menu price fr £23 Av 3 course à la carte fr £25 ⊕ FREE
HOUSE ◼ Deuchars IPA, Cairngorm Trade Winds, Cairngorm
Black Gold, Atlas Nimbus, Schiehallion Ŏ Thistly Cross
Cider. **Facilities** Children welcome Children's portions Dogs
allowed Garden Parking Wi-fi

BADACHRO — Map 4 NG77

The Badachro Inn

IV21 2AA ☎ 01445 741255 📠 01445 741319
e-mail: Lesley@badachroinn.com
dir: From Kinlochewe A832 towards Gairloch. Onto B8056, right to Badachro after 3.25m, towards quay

Expect great views from one of Scotland's finest anchorages at this convivial waterside pub, which has two moorings for visitors. Decking, with nautical-style sails and rigging, runs right down to the water overlooking Loch Gairloch. Interesting photographs and collages adorn the bar walls, where there is a dining area by a log fire. Friendly staff serve beers from the An Teallach or Caledonian breweries and a farm cider. A further dining conservatory overlooks the bay. Excellent fresh fish is the speciality of the house, along with dishes such as local venison terrine and chicken breast on crushed haggis, neeps and tatties.

Open all wk Closed: 25-26 Dec ⊕ FREE HOUSE ◀ Red Cullen, An Teallach, Blaven, 80/-, Guinness.
Facilities Children welcome Children's portions Dogs allowed Garden Parking Wi-fi

BALLACHULISH — Map 4 NN05

Lyn-Leven

★★★★ GUEST HOUSE

West Laroch PH49 4JP
☎ 01855 811392 📠 01855 811600
e-mail: macleodcilla@aol.com
web: www.lynleven.co.uk
dir: Off A82 signed on left West Laroch

Genuine Highland hospitality and high standards are part of the appeal of this comfortable guest house. The attractive bedrooms vary in size, are well equipped, and offer many thoughtful extra touches. There is a spacious lounge, and a smart dining room where delicious home-cooked breakfasts are served at individual tables.

Rooms 8 en suite 4 annexe en suite (3 fmly) (12 GF) S £45-£55; D £56-£70* Facilities TVL tea/coffee Cen ht Licensed Parking 12 Notes LB Closed Xmas

The Isles of Glencoe Hotel & Leisure Centre

★★★ 72% HOTEL

☎ 0845 906 9966 & 0844 855 9134 📠 01855 811 770
PH49 4HL
e-mail: reservations@akkeronhotels.com
web: www.akkeronhotels.com
dir: A82 N, slip road on left into village, 1st right, hotel in 600yds

This hotel enjoys a spectacular setting beside Loch Leven. This friendly modern establishment has spacious bedrooms and guests have a choice of Loch or Mountain View rooms. Public areas include a popular restaurant and a family friendly leisure centre.

Rooms 59 (21 fmly) (21 GF) S £59-£155; D £59-£165 (incl. bkfst)* Facilities STV ⊛ Gym Hydroseat Bio-sauna ♫ Xmas New Year Wi-fi Conf Class 40 Board 20 Thtr 40 Del from £70 to £140* Parking 100 Notes LB Civ Wed 100

BEAULY — Map 5 NH54

Priory

★★★ 74% HOTEL

☎ 01463 782309 📠 01463 782531
The Square IV4 7BX
e-mail: reservations@priory-hotel.com
web: www.priory-hotel.com
dir: Signed from A832, into Beauly, hotel in square on left

This popular hotel occupies a central location in the town square. Standard and executive rooms are on offer, both providing a good level of comfort and range of facilities. Food is served throughout the day in the open-plan public areas, with menus offering a first rate choice.

Rooms 37 (3 fmly) (1 GF) S £55-£62.50; D £70-£95 (incl. bkfst)* Facilities STV FTV Xmas New Year Wi-fi Conf Class 40 Board 30 Thtr 40 Del from £75 to £85* Services Lift Parking 20 Notes LB ⊗

Lovat Arms

★★★ 73% HOTEL

☎ 01463 782313 📠 01463 782862
IV4 7BS
e-mail: info@lovatarms.com
web: www.lovatarms.com
dir: From The Square past Royal Bank of Scotland, hotel on right

This fine family run hotel enjoys a prominent position in this charming town which is a short drive from Inverness. The bedrooms are comfortable and well appointed. The spacious foyer has a real fire and comfortable seating, while the Strubag lounge is ideal for informal dining.

Rooms 33 (12 annexe) (4 fmly) (6 GF) **Facilities** STV FTV Xmas New Year Wi-fi **Conf** Class 26 Board 40 Thtr 80 Del from £120 to £150* **Parking** 25 **Notes** Civ Wed 60

BOAT OF GARTEN   Map 5 NH91

Boat Hotel

★★★   80%   HOTEL

◉◉ Modern Scottish ☝

Modern bistro classics in a majestic Cairngorm setting

☎ 01479 831258   & 831696   🖹 01479 831414
PH24 3BH
e-mail: info@boathotel.co.uk
dir: Off A9 N of Aviemore onto A95, follow signs to Boat of Garten

With golf next door and skiing in the Cairngorms just a short drive from this beautifully-sited Victorian hotel, there's never an excuse for coming to table without a keenly-honed appetite. In such a traditional Scottish country hotel setting, you might expect the full best-bib-and-tucker formal approach to dining to be in force, but the panelled Osprey Bistro has moved with the times and gone for a more unbuttoned ambience with tealights on unclothed wooden tables and relaxed service led by a smartly turned-out young team. Excellent ingredients underpin the kitchen's appealing repertoire of unpretentious modern classics: smoked Rannoch Moor venison is tender enough to be served as carpaccio with rocket, fresh parmesan, and olive oil and thyme dressing, while braised lamb shank is teamed heartily with dauphinoise potatoes, crunchy sautéed mange-tout, and garlic and rosemary gravy. A richly indulgent finale involves dark chocolate fondant with walnut ice cream and Baileys crème anglaise. Individually styled bedrooms reflect the unique character of the hotel; all are comfortable and well equipped.

Rooms 34 (2 fmly) **Facilities** FTV Xmas New Year Wi-fi **Conf** Class 30 Board 25 Thtr 40 **Parking** 36 **Notes** Civ Wed 40

Chef Joseph Zilan **Owner** Mr J Erasmus & Mr R Drummond **Times** 12-3/7-9 Closed Dec-Feb (bookings only) **Prices** Starter £9.25-£9.95, Main £9.95-£24.95, Dessert £5.95-£7.25, Service optional **Wines** 40 bottles over £20, 6 bottles under £20, 8 by glass **Notes** Sunday L, Vegetarian available **Seats** 70, Pr/dining room 40 **Children** Portions, Menu

BONAR BRIDGE   Map 5 NH69

Kyle House

★★★ GUEST ACCOMMODATION

Dornoch Rd IV24 3EB
☎ 01863 766360
e-mail: kylehouse360@msn.com
dir: On A949 N from village centre

A spacious house with splendid views of the Kyle of Sutherland and the hills beyond. Bedrooms are comfortably furnished in traditional style and equipped with all the expected facilities. There is a lounge, and hearty breakfasts are enjoyed in the dining room.

Rooms 5 rms (3 en suite) (2 fmly) S £30-£50; D £60* **Facilities** FTV TVL tea/coffee Cen ht **Parking** 5 **Notes** ⊗ No Children 5yrs Closed Dec-Jan RS Oct & Apr Occasional closure (phone in advance) ✆

BRACHLA   Map 5 NH53

Loch Ness Lodge

★★★★★ 🛏 RESTAURANT WITH ROOMS

◉◉ French, Scottish

Modern Highland cooking overlooking Loch Ness

Loch Ness-Side IV3 8LA
☎ 01456 459469   🖹 01456 459439
e-mail: escape@loch-ness-lodge.com
web: www.loch-ness-lodge.com
dir: From A9 Inverness onto A82 signed Fort William, after 9m & 30mph speed sign, Lodge on right immediately after Clansman Hotel

A big white house on top of steeply shelving grounds on the western flank of Loch Ness, the Lodge makes an elegant contemporary restaurant with rooms, and each of the individually designed bedrooms enjoys views of the loch. The bedrooms are of the highest standard, and are beautifully presented with a mix of traditional luxury and up-to-date technology, including Wi-fi. There is a spa with a hot tub, sauna and a therapy room offering a variety of treatments. The rose-pink dining room has large picture windows commanding views of the Loch, the better to scan the waters for any sight of their most famous resident. A five-course dinner menu is the evening drill, with modern Scottish dishes making the most of fine Highland produce. Spring might see asparagus velouté with crispy snails start things off, to be followed by caramelised Moray pork belly with pickled fennel and shallot purée. Main course could be either rose veal with morels, or roasted monkfish tail on crushed potato in curry cream. A cheese course then precedes the dessert choice, which may include a spectacular burnt caramel soufflé with bitter chocolate sorbet.

continued

BRACHLA CONTINUED

Rooms 7 en suite (1 GF) S £204-£369; D £254-£419* (incl. dinner) **Facilities** Dinner available Direct Dial Cen ht Wi-fi Golf 18 Fishing Sauna Hot tub Therapy room **Conf** Max 14 Thtr 14 Class 10 Board 14 **Parking** 10 **Notes** LB ⊗ No Children 16yrs Closed 2-31 Jan No coaches Civ Wed 24

Chef Ross Fraser **Owner** Scott & Iona Sutherland **Times** 7-9 Closed 2-31 Jan, L all week (except by arrangement) **Prices** Fixed D 3 course £35, Service optional **Wines** 45 bottles over £20, 6 by glass **Notes** Fixed D 5 course £55, Dress restrictions, Smart casual **Seats** 14 **Children** Portions

| BRORA | Map 5 NC90 |

Royal Marine Hotel, Restaurant & Spa

★★★★ 77% HOTEL

◉ Modern Scottish

Traditional Highland hotel with reliable cooking

☎ 01408 621252   ▤ 01408 621181
Golf Rd KW9 6QS
e-mail: info@royalmarinebrora.com
web: www.royalmarinebrora.com
dir: Off A9 in village towards beach & golf course

With Brora's renowned golf course on its doorstep it is no surprise that this smartly refurbished Edwardian country-house hotel does service as the 19th hole. A modern bedroom wing complements the original bedrooms, which retain period style. There are also luxury apartments just a short walk away. If the action on the fairways is not your bag, there are splendid beaches and the charming village itself to help while away the hours until hunger strikes and dinner awaits in the natty traditional setting of Lorimer's Restaurant. Expect fine Scottish produce given a gently contemporary tweak in dishes that aim for all-round satisfaction - perhaps a trio of rabbit confit, caramelised pork belly, and local black pudding ballottine served with salsa verde, followed by Aberdeen Angus beef with a crisp haggis cake and creamy malt whisky sauce.

Rooms 21 (1 fmly) (2 GF) **Facilities** FTV 🏊 🎱 Putt green Fishing 🏌 Gym Steam room Sauna Xmas New Year Wi-fi **Conf** Class 40 Board 40 Thtr 70 **Parking** 40 **Notes** Civ Wed 60

Times 12-2/6.30-8.45 Closed L (pre booking only)

| CARRBRIDGE | Map 5 NH92 |

The Pines Country House

★★★ BED AND BREAKFAST

Duthil PH23 3ND
☎ 01479 841520   ▤ 01479 841520
e-mail: lynn@thepines-duthil.co.uk
dir: 2m E of Carrbridge in Duthil on A938

A warm welcome is assured at this comfortable home in the Cairngorms National Park. The bright bedrooms are traditionally furnished and offer good amenities. Enjoyable home-cooked fare is served around a communal table. Guests can relax in the conservatory-lounge and watch squirrels feed in the nearby wood.

Rooms 3 en suite (1 fmly) S £41.50-£45; D £60-£63.50* **Facilities** STV tea/coffee Dinner available Cen ht Wi-fi ch fac **Parking** 5 **Notes** LB

The Cairn

PH23 3AS ☎ 01479 841212   ▤ 01479 841362
e-mail: info@cairnhotel.co.uk
dir: In village centre

The Highland village of Carrbridge and this family-run inn make the perfect base for exploring the Cairngorms, the Moray coast and the Malt Whisky Trail. In the homely, tartan-carpeted bar, you'll find cracking Isle of Skye and Cairngorm ales on handpump, blazing winter log fires, all-day sandwiches, and hearty bar meals, including sweet marinated herring with oatcakes, venison sausage casserole, and sticky toffee pudding. Change of hands.

Open all day all wk 11-11 (Fri-Sat 11am-1am) ⊕ FREE HOUSE ◀ Cairngorm, Black Isle, Guest ales. **Facilities** Children welcome Children's menu Children's portions Dogs allowed Garden Parking Wi-fi

| CAWDOR | Map 5 NH85 |

Cawdor Tavern 🍷

The Lane IV12 5XP ☎ 01667 404777   ▤ 01667 404584
e-mail: enquiries@cawdortavern.co.uk
web: www.cawdortavern.co.uk
dir: From A96 (Inverness-Aberdeen) take B9006 & follow Cawdor Castle signs. Tavern in village centre

Tucked away in the heart of Cawdor's pretty village, the Tavern's near neighbour is the castle where Macbeth held court. Nairn's pretty wooded countryside slides away from the pub, offering umpteen opportunities for easy rambles before retiring to consider the welcoming mix of fine Scottish food and island micro-brewery ales that makes the pub a destination in its own right. There's an almost baronial feel to the bars, created from the Cawdor Estate's joinery workshop and featuring wonderful panelling which originated in the castle; log fires and stoves add winter warmth, as does the impressive list of Highland and Island malts. A highly accomplished menu balances meat, fish, game and vegetarian options, prepared in a modern Scottish style with first class Scottish produce. Settle in with a pint of Raven Ale from the respected Orkney Brewery and contemplate a starter of seafood platter, appetizers for mains covering pan-fried fillet of sea bream served on spinach crayfish-tail risotto, fillet of Moray pork encased in a sage and onion mousse, or local Brie, cranberry and chestnut risotto.

Open all wk 11-3 5-11 (Sat 11am-mdnt Sun 12.30-11) all day in summer Closed: 25 Dec, 1 Jan, 2wks mid Jan **Bar Meals** L served Mon-Sat 12-2, Sun 12.30-3 D served all wk 5.30-9 **Restaurant** L served Mon-Sat 12-2, Sun 12.30-3 booking required D served all wk 5.30-9 booking required ⊕ FREE HOUSE ◀ Red MacGregor, Three Sisters, Orkney Dark Island, Raven Ale, Latitude Highland Pilsner, Nimbus ♂ Thatchers Gold. ♟ 9 **Facilities** Children welcome Children's menu Children's portions Dogs allowed Garden Parking

DINGWALL — Map 5 NH55

Tulloch Castle

★★★★ 74% HOTEL

☎ 01349 861325 🗎 01349 863993
Tulloch Castle Dr IV15 9ND
e-mail: reservations.tulloch@ohiml.com
web: www.oxfordhotelsandinns.com
dir: A9 N, Tore rdbt 2nd left signed Dingwall, at Dingwall turn left at 4th lights, hotel signed

Overlooking the town of Dingwall this 12th-century castle is still the gathering place of the Clan Davidson and boasts its own ghost in the shape of the Green Lady. The friendly team are very helpful and love to tell you about the history of the castle; the ghost tour after dinner is a must. The hotel has a self contained suite and a number of bedrooms with four-posters.

Rooms 20 (2 fmly) **Facilities** FTV Xmas New Year Wi-fi **Conf** Class 70 Board 70 Thtr 120 Del from £160 to £180* **Parking** 50 **Notes** Civ Wed 110

DORNOCH — Map 5 NH78

Dornoch Castle Hotel

★★★ 75% HOTEL

◉ Modern Scottish ♥

Country-house cooking in a restored medieval castle

☎ 01862 810216 🗎 01862 810981
Castle St IV25 3SD
e-mail: enquiries@dornochcastlehotel.com
web: www.dornochcastlehotel.com
dir: 2m N of Dornoch Bridge on A9, turn right to Dornoch. Hotel in village centre

A mighty presence in a pretty town, Dornoch Castle was the former bishop's palace for the 12th-century cathedral that sits across the market square. Smartly restored and packed with baronial Scottish character, this ancient castle is a popular wedding venue. Within the original castle are some splendid themed bedrooms, and elsewhere the more modern bedrooms have all of the expected facilities. The dining room was once the bishop's kitchen, and has a crackling log fire in an 11-foot fireplace as a grand centrepiece, but equally inviting is the modern conservatory-style Garden restaurant which looks into the castle's walled garden. The kitchen deals in modern Scottish dishes, starting with a tender seared loin of rabbit on a ragoût of Puy lentils, carrot and thyme, following by excellent local cod, pan-fried and partnered with colourful vegetable ribbons, saffron cocotte potatoes, and lemon and herb butter sauce; local meat fans might find roast rack of Dornoch lamb sharing a plate with fondant potato, aubergine caviar and fresh thyme jus.

Rooms 22 (3 fmly) (4 GF) **Facilities** FTV New Year Wi-fi Child facilities **Conf** Class 40 Board 30 Thtr 60 **Parking** 16 **Notes** LB ✪ Closed 24-26 Dec & 2nd wk Jan

Chef Mikael Helies **Owner** Colin Thompson
Times 12-3/6-9.30 Closed 25-26 Dec **Prices** Fixed L 2 course £12.95, Fixed D 3 course £30-£35, Starter £6-£8.75, Main £17-£22, Dessert £7-£9, Service optional **Wines** 25 bottles over £20, 22 bottles under £20, 6 by glass **Notes** Early D special menu, Sunday L, Vegetarian available **Seats** 75, Pr/dining room 25 **Children** Portions, Menu

DORNOCH CONTINUED

2 Quail

★★★★★ GUEST ACCOMMODATION

Castle St IV25 3SN
☎ 01862 811811
e-mail: theaa@2quail.com
dir: On main street, 200yds from cathedral

The saying 'small is beautiful' aptly applies to this guest accommodation. Set in the main street the careful renovation of its Victorian origins transports guests back in time. Cosy public rooms are ideal for conversation, but there are masses of books for those just wishing to relax. The stylish, individual bedrooms match the character of the house but are thoughtfully equipped to include DVD players.

Rooms 3 en suite (1 fmly) S £70-£110; D £80-£120*
Facilities FTV tea/coffee Direct Dial Cen ht Licensed Wi-fi
Notes LB ⊗ No Children 8yrs Closed Xmas & 2 wks Feb/Mar
RS Nov-Mar winter hours - check when booking

DRUMNADROCHIT   Map 5 NH53

Ferness Cottage

★★★★ BED AND BREAKFAST

Lewiston IV63 6UW
☎ 01456 450564
e-mail: info@lochnessaccommodation.co.uk
web: www.lochnessaccommodation.co.uk
dir: A82, from Inverness turn right after Esso service station; from Fort William left before Esso service station, 100mtrs phone box on left. 100mtrs on right

This rose-covered cottage dating from the 1840s has a peaceful location and is within easy walking distance of the village centre. The two charming bedrooms are well equipped, with many thoughtful extra touches. Traditional breakfasts in the cosy lounge-dining room feature the best of local produce. Guests can use the grass area, with seating, beside the River Coiltie, where fishing is available.

Rooms 2 rms (1 en suite) (1 pri facs) S £50-£70; D £50-£70
Facilities STV tea/coffee Cen ht Wi-fi Fishing **Parking** 2
Notes LB ⊗ No Children 10yrs

EVANTON   Map 5 NH66

Kiltearn House

★★★★ A GUEST HOUSE

Kiltearn, Dingwall IV16 9UY
☎ 01349 830617   ▤ 01349 830617
e-mail: info@kiltearn.co.uk
dir: Off A9 towards Evanton, follow signs for burial ground

Rooms 5 en suite S £72-£84; D £120-£150* **Facilities** FTV TVL tea/coffee Dinner available Cen ht Licensed Wi-fi
Parking 6 **Notes** LB ⊗ No Children 12yrs

FORT AUGUSTUS   Map 5 NH30

Inchnacardoch Lodge Hotel

★★★ 73% SMALL HOTEL

◉ Modern Scottish

Loch Ness views, confident cooking

☎ 01456 450900   ▤ 01320 366294
Inchnacardoch Bay PH32 4BL
e-mail: info@inchhotel.com
web: www.inchhotel.com

Known as The Inch, this hotel has a fantastic setting on the shore of Loch Ness within the Great Glen. The 150-year old hunting lodge turned country-house hotel is traditionally done out; the bedrooms are very individual in style and the Bridal Suite has stunning views. Guests can expect the finest of highland hospitality here from staff that are always eager to please. The Yard restaurant has high ceilings, polished wooden floors, smartly set tables, and local artwork on the walls (available to buy). Oh yes, and fabulous views over Loch Ness. The menu is based on quality local produce cooked with a degree of refinement. Start with a visually impressive roast boudin of wild rabbit with carrot and cumin purée, garlic confit and pea salsa, before boned and rolled oxtail wrapped in crispy Parma ham, and served with sautéed curly kale, confit new potatoes and oxtail jus. Save room for Glenmorangie bread-and-butter pudding with vanilla pod ice cream. There's an impressively stocked whisky bar, too.

Rooms 14 (2 fmly) **S** £69.99-£89.99; **D** £69.99-£140 (incl. bkfst)* **Facilities** FTV Fishing Xmas New Year Wi-fi
Conf Class 26 Board 18 Thtr 20 Del from £179 to £239*
Parking 30 **Notes** LB Civ Wed 40

Times 7-10

FORTROSE   Map 5 NH75

The Anderson ♥

Union St IV10 8TD ☎ **01381 620236**
e-mail: info@theanderson.co.uk
dir: From Inverness take A9 N signed Wick. Right onto B9161
signed Munlochy, Cromarty A832. At T-junct right onto A832
to Fortrose

In a tranquil seaside setting on the beautiful Black Isle to
the north of Inverness; a short walk from the striking black-
and-white painted pub passes the gaunt, ruined cathedral
before happening on the picturesque harbour at Fortrose,
with sweeping views across the Moray Firth. Nearby
Chanonry Point lighthouse is renowned as one of the best
places from which to watch the dolphins of the Firth. But
why leave an inn famed for its classic range of finest
Scottish micro-brewery beers, vast array of Belgian beers
and 230 single malts selected by American proprietor and
head mop slinger Jim Anderson?! The 'Global cuisine'
created with freshest Scottish produce is equally
comprehensive. Aberdeen beef, West Coast seafood and
Highland game are amongst dishes that may inhabit the
daily-changing menu: Manhattan seafood chowder or peat-
smoked haddock fritters an opening indulgence to be
followed by Stornoway guinea fowl stuffed with local white
pudding with a creamy leek and Somerset cider sauce, or
baby beef stew cooked in Timmerman's Lambicus beer. Co-
owner Anne Anderson trained as a chef in New Orleans, so
expect unexpected twists to add spice.

Open all wk 4pm-11.30pm (Sun 12.30-11.30) Closed: 10
Nov-18 Dec **Bar Meals** L served Sun fr 1pm D served all wk
fr 6pm booking required Av main course £11 **Restaurant** L
served Sun fr 1pm D served all wk fr 6pm booking required
Av 3 course à la carte fr £21 ⊞ FREE HOUSE ◀ Rotating
ales ⊘ Westons 1st Quality, Gwynt y Ddraig Black Dragon.
♥ 13 **Facilities** Children welcome Children's menu Dogs
allowed Garden Beer festival Parking Wi-fi

FORT WILLIAM   Map 5 NN17

See also Spean Bridge

Inverlochy Castle

★★★★★ COUNTRY HOUSE HOTEL

◉◉◉ Modern British **V** ♦ NOTABLE WINE LIST

Stunning country-house hotel in the foothills of Ben Nevis

☎ 01397 702177   📄 01397 702953
Torlundy PH33 6SN
e-mail: info@inverlochy.co.uk
web: www.inverlochycastlehotel.com
dir: Accessible from either A82 (Glasgow-Fort William) or A9
(Edinburgh-Dalwhinnie). Hotel 3m N of Fort William on A82,
in Torlundy

Queen Victoria described this place as 'one of the loveliest
and most romantic spots' and monarchs are not wont to be
sycophantic - it is indeed a gem of a location. The grand pile
(castle is a worthy moniker) built in the foothills of Ben
Nevis to the highest of Victorian spec is surrounded by 600
acres of beautifully landscaped gardens and stands beside
its own loch. If the outside makes a good impression, the
inside is no less memorable: the hotel is luxuriously done out
in the traditional manner with fine antiques and lavish
furnishings. Lavishly appointed in classic country-house
style, spacious bedrooms are extremely comfortable and
boast flat-screen TVs and laptops with internet access. The
furniture in the three dining rooms was a gift from the King
of Norway and continues the theme of sumptuous splendour
in rooms of fine period detail. So...a smart setting for some
traditional food? Not quite. Chef Philip Carnegie is an
exponent of refined modern cooking and produces the likes
of spatchcock quail with ginger-spiced vegetables and a soy
and lemongrass jus, or another first-course of seared skate
wing with speck-wrapped fennel and chorizo foam. Excellent
use is made of the local larder and some produce is home-
grown. Main-course corn-fed pigeon might come with petit
pois tortellini, morels and pea shoots, and to finish, perhaps
a trio of sorbets with fresh fruit and lime syrup. This is a
formal affair and jackets and ties are required, gents.

Rooms 17 (6 fmly) **S** £375-£695; **D** £440-£695 (incl. bkfst)*
Facilities STV 🏊 ⛳ Fishing on loch Massage Riding
Hunting Stalking Clay pigeon shooting Archery ♫ Xmas New
Year Wi-fi **Conf** Class 20 Board 20 Thtr 50 **Parking** 17
Notes LB Civ Wed 80

Chef Philip Carnegie **Owner** Inverlochy Hotel Ltd
Times 12.30-1.45/6.30-10 **Prices** Fixed L 2 course £28,
Fixed D 4 course £67, Service added but optional **Wines** 283
bottles over £20, 8 by glass **Notes** Vegetarian menu, Dress
restrictions, Jacket & tie for D **Seats** 40, Pr/dining room 20
Children Portions, Menu

Ben Nevis, as seen from Bonarie, Highlands

Moorings

★★★ 82% HOTEL

◉ Modern European

Popular Highland hotel with accomplished cooking

☎ 01397 772797 📄 01397 772441
Banavie PH33 7LY
e-mail: reservations@moorings-fortwilliam.co.uk
web: www.moorings-fortwilliam.co.uk
dir: Take A830 (N from Fort William), cross Caledonian
Canal, 1st right

Considering its tranquil location, there's plenty going on
around the Moorings Hotel. You could hike in the steps of
World War II commandos who trained in the Great Glen,
watch boats climbing the heroic flight of locks known as
Neptune's Staircase on the Caledonian Canal as it leaves
Loch Linnhe, or turn up to wave at the Jacobite train as it
steams past on its way to the fishing port of Mallaig.
Accommodation comes in two distinct styles and the newer
rooms are particularly appealing. The beamed restaurant
offers the pick of local seafood and game in a menu of
uncomplicated modern Scottish dishes. Start, perhaps, with
a trio of Highland salmon - gravad lax with mustard cream,
hot-smoked, and salmon tartare with dill mayonnaise -
followed by roast rump of lamb with buttered cabbage,
fondant potato and garlic and rosemary jus. Finish with malt
whisky cranachan with raspberries and home-made
shortbread.

Rooms 27 (2 fmly) (1 GF) **S** £49-£138; **D** £70-£148 (incl.
bkfst)* **Facilities** STV Gym New Year Wi-fi **Conf** Class 60
Board 40 Thtr 140 Del from £90 to £120* **Parking** 60
Notes LB Closed 24-26 Dec Civ Wed 120

Chef Paul Smith **Owner** Mr S Leitch **Times** 7-9.30
Closed 24-26 Dec, L all week **Prices** Fixed D 3 course fr £30,
Service optional **Wines** 17 bottles over £20, 28 bottles under
£20, 7 by glass **Notes** Vegetarian available, Dress
restrictions, Smart casual **Seats** 60, Pr/dining room 120
Children Portions

Lime Tree Hotel & Restaurant

★★★ 78% SMALL HOTEL

◉◉ Modern European

Modern cooking in charming restaurant and art gallery

☎ 01397 701806 📄 01397 701806
Lime Tree Studio, Achintore Rd PH33 6RQ
e-mail: info@limetreefortwilliam.co.uk
web: www.limetreefortwilliam.co.uk
dir: On A82 at entrance to Fort William

A stylish amalgam of boutique hotel, restaurant and art
gallery, the Lime Tree sits in the heart of Fort William, and
comes with uplifting views of Loch Linnhe and the
mountains beyond. The old stone manse has been reworked
in a modern, pared-back style, and individually designed
bedrooms are spacious, with some nice little personal
touches courtesy of the artist owner. In the restaurant the
neutral-hued walls are hung with an ever-changing cast of
local artists' work above wooden floors and unclothed tables.
The kitchen has earned itself a fiercely loyal local fan base
who come for the vibrant modern Scottish cooking built from
pedigree local ingredients. A good-looking starter teams
smoked ham hock and parsley terrine with herb purée and
apple chutney, while braised artichokes, violet potatoes and
salsa verde add similarly colourful impact to a main-course
starring pan-fried sea bass. Poached rhubarb crowdie
cheesecake mousse with ginger honeycomb finishes in style
with an entertaining array of flavours and textures.

Rooms 9 (4 fmly) (4 GF) **S** £110; **D** £110 (incl. bkfst)*
Facilities New Year Wi-fi **Conf** Class 40 Board 30 Thtr 60
Del from £200* **Parking** 9 **Notes** Closed 24-26 Dec

Chef Ross Sutherland **Owner** David Wilson & Charlotte
Wright **Times** 6.30-9 Closed 24-26 Dec, L all week
Prices Fixed D 4 course £29.95, Service optional **Wines** 14
bottles over £20, 17 bottles under £20, 5 by glass
Notes Vegetarian available, Civ Wed 50 **Seats** 30
Children Portions

Alexandra Hotel

★★★ 75% HOTEL

☎ 01397 702241 📠 01397 705554
The Parade PH33 6AZ
e-mail: salesalexandra@strathmorehotels.com
dir: Off A82. Hotel opposite railway station

This charming old hotel enjoys a prominent position in the town centre and is just a short walk from all the major attractions. Front-facing bedrooms have views over the town and the spectacular Nevis mountain range. There is a choice of restaurants, including a bistro serving meals until late, along with several stylish and very comfortable lounges.

Rooms 93 (2 fmly) **S** £69-£89; **D** £99-£120 (incl. bkfst)*
Facilities Free use of nearby leisure club ♫ Xmas New Year Wi-fi **Conf** Class 100 Board 40 Thtr 120 **Services** Lift **Parking** 50 **Notes** LB

Ben Nevis Hotel & Leisure Club

★★ 75% HOTEL

☎ 01397 702331 📠 01397 700132
North Rd PH33 6TG
e-mail: bennevismanager@strathmorehotels.com
dir: Off A82

This popular hotel is ideally situated on the outskirts of Fort William. It provides comfortable, well equipped bedrooms; many with views of the impressive Nevis mountains. The hotel's leisure centre is a firm favourite with guests at the hotel.

Rooms 119 (3 fmly) (30 GF) **Facilities** ⊛ supervised Gym Beauty salon ♫ Xmas New Year Wi-fi **Conf** Class 60 Board 40 Thtr 150 **Parking** 100 **Notes** Civ Wed 60

Croit Anna

★★ 71% HOTEL

☎ 01397 702268 📠 01397 704099
Achintore Rd, Drimarben PH33 6RR
e-mail: croitanna.fortwilliam@alfatravel.co.uk
dir: From Glencoe on A82 into Fort William, hotel 1st on right

Located on the edge of Loch Linnhe, just two miles out of town, this hotel offers some spacious bedrooms, many with fine views over the loch. There is a choice of two comfortable lounges and a large airy restaurant. The hotel appeals to coach parties and independent travellers alike.

Rooms 92 (5 fmly) (13 GF) **S** £37-£52; **D** £58-£88 (incl. bkfst) **Facilities** FTV Pool table ♫ Xmas New Year **Parking** 25 **Notes** LB ⊗ Closed Dec-Jan (ex Xmas) RS Nov, Feb, Mar

Premier Inn Fort William

BUDGET HOTEL

☎ 0871 527 8402 📠 0871 527 8403
Loch Iall, An Aird PH33 6AN
web: www.premierinn.com
dir: N end of Fort William Shopping Centre, just off A82 (ring road)

High quality, budget accommodation ideal for both families and business travellers. Spacious, en suite bedrooms feature tea and coffee-making facilities, and Freeview TV in most hotels. Internet access and Wi-fi are available for a small fee. The adjacent family restaurant features a wide and varied menu.

Rooms 40 **D** £69*

Distillery Guest House

★★★★ GUEST HOUSE

Nevis Bridge, North Rd PH33 6LR
☎ 01397 700103
e-mail: disthouse@aol.com
dir: A82 from Fort William towards Inverness, on left after Glen Nevis rdbt

Situated in the grounds of the former Glenlochy Distillery, this friendly guest house was once the distillery manager's home. Bedrooms are attractively decorated, comfortably furnished and very well equipped. There is a relaxing lounge, which features a superb range of games, and a bright airy dining room where traditional Scottish breakfasts are served at individual tables.

Rooms 10 en suite (1 fmly) (1 GF) **Facilities** tea/coffee Cen ht Licensed **Parking** 21 **Notes** ⊗

Mansefield Guest House

★★★★ GUEST HOUSE

Corpach PH33 7LT
☎ 01397 772262 & 0845 6449432
e-mail: mansefield@btinternet.com
web: www.fortwilliamaccommodation.com
dir: 2m N of Fort William A82 onto A830, house 2m on A830 in Corpach

Peacefully set in its own well-tended garden this friendly, family-run guest house provides comfortable, attractively decorated and well-equipped accommodation. There is a cosy lounge, where a roaring coal fire burns on cold evenings, and an attractive dining room where delicious, home-cooked evening meals and breakfasts are served at individual tables.

Rooms 6 en suite (1 GF) S £35-£40; D £60-£65 **Facilities** FTV TVL tea/coffee Dinner available Cen ht Wi-fi Golf 18 **Parking** 7 **Notes** LB ⊗ No Children 12yrs

Stobhan B&B

★★★ BED AND BREAKFAST

Fassifern Rd PH33 6BD
☎ 01397 702790 📠 01397 702790
e-mail: boggi@supanet.com
dir: In town centre. A82 onto Victoria Rd beside St Mary's Church, right onto Fassifern Rd

Stobhan B&B occupies an elevated location overlooking Loch Linnhe and offers comfortable, good-value accommodation. Bedrooms, one of which is on the ground floor, are traditionally furnished and have en suite facilities. Breakfast is served in the ground-floor dining room, which is adjacent to the lounge.

Rooms 4 en suite (1 GF) S £28-£35; D £56-£70
Facilities FTV tea/coffee Cen ht

FOYERS   Map 5 NH42

Craigdarroch House

★★★★ 🍴 RESTAURANT WITH ROOMS

IV2 6XU
☎ 01456 486400 📠 01456 486444
e-mail: info@hotel-loch-ness.co.uk
dir: Take B862 from either end of loch, then B852 signed Foyers

Craigdarroch is located in an elevated position high above Loch Ness on the south side. Bedrooms vary in style and size but all are comfortable and well equipped; those that are front-facing have wonderful views. Dinner is well worth staying in for, and breakfast is also memorable.

Rooms 8 en suite (1 fmly) S £65-£95; D £99-£160
Facilities FTV TVL tea/coffee Dinner available Direct Dial Cen ht Wi-fi **Conf** Max 30 Thtr 30 Class 30 Board 30
Parking 24 **Notes** No coaches Civ Wed 30

Foyers Bay Country House

★★★ GUEST HOUSE

Lochness IV2 6YB
☎ 01456 486624
e-mail: enquiries@foyersbay.co.uk
dir: Off B852 into Lower Foyers

Situated in sloping grounds with pines and abundant colourful rhododendrons, this delightful Victorian villa has stunning views of Loch Ness. The attractive bedrooms vary in size and are well equipped. There is a comfortable lounge next to the plant-filled conservatory-café, where delicious evening meals and traditional breakfasts are served.

Rooms 6 en suite (1 GF) S £55-£65; D £70-£95*
Facilities FTV TVL tea/coffee Dinner available Cen ht Licensed Wi-fi **Conf** Max 20 Thtr 20 Class 20 Board 20
Parking 6 **Notes** LB ⊗ No Children 16yrs Civ Wed 20

GAIRLOCH   Map 4 NG87

The Old Inn

IV21 2BD ☎ 01445 712006 📠 01445 712933
e-mail: info@theoldinn.net
web: www.theoldinn.net
dir: Just off A832, near harbour at south end of village

This former changing house for horses enjoys a wonderful setting at the foot of the Flowerdale valley. Built in 1750, Gairloch's oldest hostelry boasts views of Outer Hebrides and attracts many outdoor enthusiasts especially walkers. Long established as a real ale pub, owner Alastair Pearson has now opened the pub's very own on-site micro-brewery so expect the pints of Slattadale and Flowerdale to be in tip-top condition at the bar; more ales are planned. Fresh local seafood features prominently on the menu, which also includes home-made pies, oven bakes and casseroles. Typical choices include Highland lamb pie; West Coast seafood platter; grilled or steamed local mussels; and braised beef ribs. Picnic tables on the large grassy area by the stream make an attractive spot for eating and enjoying the views. Dogs are welcomed with bowls, baskets and rugs to help them feel at home.

Open all day all wk 11am-mdnt (Sun noon-mdnt) **Bar Meals** L served all wk 12-2.30 (summer 12-4.30) D served all wk 5-9.30 Av main course £12 **Restaurant** D served all wk 6-9.30 booking required Fixed menu price fr £27.50 ⊕ **FREE HOUSE** 🍺 Adnams Bitter, An Teallach, Deuchars IPA, Wildcat, Erradale, Flowerdale, Crofters, Trade Winds, Slattadale, Three Sisters. **Facilities** Children welcome Children's menu Children's portions Play area Family room Dogs allowed Garden Parking Wi-fi

GLENCOE   Map 4 NN15

Lyn-Leven

★★★★ GUEST HOUSE

West Laroch PH49 4JP
☎ 01855 811392   📄 01855 811600
e-mail: macleodcilla@aol.com
web: www.lynleven.co.uk

(For full entry see Ballachulish)

Scorrybreac

★★★★ GUEST ACCOMMODATION

PH49 4HT
☎ 01855 811354
e-mail: info@scorrybreac.co.uk
web: www.scorrybreacglencoe.com
dir: Off A82 just outside village, 500yds from River Coe bridge

With a stunning location above the village and overlooking the loch, this charming family-run guest accommodation offers guests a warm welcome. Bedrooms are attractive, well equipped and comfortably furnished. There is a cosy lounge with plenty of books, board games and maps, and a bright airy dining room where delicious breakfasts are served at individual tables.

Rooms 6 en suite (6 GF) Facilities tea/coffee Cen ht Parking 7 Notes ⊗ Closed 25-26 Dec

GLENFINNAN   Map 4 NM98

The Prince's House

★★★ 75% SMALL HOTEL

◉◉ Modern British ☙

Confident Scottish cooking in an old coaching inn

☎ 01397 722246   📄 01397 722323
PH37 4LT
e-mail: princeshouse@glenfinnan.co.uk
web: www.glenfinnan.co.uk
dir: On A830, 0.5m on right past Glenfinnan Monument. 200mtrs from railway station

Privately run and with bags of character, this hotel is in a fantastic Highland spot in the heart of Bonnie Prince Charlie country. Dating back to the 17th century, the restaurant is in the oldest part of the hotel and makes a feature of the log-burning fireplace, while the adjoining conservatory is the place to kick-back after a meal. Chef-proprietor Keiron Kelly runs the kitchen, often singlehandedly, serving up local ingredients from the land and sea. To begin, West Coast scallops come in a fashionable partnership with braised belly pork, plus wilted baby gem lettuce and thyme gravy,

while main-course pan-seared loin of Lochaber lamb comes with parsnip fondant, red wine-baked mushrooms and green peppercorn jus. The cooking shows sound technique right the way to the end; excellent pastry skills, for example, witnessed in a light apple and almond tart with vanilla mascarpone sorbet.

Rooms 9 S £65-£75; D £95-£140 (incl. bkfst)*
Facilities STV FTV Fishing New Year Wi-fi Conf Class 20 Thtr 40 Parking 18 Notes LB Closed Xmas & Jan-Feb (ex New Year) RS Nov-Dec & Mar

Chef Kieron Kelly Owner Kieron & Ina Kelly Times 7-9 Closed Xmas, Jan-Feb, Low season - booking only, L all week Prices Fixed D 3 course £38-£45, Service included Wines 70 bottles over £20, 12 bottles under £20, 8 by glass Notes Vegetarian available Seats 30 Children Portions

GOLSPIE   Map 5 NC80

Granite Villa Guest House

★★★★ GUEST ACCOMMODATION

Fountain Rd KW10 6TH
☎ 01408 633146
e-mail: info@granite-villa.co.uk
dir: Left from A9 (N'bound) onto Fountain Rd, immediately before pedestrian crossing lights

Originally built in 1892 for a wealthy local merchant, this traditional Victorian house has been sympathetically restored in recent years. Bedrooms are comfortable and all come with a range of thoughtful extras. Guests can relax in the large lounge, with its views over the landscaped garden where complimentary tea and coffee is often served. A warm welcome is assured in this charming period house.

Rooms 5 en suite (1 fmly) (1 GF) (2 smoking) S £45-£50; D £70* Facilities FTV tea/coffee Cen ht Wi-fi Golf 18 Parking 6 Notes ♨

GRANTOWN-ON-SPEY   Map 5 NJ02

Grant Arms Hotel

★★★ 79% HOTEL

☎ 01479 872526   📄 01479 873589
25-27 The Square PH26 3HF
e-mail: info@grantarmshotel.com
web: www.grantarmshotel.com
dir: Exit A9 N of Aviemore onto A95

Conveniently located in the centre of the town, this fine hotel has now been refurbished and upgraded to a high standard yet still retains the building's traditional character. The spacious bedrooms are stylishly presented and very well equipped. The Garden Restaurant is a popular venue for dinner, and lighter snacks can be enjoyed in the comfortable

continued

bar. Modern conference facilities are available and the hotel is very popular with birdwatchers and wildlife enthusiasts.

Rooms 50 (4 fmly) **S** £45-£80; **D** £90-£160 (incl. bkfst) **Facilities** STV FTV Home to Birdwatching & Wildlife Club ♫ Xmas New Year Wi-fi **Conf** Class 30 Board 16 Thtr 70 Del from £95 to £125 **Services** Lift **Notes** LB

An Cala

★★★★★ 🅰 GUEST HOUSE

Woodlands Ter PH26 3JU
☎ 01479 873293 📄 01479 873610
e-mail: ancala@globalnet.co.uk
web: www.ancalaguesthouse.co.uk
dir: From Aviemore on A95 left onto B9102 at rdbt outside Grantown. After 400yds, 1st left, An Cala opposite

Rooms 4 en suite (1 fmly) **D** £80-£86* **Facilities** FTV TVL tea/coffee Dinner available Cen ht Wi-fi **Parking** 7 **Notes** LB ⊗ No Children 3yrs Closed Xmas RS Nov-Mar Phone/e-mail bookings only

Holmhill House

★★★★ GUEST ACCOMMODATION

Woodside Av PH26 3JR
☎ 01479 873977
e-mail: enquiries@holmhillhouse.co.uk
web: www.holmhillhouse.co.uk
dir: S of town centre off A939 Spey Av

Built in 1895, and situated in a large well-tended garden within walking distance of the town centre, Holmhill House combines Victorian character with modern comforts. The attractive bedrooms are well equipped, and en suite. There a ramp and lift available for easier access plus a specially equipped bathroom.

Rooms 3 en suite **D** £80-£90* **Facilities** FTV tea/coffee Cen ht Lift Wi-fi **Parking** 9 **Notes** ⊗ No Children 12yrs Closed Nov-Mar

Glengarry Castle

★★★ 82% COUNTRY HOUSE HOTEL

 Scottish, International

Country-house comfort food by Loch Oich

☎ 01809 501254 📄 01809 501207
PH35 4HW
e-mail: castle@glengarry.net
web: www.glengarry.net
dir: On A82, 0.5m from A82/A87 junct

The house was built in the 1860s for the Ellice family, who had got rich in the Canada fur and logging trades. It stands on the wooded shore of Loch Oich, barely a stone's throw from the ruined castle of the same name, from where Bonnie Prince Charlie planned his getaway to France. History lessons absorbed, we can settle to enjoying the sumptuous views, and the high-toned Victorian style of the dining room with its striped upholstery and crisp table linen. Fixed-price dinner menus might start with hot-smoked salmon seasoned with honey and ginger in tomato and dill dressing, pause for a soup or sorbet, and then proceed with roast pork loin stuffed with apple and chestnuts in red wine jus. A properly luxurious rendition of cranachan, with all its canonical ingredients present and correct, is the way to finish. The smart bedrooms vary in size and style but all boast magnificent loch or woodland views.

Rooms 26 (2 fmly) **S** £67-£77; **D** £118-£180 (incl. bkfst) **Facilities** FTV 🎣 Fishing Wi-fi **Parking** 30 **Notes** Closed mid Nov-mid Mar

Chef John McDonald **Owner** Mr & Mrs MacCallum **Times** 12-1.45/7-8.30 Closed mid Nov-mid Mar, L all week **Prices** Food prices not confirmed for 2012. Please telephone for details **Wines** 32 bottles over £20, 20 bottles under £20, 9 by glass **Notes** Vegetarian available **Seats** 40 **Children** Portions, Menu

Forest Lodge Guest House

★★★ Ⓐ GUEST HOUSE

South Laggan PH34 4EA
☎ **01809 501219 & 07790 907477**
e-mail: info@flgh.co.uk
web: www.flgh.co.uk
dir: 2.5m S of Invergarry. Off A82 in South Laggan

Rooms 8 rms (7 en suite) (1 pri facs) (3 fmly) (4 GF) S £38-£40; D £60-£64* **Facilities** TVL TV1B tea/coffee Dinner available Cen ht Wi-fi **Parking** 10 **Notes** LB Closed 20 Dec-7 Jan

The Invergarry Inn

PH35 4HJ ☎ **01809 501206** 📄 **01809 501400**
e-mail: info@invergarryhotel.co.uk
dir: At junct of A82 & A87

A real Highland atmosphere pervades this refurbished roadside inn set in glorious mountain scenery between Fort William and Fort Augustus. Spruced-up bars make it a great base from which to explore Loch Ness, Glencoe and the West Coast. Relax by the crackling log fire with a wee dram or a pint of Garry Ale, then tuck into a good meal. Perhaps try Lochaber haggis, bashit neeps and tatties to start; followed by sea bream en papiette or a succulent 10oz rib-eye Scottish beef and hand-cut chips. Good lunches and excellent walks from the front door.

Open all day all wk Closed: Dec-Jan **Bar Meals** L served all day 8am-9.30pm booking required for D Av main course £14 food served all day **Restaurant** L served all day 8am-9.30pm booking required for D food served all day ⊕ FREE HOUSE ◀ Garry Ale, Timothy Taylor, Guinness. **Facilities** Children welcome Children's menu Children's portions Family room Garden Parking

INVERGORDON   Map 5 NH76

Kincraig Castle Hotel

★★★★ 78% COUNTRY HOUSE HOTEL

◎◎ Traditional British

Scottish fine dining in a splendid castle setting

☎ 01349 852587 📄 01349 852193
IV18 0LF
e-mail: info@kincraig-house-hotel.co.uk
web: www.kincraig-house-hotel.co.uk
dir: Off A9 past Alness towards Tain. Hotel on left 0.25m past Rosskeen Church

Superb views over to the Cromarty Firth and Black Isle from a baronial castle complete with mini turrets and gables makes for a memorable spot. Once the family home of the Mackenzie clan, the hotel is set in mature private grounds and does not lack for authentic atmosphere on the inside

either - a stone fireplace takes centre stage in the discreet, candlelit restaurant, set against red walls and generously-sized linen-clad tables, while antiques and period features are resplendent throughout the hotel. During dinner traditional Scottish music plays and local produce plays a leading role in dishes that are modernised with clever techniques and some nice little touches in the presentation. Start with Dalmore-cured Shetland salmon with cucumber, tomato jelly, herbs and quail's egg, before moving on to sirloin of Highland beef with a mushroom tarte Tatin, roast plum tomato and onion rings.

Rooms 15 (1 fmly) (1 GF) **Facilities** STV Xmas Wi-fi
Conf Class 30 Board 24 Thtr 50 **Parking** 30
Notes Civ Wed 70

Times 12.30-2/6.45-9

INVERIE   Map 4 NG70

The Old Forge

PH41 4PL ☎ **01687 462267** 📄 **01687 462267**
e-mail: info@theoldforge.co.uk
dir: From Fort William take A830 (Road to the Isles) towards Mallaig. Take ferry from Mallaig to Inverie (boat details on website)

Accessible only by boat, The Old Forge is Britain's most remote mainland pub. It stands literally between heaven and hell; Loch Nevis is Gaelic for heaven and Loch Hourn is Gaelic for hell. It's popular with everyone from locals to hill walkers, and is renowned for its impromptu ceilidhs. It is also the ideal place to sample local fish and seafood and there's no better way than choosing the seafood platter of rope mussels, langoustines, oak-smoked salmon and smoked trout; other specialities include slow roasted belly of Scottish pork with a home-made brandy and apple sauce; and slow-cooked lamb shank with clapshot. There are twelve boat moorings and a daily ferry from Mallaig.

Open all day all wk **Bar Meals** L served all wk 12-3 D served all wk 6-9.30 Av main course £10 **Restaurant** L served all wk 12-3 D served all wk 6-9.30 ⊕ FREE HOUSE ◀ Guinness, Calders 80/, Guest ales. **Facilities** Children welcome Children's menu Children's portions Play area Family room Dogs allowed Garden Parking Wi-fi

INVERNESS — Map 5 NH64

Culloden House

★★★★ 80% HOTEL

◉◉ Modern British 🌱

Seriously creative Scottish cuisine in historic setting

☎ 01463 790461 📠 01463 792181
Culloden IV2 7BZ
e-mail: info@cullodenhouse.co.uk
web: www.cullodenhouse.co.uk
dir: A96 from Inverness, right for Culloden. 1m after 2nd lights, left at church

You'll be following in the footsteps of royalty with a visit to the magnificent Palladian mansion that is Culloden House. Bonnie Prince Charlie spent the night here before his army was defeated at the battle of Culloden in 1746, and the sense of history inside the handsome ivy-covered building is palpable. Grand it certainly is, with crystal chandeliers hanging from lofty ceilings garlanded with ornate plasterwork, and many fine antiques, but the friendly staff make sure the place doesn't ever feel stuffy. Bedrooms come in a range of sizes and styles, with a number situated in a separate house. Chef Michael Simpson showcases Scotland's excellent produce - most of it local, including fruit and herbs from the hotel's own garden - in classic dishes with a modern spin. To start, perhaps herb- and spice-rolled carpaccio of Highland venison with petit Caesar salad and garlic-infused olive oil, following on with fillet of sea trout with crispy seaweed, shellfish and vanilla risotto, scallop butter and wasabi foam.

Rooms 28 (5 annexe) (1 fmly) (3 GF) **S** £95-£175; **D** £125-£270 (incl. bkfst)* **Facilities** FTV Putt green Boules Badminton Golf driving net Putting green New Year Wi-fi **Conf** Class 40 Board 30 Thtr 60 Del from £120 to £170* **Parking** 50 **Notes** LB No children 10yrs Closed 24-28 Dec Civ Wed 65

Chef Michael Simpson **Owner** Culloden House Ltd **Times** 12.30-2/7-9 Closed 25-26 Dec **Prices** Food prices not confirmed for 2012. Please telephone for details **Wines** 76 bottles over £20, 8 by glass **Notes** Vegetarian available, Dress restrictions, Smart casual **Seats** 50, Pr/dining room 17 **Children** Portions

Loch Ness Country House Hotel

★★★★ 79% SMALL HOTEL

◉ Modern British

Small-scale country house with appealing modern cuisine

☎ 01463 230512 📠 01463 224532
Loch Ness Rd IV3 8JN
e-mail: info@lochnesscountryhousehotel.co.uk
web: www.lochnesscountryhousehotel.co.uk
dir: On A82, 1m from Inverness town boundary

Built in 1710 as a shooting lodge, this charming country-house hotel in landscaped gardens on the outskirts of Inverness has been given a gentle modern facelift in recent years. The hotel has luxurious bedrooms, including some in the garden suite cottages. It is an intimate, small-scale operation with friendly, smartly-turned-out staff on hand to ensure a relaxed informal mood. The dining room looks good in understated neutral tones twinned with bold designer wallpaper, and there's a new chef in the kitchen who brings a lightness of touch to excellent local fish, seafood and game. Flair and imagination are there from the off in a trio of Scottish salmon that brings the fish peat-smoked, hot-smoked, roasted, and served with confit fillet, cucumber yoghurt and caviar, while a main course of monkfish with cannellini beans, chorizo, winter cabbage ragoût and piquant salsa verde continues in the modern Scottish idiom. Moist sticky toffee pudding with ginger ice cream makes a great finale. The garden terrace is ideal for relaxing and has splendid views over the landscaped gardens towards Inverness.

Rooms 13 (2 annexe) (8 fmly) (3 GF) **S** £85-£165; **D** £125-£215 (incl. bkfst)* **Facilities** FTV Xmas New Year Wi-fi **Conf** Class 30 Board 20 Thtr 50 Del from £135 to £175* **Parking** 50 **Notes** Civ Wed 120

Chef Chris Crombie **Owner** Loch Ness Hospitality Ltd **Times** 12-2.30/6-9 **Prices** Fixed L 2 course £9.95-£14.50, Fixed D 3 course £28.50-£31.50, Starter £4.50-£9.50, Main £13.95-£24.50, Dessert £4.50-£8.50, Service optional **Wines** 19 bottles over £20, 12 bottles under £20, 9 by glass **Notes** Sunday L, Vegetarian available **Seats** 42, Pr/dining room 14 **Children** Portions, Menu

The New Drumossie

★★★★ 78% HOTEL

◉◉ Modern Scottish

Seasonal cooking at an art-deco hotel

☎ 01463 236451 & 0870 194 2110 📄 01463 712858
Old Perth Rd IV2 5BE
e-mail: stay@drumossiehotel.co.uk
web: www.drumossiehotel.co.uk
dir: From A9 follow signs for Culloden Battlefield, hotel on left after 1m

A few miles out of Inverness, the hotel is a sparkling-white art-deco beauty, as anyone familiar with the period style of its cleanly flowing bowed façade will readily attest. Service is friendly and attentive and the bedrooms spacious and well presented. The extensive grounds and lake are a tonic for the world weary, and all is well-oiled serenity in the Grill Room too, where a polished team delivers high-class, seasonal Scottish cooking. The grill itself delivers fine rib-eye and sirloin steaks, or rack of Blackface lamb, with a choice of sauces that includes Arran mustard as well as whisky cream. Otherwise, look to the main menus for the likes of king scallops partnered with Stornoway black pudding, crispy ham and a 'tattie scone', followed by Glen Affric venison with braised red cabbage, honey-roast roots and a juniper-scented sauce. Regional cheeses, as well as a dessert selection that wanders into the realms of green tea crème brûlée with Malibu-soaked apricots and coconut ice, maintain true breadth of choice to the end.

Rooms 44 (10 fmly) (6 GF) **Facilities** STV Fishing New Year Wi-fi **Conf** Class 200 Board 40 Thtr 500 Del from £145* **Services** Lift **Parking** 200 **Notes** ⊗ Civ Wed 400

Chef Kenny McMillan **Owner** Ness Valley Leisure **Times** 12.30-2/7-9.30 **Prices** Food prices not confirmed for 2012. Please telephone for details **Wines** 2 bottles over £20, 2 bottles under £20, 13 by glass **Notes** Vegetarian available, **Seats** 90, Pr/dining room 30 **Children** Portions, Menu

Glenmoriston Town House Hotel

★★★★ 76% HOTEL

◉◉◉ Modern French **V**

Imaginative avant-garde cooking by the riverside

☎ 01463 223777 📄 01463 712378
20 Ness Bank IV2 4SF
e-mail: reception@glenmoristontownhouse.com
web: www.glenmoristontownhouse.com
dir: On riverside opposite theatre

Bold contemporary designs blend seamlessly with the classical architecture of this stylish townhouse hotel, situated on the banks of the River Ness. The sleek, modern, individually designed bedrooms have many facilities including free Wi-fi, DVD players and flat-screen TVs, while delightful day rooms include a piano bar and two eating options. Abstract is the alternative dining space to the Contrast Brasserie (see entry below) and for a city address, the views are lovely (get a window table if you can). Bruce Morrison offers a chef's table for up to six diners, but the fact is, you'll likely be dazzled whether you see the brigade at work or not. This is technically highly polished cooking in the modern European vein, with immaculate presentation skills and a strong seam of imaginative energy running through it. Smoked eel often finds its way into a meaty terrine these days, and here it just about holds its own in the company of foie gras with glazed walnuts and Sauternes jelly. Main course might deliver a daring meat and fish combination that is brought off with great panache, as when halibut poached in red wine sits alongside a serving of duck en crépinette with smoked bacon vinaigrette, and a serving of pomme purée to unite the dish's two halves. Dessert may look to the pasta repertoire for inspiration, for a raspberry and pistachio lasagne with raspberry sorbet and a slick of foaming bubbles flavoured with lemon thyme. The eight-stage tasting menu contains an array of surprises, even shocks, including 'full Scottish breakfast' and the alliterative delights of pork pie purée and popping popcorn pannacotta.

Rooms 30 (15 annexe) (1 fmly) (6 GF) **Facilities** STV ♫ Xmas New Year Wi-fi **Conf** Class 10 Board 10 Thtr 15 **Parking** 40 **Notes** ⊗ Closed 26-28 Dec & 4-6 Jan Civ Wed 70

Chef Bruce Morrison **Owner** Larsen & Ross South **Times** 6-10 Closed 26-28 Dec, Sun-Mon, L all week **Prices** Food prices not confirmed for 2012. Please telephone for details **Wines** 90% bottles over £20, 10% bottles under £20, 11 by glass **Notes** Vegetarian menu **Seats** 26, Pr/dining room 15 **Children** Portions, Menu

Contrast Brasserie

◉ Modern, Traditional

Riverside brasserie with resourceful cooking

☎ 01463 223777
Glenmoriston Town House Hotel, 20 Ness Walk IV2 4SF
e-mail: reception@glenmoristontownhouse.com
dir: On riverside opposite theatre

Observant locals will have noticed that the Contrast used to be next door to the Glenmoriston Town House Hotel, but was incorporated into it a couple of years ago. What hasn't changed is the relaxing location, a short walk from the city centre on a bank of the Ness. With an outdoor terrace offering stunning Highland views, it's a very welcoming ambience for some self-assured modern brasserie cooking. A meal might open with a quartet of evenly seared scallops, seasoned with cumin and confit lemon, and served with braised fennel. Local free-range pork belly comes in Thai

continued

guise, with a warm noodle salad, pickled cucumber and fried tiger prawns, and then there might be a trio of crème brûlée variations: au naturel, with Baileys, and subtly spiced with cardamom.

Chef Geoffrey Malmedy **Owner** Barry Larsen
Times 12-2.30/5-10 **Prices** Food prices not confirmed for 2012. Please telephone for details **Wines** 40 bottles over £20, 5 bottles under £20, 8 by glass **Notes** Sunday L, Vegetarian available, Civ Wed 90 **Seats** 70, Pr/dining room 20 **Children** Portions, Menu **Parking** 40

Bunchrew House

★★★★ 74% COUNTRY HOUSE HOTEL

🌸🌸 Modern, Traditional

Stunning sea views and well-conceived dishes

☎ 01463 234917 📄 01463 710620
Bunchrew IV3 8TA
e-mail: welcome@bunchrewhousehotel.com
web: www.bunchrewhousehotel.com
dir: W on A862. Hotel 2m after canal on right

In 20 acres of gardens and woodland, right on the edge of the Beauly Firth, Bunchrew House is a 400-year-old baronial-style mansion, now a plush country-house hotel, complete with turrets and a portico over the front door. Individually styled bedrooms are spacious and tastefully furnished, and there is a choice of comfortable lounges complete with real fires. The panelled restaurant has spectacular views over the water to the mountains beyond, and this is the setting for some modern Scottish cooking using fine local ingredients and produce from the hotel's own garden. Ragout of seafood spiked with caviar and herbs gets a meal off to a flying start, followed perhaps by pork loin wrapped in Parma ham with pancetta sauce and a stack of local black pudding and apple. The kitchen looks beyond the confines of Europe in some dishes, accompanying pink breast of wood pigeon with spiced couscous and Madeira sauce, and dusting baked fillet of salmon in Thai-style spices and serving it with lemongrass sauce.

Rooms 16 (4 fmly) (1 GF) **S** £115-£139; **D** £170-£178 (incl. bkfst)* **Facilities** FTV Fishing New Year Wi-fi **Conf** Class 30 Board 30 Thtr 80 Del from £128.50 to £144.50* **Parking** 40 **Notes** LB ⊗ Closed 24-27 Dec Civ Wed 92

Chef Walter Walker **Owner** Terry & Irina Mackay
Times 12-1.45/7-9 Closed 23-26 Dec **Prices** Fixed L 3 course fr £23.50, Fixed D 3 course fr £39.50, Service optional **Wines** 56 bottles over £20, 19 bottles under £20, 4 by glass **Notes** Sunday L, Vegetarian available **Seats** 32, Pr/dining room 14 **Children** Portions, Menu

Columba

★★★★ 74% HOTEL

☎ 08444 146 522 📄 08444 146 521
Ness Walk IV3 5NF
e-mail: reservations.columba@ohiml.com
web: www.oxfordhotelsandinns.com
dir: From A9, A96 follow signs to town centre, pass Eastgate shopping centre into Academy St, at bottom left into Bank St, right over bridge, hotel 1st left

Originally built in 1881 and with many original features retained, the Columba Hotel lies in the heart of Inverness overlooking the fast flowing River Ness. The bedrooms are very stylish, and public areas include a first-floor restaurant and lounge. A second dining option is the ever popular McNabs bar bistro, which is ideal for less formal meals.

Rooms 76 (4 fmly) **Facilities** FTV 🎵 Xmas New Year Wi-fi **Conf** Class 100 Board 60 Thtr 200 **Services** Lift **Notes** Civ Wed 120

River Avon and the Cairngorms, Tomintoul Cairngorms National Park

Royal Highland

★★★ 77% HOTEL

☎ 01463 231926 & 251451 📠 01463 710705
Station Square, Academy St IV1 1LG
e-mail: info@royalhighlandhotel.co.uk
web: www.royalhighlandhotel.co.uk
dir: From A9 into town centre. Hotel next to rail station & Eastgate Retail Centre

Built in 1858 adjacent to the railway station, this hotel has the typically grand foyer of the Victorian era with comfortable seating. The contemporary ASH Brasserie and bar is a refreshing venue for both eating and drinking throughout the day. The generally spacious bedrooms are comfortably equipped especially for the business traveller.

Rooms 85 (12 fmly) (2 GF) (25 smoking) **Facilities** FTV Xmas New Year Wi-fi **Conf** Class 80 Board 80 Thtr 200 **Services** Lift **Parking** 8 **Notes** Civ Wed 200

Thistle Inverness

★★★ 77% HOTEL

☎ 0871 376 9023 📠 0871 376 9123
Millburn Rd IV2 3TR
e-mail: inverness@thistle.co.uk
web: www.thistlehotels.com/inverness
dir: From A9 take Raigmore Interchange exit (towards Aberdeen), 3rd left towards centre. Hotel opposite

Well located within easy distance of the town centre. This well presented hotel offers modern bedrooms including three suites. There is a well equipped leisure centre along with an informal brasserie and open-plan bar and lounge. Ample parking is an added benefit.

Rooms 118 **Facilities** 🏊 supervised Gym Sauna Steam room Xmas New Year Wi-fi **Conf** Class 70 Board 50 Thtr 120 **Services** Lift **Parking** 80 **Notes** ⊗ Civ Wed 120

Best Western Palace Hotel & Spa

★★★ 75% HOTEL

☎ 01463 223243 📠 01463 236865
8 Ness Walk IV3 5NG
e-mail: palace@miltonhotels.com
web: www.invernesspalacehotel.co.uk
dir: A82 Glenurquhart Rd onto Ness Walk. Hotel 300yds on right opposite Inverness Castle

Set on the north side of the River Ness close to the Eden Court theatre and a short walk from the town, this hotel has a contemporary look. Bedrooms offer good levels of comfort and equipment, and a smart leisure centre attracts a mixed market.

Rooms 88 (48 annexe) (3 fmly) (5 smoking)
S £69.90–£189.90; **D** £99.90–£249.90 **Facilities** Spa FTV 🏊 supervised Gym Beautician Sauna Steam room Xmas New Year Wi-fi **Conf** Class 40 Board 30 Thtr 80 Del from £129.90 to £159.90 **Services** Lift **Parking** 38 **Notes** LB

Ramada Encore Inverness City Centre

★★★ 75% HOTEL

☎ 01463 228850 📠 01463 228879
63 Academy St IV1 1LU
e-mail: reservations@encoreinverness.co.uk
dir: A9, A82, B865, hotel on right

This hotel is ideally located, as its name suggests, close to the main shopping district, railway station and the tourist attractions of Inverness. The contemporary bedrooms have a bright stylish design and all rooms are equipped with Wi-fi along with an extensive choice of TV channels and movies. Public areas include a modern restaurant and a light-filled lounge area with comfortable seating. There is a choice of ground-floor business suites which makes the hotel very popular with corporate guests.

Rooms 90 (20 fmly) **Facilities** STV FTV Wi-fi **Conf** Class 20 Board 20 Thtr 34 **Services** Lift **Notes** ⊗

Glen Mhor

★★★ 72% HOTEL

☎ 01463 234308 📠 01463 218018
8-15 Ness Bank IV2 4SG
e-mail: enquires@glen-mhor.com
web: www.glen-mhor.com
dir: On east bank of River Ness, below Inverness Castle

This hotel is a short walk from the city centre and overlooks the beautiful River Ness. This fine old property offers bedrooms and several suites that are up-to-the-minute in design. The public areas include a cosy bar and a comfortable lounge with a log fire.

Rooms 52 (34 annexe) (3 fmly) (12 GF) **S** £39-£89; **D** £59-£149 (incl. bkfst)* **Facilities** FTV ♫ Xmas New Year Wi-fi **Conf** Class 30 Board 35 Thtr 60 **Parking** 26 **Notes** LB ⊗ Civ Wed 60

Express by Holiday Inn Inverness

BUDGET HOTEL

☎ 01463 732700 📄 01463 732732
Stoneyfield IV2 7PA
e-mail: inverness@expressholidayinn.co.uk
web: www.hiexpress.com/inverness
dir: From A9 follow A96 & Inverness Airport signs, hotel on right

A modern hotel ideal for families and business travellers. Fresh and uncomplicated, the spacious rooms include Sky TV, power shower and tea and coffee-making facilities. Continental buffet breakfast is included in the room rate; other meals may be taken at the nearby family pub or restaurant.

Rooms 94 (43 fmly) (24 GF) (10 smoking) **Conf** Class 20 Board 15 Thtr 35

Premier Inn Inverness Centre (Milburn Rd)

BUDGET HOTEL

☎ 0871 527 8544 📄 0871 527 8545
Millburn Rd IV2 3QX
web: www.premierinn.com
dir: From A9 & A96 junct (Raigmore Interchange, signed Airport/Aberdeen), take B865 towards town centre, hotel 100yds after next rdbt

High quality, budget accommodation ideal for both families and business travellers. Spacious, en suite bedrooms feature tea and coffee-making facilities, and Freeview TV in most hotels. Internet access and Wi-fi are available for a small fee. The adjacent family restaurant features a wide and varied menu.

Rooms 55 **D** £65-£70*

Premier Inn Inverness East

BUDGET HOTEL

☎ 0871 527 8546 📄 0871 527 8547
Beechwood Business Park IV2 3BW
web: www.premierinn.com
dir: From A9 follow Raigmore Hospital, Police HQ & Inshes Retail Park signs

Rooms 60 **D** £65-£70*

Daviot Lodge

★★★★★ 🏠 GUEST ACCOMMODATION

Daviot Mains IV2 5ER
☎ 01463 772215 📄 01463 772099
e-mail: margaret.hutcheson@btopenworld.com
dir: Off A9 5m S of Inverness onto B851 signed Croy. 1m on left

Standing in 80 acres of peaceful pasture land, this impressive establishment offers attractive, well-appointed and equipped bedrooms. The master bedroom is furnished with a four-poster bed. There is a tranquil lounge with deep sofas and a real fire, and a peaceful dining room where hearty breakfasts featuring the best of local produce are served. Full disabled access for wheelchairs.

Rooms 4 en suite (1 GF) **S** £40-£50; **D** £80-£100* **Facilities** FTV TVL tea/coffee Direct Dial Cen ht Licensed Wi-fi **Parking** 10 **Notes** LB No Children 5yrs Closed 23 Dec-2 Jan

Trafford Bank

★★★★★ 🏠 GUEST HOUSE

96 Fairfield Rd IV3 5LL
☎ 01463 241414
e-mail: enquiries@invernesshotelaccommodation.co.uk
dir: Off A82 at Kenneth St, Fairfield Rd 2nd left, 600yds on right

This impressive Victorian house lies in a residential area close to the canal. Lorraine Freel has utilised her interior design skills to blend the best in contemporary styles with the house's period character and the results are simply stunning. Delightful public areas offer a choice of lounges, while breakfast is taken in a beautiful conservatory featuring eye-catching wrought-iron chairs. Each bedroom is unique in design and has TV, DVD and CDs, sherry, silent mini-fridges and much more.

Rooms 5 en suite (2 fmly) **Facilities** STV FTV TVL tea/coffee Cen ht Wi-fi **Parking** 10 **Notes** ⊗

Avalon Guest House

★★★★ GUEST HOUSE

79 Glenurquhart Rd IV3 5PB
☎ 01463 239075 📄 01463 709827
e-mail: avalon@inverness-loch-ness.co.uk
web: www.inverness-loch-ness.co.uk
dir: Exit A9 at Longman rdbt, 1st exit onto A82, at Telford St rdbt, 2nd exit. Right at lights onto Tomnahurich St/Glenurquhart Rd

Avalon Guest House is just a short walk from the city centre, and five minutes drive from Loch Ness. Each bedroom has a

continued

flatscreen LCD TV with Freeview (some with DVD), Wi-fi, fluffy white towels and complimentary toiletries; bathrobes and slippers are available on request as well as various other useful items. A delicious breakfast, freshly cooked from a varied menu, is served in the dining room; most dietary requirements can be catered for. Public areas include a guest lounge; and the owners have a range of maps, guidebooks and brochures that guests can refer to.

Rooms 6 rms (5 en suite) (1 pri facs) (4 GF) S £45-£75; D £60-£85 **Facilities** FTV TVL tea/coffee Cen ht Wi-fi **Parking** 12 **Notes** LB ⊗ No Children 12yrs

Ballifeary Guest House

★★★★ 🏠 GUEST HOUSE

10 Ballifeary Rd IV3 5PJ
☎ **01463 235572** 📄 **01463 717583**
e-mail: william.gilbert@btconnect.com
web: www.ballifearyguesthouse.co.uk
dir: Off A82, 0.5m from town centre, turn left onto Bishops Rd & sharp right onto Ballifeary Rd

This charming detached house has a peaceful residential location within easy walking distance of the town centre and Eden Court Theatre. The attractive bedrooms are carefully appointed and well equipped. There is an elegant ground-floor drawing room and a comfortable dining room, where delicious breakfasts, featuring the best of local produce, are served at individual tables.

Rooms 7 en suite (1 GF) S £40-£70; D £70-£85 **Facilities** FTV TV6B tea/coffee Cen ht Wi-fi **Parking** 6 **Notes** LB ⊗ No Children 15yrs Closed 24-28 Dec

The Ghillies Lodge

★★★★ 🏠 BED AND BREAKFAST

16 Island Bank Rd IV2 4QS
☎ **01463 232137** & **07817 956533**
e-mail: info@ghillieslodge.com
dir: 1m SW from town centre on B862, pink house facing river

Situated on the banks of the River Ness not far from the city centre, Ghillies Lodge offers comfortable accommodation in a relaxed, peaceful environment. The attractive bedrooms, one of which is on the ground floor, are all en suite, and are individually styled and well equipped. There is a comfortable lounge-dining room, and a conservatory that overlooks the river.

Rooms 3 en suite (1 GF) S £40-£55; D £62-£72 **Facilities** STV tea/coffee Cen ht Wi-fi **Parking** 4 **Notes** ⊗

Moyness House

★★★★ 🏠 GUEST ACCOMMODATION

6 Bruce Gardens IV3 5EN
☎ **01463 233836** 📄 **01463 233836**
e-mail: stay@moyness.co.uk
web: www.moyness.co.uk
dir: Off A82 (Fort William road), almost opp Highland Regional Council headquarters

Situated in a quiet residential area just a short distance from the city centre, this elegant Victorian villa dates from 1880 and offers beautifully decorated, comfortable bedrooms and well-appointed bathrooms. There is an attractive sitting room and an inviting dining room, where traditional Scottish breakfasts are served. Guests are welcome to use the secluded and well-maintained back garden.

Rooms 6 en suite (1 fmly) (2 GF) S £60-£85; D £68-£100* **Facilities** FTV tea/coffee Cen ht Wi-fi **Parking** 10 **Notes** LB ⊗ No Children 5yrs

The Alexander

★★★★ 🏠 GUEST HOUSE

16 Ness Bank IV2 4SF
☎ **01463 231151** 📄 **01463 232220**
e-mail: info@thealexander.net
web: www.thealexander.net
dir: On E bank of river, opposite cathedral

Built in 1830 this impressive house has been extensively renovated by the current owners and many of the original Georgian features have been retained. Bedrooms are simply furnished and beds have luxurious mattresses dressed in fine Egyptian cotton. All rooms have flatscreen TVs with DVD players, there is a payphone in the hall, and ironing facilities are available. Light sleepers will welcome the silent running fridges in each room. Public rooms include a charming lounge with views over the River Ness and the house is a short walk from the city centre.

Rooms 7 en suite 3 annexe en suite (1 GF) S £45-£60; D £75-£95* **Facilities** FTV tea/coffee Cen ht Wi-fi **Parking** 8 **Notes** ⊗

Lyndon Guest House

★★★★ GUEST HOUSE

50 Telford St IV3 5LE
☎ **01463 232551** 📠 **01463 225827**
e-mail: lyndon@invernessbedandbreakfast.com
web: www.invernessbedandbreakfast.com
dir: From A9 onto A82 over Friars Bridge, right at rdbt onto Telford St. House on right

A warm Highland welcome awaits at this family-run accommodation close to the centre of Inverness. All rooms are en suite and are equipped with plenty of useful facilities including full internet access. Gaelic Spoken.

Rooms 6 en suite (4 fmly) (2 GF) S £28-£40; D £56-£80*
Facilities STV FTV TVL tea/coffee Cen ht Wi-fi **Parking** 6
Notes ⊗ Closed 20 Dec-5 Jan

Westbourne

★★★★ ⚲ GUEST ACCOMMODATION

50 Huntly St IV3 5HS
☎ **01463 220700** 📠 **01463 220700**
e-mail: richard@westbourne.org.uk
dir: A9 onto A82 at football stadium over 3 rdbts, at 4th rdbt 1st left onto Wells St & Huntly St

The immaculately maintained Westbourne looks across the River Ness to the city centre. This friendly, family-run house has bright modern bedrooms of varying size, all attractively furnished in pine and very well equipped. A relaxing lounge with internet access, books, games and puzzles is available.

Rooms 9 en suite (2 fmly) S £45-£55; D £80-£90*
Facilities FTV tea/coffee Cen ht Wi-fi **Parking** 6 **Notes** LB
Closed Xmas & New Year

Sunnyholm

★★★ GUEST ACCOMMODATION

12 Mayfield Rd IV2 4AE
☎ **01463 231336**
e-mail: sunnyholm@aol.com
web: www.invernessguesthouse.com
dir: 500yds SE of town centre. Off B861 Culduthel Rd onto Mayfield Rd

Situated in a peaceful residential area within easy walking distance of the city centre, Sunnyholm offers comfortably proportioned and well-equipped bedrooms. A spacious conservatory-lounge overlooks the rear garden, and there is a another lounge next to the bright, airy dining room.

Rooms 4 en suite (4 GF) S £38-£42; D £60-£64*
Facilities FTV tea/coffee Cen ht Wi-fi **Parking** 6 **Notes** ⊗ No Children 3yrs

Acorn House

★★★ GUEST HOUSE

2A Bruce Gardens IV3 5EN
☎ **01463 717021** & **240000** 📠 **01463 714236**
e-mail: enquiries@acorn-house.freeserve.co.uk
web: www.acorn-house.freeserve.co.uk
dir: From town centre onto A82, on W side of river, right onto Bruce Gardens

This attractive detached house is just a five-minute walk from the town centre. Bedrooms are smartly presented and well equipped. Breakfast is served at individual tables in the spacious dining room.

Rooms 6 en suite (2 fmly) **Facilities** STV TVL tea/coffee Cen ht Wi-fi Sauna Hot tub **Parking** 7 **Notes** Closed 25-26 Dec

Fraser House

★★★ GUEST ACCOMMODATION

49 Huntly St IV3 5HS
☎ **01463 716488** & **07900 676799** 📠 **01463 716488**
e-mail: fraserlea@btopenworld.com
dir: A82 W over bridge, left onto Huntly St, house 100yds

Situated on the west bank of the River Ness, Fraser House has a commanding position overlooking the city, and is within easy walking distance of the central amenities. Bedrooms, all en suite, vary in size and are comfortably furnished and well equipped. The ground-floor dining room is the setting for freshly cooked Scottish breakfasts.

Rooms 5 en suite (2 fmly) S £30-£35; D £50-£60*
Facilities FTV tea/coffee Cen ht Wi-fi **Notes** Closed Feb-Mar

Riverhouse

◉ British, Seafood **V** ✑

Super Scottish ingredients by the River Ness

☎ 01463 222033
1 Greig St IV3 5PT
e-mail: riverhouse.restaurant@unicombox.co.uk
web: www.riverhouseinverness.co.uk
dir: On corner of Huntly St & Greig St

Views of the River Ness are a treat at this intimately charming restaurant in the heart of the town. Chef-proprietor Allan Little will quite likely welcome you personally such is the charming nature of the place. The open-plan kitchen is a focal point in the dining room where piscine art gives a clue as to what's cooking. A warm colour scheme, bench style seating and crisply laid tables featuring sparkling glasses and good silverware bring to mind a bistro, while imaginatively presented modern Scottish food

continued

with a strong emphasis on local seafood impresses without being pretentious; Kyle of Tongue oysters, perhaps, or Orkney crab pâté with cucumber and caper salad and toasted brioche. Move on to bouillabaise of Arisaig mussels, king prawns and sea bream, or a prime Scottish rump steak with rocket and parmesan salad and potato wedges.

Chef Allan Little **Owner** Allan Little **Times** 12-2/5.30-late Closed 25-26 Dec, Sun, L Mon-Thu **Prices** Fixed L 2 course £13.50, Starter £6.95-£30.25, Main £14.50-£23, Dessert £5.95-£7.95 **Wines** 10 bottles over £20, 5 bottles under £20, 15 by glass **Notes** Pre-theatre menu 2 course £13.50, Vegetarian menu **Seats** 32 **Children** Portions **Parking** On street

Rocpool

◉◉ Modern European

Modern Scottish cooking in a cool city-centre venue

☎ 01463 717274
1 Ness Walk IV3 5NE
e-mail: info@rocpoolrestaurant.com
web: www.rocpoolrestaurant.com
dir: On W bank of River Ness close to the Eden Court Theatre

Rocpool positively bristles with contemporary design flair. Glassed on two sides, it sits on a corner site on the west bank of the Ness, with floodlit views of the Castle after dark. As much as the location delights the eye, the lengthy menus of many-layered modern Scottish cooking will stimulate the imagination. A Thai red curry of mussels sounds straightforward enough, but there might also be seared pigeon breast dressed in sherry vinegar, pine nuts and sultanas, with Jerusalem artichoke and pancetta. Then it's on to crisp-fried sea bream with roasted peppers, spinach, basil and capers, or calves' liver Venetian style, with sweet onions, garlic and rosemary potatoes and artichokes. Desserts aim to please with the likes of pecan pie and maple syrup ice cream, or passionfruit Pavlova with thick cream.

Chef Steven Devlin **Owner** Mr Devlin **Times** 12-2.30/5.45-10 Closed 25-26 Dec, 1-2 Jan, Sun (Oct-Jun), L Sun **Prices** Fixed L 2 course fr £11.95, Fixed D 2 course fr £13.95, Starter £3.95-£8.95, Main £11.95-£22.95, Dessert £5.95-£7.90, Service optional **Wines** 42 bottles over £20, 3 bottles under £20, 13 by glass **Notes** Early D 2 course £13.95 5.45-6.45pm, Vegetarian available **Seats** 55 **Children** Portions **Parking** On street

The Cross at Kingussie

★★★★★ ⓘ RESTAURANT WITH ROOMS

◉◉◉ Modern Scottish 🍷 NOTABLE WINE LIST

First-class restaurant with rooms in an idyllic setting

Tweed Mill Brae, Ardbroilach Rd PH21 1LB
☎ 01540 661166   📠 01540 661080
e-mail: relax@thecross.co.uk
dir: From lights in Kingussie centre along Ardbroilach Rd, 300yds left onto Tweed Mill Brae

If you've got the weather on your side you might never want to leave the terrace by the waters of the Gynack Burn, where wildlife puts on its own show and your aperitif has never tasted quite so good. That's the importance of a good location, and The Cross has a splendid one in the Cairngorm National Park surrounded by four acres of pretty gardens and woodland. You will get up from the terrace, though, as you really wouldn't want to miss out on the food, which takes the very best Scottish produce around and turns it into carefully considered dishes that allow the ingredients to shine. The Cross is the whole package - there are eight attractive bedrooms so you don't have to rush off home, and the place is done out in such a way that it has kept the essence of its Victorian heritage but is imbued with an understated contemporary charm. The fixed-price menu offers a couple of choices at each course, which helps to ensure the focus is on the best seasonal produce, and the combinations of flavours and textures are acutely judged. An appetiser kicks things off; escabèche of sea bream, for example, with mushroom and spring truffle, or langoustine soup with chive cream. First-course tartlet of organic salmon, naturally-smoked haddock and Shetland crab is full of Scotland's finest seafood, partnered with wild leek pesto and vine tomato salad, while main course might see seared fillet and braised shin of Haddington White Park beef partnered with caramelised silverskin onions, Savoy cabbage, baby carrots, Yetholm Gypsy potato purée and finished with a Madeira jus. Upside-down Black Isle plum cake with plum sorbet and vanilla custard is one way to finish. The service is refreshingly easygoing but thoroughly well informed, and the magnificent wine list shows real passion and knowledge for the subject and is full of little treasures.

Rooms 8 en suite (1 fmly) S £140-£165; D £180-£280* (incl.dinner) **Facilities** FTV tea/coffee Dinner available Direct Dial Cen ht Wi-fi Golf 18 Petanque **Conf** Max 20 Thtr 20 Class 20 Board 20 **Parking** 12 **Notes** LB ⊗ No Children 8yrs Closed Xmas & Jan (ex New Year) RS Sun & Mon Accommodation/dinner not available No coaches

Chef Becca Henderson, David Young **Owner** David & Katie Young **Times** 7-8.30 Closed Xmas & Jan (excl New Year), Sun-Mon, L all week **Prices** Fixed D 3 course £50, Service included, Groups min 6 service 10% **Wines** 200 bottles over £20, 20 bottles under £20, 4 by glass **Notes** Vegetarian available **Seats** 20

Allt Gynack Guest House

★★★ **A** GUEST HOUSE

Gynack Villa, 1 High St PH21 1HS
☎ 01540 661081
e-mail: alltgynack@tiscali.co.uk
web: www.alltgynack.com
dir: A9 onto A86 through Newtonmore, 2m to Kingussie, on left after bridge

Rooms 5 rms (3 en suite) (2 pri facs) (1 fmly) S £30-£32; D £56-£64* **Facilities** FTV tea/coffee Cen ht Wi-fi Golf 18 **Parking** 5 **Notes** LB No Children 14yrs

KYLE OF LOCHALSH　　　　　Map 4 NG72

The Waterside Seafood Restaurant

◉ Modern, Traditional Seafood

Simple fresh seafood dishes in the old railway booking-hall

☎ 01599 534813
Railway Station Buildings, Station Rd IV40 8AE
e-mail: seafoodrestaurant@btinternet.com
dir: Off A87

In what was once the booking hall of the railway station at one end of Scotland's most unforgettable train journey (Inverness to Lochalsh), the Waterside is an honest-to-goodness fish restaurant specialising in the freshest of west coast provender. Dishes are subjected to the minimum of intervention, dressing grilled queenies in lemon herb butter or steaming mussels in Thai spices, before flashing baked cod on the grill under a layer of spinach pesto, or salmon under a spiced red pepper crust. Specials based on the morning's catch are chalked on the board. Sirloin steaks with mushrooms in whisky cream sauce should satisfy the non-fish constituency, while warm chocolate and almond cake is a well-received finisher.

Chef Jann MacRae **Owner** Jann MacRae **Times** 11-3/5-9.30 Closed end Oct-beginning Mar, Sun (please phone to confirm opening hrs), L Sat **Prices** Fixed L 2 course £10-£20, Starter £3.95-£8.95, Main £9.95-£16.95, Dessert £3.95-£5.50, Service optional **Wines** 2 bottles over £20, 15 bottles under £20, 2 by glass **Notes** Vegetarian available **Seats** 35 **Children** Portions, Menu **Parking** 5

KYLESKU　　　　　Map 4 NC23

Kylesku Hotel

IV27 4HW ☎ 01971 502231
e-mail: info@kyleskuhotel.co.uk
web: www.kyleskuhotel.co.uk
dir: A835, then A837 & A894 into Kylesku. Hotel at end of road at Old Ferry Pier

Bypassed by the new bridge over Loch Glencoul in the early 80s, the former 17th-century coaching inn enjoys a glorious location down by the old ferry slipway where boats land the local seafood that forms the backbone of the daily chalkboard menu. It's a delightful spot on the shores of Loch Glendhu and Glencoul and the views from the bar and restaurant are truly memorable. Legendary fell-walking writer Alfred Wainwright once wrote of this village: 'Anyone with an eye for impressive beauty will not regard time spent at Kylesku as wasted.' You can understand why as the hotel is at the centre of the North West Highlands Global Geopark, 2,000-square kilometres of lochs, mountains and wild coast. The day's catch - langoustines, spineys, lobster, crab, hand-dived scallops, haddock, monkfish, John Dory and rope-grown mussels certainly don't have far to travel before ending up in the kitchen. Salmon is hot- and cold-smoked in-house, beef and lamb fillets are from animals reared in the Highlands, and all the venison is wild. The bar menu offers starters of Cullen skink (smoked haddock, potato and chive crème fraîche chowder); hand-dived scallops with garlic butter; whole cracked crab straight from the loch; and a pint of langoustines with Marie Rose dressing. Main courses may include mussels in a Thai coconut broth with lime and coriander (also available as a starter); fishcakes in a mussel sauce; grilled langoustine; John Dory with colcannon, lemongrass and dill butter sauce; and monkfish with sun-dried tomato risotto. The Kylesku signature dish is the local seafood platter. Puddings range from lime cheesecake to sticky toffee pudding to platters of Isle of Mull Cheddar with celery and spicy apricot sauce. To drink, there are two An Teallach real ale on tap, bottled beers from the Isle of Skye, 40 wines and 50 malt whiskies.

Open all day all wk Closed: Nov-Feb **Bar Meals** L served all wk 12-6 D served all wk 6-9 Av main course £13 food served all day **Restaurant** D served all wk 7-9 booking required Fixed menu price fr £28 Av 3 course à la carte fr £33 ⊕ FREE HOUSE ◧ Tennent's Ember 80/-, Selection of Black Isle Brewery and Skye Cuillin bottled ales, An Teallach Real Ale. **Facilities** Children welcome Children's menu Children's portions Dogs allowed Garden Wi-fi

LOCHINVER | Map 4 NC02

Inver Lodge

 ★★★★ HOTEL

◉◉ Traditional French **V**

Classic French cooking in stunning Highland location

☎ 01571 844496 📠 01571 844395
IV27 4LU
e-mail: stay@inverlodge.com
web: www.inverlodge.com
dir: A835 to Lochinver, through village, left after village hall, follow private road for 0.5m

Perched above the tranquil fishing village of Lochinver, this smart modern hotel has jaw-dropping views from bedrooms and public areas - in the restaurant you can see across the bay to the wild ocean, where the Western Isles might be glimpsed on a clear day. When it comes to fine dining the Roux dynasty needs no introduction, and the Monsieur Roux in question is Albert, who oversees the culinary output of the Chez Roux restaurant. The Auld Alliance is in fine fettle here: robust French country cooking built on Scottish ingredients is the deal, and the chefs are certainly off to a flying start with superb regional produce: fish and crustaceans are landed practically on the doorstep, and Highland lamb, venison and beef don't have far to come. Pike quenelle with duxelle of mushroom and brown shrimp and lobster sauce shows the style, and could be followed by a classic rib-eye of Buccleuch beef with sauce béarnaise and Pont-Neuf potatoes, or a full-flavoured 'surf n' turf' pairing of halibut fillet with Puy lentils and slow-braised oxtail, and sauce vierge. Stick to the Gallic theme and finish with Roux's signature caramelised lemon tart with raspberry sorbet.

Rooms 21 (11 GF) **S** £115-£150; **D** £215-£480 (incl. bkfst)*
Facilities FTV Sauna Wi-fi **Parking** 30 **Notes** LB Closed Nov-Mar Civ Wed 50

Chef Albert Roux, Lee Pattie **Owner** Robin Vestey
Times 12-6/7-9.30 Closed Nov-Mar **Prices** Fixed D 3 course £40, Starter £10-£12, Main £16.50-£22, Dessert £7.50-£8, Service optional **Wines** 62 bottles over £20, 6 by glass
Notes Fixed L 4 course from £15.50, Vegetarian menu **Seats** 50 **Children** Portions, Menu

LYBSTER | Map 5 ND23

Portland Arms

 ★★★★ ⊜ INN

Main St KW3 6BS
☎ 01593 721721 📠 01593 721722
e-mail: manager@portland-arms.co.uk
web: www.portlandarms.co.uk
dir: On A99, 4m N of Thurso junct

Just half a mile from the North Sea coastline, this former coaching inn was built in the 1850s and offers a range of stylish, comfortable bedrooms - those at the front have wonderful sea views. Fine dining can be enjoyed in the refurbished Library restaurant while more informal meals are served in the Farmhouse Kitchen. Menus cater for all tastes, with everything from home-made soup with freshly baked baguette to flash-fried langoustine in garlic and brandy butter. Look out for delicious desserts and home baking with morning coffee and afternoon tea. Sunday lunch is a speciality. The resident's lounge has a range of comfortable seating and an open log fire burns brightly in the colder months.

Rooms 23 en suite (4 fmly) (4 GF) **Facilities** FTV tea/coffee Dinner available Direct Dial Cen ht Wi-fi ch fac Golf 9 **Conf** Max 150 Thtr 150 Class 150 Board 50 **Parking** 72 **Notes** ⊗ Civ Wed 280

Open all day all wk 7am-11pm ⊕ FREE HOUSE ◀ McEwans 70/-, Guinness, Belhaven Best, John Smith's.
Facilities Children welcome Children's menu Children's portions Family room Garden Parking **Rooms** 23

MUIR OF ORD | Map 5 NH55

Ord House

★★ 72% SMALL HOTEL

◉ Traditional British

Country-house comforts and fresh local produce

☎ 01463 870492 📠 01463 870297
IV6 7UH
e-mail: admin@ord-house.co.uk
dir: Off A9 at Tore rdbt onto A832. 5m, through Muir of Ord. Left towards Ullapool (A832). Hotel 0.5m on left

The setting of this elegant 17th-century manor house, in 60 acres of walled, formal and vegetable gardens, provides both views and tranquillity. Elegantly converted into a small hotel, it retains period features, with open fires and some fine antique pieces, and a relaxing atmosphere. Bedrooms are brightly furnished and well-proportioned, while the comfortable day rooms reflect the character and charm of the house, with inviting lounges, a cosy snug bar and an elegant dining room. Own-grown produce gives strength to the commitment to local produce and the focus of the kitchen is simple, traditional country-house cooking prepared from fresh seasonal ingredients. Take potted shrimps or home-smoked salmon pâté to start, followed by charcoal-grilled Aberdeen Angus sirloin steak with pepper sauce, or baked cod with lemon butter sauce, and comforting desserts like sticky toffee pudding.

Rooms 12 (3 GF) **S** £60-£85; **D** £100-£150 (incl. bkfst)*
Facilities Putt green 🎯 Clay pigeon shooting Wi-fi
Parking 30 **Notes** LB Closed Nov-Apr

Chef Eliza Allen **Owner** Eliza & John Allen **Times** 7-9
Closed Nov-end Feb **Prices** Fixed D 3 course £28, Starter £6-£12, Main £14-£23, Dessert £4.95-£8.50, Service included
Wines 14 bottles over £20, 18 bottles under £20,
4 by glass **Notes** Vegetarian available **Seats** 26
Children Portions

Carndaisy House

★★★★ BED AND BREAKFAST

Easter Urray IV6 7UL
☎ **01463 870244 & 07780 923316** 📄 **0808 280 1771**
e-mail: info@carndaisyhouse.co.uk
dir: A9, at Tore rdbt 1st left onto A832 to Muir of Ord. At junct with A862 turn right over bridge, then 1st left onto A832. 2m W, turn right, 0.5m on left

Carndaisy House offers very comfortable bed and breakfast in Easter Urray a short drive from Muir of Ord just outside Inverness. Accommodation includes three en suite rooms including a large family room with its own entrance and patio. All bedrooms are contemporarily decorated, and finished to a high standard. A well-cooked traditional Scottish breakfast provides a good start to the day.

Rooms 3 en suite (2 fmly) (1 GF) S £29-£49; D £49-£75*
Facilities FTV tea/coffee Cen ht Wi-fi Riding **Parking** 5
Notes LB ⊗ ⊚

NAIRN
Map 5 NH85

Newton

★★★★ 74% HOTEL

◉ Traditional European

Enjoyable food in baronial-style hotel

☎ 01667 453144 📄 01667 454026
Inverness Rd IV12 4RX
e-mail: newton.frontdesk@ohiml.com
web: www.oxfordhotelsandinns.com
dir: A96 from Inverness to Nairn, through 3 sets of lights, at 4th right to Newton Gate

This baronial pile, set in 21 acres of mature parkland and bordering Nairn's championship golf course overlooks the Moray Firth and has a 350-seat conference centre. Bedrooms are of a high standard, and many of the front-facing rooms have splendid sea views. The oldest part of Newton House sprouts fantasy turrets and a crenellated tower, and that, together with the splendid setting, once attracted the likes of Harold Macmillan and Charlie Chaplin on their hols (not together, of course). When it comes to dining, modern visitors can choose between the casual contemporary setting of Chaplin's bistro, or the fine-dining Ellis restaurant, where straightforward modern dishes are assembled from fresh, locally-sourced ingredients. Expect starters such as vegetarian haggis croquettes with pepper cream sauce, followed by rack of lamb served with Parisienne potatoes, rosemary jus and poached pear filled with stilton. End in the comfort zone with sticky toffee pudding with butterscotch sauce and vanilla ice cream.

Rooms 56 (4 fmly) **Facilities** STV Xmas New Year Wi-fi
Conf Class 220 Board 90 Thtr 450 Del from £130 to £180*
Services Lift **Parking** 150 **Notes** Civ Wed 250

Times 12-2.30/6-9 Closed Xmas & New Year

Golf View Hotel & Leisure Club

★★★★ 72% HOTEL

◉ Traditional **V**

Sound modern Scottish cooking in hotel with sea views

☎ 01667 452301   📄 01667 455267
The Seafront IV12 4HD
e-mail: golfview@crerarhotels.com
dir: Off A96 into Seabank Rd, hotel at end on right

The Golf View Hotel's name may nail its colours to the mast, but you don't have to be a fan of the game to revel in the timeless appeal of strolling the sandy beaches of the Moray Firth and soaking up the views across to the Black Isle. When you head indoors from the pleasures of the seashore or the world-renowned Nairn golf courses, those glorious coastal panoramas are still there, viewed through sweeping picture windows in the hotel's restaurant. Classic French techniques underpin the contemporary Scottish cooking, with a good showing of top-class local ingredients at the heart of it all. Expect the likes of roasted mussels with garlic and chervil butter, followed by grilled red mullet fillets served with sun-blushed tomato risotto, aubergine caviar and sauce vierge. To finish, there may be mango pannacotta with pineapple and chilli salsa and caramelised brioche toast. Bedrooms are of a very high standard and there's a well-equipped leisure complex and swimming pool.

Rooms 42 (6 fmly) **S** £95-£130; **D** £130-£200 (incl. bkfst)*
Facilities Spa FTV 🏊 supervised 🏌 Gym Sauna Steam room
Xmas New Year Wi-fi **Conf** Class 40 Board 40 Thtr 100
Del from £125 to £195* **Services** Lift **Parking** 40 **Notes** LB
Civ Wed 100

Chef Stuart Urghart **Owner** Crerar Hotels **Times** 6.45-9
Closed L Mon-Sat **Prices** Fixed D 3 course £32-£43, Service
optional **Wines** 22 bottles over £20, 23 bottles under £20, 8
by glass **Notes** Vegetarian menu, Dress restrictions, Smart
casual **Seats** 50 **Children** Portions, Menu

Boath House

★★★ HOTEL

◉◉◉◉ Modern British 🏵

Small luxury country-house hotel with an outstanding restaurant

☎ 01667 454896   📄 01667 455469
Auldearn IV12 5TE
e-mail: info@boath-house.com
web: www.boath-house.com
dir: 2m past Nairn on A96, E towards Forres, signed on main road

Looking at this elegant vision of Palladian design by the celebrated architect Archibald Simpson, it is almost impossible to imagine it gone to rack and ruin, but that's how it was in the early 1990s before salvation came in the form of Don and Wendy Matheson. They set about a restoration that not only saved a national treasure, but has provided Scotland with a world-class country-house hotel. Wendy Matheson is a garden designer so it will come as no surprise that the 20 acres of grounds are rather on the impressive side, with walled gardens, an ornamental lake, sweeping lawns, woodland, streams, and pathways to link them all together. The gardens play their part in supplying the kitchen - bee hives afford honey, the earth brings forth a myriad of organic fruits, herbs and vegetables. The house is designated an art gallery, displaying the works of 30 or so Scottish artists (there are sculptures in the gardens, too), and the public rooms are decorated with warm colours and furnished with an eclectic mix of handsome antiques, while bedrooms are striking, comfortable, and include many fine antique pieces. It is in this magnificent setting that chef Charles Lockley has worked since the hotel opened its doors. An advocate of slow food, what cannot be grown in the hotel's gardens or foraged from the woods is sourced locally by the chef with due diligence, and what appears on the plate is refined, intelligent dishes where flavour is king. The six-course fixed-price menu is served up to a maximum of 26 people in the candlelit dining room, with its generous Regency proportions, fine features, and French windows looking across the gardens to the lake. Carrot soup with black olive crumb has an intensity of flavour that shows what this kitchen is all about - the carrot is not overwhelmed or lost, simply enhanced by its pairing with olives and crisp crumb. Acute technical skills and well-thought-out combinations run through from pig's trotter with snails and wild garlic, to breast of ruby veal with lingot beans and celeriac. The seldom seen chickweed comes with scallops, leek and hazelnuts, while halibut is partnered with langoustines, spelt and celery. There's a cheese course before dessert - Ticklemore goats' cheese with crispbreads, for example - which might be a deliciously moist pistachio cake with a pineapple shooter. Charles Lockley's cooking shows considerable balance and a rare appreciation of nature's bounty.

Rooms 8 (1 fmly) (1 GF) **S** £260-£330; **D** £345-£450 (incl. bkfst & dinner) **Facilities** FTV Fishing 🏊 Beauty salon Xmas New Year Wi-fi **Conf** Class 10 Board 10 Thtr 15 **Parking** 20 **Notes** LB Civ Wed 28

Chef Charles Lockley **Owner** Mr & Mrs D Matheson **Times** 12.30-1.15/7-7.30 **Prices** Fixed L 2 course £24, Service included **Wines** 125 bottles over £20, 9 by glass **Notes** Fixed D 6 course £70, Sunday L, Vegetarian available, Dress restrictions, Smart casual, no shorts/T-shirts/jeans, **Seats** 28, Pr/dining room 8 **Children** Portions

North End

★★★★ BED AND BREAKFAST

18 Waverley Rd IV12 4RQ
☎ **01667 456338**
e-mail: reservations@northendnairn.co.uk
dir: On corner of A96 (Academy St) & Waverley Rd

Built in 1895, North End is a delightful Victorian villa that has been sympathetically restored in recent years. The spacious bedrooms are comfortable and well equipped. The cosy lounge has a wood-burning stove and the original features of the house are complemented by contemporary furnishings. The house is within easy walking distance of Nairn and is a 20-minute drive from Inverness.

Rooms 3 rms (2 en suite) (1 pri facs) **Facilities** TVL tea/coffee Cen ht **Parking** 4 **Notes** ⊗ Closed Sep-Apr ⊛

NETHY BRIDGE   Map 5 NJ02

Nethybridge

★★★ 68% HOTEL

☎ 01479 821203   📠 01479 821686
PH25 3DP
e-mail: salesnethybridge@strathmorehotels.com
dir: A9 onto A95, onto B970 to Nethy Bridge

This popular tourist and coaching hotel enjoys a central location amidst the majestic Cairngorm Mountains. Bedrooms are stylishly furnished in bold tartans whilst traditionally styled day rooms include two bars and a popular snooker room. Staff are friendly and keen to please.

Rooms 69 (3 fmly) (7 GF) **Facilities** Putt green Bowling green ♫ Xmas New Year **Conf** Thtr 100 **Services** Lift **Parking** 80

The Mountview Hotel

★★ 78% HOTEL

◉◉ Modern British

Highland retreat with scenery as appetising as the cooking

☎ 01479 821248   📠 01479 821515
Grantown Rd PH25 3EB
e-mail: info@mountviewhotel.co.uk
dir: From Aviemore follow signs through Boat of Garten to Nethy Bridge. On main road through village, hotel on right

Picture the scene: the snow-sprinkled peaks of the Cairngorm National Park rise above the Caledonian pines of the RSPB-owned Abernethy Forest. This grand Victorian country-house hotel has elemental nature on its very doorstep, and specialises in guided holidays making it a favoured base for birdwatching and for walking groups. The River Spey is close at hand - and that means whisky mecca in Grantown-on-Spey for aficionados of single malts. The Mountview's restaurant makes the most of this dramatic landscape, which is there as a wide-screen backdrop to the accomplished modern cooking. The kitchen here is dedicated to procuring all things local and bringing this superlative produce together in well-considered combinations - seared west coast scallops with minted pea purée and crispy pancetta, perhaps, followed by slow-cooked pork belly infused with thyme and garlic, and teamed with buttered kale and sweet potato purée. Dessert might be rhubarb and ginger crème brûlée with shortbread.

Rooms 12 (1 GF) **Facilities** FTV **Parking** 20 **Notes** ⊗

Times 6-11 Closed 25-26 Dec, Mon, L all week

NEWTONMORE — Map 5 NN79

Crubenbeg House

★★★★ GUEST HOUSE

Falls of Truim PH20 1BE
☎ 01540 673300
e-mail: enquiries@crubenbeghouse.com
web: www.crubenbeghouse.com
dir: 4m S of Newtonmore. Off A9 for Crubenmore, over
railway bridge & right, signed

Set in a peaceful rural location, Crubenbeg House has
stunning country views and is well located for touring the
Highlands. The attractive bedrooms are individually styled
and well equipped, while the ground-floor bedroom provides
easier access. Guests can enjoy a dram in front of the fire in
the inviting lounge, while breakfast features the best of
local produce in the adjacent dining room.

Rooms 4 rms (3 en suite) (1 pri facs) (1 GF) S £33-£40; D
£55-£87* **Facilities** STV tea/coffee Dinner available Cen ht
Licensed Wi-fi **Parking** 10 **Notes** LB No Children 12yrs

NORTH BALLACHULISH — Map 4 NN06

Loch Leven Hotel

Old Ferry Rd PH33 6SA ☎ 01855 821236   📄 01855 821550
e-mail: reception@lochlevenhotel.co.uk
web: www.lochlevenhotel.co.uk
dir: Off A82, N of Ballachulish Bridge

The slipway into Loch Leven at the foot of the garden recalls
the origins of this 17th century inn as one staging point on
the old ferry linking the Road to The Isles. This extraordinary
location, near the foot of Glencoe and with horizons
peppered by Munro peaks rising above azure sea lochs, is
also gifted with superb seafood from the local depths; such
as scampi and haddock, or indulge in a chunky lamb Celtic
casserole. Sip beers from Cairngorm Brewery or a wee dram
from a choice of over 75 malts, making the best of the sun
terrace which must have one of Scotland's most idyllic
views.

Open all day all wk 11-11 (Thu-Sat 11am-mdnt Sun
12.30-11) **Bar Meals** L served all wk 12-3 D served all wk
6-9 Av main course £12 **Restaurant** L served all wk 12-3 D
served all wk 6-9 Fixed menu price fr £25 Av 3 course à la
carte fr £25 ⊕ FREE HOUSE ◀ Cairngorm Brewery, Atlas
Brewery, small micro-brewery. **Facilities** Children welcome
Children's menu Children's portions Play area Family room
Dogs allowed Garden Parking Wi-fi

ONICH — Map 4 NN06

Onich

★★★ 78% HOTEL

◎ Traditional Scottish

Lochside dining in a charming little hotel

☎ 01855 821214   📄 01855 821484
PH33 6RY
e-mail: enquiries@onich-fortwilliam.co.uk
web: www.onich-fortwilliam.co.uk
dir: Beside A82, 2m N of Ballachulish Bridge

Set in its own landscaped gardens in a spectacular position
overlooking Loch Linnhe, this charming little hotel makes a
great base for exploring the nearby glens and lochs.
Bedrooms, with pleasing colour schemes, are comfortably
modern, and panoramic views over the Loch to the Glencoe
Mountains and Morvern and the Isle of Mull are inspiring,
whether you choose to eat traditional bar food by the fire, on
the terrace, or in the sun lounge. The Loch View restaurant is
a popular spot and a lovely place to tuck into top-quality
Scottish produce in flavoursome dishes that reveal good
technical expertise in the kitchen. Tea-smoked duck is
accompanied by medallions of orange-and-rosemary-
scented jelly, with a light apple and honey syrup, while
poached smoked haddock fillet keeps things relatively
simple with chive mash, seasonal roasted vegetables and a
tomato velouté.

Rooms 26 (6 fmly) **Facilities** STV Games room ♬ Xmas New
Year Wi-fi **Conf** Board 40 Thtr 150 **Parking** 50 **Notes** LB
Civ Wed 120

Times 7-9 Closed 24 Dec, 26 Dec, L all week

Old St Peter's Kirk, Thurso's old town, Highlands

PLOCKTON

Map 4 NG83

The Plockton

★★★ 75% SMALL HOTEL

☎ 01599 544274 📠 01599 544475
41 Harbour St IV52 8TN
e-mail: info@plocktonhotel.co.uk
web: www.plocktonhotel.co.uk
dir: 6m from Kyle of Lochalsh. 6m from Balmacara

The Pearson family – Dorothy, Tom, Alan and Ann-Mags – have been running this award-winning harbourside hotel for more than twenty years. It's easy to see why they stay (and indeed why so many guests return again and again) because as you walk down the main street a surprising panorama opens up: to one side the watchful mountains, to the other the deep blue waters of Loch Carron lapping at the edge of a sweep of whitewashed Highland cottages. There are palm trees too, courtesy of the Gulf Stream. The building dates from 1827 and later became a ship's chandlery, from which it was converted into a hotel in 1913. Stylish bedrooms offer individual, pleasing decor and many have spacious balconies or panoramic views, two family suites are also available, along with a cottage annexe nearby. In the dining room and hotel bar the speciality is seafood, including locally caught langoustines and fresh fish landed at Gairloch and Kinlochbervie. Succulent Highland steaks and locally reared beef also add to the wealth of other tempting Scottish produce. Example starters from a recent menu are Talisker whisky pâté and Plockton mackerel smokies, while from among the mains there might be pan-fried medallions of pork with brandied apricots in cream sauce; casserole of Highland venison in red wine, juniper berries and redcurrant jelly; supreme of chicken stuffed with Argyle smoked ham in sun-dried tomato, garlic and basil sauce; and chargrilled Plockton prawns. Vegetarian dishes are detailed on the blackboard. Basket meals, such as beer-battered fish and chips and breaded scampi tails, are served nightly. Well kept ales and a fine range of malts is available to round off that perfect Highland day.

Rooms 15 (4 annexe) (1 fmly) (1 GF) **S** £55-£90; **D** £80-£130 (incl. bkfst)* **Facilities** STV Pool table 🎵 New Year Wi-fi **Notes** ⊗ Closed 25 Dec & 1 Jan

Open all day all wk 11am-mdnt (Sun 12.30pm-11pm) Closed: 25 Dec, 1 Jan **Bar Meals** L served all wk 12-2.15 D served all wk 6-10 Av main course £14 **Restaurant** L served all wk 12-2.15 D served all wk 6-10 booking required Av 3 course à la carte fr £20 ⊕ FREE HOUSE ◀ Plockton Bay, Crags Ale, Trade Winds. **Facilities** Children welcome Children's menu Children's portions Family room Garden

Plockton Inn & Seafood Restaurant

Innes St IV52 8TW ☎ **01599 544222** 📠 **01599 544487**
e-mail: info@plocktoninn.co.uk
web: www.plocktoninn.co.uk
dir: On A87 to Kyle of Lochalsh take turn at Balmacara. Plockton 7m N

Just 100 metres from the harbour, this attractive stone-built free house is run by Mary Gollan, her brother Kenny and his partner, Susan Trowbridge. Mary and Kenny's great-grandfather built it as a manse, and they themselves were born and bred in Plockton. Since buying the business in 1997, Mary, Susan and Kenny have turned it into an inveterate award-winner, the ladies sharing the role of chef, while Kenny runs the bar. An easygoing atmosphere is apparent throughout, with winter fires in both bars, and a selection of over 50 malt whiskies. A meal in the reasonably formal Dining Room, or the more relaxed Lounge Bar, is a must, with a wealth of freshly caught local fish and shellfish, West Highland beef, lamb, game and home-made vegetarian dishes on the set menu, plus daily specials. Martin, the barman, lands the Plockton prawns (langoustines here) himself, then Kenny takes them and other seafood off to his smokehouse, to feature later in the seafood platter, perhaps. Starters include a vegetable or fish-based soup; oysters with vodka, tomato juice and herbs; edamame (baby soya beans), asparagus and pea salad; and both meat and vegetarian antipasti. Among the main dishes are those langoustines Martin caught in Loch Carron, served hot with garlic, or cold with Marie Rose sauce; Scottish salmon fillet; hand-dived king scallops; lamb shank; Moorish pork kebabs; chicken and bacon salad; and spinach and ricotta gnocchi. Desserts include lemon and ginger crunch pie; cranachan ice cream; and Scottish cheeses served with Orkney oatcakes. The public bar is alive on Tuesdays and Thursdays with music from local musicians, who are often joined by talented youngsters from the National Centre of Excellence in Traditional Music.

Open all day all wk **Bar Meals** L served all wk 12-2.30 D served all wk 6-9 booking required Av main course £12 **Restaurant** D served all wk 6-9 booking required Av 3 course à la carte fr £20 ⊕ FREE HOUSE ◀ Greene King Abbot Ale, Fuller's London Pride, Young's Special, Plockton Crag Ale, Plockton Bay. **Facilities** Children welcome Children's menu Children's portions Play area Dogs allowed Garden Parking Wi-fi

POOLEWE — Map 4 NG88

Pool House

★★★★★ GUEST ACCOMMODATION

IV22 2LD
☎ **01445 781272** 📠 **01445 781403**
e-mail: stay@pool-house.co.uk
dir: 6m N of Gairloch on A832 in the centre of village by bridge

Set on the shores of Loch Ewe where the river meets the bay, the understated roadside façade gives little hint of its splendid interior, nor of the views facing the bay. Memorable features are its delightful public rooms and stunningly romantic suites, each individually designed and with feature bathrooms. Pool House is run very much as a country house - the hospitality and guest care by the Harrison Family are second to none.

Rooms 5 en suite 1 annexe en suite (2 GF) S £125-£150; D £250-£300* **Facilities** FTV tea/coffee Dinner available Direct Dial Cen ht Licensed Wi-fi Fishing Snooker **Parking** 12 **Notes** LB ⊗ No Children 16yrs Closed 6 Jan-12 Feb RS Mon closed

ROY BRIDGE — Map 4 NN28

Best Western Glenspean Lodge Hotel

★★★ 83% HOTEL

☎ 01397 712223 📠 01397 712660
PH31 4AW
e-mail: reservations@glenspeanlodge.co.uk
web: www.glenspeanlodge.com
dir: 2m E of Roy Bridge, exit A82 at Spean Bridge onto A86

With origins as a hunting lodge dating back to the Victorian era, this hotel sits in gardens in an elevated position in the Spean Valley. Accommodation is provided in well laid out bedrooms, some suitable for families. Inviting public areas include a comfortable lounge bar and a restaurant that enjoys stunning views of the valley.

Rooms 17 (4 fmly) **Facilities** Gym Sauna Xmas New Year Wi-fi **Conf** Class 16 **Parking** 60 **Notes** Civ Wed 60

The Stronlossit Inn

★★★ 77% SMALL HOTEL

☎ 01397 712253 📠 01397 712641
PH31 4AG
e-mail: stay@stronlossit.co.uk
web: www.stronlossit.co.uk
dir: Exit A82 at Spean Bridge onto A86, signed Roy Bridge. Hotel on left

Appointed to modern standards with the character and hospitality of a traditional hostelry, The Stronlossit Inn is proving quite a draw for the discerning Highland tourist. The spacious bar is the focal point, with a peat burning fire providing a warm welcome in cooler months; guests can eat in the attractive restaurant. Bedrooms come in a mix of sizes and styles, most being smartly modern and well equipped.

Rooms 10 (5 GF) **S** £60-£70; **D** £85-£100 (incl. bkfst) **Facilities** Wi-fi **Conf** Class 12 Board 10 Thtr 20 Del from £90 to £120 **Parking** 30 **Notes** LB ⊗ No children 17yrs Closed 1-15 Dec

SCOURIE — Map 4 NC14

Scourie

★★★ 73% SMALL HOTEL

☎ 01971 502396 📠 01971 502423
IV27 4SX
e-mail: patrick@scourie-hotel.co.uk
dir: N'bound on A894. Hotel in village on left

This well-established hotel is an angler's paradise with extensive fishing rights available on a 25,000-acre estate. Public areas include a choice of comfortable lounges, a cosy bar and a smart dining room offering wholesome fare. The bedrooms are comfortable and generally spacious. The resident proprietors and their staff create a relaxed and friendly atmosphere.

Rooms 20 (2 annexe) (2 fmly) (5 GF) **S** £43-£54; **D** £82-£102 (incl. bkfst)* **Facilities** Fishing Wi-fi **Parking** 30 **Notes** LB Closed mid Oct-end Mar RS winter evenings

SHIEL BRIDGE — Map 4 NG91

Grants at Craigellachie

★★★★ RESTAURANT WITH ROOMS

🌸 Modern Scottish 🌶️

Stunning backdrop for bold modern Scottish cooking
Craigellachie, Ratagan IV40 8HP
☎ 01599 511331
e-mail: info@housebytheloch.co.uk
dir: From A87 exit for Glenelg, 1st right to Ratagan, opposite
Youth Hostel sign

Billed as 'The Little Restaurant with Rooms', Grants sits in the rural idyll of Craigellachie with uplifting views of Loch Duich and the Five Sisters mountains from its cosy conservatory setting. Chef-patron Tony Taylor knows where to get his hands on the best spanking-fresh fish and seafood and the finest local meat and game, which he sends out in plates of big, bold modern Scottish flavours. The friendly team keep things ticking over at a nicely relaxed pace, delivering starters such as chargrilled baby squid stuffed with salami, mozzarella and green olives, ahead of pan-roasted tenderloin of organic Isle of Raasay pork wrapped in fresh sage and prosciutto, flamed with Calvados and served with pears and walnuts. Finish with Highland and island cheeses, or on a sweet note with clementine and whisky pannacotta with caramelised fruits. Bedrooms are stylish and have all the creature comforts, and guests are guaranteed a warm welcome at this charming house.

Rooms 2 en suite 2 annexe en suite (3 GF)
S £92.50–£112.50; D £155–£240* (incl.dinner)
Facilities STV tea/coffee Dinner available Cen ht Wi-fi
Riding **Parking** 8 **Notes** LB No Children 12yrs Closed Dec-mid Feb RS Oct-Apr reservation only No coaches

Chef Tony Taylor **Owner** Tony & Liz Taylor **Times** 7-11
Closed Dec-mid Feb, L all week, D Sun **Prices** Food prices not confirmed for 2012. Please telephone for details
Wines 51 bottles over £20, 12 bottles under £20, 7 by glass
Notes Restaurant open only by reservation, Vegetarian available **Seats** 12 **Children** Portions

SHIELDAIG — Map 4 NG85

Tigh an Eilean

★ SMALL HOTEL

🌸🌸 Modern Scottish **V** 🌶️

Innovative cooking in a lochside inn
☎ 01520 755251   📄 01520 755321
IV54 8XN
e-mail: tighaneilean@keme.co.uk
web: www.shieldaigbarandcoastalkitchen.co.uk
dir: Exit A896 into Shieldaig, hotel in village centre

Tigh an Eilean is in an utterly stunning location beside Loch Shieldaig; the bulk of Upper Loch Torridon and its astonishing mountains are literally just round the corner, whilst the lane to the remote Applecross Peninsula curves round the bay from the inn. Patrons have been left speechless by the abundance of wildlife visible from this extraordinary waterside setting; otters and seals abound and there's a nesting pair of white-tailed sea eagles here too. And you know you're onto a good thing when the tea and scones appear on arrival; this welcoming, hands-on approach is a hallmark of the way in which Chris and Cathryn Field run the whole operation. It can be a long drive to get here but the journey is more than worth the effort. The brightly decorated bedrooms are comfortable - but don't expect television, except in one of the lounges. The dining room basks in fabulous views of islands and hills to the open sea beyond the loch - the perfect spot, then, for sourcing the spectacular ingredients that drive Chris's daily-changing dinner menus. Unsurprisingly, there's a strong line in seafood, with fish and hand-dived scallops and clams delivered straight from the village jetty to the kitchen door. A rich gratin of Loch Torridon crab offset by zesty pink grapefruit gets things under way, ahead of cannon of venison teamed with roasted beetroot, sauté potatoes and a red wine and thyme jus. The contrasting textures and temperatures of warm roasted plums served in a chilled plum soup with home-made double ginger ice cream make a great finale. There's also a traditional bar, where live music and certainly ceilidhs add a weekend buzz to the village, and upstairs the Coastal Kitchen offers more informal dining, majoring on the bountiful fruits of the sea; sourced by environmentally-responsible methods such as creel-fishing or hand-diving. Razor clam fritters or langoustines à la plancha are a great introduction to the menu and specials choices cooked in the open kitchen here. The wood-burning oven gives a flavoursome edge to the hand-made pizzas like the 'from the sea' feast of crayfish, squid, shrimps, wood-fired langoustines, onion and orange-braised fennel; or try a trio of hand-dived scallops, oven-seared and served on a bed of dressed leaves with lemon and chilli butter.

Rooms 11 (1 fmly) **S** fr £70; **D** fr £140 (incl. bkfst)*

Facilities Birdwatching Kayaks Astronomical telescope
Xmas New Year Wi-fi **Parking** 15 **Notes** LB RS late Oct-mid
Mar

Chef Christopher Field **Owner** Christopher & Cathryn Field
Times 7-9 Closed end Oct-mid Mar (except private booking),
L all week **Prices** Fixed D 4 course £45, Service optional
Wines 50 bottles over £20, 20 bottles under £20, 14 by glass
Notes Vegetarian menu **Seats** 28, Pr/dining room 28
Children Portions, Menu

SOUTH BALLACHULISH	Map 4 NN05

The Ballachulish Hotel

★★★ 75% HOTEL

☎ 0845 609 9966 📠 01855 811629
PH49 4JY
e-mail: reservations@akkeron-hotels.com
web: www.akkeron-hotels.com
dir: On A828 (Fort William-Oban road), 3m N of Glencoe

On the shores of Loch Linnhe and at the foot of dramatic
Glencoe, guests are assured of a warm welcome here. A
selection of bar meals is available at lunchtime, and
evening meals are served in the Bulas Bistro which
overlooks the stunning mountain scenery. The tastefully
decorated bedrooms include the six Chieftain Rooms which
are particularly comfortable.

Rooms 53 (2 fmly) (7 GF) **Facilities** Xmas New Year Wi-fi
Conf Board 20 **Parking** 60 **Notes** Civ Wed 65

Craiglinnhe House

★★★★ GUEST HOUSE

Lettermore PH49 4JD
☎ 01855 811270
e-mail: info@craiglinnhe.co.uk
web: www.craiglinnhe.co.uk
dir: From village A82 onto A828, Craiglinnhe 1.5m on left

Built during the reign of Queen Victoria, Craiglinnhe House
enjoys an elevated position with stunning views across Loch
Linnhe to the village of Onich, and up to the Ballachulish
Bridge and the Pap of Glencoe. The attractive bedrooms vary
in size, are stylishly furnished, and are well equipped. There
is a ground-floor lounge and a charming dining room where
delicious breakfasts, and evening meals by arrangement,
are served at individual tables.

Rooms 5 en suite S £48-£55.50; D £60-£85 **Facilities** FTV
tea/coffee Dinner available Cen ht Licensed Wi-fi **Parking** 5
Notes LB ⊗ No Children 13yrs Closed 24-26 Dec

SPEAN BRIDGE	Map 4 NN28

Corriechoille Lodge

★★★★ 🍴 GUEST HOUSE

PH34 4EY
☎ 01397 712002
web: www.corriechoille.com
dir: Off A82 signed Corriechoille, 2.5m, left at fork (10mph
sign). At end of tarmac, turn right up hill & left

This fine country house stands above the River Spean. There
are magnificent views of the Nevis range and surrounding
mountains from the comfortable first-floor lounge and some
of the spacious, well-appointed bedrooms. Friendly and
attentive service is provided, as are traditional breakfasts
and delicious evening meals by arrangement.

Rooms 4 en suite (2 fmly) (1 GF) S £42-£48; D £64-£76*
Facilities STV FTV tea/coffee Dinner available Cen ht
Licensed Wi-fi **Parking** 7 **Notes** ⊗ No Children 7yrs Closed
Nov-Mar RS Sun-Mon closed

Smiddy House

★★★★ 🛏 RESTAURANT WITH ROOMS

◉◉ Modern Scottish

Highland hospitality and fine Scottish produce

Roy Bridge Rd PH34 4EU
☎ 01397 712335 📠 01397 712043
e-mail: enquiry@smiddyhouse.co.uk
web: www.smiddyhouse.co.uk
dir: In village centre, A82 onto A86

On the main road through Spean Bridge, this imposing
building turned luxury bed and breakfast, housed in what
used to be the village blacksmiths, and is now a very
friendly restaurant with rooms. The attractive bedrooms,
named after places in Scotland, are comfortably furnished
and well equipped. The local sights of Ben Nevis and the
Great Glen are on the doorstep, but there's plenty of interest
inside too. Original features are married with high quality
tablecloths, fresh flowers and glassware, while the service
team set a friendly tone. The small kitchen team keeps
things relatively simple and allow flavours to sing out, which

continued

SPEAN BRIDGE CONTINUED

is always a good thing, but particularly so when ingredients are as fresh and local as these. Seared Mallaig king scallops with tomato salsa and lemon butter sauce sets the high standard of modern Scottish cuisine on offer, before the likes of herb-crusted rack of lamb with fine ratatouille, glazed shallots and basil mustard dressing. To finish, apple parfait with green apple granité, honeycomb and milk ice cream is bursting with flavour.

Rooms 4 en suite (1 fmly) **Facilities** tea/coffee Dinner available Wi-fi **Parking** 15 **Notes** No coaches

Chef Glen Russell **Owner** Glen Russell, Robert Bryson **Times** 6-9 Closed 2 days a week (Nov-Apr), L all week **Prices** Fixed D 3 course £33.50-£39.50, Service optional **Wines** 26 bottles over £20, 10 bottles under £20, 5 by glass **Notes** Sunday L, Vegetarian available, Dress restrictions, Smart casual **Seats** 38 **Children** Portions, Menu

Achnabobane *(NN195811)*

 ★★★ FARMHOUSE

PH34 4EX
☎ **01397 712919   Mr and Mrs N Ockenden**
e-mail: enquiries@achnabobane.co.uk
web: www.achnabobane.co.uk
dir: 2m S of Spean Bridge on A82

With breathtaking views of Ben Nevis, Aonach Mhor and the Grey Corries, the farmhouse offers comfortable, good-value accommodation in a friendly family environment. Bedrooms are traditional in style and well equipped. Breakfast and evening meals are served in the conservatory-dining room.

Rooms 4 rms (1 en suite) (1 fmly) (1 GF) S £30-£34; D £60-£68* **Facilities** TVL tea/coffee Dinner available Cen ht Wi-fi **Parking** 5 **Notes** Closed Xmas red deer/woodland

STRATHPEFFER   Map 5 NH45

Inver Lodge

★★★ GUEST HOUSE

IV14 9DL
☎ **01997 421392**
e-mail: derbyshire@inverlg.fsnet.co.uk
dir: A834 through Strathpeffer centre, turn beside Spa Pavilion signed Bowling Green, Inver Lodge on right

You are assured of a warm welcome at this Victorian lodge, secluded in its own tree-studded gardens yet within easy walking distance of the town centre. Bedrooms are comfortable and well equipped, and the cosy lounge is ideal for relaxation. Breakfasts, and evening meals (by arrangement), are served at a communal table.

Rooms 2 rms (1 fmly) S £32.50; D £50* **Facilities** FTV tea/coffee Dinner available Cen ht Wi-fi **Parking** 2 **Notes** LB ⊗ Closed Xmas & New Year ⊠

STRONTIAN   Map 4 NM86

Kilcamb Lodge

★★★ COUNTRY HOUSE HOTEL

  Modern European, Scottish **V** ⌖

Idyllically situated lodge with highly accomplished cooking

☎ 01967 402257   📄 01967 402041
PH36 4HY
e-mail: enquiries@kilcamblodge.co.uk
web: www.kilcamblodge.co.uk
dir: Off A861, via Corran Ferry

Kilcamb Lodge is in an unparalleled location even for the Scottish Highlands, perched on the shores of the stunning Loch Sunart, with wonderful views of this loch and the mountains that surround it. It's unbelievably tranquil and a great getaway. The suites and bedrooms, with either loch or garden views, are stylishly decorated using designer fabrics and have flat-screen TVs, DVD/CD players, plus bath robes, iced water and even guest umbrellas. The restaurant does well to live up to its idyllic location with some extremely refined cooking. There's a focus on local game and shellfish, often sourced from local estates and fishing boats. Start perhaps with pan-fried partridge breast with Puy lentils, garlic purée and game jus, followed by a trio of West Coast shellfish with creamed leeks, potato purée and shellfish sauce, and finish with a dessert such as lemon tart and lemon soufflé with clotted cream ice cream.

Rooms 10 (2 fmly) **S** £145-£208; **D** £229-£369 (incl. bkfst & dinner)* **Facilities** FTV Fishing Boating Hiking Bird/whale/otter watching Stalking Clay pigeon shooting Xmas New Year Wi-fi **Conf** Class 18 Board 18 Thtr 18 **Parking** 20 **Notes** LB No children 10yrs Closed 2 Jan-1 Feb Civ Wed 120

Chef Gary Phillips **Owner** Sally & David Fox **Times** 12-1.30/7.30-9.30 Closed Jan-1 Feb **Prices** Fixed L 2 course £14.50, Fixed D 4 course £49.50, Service optional, Groups min 10 service 10% **Wines** 45 bottles over £20, 20 bottles under £20, 10 by glass **Notes** Chef's tasting menu available Mon-Fri, Sunday L, Vegetarian menu, Dress restrictions, Smart casual, no jeans, T-shirts or trainers **Seats** 26

TAIN — Map 5 NH78

Glenmorangie Highland Home at Cadboll

 ★★★ COUNTRY HOUSE HOTEL

 British, French 🍴

House party-style dining in Highland hideaway

☎ 01862 871671 📄 01862 871625
Cadboll, Fearn IV20 1XP
e-mail: relax@glenmorangie.co.uk
web: www.theglenmorangiehouse.com
dir: A9 onto B9175 towards Nigg. Follow tourist signs

The very name of Glenmorangie should make whisky fans' ears prick up, and this splendid operation caters for malt-loving foodies in fine style. The 17th-century house is a secluded bolt-hole sitting amid the ruins of a castle with its own beach on the wild Dornoch Firth. Stylish bedrooms are divided between the traditional main house and some cosy cottages in the grounds. Expect a chatty sort of occasion, as you dine house-party style at a long banqueting table decked out with candles, fresh flowers, silver and crystal after meeting other diners over drinks in the drawing room. It's a supremely accomplished set-up. Produce is A1 throughout, drawing on fresh ingredients from the walled kitchen gardens and orchards, fish from local boats, and game from nearby estates. A classically-trained team delivers dishes in a modern Scottish idiom: dinner might kick off with confit duck leg and foie gras with Madeira jelly and toasted brioche, then move on to roast fillet and braised shin of beef with fondant potatoes and port wine jus, and finish with roasted peach with cherries and pistachio cream.

Rooms 9 (3 annexe) (4 fmly) (3 GF) **S** £225; **D** £350-£400 (incl. bkfst & dinner)* **Facilities** FTV 🏊 Archery Beauty treatments Clay pigeon shooting Falconry Xmas New Year Wi-fi **Conf** Board 12 **Parking** 60 **Notes** LB ⊗ No children 15yrs Civ Wed 60

Chef David Graham **Owner** Glenmorangie Ltd **Times** 8 Closed L except by prior arrangement **Prices** Service optional **Wines** 38 bottles over £20, 5 bottles under £20, 15 by glass **Notes** Fixed D 5 course £55, Vegetarian available, Dress restrictions, Smart casual, no jeans or T-shirts **Seats** 30, Pr/dining room 12

THURSO — Map 5 ND16

Forss House

★★★★ 76% SMALL HOTEL

⊚⊚ Modern Scottish 🍴

Elegant dining in spectacular Highland surroundings

☎ 01847 861201 📄 01847 861301
Forss KW14 7XY
e-mail: anne@forsshousehotel.co.uk
web: www.forsshousehotel.co.uk
dir: On A836 between Thurso & Reay

Forss House is a Georgian shooting lodge suffused with congenial hospitality and offering nirvana for outdoor types. Secluded in 20 acres of wooded glen beneath a waterfall, a better base for de-stressing while fishing, stalking, hiking and biking is hard to imagine. The hotel offers a choice of bedrooms, from the traditional styled rooms in the main house to the more contemporary annexe rooms in the grounds. All rooms are very well equipped and well appointed. A day spent enjoying all that fresh air and exertion should sharpen the appetite for the accomplished modern Scottish cooking on offer in the seductively classy dining room. The kitchen has the confidence to treat exemplary local produce with a light hand, leaving the sheer quality of the raw materials to work their magic. Dinner might start with roast pigeon breast with beetroot, wilted greens and salsify crisps, then go on to clementine-glazed pork belly with smoked bacon, creamy cabbage and potato purée, or seared John Dory with parsnip purée, braised leeks and light curry sauce. Desserts wind things up with a comforting treacle tart with vanilla cream, or excellent Highland cheeses with oat cookies and spicy chutney.

Rooms 14 (6 annexe) (1 fmly) (7 GF) **S** £97-£115; **D** £130-£165 (incl. bkfst)* **Facilities** FTV Fishing Wi-fi **Conf** Class 12 Board 14 Thtr 20 Del from £155 to £170 **Parking** 14 **Notes** LB Closed 23 Dec-3 Jan Civ Wed 26

Chef Darren Sivewright **Owner** Ian & Sabine Richards **Times** 7-9 Closed 23 Dec-4 Jan, L all week **Prices** Starter £5.95-£7.95, Main £18.50-£24, Dessert £4.95-£6.95, Service optional **Wines** 34 bottles over £20, 6 bottles under £20, 2 by glass **Notes** Vegetarian available **Seats** 26, Pr/dining room 14 **Children** Portions

TOMATIN — Map 5 NH82

Glenan Lodge

★★★★ GUEST HOUSE

IV13 7YT
☎ 01808 511217 📠 08082 801125
e-mail: enquiries@glenanlodge.co.uk
web: www.glenanlodge.co.uk
dir: Off A9 to Tomatin, turn left to distillery, then right into distillery drive. Proceed to top of hill, take right fork & follow road to Glenan Lodge

Peacefully located on the edge of the village, this relaxed and homely guest house offers a warm welcome. The comfortable bedrooms are traditionally furnished and suitably equipped. An inviting lounge is available, and delicious home-cooked evening meals and breakfasts are served in the dining room. A two mile stretch of the River Findhorn is available for fly-fishing, and golfers, walkers and bird watchers are also well provided for locally.

Rooms 7 en suite (2 fmly) S £31-£41; D £62-£72*
Facilities FTV TVL tea/coffee Dinner available Cen ht Licensed Wi-fi Fishing Parking 7 Notes LB ⊗ No Children 5yrs

TORRIDON — Map 4 NG95

The Torridon

★★★★ COUNTRY HOUSE HOTEL

🌹🌹🌹 Modern British V 🍷NOTABLE WINE LIST 🖐

A piece of loch-side Highland luxury

☎ 01445 791242 📠 01445 712253
By Achnasheen, Wester Ross IV22 2EY
e-mail: info@thetorridon.com
web: www.thetorridon.com
dir: From A832 at Kinlochewe, A896 towards Torridon. (NB do not turn into village) 1m, hotel on right

The drive along winding hilly roads only adds to the sense of anticipation of a visit to The Torridon, and what greets you on arrival more than lives up to expectations. The beautiful old shooting lodge looks the part, right down to the soaring tower and position looking across a sea loch (Upper Loch Torridon). There are 58 acres of wooded grounds to explore, so every opportunity to work up an appetite. The hotel is smartly done-out, avoiding cliché, and successfully blending traditional features with contemporary style. The attractive bedrooms are all individually furnished and most enjoy stunning Highland views. Comfortable day rooms feature fine wood panelling and roaring fires in cooler months and outdoor activities include shooting, cycling and walking. The whisky bar offers a selection of over 350 malts, which should be enough to satisfy even the most ardent connoisseur, and the restaurant is a fitting setting for the

first-class cooking of chef 'Bruno' Birkbeck: acres of magnificent oak panelling on the walls and top quality linen on the tables set the scene, ably supported by magnificent views. The service is a credit to the place, being both charming and completely clued-up about the food. The modern Scottish cooking puts the fabulous regional produce to the fore, kicking off with canapés in the elegant drawing room or whisky bar; crisp goujons of lemon sole, perhaps, with lemon mayonnaise. Impeccable timing and seasoning is on display in a first-course risotto of Bayonne ham and sage, served with a quail's egg covered in crisp breadcrumbs, topped with a sage foam. Next up, a ravioli of lobster claw with shellfish foam, followed by roast loin of cod with smoked chicken and a pearl barley broth. Chocolate fondant is as perfect as can be, served up in the classic manner with vanilla ice cream, albeit with some caramel pieces to add another dimension.

Rooms 19 (2 GF) S £140; D £215-£425 (incl. bkfst)*
Facilities STV Fishing 🎣 Abseiling Archery Climbing Falconry Kayaking Mountain biking Xmas New Year Wi-fi Conf Board 16 Thtr 42 Del from £325 to £425* Services Lift Parking 20 Notes ⊗ Closed 2 Jan-9 Feb RS Nov-14 Mar Civ Wed 42

Chef Jason 'Bruno' Birkbeck Owner Daniel & Rohaise Rose-Bristow Times 12-2/7-9 Closed 2 Jan for 5 wks, L all week Prices Fixed L 3 course £30, Service optional Wines 156 bottles over £20, 27 bottles under £20, 8 by glass Notes Fixed D 5 course £50, Vegetarian menu, Dress restrictions, No jeans or trainers Seats 38, Pr/dining room 16 Children Portions, Menu

The Torridon Inn

★★★ 🍴 INN

IV22 2EY
☎ 01445 791242 📠 01445 712253
e-mail: inn@thetorridon.com
web: www.thetorridon.com/inn
dir: From Inverness take A9 N, then follow signs to Ullapool. Take A835 then A832. In Kinlochewe take A896 to Annat. Pub 200yds on right after village

Set in 58 acres of parkland and created by converting the stable block, buttery and farm buildings on the Torridon Estate, this informal inn stands in an idyllic location overlooking Loch Torridon and surrounded by lofty mountains on all sides. The inn is very popular with walkers, and guests can also avail themselves of the many outdoor pursuits that are provided at the Torridon Hotel (see entry above). Each of the spacious bedrooms are well equipped and comfortable. In the convivial bar you can replay the day's adventures over one of the 60 malt whiskies, including local favourites Talisker and Glen Ord, or a pint of real ale from the An Teallach, Isle of Skye or Cairngorm breweries. The inn has its own separate restaurant, where at any time you can sample the high quality, locally sourced food in which it specialises.

During the day you can tuck into hearty soups, sandwiches and bar meals, while in the evening menus are likely to feature salmon and other local fish, venison, haggis and a variety of home-made specials. Dinner could therefore begin with seared scallops with celeriac purée, rocket salad and balsamic dressing; followed by fish pie; or gammon steak, pineapple and chips. Round off with sticky toffee pudding with butterscotch sauce and vanilla ice cream. Live traditional music is laid on regularly and there is a beer festival late September.

Rooms 12 en suite (3 fmly) (5 GF) S £99; D £99* **Facilities** STV tea/coffee Dinner available Cen ht Wi-fi ♨ Fishing Pool table Outdoor adventure activities available **Parking** 12 **Notes** LB Closed Jan

Open all day all wk Closed: Jan **Bar Meals** Av main course £10 food served all day **Restaurant** Av 3 course à la carte fr £24 food served all day ⏣ FREE HOUSE ◀ Isle of Skye Brewery - Red Cuillin, Torridon Ale, Cairngorm Brewery Tradewinds, An Teallach, Crofters Pale Ale. **Facilities** Children welcome Children's menu Children's portions Play area Dogs allowed Garden Beer festival

ULLAPOOL	Map 4 NH19

The Arch Inn

★★★ INN

 Modern British

- -

Great views and fantastic seafood

10-11 West Shore St IV26 2UR
☎ **01854 612454**
e-mail: info@thearchinn.co.uk

Just two minutes' walk from the main Outer Hebrides ferry terminal, this white-painted inn is on the site of the first building built by the British Fishing Society when Ullapool was established over 200 years ago. The accommodation provided is comfortable and most rooms have stunning views over the loch to the mountains in the distance. Two dining options are available - the relaxed bar and grill on the ground floor, and a more formal Seafood Restaurant on the first floor, with fantastic elevated views over Loch Broom. This airy room features a large commemorative collection of Bells whisky and the young team are engaging. Both chefs have a great pedigree and the menu demonstrates confidence and a belief in the quality of their ingredients. A starter of langoustines might come with parsley mayonnaise and new potatoes, an extra dimension added by the inclusion of a sharp, citrussy carpaccio of langustine. Main course 'tasting of Leckmelm Farm lamb' is the perfect way to show off the fantastic local meat, the shoulder perfectly braised to melt in the mouth, while chocolate coulant with milk ice cream and peanut brittle is a great finale.

Rooms 10 en suite (1 fmly) (2 GF) S fr £40; D fr £80* **Facilities** FTV tea/coffee Dinner available Cen ht Wi-fi Pool

table **Conf** Max 60 Thtr 40 Class 30 Board 35 **Parking** 5 **Notes** ⊗

Chef Karen Szymik, Maciej Szymek **Owner** Karen & Maciej Szymek **Times** 6-9.30 Closed Oct-Apr, Sun-Mon **Prices** Service optional **Wines** 35 bottles over £20, 14 bottles under £20, 7 by the glass **Notes** Vegetarian available Seats 22 ⊛ **Children** Portions

WHITEBRIDGE	Map 5 NH41

Whitebridge Hotel

★★ 69% HOTEL

- -

☎ 01456 486226 ▤ 01456 486413
IV2 6UN
e-mail: info@whitebridgehotel.co.uk
dir: A9 onto B851, follow signs to Fort Augustus. Or A82 onto B862 at Fort Augustus

Close to Loch Ness and set amid rugged mountain and moorland scenery, this hotel is popular with tourists, fishermen and deerstalkers. Guests have a choice of more formal dining in the restaurant or lighter meals in the popular cosy bar. Bedrooms are thoughtfully equipped and brightly furnished.

Rooms 12 (3 fmly) **S** £50-£60; **D** £75-£85 (incl. bkfst)* **Facilities** Fishing Wi-fi **Parking** 32 **Notes** Closed 11 Dec-9 Jan

WICK	Map 5 ND35

Mackay's

★★★ 75% HOTEL

- -

☎ 01955 602323 ▤ 01955 605930
Union St KW1 5ED
e-mail: info@mackayshotel.co.uk
dir: Opposite Caithness General Hospital

This well-established hotel is situated just outside the town centre overlooking the River Wick. MacKay's provides well-equipped, attractive accommodation, suited to both the business and leisure guest. There is a stylish bistro offering food throughout the day and a choice of bars that also offer food.

continued

WICK CONTINUED

Rooms 30 (2 fmly) **S** £75-£85; **D** £99-£150 (incl. bkfst)*
Facilities FTV 🎵 Wi-fi **Conf** Class 100 Board 60 Thtr 100
Del from £115 to £150* **Services** Lift **Notes** LB ⊗ Closed
24-26 Dec & 1-3 Jan

The Clachan

★★★★ BED AND BREAKFAST

13 Randolph Place, South Rd KW1 5NJ
☎ **01955 605384 & 600467**
e-mail: enquiry@theclachan.co.uk
dir: Off A99 0.5m S of town centre

A warm welcome is assured at this immaculate detached
home, by the main road on the south edge of the town. The
bright, airy bedrooms (all on the ground floor) though
compact, are attractively furnished to make good use of
available space. Breakfast offers an extensive choice and is
served at individual tables in the cosy dining room.

Rooms 3 en suite (3 GF) **S** £35-£55; **D** £64-£70*
Facilities FTV tea/coffee Cen ht Wi-fi **Parking** 3 **Notes** ⊗ No
Children 12yrs Closed Xmas & New Year ☺

INVERCLYDE

GREENOCK   **Map 2 NS27**

Holiday Inn Express Greenock

BUDGET HOTEL

☎ 01475 786666   🖹 01475 786777
Cartsburn PA15 1AE
e-mail: greenock@holidayinnexpress.org.uk
web: www.hiexpressgreenock.co.uk
dir: M8 junct 31, A8 to Greenock, right at 5th rdbt, hotel on
right

A modern hotel ideal for families and business travellers.
Fresh and uncomplicated, the spacious rooms include Sky
TV, power shower and tea and coffee-making facilities.
Continental buffet breakfast is included in the room rate;
other meals may be taken at the nearby family pub or
restaurant.

Rooms 71 (15 fmly) (6 GF) (20 smoking) **Conf** Class 48
Board 32 Thtr 70

Premier Inn Greenock

BUDGET HOTEL

☎ 0871 527 8476   🖹 0871 527 8477
The Point, 1-3 James Watt Way PA15 2AD
web: www.premierinn.com
dir: A8 to Greenock. At rdbt junct of East Hamilton St & Main
St (McDonalds visable on right) take 3rd exit. Hotel on left

High quality, budget accommodation ideal for both families
and business travellers. Spacious, en suite bedrooms
feature tea and coffee-making facilities, and Freeview TV in
most hotels. Internet access and Wi-fi are available for a
small fee. The adjacent family restaurant features a wide
and varied menu.

Rooms 17 **D** £57-£78*

KILMACOLM   **Map 2 NS37**

Windyhill Restaurant

 Modern British **V** ✋

Carefully-sourced contemporary British cuisine

☎ 01505 872613
4 St James Ter, Lochwinnoch Rd PA13 4HB
e-mail: matthewscobey@hotmail.co.uk
dir: From Glasgow Airport, A737 take Bridge of Weir exit.
Onto A761 to Kilmacolm. Left into High Street

Taking its name from the art nouveau home built in
Kilmacolm by the renowned architect and designer Charles
Rennie Mackintosh, Windyhill is a smartly casual
contemporary restaurant run by welcoming, hands-on
owners. Inside, bare darkwood tables and leather chairs look
slick, and modern artwork adds splashes of colour to
pristine white walls; a scattering of tealights and fairy
lights, and laid-back jazz in the background make for a
romantic ambience. The cooking follows a modern course,
with local produce a feature on straightforward, well-
thought-through monthly menus. Haggis and smoked
pancetta beignets with root vegetable purée and pepper
sauce is an attention-grabbing starter, then roast rump of
lamb might follow, partnered by roast cocotte potatoes,
Chantenay carrots, sweet braised red cabbage and tarragon
jus. Don't skimp on pudding, especially when it could be
warm sticky toffee and walnut tart with caramel ice cream
and toffee sauce.

Chef Matthew Scobey **Owner** Matthew Scobey & Careen
McLean **Times** 6-10 Closed Xmas-New Year, last wk Jul, 1st
wk Aug, Sun-Mon, L all week **Prices** Fixed L 2 course £16,
Fixed D 3 course £21, Starter £3.95-£6.50, Main £9.95-
£19.95, Dessert £4.95-£6.95 **Wines** 18 bottles over £20, 8
bottles under £20, 6 by glass **Notes** Vegetarian menu
Seats 45 **Children** Portions, Menu **Parking** On street, car
park opposite

NORTH LANARKSHIRE

AIRDRIE
Map 3 NS76

Shawlee Cottage

★★★ Ⓐ BED AND BREAKFAST

108 Lauchope St, Chapelhall ML6 8SW
☎ 01236 753774 📄 01236 749300
e-mail: shawleecottage@blueyonder.co.uk
web: www.airdriebedbreakfast.co.uk
dir: M8 junct 6, A73 to Chapelhall, left onto B799, Shawlee 600yds on right

Rooms 5 en suite (5 GF) S £36-£46; D £55-£75* **Facilities** tea/coffee Direct Dial Cen ht Wi-fi Golf 18 **Parking** 6 **Notes** ⊗

COATBRIDGE
Map 2 NS76

Auchenlea

★★★ GUEST HOUSE

153 Langmuir Rd, Bargeddie G69 7RT
☎ 0141 771 6870 & 07775 791381 📄 0141 771 6870
e-mail: helenbarr06@btinternet.com
dir: N off A8 onto A752 for 0.4m

Backing onto farmland, yet only a short distance from the motorway, this detached house is well placed for Glasgow and Edinburgh. Satisfying, well-cooked breakfasts are served at a communal table in the bright dining room, and there is an attractive conservatory and adjoining lounge. The bedrooms, all on the ground floor, are modern in style with one designed for easier access.

Rooms 6 en suite (1 fmly) (6 GF) **Facilities** FTV TVL tea/coffee Cen ht **Parking** 10 **Notes** ⊗

CUMBERNAULD
Map 3 NS77

The Westerwood Hotel & Golf Resort

★★★★ 81% HOTEL

◉ Modern Scottish ✿

Confident modern cooking and superlative service

☎ 01236 457171 📄 01236 738478
1 St Andrews Dr, Westerwood G68 0EW
e-mail: westerwood@qhotels.co.uk
web: www.qhotels.co.uk
dir: A80 junct signed Dullatur, from junct follow signs fo hotel

It is hard to believe that the centre of Glasgow is a mere 15-minute drive from this stylish contemporary golf and spa-oriented hotel set in 400 acres at the foot of the Campsie Hills. Accommodation is provided in spacious, bright bedrooms, many with super bathrooms, day rooms include sumptuous lounges and extensive golf, fitness and conference facilities are available. But location and tip-top facilities are only one side of the coin: what makes Westerwood House stand out from the pack is the excellent professional team who make every aspect of the experience run smoothly. On the food front, Fleming's Restaurant fits in with the sophisticated modern tone of the hotel, kitted out with darkwood tables and seats clad in warm hues of tangerine and sage-green, and run with aplomb by smartly-turned-out, knowledgeable staff. Much of the food runs along familiar modern Scottish lines, with sparks of off-the-wall creativity to grab the attention. Orkney scallops with black pudding, pancetta, and olive mash is a crowd-pleaser done right, followed by a creative teaming of roast breast of duck with dauphinoise potatoes, pickled wild mushrooms, and juniper and bramble jus.

Rooms 148 (15 fmly) (49 GF) **Facilities** Spa STV 🏹 ♨ 18 🏊 Putt green Gym Beauty salon Relaxation room Sauna Steam room Xmas New Year Wi-fi **Conf** Class 120 Board 60 Thtr 400 Del from £115 to £190 **Services** Lift **Parking** 250 **Notes** Civ Wed 350

Chef Stewart Goldie **Owner** Q Hotels **Times** 6-9.30 Closed Sun-Mon, L all week **Prices** Food prices not confirmed for 2012. Please telephone for details **Notes** Vegetarian available, Air con **Seats** 180, Pr/dining room 60 **Children** Portions, Menu

Premier Inn Glasgow (Cumbernauld)

BUDGET HOTEL

☎ 0871 527 8424 📄 0871 527 8425
4 South Muirhead Rd G67 1AX
web: www.premierinn.com
dir: From A80, A8011 follow Cumbernauld & town centre signs. Hotel opposite Asda & McDonalds

High quality, budget accommodation ideal for both families and business travellers. Spacious, en suite bedrooms feature tea and coffee-making facilities, and Freeview TV in most hotels. Internet access and Wi-fi are available for a small fee. The adjacent family restaurant features a wide and varied menu.

Rooms 37 D £54-£60*

Castlecary House Hotel 🍷

Castlecary Rd G68 0HD ☎ 01324 840233
📄 01324 841608
e-mail: enquiries@castlecaryhotel.com
dir: A80 onto B816 between Glasgow & Stirling. 7m from Falkirk, 9m from Stirling

Run by the same family for over 30 years, this friendly hotel is located close to the historic Antonine Wall and Forth and Clyde Canal. Meals in the lounge bars plough a traditional

continued

CUMBERNAULD CONTINUED

furrow with options such as venison and port terrine; chicken tournedo (chicken stuffed with haggis and served with traditional clapshot and Arran mustard sauce); roast salmon fillet with prawn bisque and rumbledethumps. There is an excellent selection of real ales on offer, and more formal fare is available in Camerons Restaurant. A beer festival is held twice a year – contact the hotel for details of the dates.

Open all day all wk Closed: 1 Jan **Bar Meals** L served 12-9 D served 12-9 food served all day **Restaurant** L served Sun 12.30-3 D served Mon-Sat 6-9.30 booking required Fixed menu price fr £10 ⊕ FREE HOUSE ◢ Arran Blonde, Harviestoun Brooker's Bitter & Twisted, Inveralmond Ossian's Ale, Houston Peter's Well, Caledonian Deuchars IPA. ♀ 8 **Facilities** Children welcome Children's menu Children's portions Garden Beer festival Parking Wi-fi

MOTHERWELL	Map 3 NS75

Alona Hotel

★★★★ 77% HOTEL

☎ 01698 333888 ☷ 01698 338720
Strathclyde Country Park ML1 3RT
e-mail: gm@alonahotel.co.uk
web: www.alonahotel.co.uk
dir: M74 junct 5, hotel approx 250yds on left

Alona is a Celtic word meaning 'exquisitely beautiful'. This hotel is situated within the idyllic beauty of Strathclyde Country Park, with tranquil views over the picturesque loch and surrounding forests. There is a very contemporary feel, from the open-plan public areas to the spacious and well-appointed bedrooms. Wi-fi is available throughout. M&D's, Scotland's Family Theme Park, is just next door.

Rooms 51 (24 fmly) (17 GF) **Facilities** FTV ♬ Xmas New Year Wi-fi **Conf** Class 100 Board 76 Thtr 140 **Services** Lift Air con **Parking** 100 **Notes** ⊗ Civ Wed 250

Express by Holiday Inn Strathclyde Park

BUDGET HOTEL

☎ 01698 858585 ☷ 01698 852375
Hamilton Rd, Hamilton ML1 3RB
e-mail: isabella.little@ichotelsgroup.com
web: www.hiexpress.com/strathclyde
dir: M74 junct 5 follow signs for Strathclyde Country Park

A modern hotel ideal for families and business travellers. Fresh and uncomplicated, the spacious rooms include Sky TV, power shower and tea and coffee-making facilities. Continental buffet breakfast is included in the room rate; other meals may be taken at the nearby family pub or restaurant.

Rooms 120 (58 fmly) **Conf** Class 10 Board 18 Thtr 30

Premier Inn Glasgow (Motherwell)

BUDGET HOTEL

☎ 0871 527 8430 ☷ 0871 527 8431
Edinburgh Rd, Newhouse ML1 5SY
web: www.premierinn.com
dir: From S: M74 junct 5, A725 towards Coatbridge. Take A8 towards Edinburgh, exit at junct 6, follow Lanark signs. Hotel 400yds on right

High quality, budget accommodation ideal for both families and business travellers. Spacious, en suite bedrooms feature tea and coffee-making facilities, and Freeview TV in most hotels. Internet access and Wi-fi are available for a small fee. The adjacent family restaurant features a wide and varied menu.

Rooms 40 **D** £54-£60*

STEPPS	Map 2 NS66

Premier Inn Glasgow North East (Stepps)

BUDGET HOTEL

☎ 0871 527 8452 ☷ 0871 527 8453
Crowwood Roundabout, Cumbernauld Rd G33 6HN
web: www.premierinn.com
dir: M8 junct 12, A80 (becomes dual carriageway) to Crowwood rdbt, 4th exit back onto A80, hotel 1st left. Or exit M80 at Crowwood rdbt, 3rd exit signed A80 West. Hotel 1st left

High quality, budget accommodation ideal for both families and business travellers. Spacious, en suite bedrooms feature tea and coffee-making facilities, and Freeview TV in most hotels. Internet access and Wi-fi are available for a small fee. The adjacent family restaurant features a wide and varied menu.

Rooms 80 **D** £54-£60*

SOUTH LANARKSHIRE
ABINGTON MOTORWAY SERVICE AREA (M74) Map 3 NS92

Days Inn Abington - M74

BUDGET HOTEL

☎ 01864 502782 ☷ 01864 502759
ML12 6RG
e-mail: abington.hotel@welcomebreak.co.uk
web: www.welcomebreak.co.uk
dir: M74 junct 13, accessible from N'bound and S'bound carriageways

This modern building offers accommodation in smart, spacious and well-equipped bedrooms, suitable for families and business travellers, and all with en suite bathrooms. Continental breakfast is available and other refreshments may be taken at the nearby family restaurant.

Rooms 52 (50 fmly) (8 smoking) S £39.95-£59.95;
D £49.95-£69.95 Conf Board 10

| BOTHWELL | Map 2 NS75 |

Bothwell Bridge Hotel

★★★ 79% HOTEL

☎ 01698 852246 📄 01698 854686
89 Main St G71 8EU
e-mail: reception@bothwellbridge-hotel.com
web: www.bothwellbridge-hotel.com
dir: M74 junct 5 & follow signs to Uddingston, right at mini-rdbt. Hotel just past shops on left

This red-sandstone mansion house is a popular business, function and conference hotel conveniently placed for the motorway. Most bedrooms are spacious and all are well equipped. The conservatory is a bright and comfortable restaurant serving an interesting variety of Italian influenced dishes. The lounge bar offers a comfortable seating area that proves popular as a stop for coffee.

Rooms 90 (14 fmly) (26 GF) Facilities STV ♫ Xmas New Year Wi-fi Conf Class 80 Board 50 Thtr 200 Del from £90 to £103* Services Lift Parking 125 Notes ⊗ Civ Wed 250

| EAST KILBRIDE | Map 2 NS65 |

Macdonald Crutherland House

★★★★ 74% HOTEL

⊚⊚⊚ British

Smart panelled restaurant with appealing menus

☎ 0844 879 9039 📄 01355 577047
Strathaven Rd G75 0QZ
e-mail: crutherland@macdonald-hotels.co.uk
web: www.macdonaldhotels.co.uk
dir: Follow A726 signed Strathaven, straight over Torrance rdbt, hotel on left after 250yds

In 37 acres of woods and parkland, the original building dates from 1705, although the hotel now has extensive conference and leisure facilities. The bedrooms are spacious and comfortable, and staff provide good levels of attention. It's popular for weddings, while the candlelit restaurant, panelled in wood, with high-backed leather chairs, is a destination dining spot. A glance at the menu explains why this should be so: an appealing list of tempting dishes, with a kitchen strong on technique and seasonality. Grills - steaks, or lamb cutlets - are a fixture, and there might be steamed haunch of venison pudding with spiced red cabbage, or roast cod in pancetta with wilted greens and sautéed Jerusalem artichokes. Starters could include mackerel rillette with a soft-boiled quail's egg, and ham

hock and black pudding terrine with apple purée. Treacle tart with crème Chantilly, or rhubarb crumble brûlée rounds things off nicely.

Rooms 75 (16 fmly) (16 GF) S £60-£175; D £70-£185 Facilities Spa STV ® Gym Sauna Steam room Xmas New Year Wi-fi Conf Class 100 Board 50 Thtr 500 Del from £135 to £235 Services Lift Parking 200 Notes LB ⊗ Civ Wed 300

Chef Kevin Hay Owner Macdonald Hotels Times 6-9 Closed L all week Prices Food prices not confirmed for 2012. Please telephone for details Wines 53 bottles over £20, 11 bottles under £20, 15 by glass Notes Vegetarian available, Dress restrictions, Smart dress Seats 80, Pr/dining room 300 Children Portions, Menu

Holiday Inn Glasgow-East Kilbride

★★★★ 74% HOTEL

☎ 01355 236300 📄 01355 233552
Stewartfield Way G74 5LA
e-mail: salesmgr@hieastkilbride.com
web: www.hieastkilbride.com
dir: M74 junct 5, A725 then A726

A modern hotel located in East Kilbride but within easy striking distance of Glasgow. Bedrooms are nicely appointed and cater well for the needs of the modern traveller. Food is served in La Bonne Auberge with a definite French and Mediterranean bias. Good leisure facilities are an added bonus.

Rooms 101 (4 fmly) (26 GF) (8 smoking) S £39-£149; D £39-£149* Facilities Spa STV ® Gym Aerobics studio Spin-cycle studio Sauna Steam room Xmas New Year Wi-fi Conf Class 120 Board 60 Thtr 400 Del from £99 to £145* Services Lift Air con Parking 200 Notes Civ Wed 200

Premier Inn Glasgow East Kilbride

BUDGET HOTEL

☎ 0871 527 8446 📄 0871 527 8447
5 Lee's Burn Court, Nerston G74 3XB
web: www.premierinn.com
dir: M74 junct 5, follow East Kilbride/A725 signs. Into right lane, follow Glasgow/A749 signs. At lights left onto A749 signed East Kilbride Town Centre (A725). Take slip road to Lee's Burn Court

High quality, budget accommodation ideal for both families and business travellers. Spacious, en suite bedrooms feature tea and coffee-making facilities, and Freeview TV in most hotels. Internet access and Wi-fi are available for a small fee. The adjacent family restaurant features a wide and varied menu.

Rooms 44 D £52-£60*

Premier Inn Glasgow East Kilbride Central

BUDGET HOTEL

☎ 0871 527 8450 📄 0871 527 8451
Brunel Way, The Murray G75 0LD
web: www.premierinn.com
dir: M74 junct 5, follow East Kilbride A725 signs, then
Paisley A726 signs, left at Murray Rdbt, left into Brunel Way

Rooms 40 D £52-£60*

Premier Inn Glasgow East Kilbride (Peel Park)

BUDGET HOTEL

☎ 0871 527 8448 📄 0871 527 8449
Eaglesham Rd G75 8LW
web: www.premierinn.com
dir: 8m from M74 junct 5 on A726 at rdbt of B764

Rooms 42 D £52-£60*

| HAMILTON | Map 2 NS75 |

Express by Holiday Inn Hamilton

BUDGET HOTEL

☎ 0141 419 3500 📄 0141 419 3500
Keith St ML3 7BL
web: www.hiexpress.com/hamilton

A modern hotel ideal for families and business travellers.
Fresh and uncomplicated, the spacious rooms include Sky
TV, power shower and tea and coffee-making facilities.
Continental buffet breakfast is included in the room rate;
other meals may be taken at the nearby family pub or
restaurant.

Rooms 104

| LANARK | Map 3 NS84 |

Best Western Cartland Bridge Hotel

★★★ 75% COUNTRY HOUSE HOTEL

☎ 01555 664426 📄 01555 663773
Glasgow Rd ML11 9UF
e-mail: sales@cartlandbridge.co.uk
dir: A73 through Lanark towards Carluke. Hotel in 1.25m

Situated in wooded grounds on the edge of the town, this
Grade I listed mansion continues to be popular with both
business and leisure guests. Public areas feature wood
panelling, a gallery staircase and a magnificent dining
room. The well-equipped bedrooms vary in size.

Rooms 20 (2 fmly) S £40-£80; D £70-£120* Facilities FTV
Xmas New Year Wi-fi Conf Class 180 Board 50 Thtr 250

Del from £65 to £140* Parking 120 Notes LB ⊗
Civ Wed 200

| NEW LANARK | Map 3 NS84 |

New Lanark Mill Hotel

★★★ 83% HOTEL

☎ 01555 667200 📄 01555 667222
Mill One, New Lanark Mills ML11 9DB
e-mail: hotel@newlanark.org
web: www.newlanark.org
dir: Signed from all major roads, M74 junct 7 & M8

Originally built as a cotton mill in the 18th century, this
hotel forms part of a fully restored village, now a UNESCO
World Heritage Site. There's a bright modern style
throughout which contrasts nicely with features from the
original mill. There is a comfortable foyer-lounge with a
galleried restaurant above. The hotel enjoys stunning views
over the River Clyde.

Rooms 38 (5 fmly) (6 smoking) S £59-£99; D £69-£119
(incl. bkfst) Facilities STV 🏊 Gym Beauty room Steam room
Sauna Aerobics studios Xmas New Year Wi-fi Conf Class 60
Board 40 Thtr 200 Del from £99 to £139 Services Lift
Parking 75 Notes LB Civ Wed 120

| STRATHAVEN | Map 2 NS74 |

Rissons at Springvale

★★★ RESTAURANT WITH ROOMS

◉ Modern Scottish ✦

Relaxed restaurant with modern Scottish cuisine

18 Lethame Rd ML10 6AD
☎ 01357 521131 & 520234 📄 01357 521131
e-mail: info@rissons.co.uk
dir: A71 into Strathaven, W of town centre off Townhead St

Anne and Scott Baxter's small and friendly restaurant with
rooms has been keeping local gastronomes happy for a
decade since it was refurbished in a clean-cut contemporary
style. The bedrooms and bathrooms are stylish and well
equipped. The Victorian merchant's house overlooks the
local park, making for a relaxed setting in the light and airy
restaurant and adjoining conservatory. It's an easygoing
place with clued-up service, and the kitchen goes about its
business without undue fuss. The modern-bistro repertoire
matches the mood, serving up well-conceived dishes put
together with attention to detail. You might start along the
lines of roast pigeon breast with beetroot and black pudding
salad, then follow with Finnan haddock in leek sauce with
poached egg and mash, and finish indulgently with
marmalade bread pudding with Drambuie custard.

Rooms 9 en suite (1 fmly) (1 GF) S £42.50-£45; D £75-£80*
Facilities tea/coffee Dinner available Cen ht Wi-fi

Parking 10 **Notes** ⊗ Closed 1st wk Jan No coaches

Chef Scott Baxter **Owner** Scott & Anne Baxter
Times 12-2.30/6-9.30 Closed New Year, 1 wk Jan, 1st wk Jul, Mon-Tue, L Sat, D Sun **Prices** Fixed L 2 course £10.95, Fixed D 3 course £16.95, Starter £4.25-£10, Main £11-£22, Dessert £5-£6.50, Service optional **Wines** 13 bottles over £20, 23 bottles under £20, 6 by glass **Notes** Early evening menu Wed-Fri, Sunday L, Vegetarian available **Seats** 40 **Children** Portions, Menu

EAST LOTHIAN

GIFFORD   Map 3 NT56

The Old Farmhouse (NT521651)

★★★★ FARMHOUSE

Redshill Farm EH41 4JN
☎ 01620 810406 & 07971 115848 Mr G Tait
e-mail: redshill@btinternet.com
web: www.haddingtonaccomodation.com
dir: Exit A1 at Haddington onto B6369 signed to Gifford. Leaving Gifford straight across staggered xrds with golf course on right. Turn left at next xrds then 2nd right

Dating back to the early 19th century but fully refurbished The Old Farmhouse is part of a working arable farm. Bedrooms are well presented and very comfortable, with a welcoming lounge and many extras provided as standard. East Lothian, the Borders and Edinburgh are all within easy striking distance of this peaceful rural setting. A drying room is available.

Rooms 3 en suite (2 GF) S £45-£55; D £70-£80*
Facilities FTV TVL tea/coffee Cen ht Wi-fi **Parking** 6
Notes LB ⊗ 300 acres arable

GULLANE   Map 3 NT48

La Potinière

◉◉ Modern British

Admirable cooking in cottage-style restaurant

☎ 01620 843214
Main St EH31 2AA
dir: 20m SE of Edinburgh. 3m from North Berwick on A198

Keith Marley and Mary Runciman's unassuming small restaurant on Gullane's high street has a following that extends far beyond the ranks of golf widows who do lunch while their other halves hack around the world-renowned links. There are no airs and graces here: the comfortingly chintzy dining room exudes an old-school charm that makes no concessions to the ephemeral whims of fashion, in the same way that the cooking eschews faddish foams, espumas and jellies. Food miles are kept to a minimum, with exclusively local and Scottish suppliers duly name-checked on a menu of straightforward dishes. The couple both work

the stoves and clearly have a solid grounding in the classics; since they are only catering to around 20 guests and the menu is restricted to a couple of choices at each stage, execution and timing are spot on throughout. First up might be a cheese millefeuille with plum compôte, pine nut salad and red wine dressing, followed by a soup - smoked salmon with crème fraîche and lemon, say - before a choice of meat or fish at main course stage. Opt for the former, and you could get seared fillet of beef with a horseradish and brioche crust, turnip fondant, truffle and cep mash, and Madeira and beef sauce, and end exotically with mango and coconut pannacotta with mango, banana and lime compôte and ginger ice cream.

Chef Mary Runciman, Keith Marley **Owner** Mary Runciman
Times 12.30-1.30/7-8.30 Closed Xmas, Jan, BHs, Mon-Tue, D Sun (Oct-May) **Prices** Fixed L 2 course fr £19, Fixed D 4 course fr £42, Service optional **Wines** 39 bottles over £20, 8 bottles under £20, 5 by glass **Notes** Sunday L, Vegetarian available, Dress restrictions, Smart casual **Seats** 24 **Children** Portions **Parking** 10

LONGNIDDRY   Map 3 NT47

The Longniddry Inn

Main St EH32 0NF ☎ 01875 852401
e-mail: info@longniddryinn.com
dir: On A198 (Main St), near rail station

Formerly a blacksmith's forge and four cottages on Longniddry's main street, this inviting looking pub is noted locally for good food and friendly service. From the extensive menu, start with haggis, neeps and tatties, deep-fried Brie with redcurrant jelly, or pâté with Cumberland sauce, then follow with chicken and mushroom pie, lambs' liver, bacon and onion gravy, or a rib-eye steak from the grill. In warmer weather why not sit outside with a pint of Belhaven Best.

Open all day all wk ⊕ PUNCH TAVERNS ◀ Belhaven Best, Deuchars IPA. **Facilities** Children welcome Children's menu Children's portions Garden Parking Wi-fi

NORTH BERWICK   Map 3 NT58

Macdonald Marine Hotel & Spa

★★★★ 82% HOTEL

◉◉ European

Impressive Victorian pile with confident cooking

☎ 0844 879 9130   🖷 01620 894480
Cromwell Rd EH39 4LZ
e-mail: sales.marine@macdonald-hotels.co.uk
web: www.macdonaldhotels.co.uk
dir: From A198 turn into Hamilton Rd at lights, then 2nd right

On Scotland's breathtaking East Coast, the Marine Hotel is a refurbished Grade II listed Victorian manor with a delightful

continued

NORTH BERWICK CONTINUED

restaurant overlooking the East Lothian golf course. Decorated with rich fabrics and chandeliers, the feel is decadent and plush. The kitchen is rightly proud of what's on its doorstep and puts regional produce to good use on its traditional menu that also displays a few contemporary touches. Start with Arbroath smokies in a mousse and delicately flaked, or McSween's haggis with neeps and tatties. Next up, perhaps something from the 'forgotten cuts' section - slowly braised Scottish beef cheek with creamed potatoes, rosemary jus - while under 'Scottish wild fish' there might be seared fillet of halibut with sweetcorn and spinach ragout. For pudding, the burnt Scottish cream gets an exotic pairing with a fresh mango sorbet. Bedrooms come in a variety of sizes and styles, all are well equipped and some are impressively large. The hotel also boasts extensive leisure and conference facilities.

Rooms 83 (4 fmly) (4 GF) **Facilities** Spa STV ⊗ supervised Putt green Gym Indoor & outdoor salt water hydro pool Xmas New Year Wi-fi **Conf** Class 120 Board 60 Thtr 300 Del from £135 to £155* **Services** Lift **Parking** 50 **Notes** Civ Wed 150

Times 12.30-2.30/6.30-9.30

WEST LOTHIAN

BATHGATE   Map 3 NS96

Premier Inn Livingston (Bathgate)

BUDGET HOTEL

☎ 0871 527 8630 📄 0871 527 8631
Starlaw Rd EH48 1LQ
web: www.premierinn.com
dir: M8 junct 3A. At 1st rdbt 1st exit (Bathgate). Over bridge, at 2nd rdbt take 1st exit. Hotel 200yds on left

High quality, budget accommodation ideal for both families and business travellers. Spacious, en suite bedrooms feature tea and coffee-making facilities, and Freeview TV in most hotels. Internet access and Wi-fi are available for a small fee. The adjacent family restaurant features a wide and varied menu.

Rooms 74 **D** £55-£63*

BLACKBURN   Map 3 NS96

Cruachan B&B

★★★★ GUEST ACCOMMODATION

78 East Main St EH47 7QS
☎ 01506 655221 📄 01506 652395
e-mail: enquiries@cruachan.co.uk
web: www.cruachan.co.uk
dir: On A705 in Blackburn, 1m from M8 junct 4

Ideally located for both the leisure and business traveller to central Scotland, with Edinburgh only 30 minutes away by train and Glasgow only 35 minutes away by car. Cruachan is the comfortable, friendly home of the Harkins family. Bedrooms are bright, attractive and very well equipped. Breakfast, featuring the best of local produce is served at individual tables in the ground-floor dining room.

Rooms 4 rms (3 en suite) (1 pri facs) (1 fmly) S £40-£45; D £60-£65* **Facilities** FTV tea/coffee Cen ht Wi-fi **Parking** 5 **Notes** ⊗

EAST CALDER   Map 3 NT06

Ashcroft Farmhouse

★★★★★ 🔒 GUEST HOUSE

East Calder EH53 0ET
☎ 01506 881810 📄 01506 884327
e-mail: scottashcroft7@aol.com
web: www.ashcroftfarmhouse.com

(For full entry see Livingston)

Whitecroft

★★★★ BED AND BREAKFAST

7 Raw Holdings, East Calder EH53 0ET
☎ 01506 882494 📄 01506 882598
e-mail: lornascot@aol.com

(For full entry see Livingston)

FAULDHOUSE
Map 3 NS96

East Badallan Farm (NS919598)

★★★★ FARMHOUSE

EH47 9AG
☎ 01501 770251 Ms Struthers
e-mail: mary@eastbadallan.co.uk
web: www.eastbadallan.co.uk
dir: M8 junct 3 or 4 onto B7010

Equidistant from Edinburgh and Glasgow with great transportation links, this working beef farm has been in the same family since the 18th century. Inside are well appointed bedrooms with modern facilities provided as standard. Hospitality is a strength, as is the breakfast, made with award-winning local produce.

Rooms 3 en suite (1 fmly) (1 GF) S £35-£45; D £60-£80*
Facilities FTV tea/coffee Cen ht Wi-fi **Parking Notes** LB ⊗
⊜ 300 acres beef

LINLITHGOW
Map 3 NS97

Arden Country House

★★★★★ 🔔 GUEST ACCOMMODATION

Belsyde EH49 6QE
☎ 01506 670172   📄 01506 670172
e-mail: info@ardencountryhouse.com
dir: 1.3m SW of Linlithgow. A706 over Union Canal, entrance 200yds on left at Lodge Cottage

Situated in the picturesque grounds of the Belsyde Country Estate and close to the Royal Burgh of Linlithgow, Arden Country House offers immaculate, stylishly furnished and spacious bedrooms. There is a cosy ground-floor lounge and a charming dining room where delicious breakfasts feature the best of local produce.

Rooms 3 en suite (1 GF) S £54-£100; D £79-£108
Facilities FTV tea/coffee Cen ht Wi-fi **Parking** 4 **Notes** LB ⊗
No Children 12yrs Closed 25-26 Dec

Belsyde House

★★★★ 🔔 GUEST ACCOMMODATION

Lanark Rd EH49 6QE
☎ 01506 842098   📄 01506 842098
e-mail: info@belsydehouse.com
web: www.belsyde.com
dir: 1.5m SW on A706, 1st left over Union Canal

Reached by a tree-lined driveway, this welcoming farmhouse is peacefully situated in attractive grounds close to the Union Canal. There are well-proportioned double, twin and family rooms, and a cosy single. All are nicely furnished and well equipped. Breakfast, including a vegetarian menu, is served at good-sized tables in the dining room, next to the lounge.

Rooms 3 en suite (1 fmly) **Facilities** FTV TVL tea/coffee Cen ht Wi-fi **Parking** 10 **Notes** ⊗ No Children 12yrs Closed Xmas

Bomains Farm

★★★★ GUEST HOUSE

Bo'ness EH49 7RQ
☎ 01506 822188 & 822861   📄 01506 824433
e-mail: bunty.kirk@onetel.net
web: www.bomains.co.uk
dir: A706, 1.5m N towards Bo'ness, left at golf course x-rds, 1st farm on right

From its elevated location this friendly farmhouse has stunning views of the Firth of Forth. The bedrooms which vary in size are beautifully decorated, well equipped and enhanced by quality fabrics, with many thoughtful extra touches. Delicious home-cooked fare featuring the best of local produce is served in a stylish lounge-dining room.

Rooms 6 rms (4 en suite) (1 pri facs) (1 fmly) **Facilities** STV FTV TVL tea/coffee Cen ht Wi-fi Golf 18 Fishing **Parking** 12

Champany Inn

⚫⚫ Traditional British 🍷 NOTABLE WINE LIST

Upmarket steakhouse in a characterful old mill

☎ 01506 834532 & 834388
Champany Corner EH49 7LU
e-mail: reception@champany.com
web: www.champany.com
dir: 2m NE of Linlithgow. From M9 (N) junct 3, at top of slip road turn right. Champany 500yds on right

The cluster of buildings, some dating from the 16th century, houses a chophouse and bar as well as the restaurant, a large circular room that was once a mill. It's a charming place, with a vaulted roof, portraits lining the stone walls and antique wooden tables gleaming in the candlelight. There are two restaurants - the more informal is the easy chair and couch-strewn Chop and Ale House, a converted farmer's bothy which was once the public bar of an inn here. With a pint of Belhaven in hand, or a glass of the Champany's own-label South African wine, settle in your chosen spot with the bistro-style menu. Here and in the more

continued

LINLITHGOW CONTINUED

formal dining room steaks, from Aberdeen cattle, properly hung and prepared by the in-house butcher, rule supreme, and the formula is simple: chefs will select your choice - sirloin, porterhouse, Chateaubriand or whatever - and cut it for cooking on the specially designed charcoal grill. Timing is spot on, contact with the grill adds a further depth of flavour, and accompanying vegetables are well reported. A few alternatives are available - perhaps lobster, or roast chicken breast stuffed with herbs - and something from the smoke pot makes a good starter: try hot-smoked cod with beurre blanc.

Chef C Davidson, D Gibson, R Gilfillan **Owner** Mr & Mrs C Davidson **Times** 12.30-2/7-10 Closed 25-26 Dec, 1-2 Jan, Sun, L Sat **Prices** Food prices not confirmed for 2012. Please telephone for details **Wines** 650 bottles over £20, 8 bottles under £20, 8 by glass **Notes** Vegetarian available, Dress restrictions, Smart casual, no jeans or T-shirts **Seats** 50, Pr/dining room 30 **Parking** 50

Open all wk noon-2 6.30-10 (Fri-Sun noon-10) Closed: 25-26 Dec, 1 Jan **Bar Meals** L served all wk 12-2 D served all wk 6.30-10 **Restaurant** L served all wk 12.30-2 booking required D served all wk 6.30-10 booking required ⊕ FREE HOUSE ◀ Belhaven. **Facilities** Children welcome Children's portions Garden Parking

Livingston's Restaurant

◉◉ Modern Scottish **V**

Family-run restaurant with imaginative modern Scottish menu

☎ 01506 846565
52 High St EH49 7AE
e-mail: contact@livingstons-restaurant.co.uk
web: www.livingstons-restaurant.co.uk
dir: On high street opposite old post office

Although family-run Livingston's is just off Linlithgow's high street, the garden setting (complete with rabbit warrens) make it a bit of an oasis. The charming restaurant in an old stone building has bags of character, helped along by interesting objets d'art and flickering candles at dinner. If you prefer the modern look, the bare-brick walls of the bright and modern patio extension may suit. The modern Scottish menu reveals interesting flavour combinations and top-

quality produce; marbled terrine of confit game to start, perhaps, with Livingston's 'Branston', tomato bread and hazelnuts. Next up, poached loin and slow-cooked belly of Tamworth pork comes with creamed cabbage, black pudding bon bon and sage jus. The skilful cooking and modish inventiveness continues in the desserts: glazed apple pressing with apple purée and jelly, miniature doughnuts and apple sorbet.

Chef Max Hogg **Owner** The Livingston Family **Times** 12-2.30/6-9.30 Closed 1 wk Jun, 1 wk Oct, 2 wks Jan, Sun, (ex Mothering Sun) Mon **Prices** Fixed D 3 course fr £105, Service optional, Groups min 8 service 10% **Wines** 37 bottles over £20, 24 bottles under £20, 6 by glass **Notes** Vegetarian menu, Dress restrictions, Smart casual **Seats** 60, Pr/dining room 15 **Children** Portions **Parking** NCP Linlithgow Cross, on street

Ship 2 Shore 24

◉ Modern Scottish ☙

Top-drawer Scottish seafood and friendly service

☎ 01506 840123
57 High St EH49 7ED
dir: On the High St, across road from the Palace

As you've no doubt sussed, seafood is the name of the game at this popular restaurant in the heart of Linlithgow. The menu comes awash with daily-landed fish from the east coast port at Eyemouth (the '24' in the name refers to the fact that the fish is caught and on your plate within 24 hours). The seafood platter (including lobster, crab, mussels, langoustine and oysters) is one of the restaurant's biggest sellers, while other fishy favourites are the beer battered haddock with hand-cut chips and home-made tartare sauce, and the linguine with crabmeat, chilli, garlic cherry tomatoes and white wine sauce. The menu is not exclusively seafood, but everything is fuss-free and main-ingredient led, and the service is friendly and relaxed. You can also stock up from their wet fish counter.

Chef Douglas Elliman **Owner** James Boyd **Times** 12-2/6-9 Closed 25 Dec, 1 Jan, Sun-Mon **Prices** Food prices not confirmed for 2012. Please telephone for details **Wines** 42 bottles over £20, 18 bottles under £20, 9 by glass **Notes** Vegetarian available **Seats** 50

The Four Marys ☙

65/67 High St EH49 7ED ☎ 01506 842171
🖹 01506 844410
dir: M9 junct 3 or 4 take A803 to Linlithgow. Pub in town centre

Named after the four ladies-in-waiting of Mary, Queen of Scots, who was born in nearby Linlithgow Palace, this town house dates from 1500, but it remained unlicensed until 1981 having previously been a chemists, newsagents and printers. It now thrives as one of Scotland top real ale pubs, serving predominantly Scottish brews and hosting popular beer festivals in May and October. Soak up the ale with a steak pie, a classic beef burger, or St Andrew's ale pork and herb sausages.

Open all day all wk **Bar Meals** L served all wk 12-5 D served all wk 5-9 Av main course £7.99 food served all day **Restaurant** L served all wk 12-5 D served all wk 5-9 Fixed menu price fr £14.99 food served all day ⊕ BELHAVEN, GREENE KING ◖ Belhaven 80/-, Greene King Old Speckled Hen, Caledonian Deuchars IPA, Stewart Edinburgh Gold. ♀ 9 **Facilities** Children welcome Children's menu Children's portions Garden Beer festival

LIVINGSTON   **Map 3 NT06**

Premier Inn Livingston M8 Jct 3

BUDGET HOTEL

☎ 0871 527 8632   📄 0871 527 8633
Deer Park Av, Deer Park, Knightsbridge EH54 8AD
web: www.premierinn.com
dir: At M8 junct 3. Hotel opposite rdbt

High quality, budget accommodation ideal for both families and business travellers. Spacious, en suite bedrooms feature tea and coffee-making facilities, and Freeview TV in most hotels. Internet access and Wi-fi are available for a small fee. The adjacent family restaurant features a wide and varied menu.

Rooms 83 **D** £55-£63*

Ashcroft Farmhouse

★★★★★ 🏠 GUEST HOUSE

East Calder EH53 0ET
☎ **01506 881810**   📄 **01506 884327**
e-mail: scottashcroft7@aol.com
web: www.ashcroftfarmhouse.com
dir: On B7015, off A71, 0.5m E of East Calder, near Almondell Country Park

With over 40 years' experience in caring for guests, Derek and Elizabeth Scott ensure a stay at Ashcroft will be memorable. Their modern home sits in lovely award-winning landscaped gardens and provides attractive and well-equipped ground-floor bedrooms. The comfortable lounge

includes a video and DVD library. Breakfast, featuring home-made sausages and the best of local produce, is served at individual tables in the stylish dining room. Free Wi-fi is now available, and a Park and Ride facility is nearby.

Rooms 6 en suite (2 fmly) (6 GF) **Facilities** FTV TVL tea/coffee Cen ht Wi-fi **Parking** 8 **Notes** ⊗ No Children 12yrs

Whitecroft

★★★★ BED AND BREAKFAST

7 Raw Holdings, East Calder EH53 0ET
☎ **01506 882494**   📄 **01506 882598**
e-mail: lornascot@aol.com
dir: A71 onto B7015, establishment on right

A relaxed and friendly atmosphere prevails at this charming modern bed and breakfast. The bedrooms, all of which are on the ground floor, are attractively colour co-ordinated, well-equipped and contain many thoughtful extra touches. Breakfast is served at individual tables in the smart dining room.

Rooms 3 en suite (3 GF) S £45-£55; D £64-£76*
Facilities FTV tea/coffee Cen ht Wi-fi **Parking** 5 **Notes** ⊗ No Children 12yrs

UPHALL   **Map 3 NT07**

Macdonald Houstoun House

★★★★ 78% HOTEL

🍴 Traditional British

Good Scottish fare in Queen Mary's old place

☎ 0844 879 9043   📄 01506 854220
EH52 6JS
e-mail: houstoun@macdonald-hotels.co.uk
web: www.macdonaldhotels.co.uk
dir: M8 junct 3 follow Broxburn signs, straight over rdbt, at mini-rdbt turn right towards Uphall, hotel 1m on right

Macdonald Houstoun House lies to the west of Edinburgh and certainly does not lack for history or character. The whitewashed pile dating from the 16th century was once home to the doomed Mary, Queen of Scots, and comes complete with plenty of tartans, stag's heads, open fires and

continued

UPHALL CONTINUED

clubby Chesterfields to set the Highland mood. Stylish bedrooms, some located around a courtyard, are comfortably furnished and well equipped. There's a sense of occasion to dining in The Tower restaurant, fostered by the ascent up a winding staircase to the panelled walls, shuttered windows and open fires spread throughout a quartet of romantic and stylish dining rooms. The kitchen cooks in a modern country-house vein with laudable emphasis on Scottish produce - pea soup with mint crème fraîche sets the ball rolling, ahead of chump of Highland lamb which arrives in the company of barley risotto and shallot gravy. Cherry pannacotta with a sesame seed tuile is a well-executed dessert.

Rooms 73 (47 annexe) (12 fmly) (12 GF) **Facilities** Spa STV FTV 🐾 ♨ Gym Health & beauty salon Xmas New Year Wi-fi **Conf** Class 80 Board 80 Thtr 400 **Parking** 250 **Notes** Civ Wed 200

Times 6.30-9.30 Closed L all week

Karma

◉ Modern Indian **V**

Modern Indian food in stylishly revamped ballroom

☎ 01501 744024 & 744243
154 West Main St EH47 0QR
e-mail: karmawhitburn@yahoo.co.uk
dir: M8 junct 5 follow signs to Whitburn for 2.5m, on right hand side before petrol station

This former ballroom and function hall has been transformed into a modern and stylish Indian restaurant. From the outside it may look uninspiring but step inside to find a stunning interior, the large, split-level bar and dining room featuring subdued lighting, red, orange and brown seating, cream walls and busts of Buddha. The contemporary Indian food displays a few twists and elements of Scottish cooking, using local produce such as haggis and monkfish tails alongside more traditional Indian foods. Dishes include haggis pakora and the signature Karma Ruby beef fillet - a meltingly tender steak barbequed in a tandoori oven - served with a Burgundy sauce. Excellent naan breads and very friendly service complete the picture.

Chef Guruinder Keemar **Owner** Amra Singh Gill **Times** 5-10 **Prices** Food prices not confirmed for 2012. Please telephone for details **Wines** 2 bottles under £20 **Notes** Vegetarian menu **Seats** 90, Pr/dining room 25 **Children** Portions **Parking** 20

The Sun Inn

★★★★ INN

◉ Modern British

Winning menus in a popular gastro-pub

Lothian Bridge EH22 4TR
☎ **0131 663 2456 & 07967 585850**
e-mail: thesuninn@live.co.uk
web: www.thesuninnedinburgh.co.uk
dir: On A7 towards Galashiels, opposite Newbattle Viaduct

'Eat, drink, relax' exhorts the motto of this gastro-pub, a former AA Pub of the Year for Scotland; and it's easy to comply, the last helped along by friendly, obliging staff and the conversion of the old building that combines modern creature comforts (it now has boutique-style bedrooms (one featuring a copper bath) and modern bathrooms) with the original features of oak beams, exposed stone and panelling. There are welcoming log fires in winter and a bright patio for summer. Scotland's larder forms the backbone of the menu, from Pittenweem smoked haddock croquettes with cheese sauce to loin of Balquhidder venison - pink and tender - with haggis, turnip fondant, Parisienne potatoes and a red wine jus, and the kitchen handles combinations with self-assurance: mussels with chorizo, garlic and tomatoes, say, or roast duck breast with a spring roll of the confit leg served with coriander pesto.

Rooms 5 en suite S £70-£100; D £85-£150* **Facilities** STV FTV tea/coffee Dinner available Cen ht Wi-fi Golf 18 Fishing **Parking** 50 **Notes** LB ⊗ No coaches

Chef Ian & Craig Minto **Owner** Bernadette McCarron **Times** 12-2/6-9 **Prices** Fixed L 2 course £10.95, Starter £5-

£8, Main £8-£22, Dessert £5-£7, Service optional **Wines** 27 bottles over £20, 24 bottles under £20, 33 by glass **Notes** Sunday L, Vegetarian available, Dress restrictions, Smart casual **Seats** 90 **Children** Portions, Menu

---

PENICUIK   Map 3 NT25

The Howgate Restaurant ♥

Howgate EH26 8PY ☎ 01968 670000 🖹 **01968 670000**
e-mail: peter@howgate.com
dir: 10m N of Peebles. 3m E of Penicuik on A6094 between Leadburn junct & Howgate

This beautifully converted farm building was formerly the home of Howgate cheeses. Its fire-warmed bar offers bistro-style meals, while the candle-lit restaurant serves a full carte. Executive and head chefs, Steven Worth and Sean Blake, respectively, use the finest Scottish produce, especially beef, with steaks from the charcoal grill, and lamb; other options might include Cullen skink; a filo 'moneybag' of haggis with a mustard and whisky jus; braised lamb shank with chive mash, honey roasted vegetables and onion gravy; or penne with asparagus and basil cream sauce. There are fine beers to enjoy and an impressively produced wine list roams the globe.

Open all wk Closed: 25-26 Dec, 1 Jan **Bar Meals** L served all wk 12-2 D served all wk 6-9.30 Av main course £9.95 **Restaurant** L served all wk 12-2 booking required D served all wk 6-9.30 booking required Fixed menu price fr £15 Av 3 course à la carte fr £30 ⊕ FREE HOUSE ◀ Belhaven Best, Hoegaarden Wheat Biere. ♥ 14 **Facilities** Children welcome Children's portions Garden Parking

---

ROSLIN   Map 3 NT26

The Original Rosslyn Inn

★★★★ INN

4 Main St EH25 9LE
☎ 0131 440 2384 🖹 **0131 440 2514**
e-mail: enquiries@theoriginalhotel.co.uk
dir: From A701 at rdbt take B7003 signed Roslin & Rosewell, into Roslin. At T-junct, inn opposite. Or from mini rdbt on A701 at Bilston take B7006 to Roslin. Inn on left

Whether on the Da Vinci Code trail or in the area on business, this property a very short walk from the famous Rosslyn Chapel which is well worth visiting. Robert Burns, the famous Scottish poet, once stayed here and wrote a poem about his stay. This delightful village inn offers well-equipped bedrooms with upgraded en suites. Four of the bedrooms have four-poster beds. Catch up with the locals in the village bar, or relax by the fire in the lounge whilst choosing from the menu. Soups, jackets and paninis are supplemented by main course options like haggis with tatties and neeps; breaded haddock and chips; and vegetarian harvester pie. Alternatively, the Grail Restaurant

offers more comprehensive dining options.

Rooms 6 en suite (2 fmly) (1 smoking) **Facilities** STV tea/coffee Dinner available Cen ht Wi-fi **Conf** Max 130 Thtr 130 Class 80 Board 60 **Parking** 8 **Notes** Civ Wed 180

Open all day all wk **Bar Meals** L served all wk 12-9.15 D served all wk 12-9.15 Av main course £9.50 food served all day **Restaurant** L served all wk 12-9.15 D served all wk 12-9.15 Fixed menu price fr £12.50 Av 3 course à la carte fr £20 ⊕ FREE HOUSE ◀ Belhaven Best. ♥ 14 **Facilities** Children welcome Children's menu Children's portions Dogs allowed Garden

---

MORAY

ARCHIESTOWN   Map 5 NJ24

Archiestown Hotel

★★★ 79% SMALL HOTEL

◎ Modern British

Country-house cooking in a Speyside village inn

☎ 01340 810218 🖹 01340 810239
AB38 7QL
e-mail: jah@archiestownhotel.co.uk
web: www.archiestownhotel.co.uk
dir: A95 Craigellachie, follow B9102 4m to Archiestown

The stone-built inn has been at the centre of the action in this Speyside village deep in single-malt country since Georgian times. The 'action' in question is of the sporting variety, as the place is a magnet for the angling community. Cosy and comfortable public rooms include a choice of lounges (there is no bar as such). Artworks depicting the local scenery adorn the bright, cheery dining room, which serves a labour-intensive version of sound country-house cooking. Expect home-smoked, whisky-cured salmon with prawns and dill mayonnaise to be followed by something like cod crusted in crabmeat and herbs on buttery mash in a creamy fish stock sauce, or chicken breast stuffed with goats' cheese and black olives on tomato tagliatelle. Then round things off with spiced apple sponge and custard. **Rooms** 11 (1 fmly) **S** £70-£80; **D** £70-£80 (incl. bkfst)* **Facilities** FTV ⬏ New Year Wi-fi **Conf** Board 12 Thtr 20 Del from £126 to £136* **Parking** 20 **Notes** LB ⊗ Closed 24-27 Dec & 3 Jan-9 Feb

Chef Robert Aspden **Owner** Alan & Jane Hunter **Times** 12-2/7-9 Closed Xmas, 3 Jan-10 Feb **Prices** Fixed L 2 course £10-£13.50, Fixed D 3 course £29.50, Service optional, Groups min 10 service 10% **Wines** 24 bottles over £20, 11 bottles under £20, 6 by glass **Notes** Sunday L, Vegetarian available, Dress restrictions, Smart casual **Seats** 35, Pr/dining room 16 **Children** Portions

CRAIGELLACHIE · Map 5 NJ24

Craigellachie

★★★★ 72% HOTEL

Ⓜ Traditional Scottish

A Scotch-lover's haven of contentment on Speyside

☎ 01340 881204 📄 01340 881253
AB38 9SR
e-mail: reservations.craigellachie@ohiml.com
web: www.oxfordhotelsandinns.com
dir: On A95 between Aberdeen & Inverness

Plumb in the heart of Speyside, one of Scotch whisky's premier appellations, this hotel is the kind of place you wouldn't mind getting snowed in at. You'd barely have made a dent in the 700 whiskies kept in the Quaich Bar (a quaich is a traditional drinking cup for Scotch) before you were rescued. Bedrooms come in various sizes but all are tastefully decorated and bathrooms are of a high specification. The ground-floor dining room is a spacious and comfortable setting for some carefully constructed country-house cooking, embracing the likes of twice-baked goats' cheese soufflé with a cream sauce, saddle of venison en croûte with roasted roots and dauphinoise in a thyme jus, and dark chocolate fondant with glaringly green mint ice cream.

Rooms 26 (1 fmly) (6 GF) **Facilities** Xmas New Year Wi-fi **Conf** Class 35 Board 30 Thtr 60 **Parking** 30 **Notes** Civ Wed 60

Chef Stuart Aitken **Owner** Oxford Hotels & Inns
Times 12-2/6-9 **Prices** Starter £5.95-£10.90, Main £16.95-£22.90, Dessert £5.95-£8.90, Service optional **Wines** 64 bottles over £20, 30 bottles under £20, 7 by glass **Notes** Booking essential for Sun L, Sunday L, Vegetarian available, Dress restrictions, Smart casual **Seats** 30, Pr/dining room 60 **Children** Portions, Menu

CULLEN · Map 5 NJ56

Cullen Bay Hotel

★★★ 75% SMALL HOTEL

☎ 01542 840432 📄 01542 840900
A98 AB56 4XA
e-mail: stay@cullenbayhotel.com
web: www.cullenbayhotel.com
dir: On A98, 1m west of Cullen

If you spot something splashing about in the water below as you look out of the Cullen Bay Hotel, it may well be a dolphin, a porpoise or even a minke whale. These marine mammals are often sighted in the Moray Firth, and this small family-run hotel has a fine vantage point, perched high above the beach. Indeed, the views through the full-length picture windows in the restaurant are truly spectacular, while the food is traditional Scottish with a few modern European influences. There's also a comfortable modern bar, a quiet lounge and a second dining room where breakfasts are served; many of the bedrooms have sea views.

Rooms 14 (3 fmly) **Facilities** New Year Wi-fi **Conf** Class 80 Board 80 Thtr 200 **Parking** 100 **Notes** ⊗ Civ Wed 200

ELGIN · Map 5 NJ26

Mansion House

★★★ 79% HOTEL

☎ 01343 548811 📄 01343 547916
The Haugh IV30 1AW
e-mail: reception@mhelgin.co.uk
web: www.mansionhousehotel.co.uk
dir: Exit A96 into Haugh Rd, then 1st left

Set in grounds by the River Lossie, this baronial mansion is popular with leisure and business guests as well as being a popular wedding venue. Bedrooms are spacious and many have views of the river. Extensive public areas include a choice of restaurants, with the bistro contrasting with the classical main restaurant. There is an indoor pool and a beauty and hair salon.

Rooms 23 (2 fmly) (5 GF) **Facilities** STV FTV ⓢ supervised Fishing Gym Hair studio New Year Wi-fi **Conf** Thtr 180 **Parking** 50 **Notes** ⊗ Civ Wed 160

Premier Inn Elgin

BUDGET HOTEL

☎ 0871 527 8372 📄 0871 527 8373
15 Linkwood Way IV30 1HY
web: www.premierinn.com
dir: On A96, 1.5m E of city centre

High quality, budget accommodation ideal for both families and business travellers. Spacious, en suite bedrooms feature tea and coffee-making facilities, and Freeview TV in most hotels. Internet access and Wi-fi are available for a small fee. The adjacent family restaurant features a wide and varied menu.

Rooms 40 **D** £54-£60*

FOCHABERS
Map 5 NJ35

Gordon Arms Hotel

80 High St IV32 7DH ☎ **01343 820508** 📠 **01343 829059**
e-mail: gordonarmsfochabers@live.co.uk
dir: A96 approx halfway between Aberdeen & Inverness, 9m from Elgin

This 200-year-old former coaching inn, close to the River Spey and within easy reach of Speyside's whisky distilleries, is understandably popular with salmon fishers, golfers and walkers. Its public rooms have been carefully refurbished, and the hotel makes an ideal base from which to explore this scenic corner of Scotland. The cuisine makes full use of local produce: venison, lamb and game from the uplands, fish and seafood from the Moray coast, beef from Aberdeenshire and salmon from the Spey - barely a stone's throw from the kitchen! Change of hands.

Open all day all wk 11-11 (Thu 11-mdnt Fri-Sat 11am-12.30am) **Bar Meals** L served all wk 12-2 D served all wk 5-8.30 **Restaurant** L served all wk 12-2 D served all wk 5-8.30 🏠 FREE HOUSE 🍺 Caledonian Deuchars IPA, John Smith's Smooth, Guest ales. **Facilities** Children welcome Dogs allowed Parking

PERTH & KINROSS

ALYTH
Map 5 NO24

Tigh Na Leigh Guesthouse

★★★★★ 🏠 🍴 GUEST ACCOMMODATION

22-24 Airlie St PH11 8AJ
☎ **01828 632372** 📠 **01828 632279**
e-mail: bandcblack@yahoo.co.uk
web: www.tighnaleigh.co.uk
dir: In town centre on B952

Situated in the heart of this country town, Tigh Na Leigh is Gaelic for 'The House of the Doctor'. Its location and somewhat sombre façade are in stunning contrast to what lies inside. The house has been completely restored to blend its Victorian architecture with contemporary interior design. Bedrooms, including a superb suite, have state-of-the-art bathrooms. There are three entirely different lounges, while delicious meals are served in the conservatory/dining room overlooking a spectacular landscaped garden.

Rooms 5 en suite (1 GF) S £42-£48; D £84-£122.50*
Facilities FTV TVL tea/coffee Dinner available Cen ht Licensed Wi-fi Golf 18 **Parking** 5 **Notes** No Children 12yrs Closed Dec-Feb

AUCHTERARDER
Map 3 NN91

The Gleneagles Hotel

★★★★★ HOTEL

Andrew Fairlie @ Gleneagles

 Modern French **V** 🍷 NOTABLE WINE LIST

France meets Scotland in luxurious Perthshire hotel

☎ 01764 662231 📠 01764 662134
PH3 1NF
e-mail: resort.sales@gleneagles.com
e-mail: andrew.fairlie@gleneagles.com
web: www.andrewfairlie.co.uk
web: www.gleneagles.com
dir: Off A9 at exit for A823 follow signs for Gleneagles Hotel

The renown of the luxurious Gleneagles Hotel, with its three championship golf courses in 850 fabulous acres of Perthshire countryside, brings in the sort of clientele for whom only the best will do. All bedrooms are appointed to a high standard and offer both traditional and contemporary styles, and the award-winning EPSA spa offers the very latest treatments to restore both body and soul. Service is always professional - the staff are friendly and nothing is too much trouble. Stylish public areas include various dining options - the Deseo 'Mediterranean Food Market' eaterie and The Strathearn, (see entry below), as well as the world-class cooking of local lad Andrew Fairlie. First, let's introduce the chef. Fairlie won the first Roux scholarship as a precocious 20 year old, then went on to train with legendary French chef Michel Guérard in Gascony, so it is no surprise that his cooking has its roots deep in French classicism. He has now been plying his trade in Gleneagles for a decade, and while the operation is set within the hotel, it is an independent business. The environment is darkly cosseting with its extravagant floor-to-ceiling silk drapes, deep brown-panelled walls and stylish banquettes emblazoned with the house's leaf motif; original artwork by Archie Frost adds an extra level that tells you that you are somewhere special. Impeccable service is equal to the setting - slick but completely unstuffy and never intrusive. The scene is thus set for the serious business of top-level dining and drinking. If the whole table is up for it, the intelligently-composed menu du marché and full-works dégustation run to six and

continued

AUCHTERARDER CONTINUED

eight courses respectively; cheese is slotted in French-style before pudding. Otherwise a carte offers five choices at each course, with plenty to knock your socks off along the way. Produce brought in from the famous Rungis market near Paris sits alongside peerless materials from Scotland as the foundation of Fairlie's uncompromisingly French ideas, all brought together with meticulous attention to detail by a battalion-strength kitchen brigade. Hand-dived scallops are perfectly timed and delivered with the vibrant flavours of sea vegetables and yuzu purée, or you might start with a signature smoked lobster that sees the crustacean smoked for 12 hours over old whisky barrels, and served simply with lime and herb butter. Main-course peppered loin of roe deer comes with beetroot and a sloe gin gel, pulling off the masterful trick of imbuing apparently simple components with deeply-layered flavours, while roast fillet of Gigha halibut could be accompanied by the delicacy of clams and a lightly-curried parsnip purée. Presentation is elegant and refined throughout, particularly at dessert when a textbook salted caramel soufflé arrives with vanilla toffee and passionfruit sorbet. The wine list is a predictably serious piece of work, with an expert sommelier to aid navigation.

Rooms 232 (115 fmly) (11 GF) **S** fr £315; **D** fr £315 (incl. bkfst)* **Facilities** Spa STV FTV ⚛ supervised ⚛ ⚓ 54 ⚓ Putt green Fishing ⚓ Gym Falconry Off-road driving Golf Archery Clay target shooting Gundog School Xmas New Year Wi-fi Child facilities **Conf** Class 240 Board 60 Thtr 360 **Services** Lift **Parking** 277 **Notes** Civ Wed 360

Chef Andrew Fairlie **Owner** Andrew Fairlie **Times** 6.30-10 Closed 24-25 Dec, 3 wks Jan, Sun, L all week **Prices** Service optional **Wines** 300 bottles over £20, 12 by glass **Notes** ALC 3 course £85, 6 course Degustation £125/Du Marché £95, Vegetarian menu, Dress restrictions, Smart casual **Seats** 54

The Strathearn

◎◎ British, French

Tableside carving and flambéing at a luxurious golf resort

☎ 01764 694270
The Gleneagles Hotel PH3 1NF
e-mail: resort.sales@gleneagles.com
web: www.gleneagles.com
dir: Off A9 at exit for A823 follow signs for Gleneagles Hotel

The main dining room of the Gleneagles golf resort (assuming we overlook Andrew Fairlie's contribution for the moment - see separate entry) is situated in what was the ballroom, in the days when people expected to be able to swing a leg as much as a five-iron. Under a grandly moulded ceiling, and with gathered drapes and formal table settings establishing the tone, the style of cooking is at once sufficiently old-school that carving and flambé trolleys can patrol the dining room as though Edward VII were still on the throne, and yet possessed of enough acuity to keep many of the dishes firmly in the modern mainstream. So mains might offer a monkfish version of osso buco, with pancetta, foie gras and paprika, or Highland venison with sweet potato gratin and wild mushroom ragoût. Fresh shellfish starters are the way to go, and dessert might be a baked Alaska made with roast banana and served with butterscotch sauce.

Chef Paul Devonshire **Owner** Diageo plc
Times 12.30-2.30/7-10 Closed L Mon-Sat **Prices** Fixed L 3 course fr £40, Fixed D 3 course fr £58, Service optional **Wines** 100% bottles over £20, 15 by glass **Notes** Sunday L, Vegetarian available, Dress restrictions, Smart casual, no jeans or trainers, Civ Wed 250 **Seats** 322 **Children** Portions, Menu **Parking** 1000

BLAIR ATHOLL   **Map 5 NN86**

Atholl Arms Hotel

★★★ 72% HOTEL

☎ 01796 481205 🖷 01796 481550
Old North Rd PH18 5SG
e-mail: hotel@athollarms.co.uk
web: www.athollarmshotel.co.uk
dir: Off A9 to B8079, 1m into Blair Atholl, hotel near entrance to Blair Castle

Situated close to Blair Castle and conveniently adjacent to the railway station, this stylish hotel has historically appointed public rooms that include a choice of bars, and a splendid baronial-style dining room. Bedrooms vary in size and style. Staff throughout are friendly and very caring.

Rooms 30 (3 fmly) **S** £51.50-£67; **D** £82-£97 (incl. bkfst)*
Facilities Fishing Rough shooting ♫ New Year Wi-fi
Conf Class 80 Board 60 Thtr 120 **Parking** 103 **Notes** LB
Civ Wed 120

BLAIRGOWRIE   Map 3 NO14

Gilmore House

★★★★ 🏠 BED AND BREAKFAST

Perth Rd PH10 6EJ
☎ **01250 872791** 📠 **01250 872791**
e-mail: jill@gilmorehouse.co.uk
dir: On A93 S

This Victorian villa stands in a well-tended garden on the south side of town. Sympathetically restored to enhance its period features it offers individual bedrooms tastefully furnished in antique pine, and thoughtfully equipped to include modern amenities such as Freeview TV. There are two inviting lounges, one of which has lovely views over the gardens. Hearty traditional breakfasts are served in the attractive dining room.

Rooms 3 en suite D £60-£80* **Facilities** FTV TVL tea/coffee Cen ht Wi-fi **Parking** 3 **Notes** Closed Xmas

COMRIE   Map 3 NN72

Royal

★★★ 83% HOTEL

🍴 Traditional British

Elegant hotel with confident cooking

☎ 01764 679200 📠 01764 679219
Melville Square PH6 2DN
e-mail: reception@royalhotel.co.uk
web: www.royalhotel.co.uk
dir: Off A9 on A822 to Crieff, then B827 to Comrie. Hotel in main square on A85

The Royal is a classic small-scale luxury hotel in the village of Comrie set amid the splendid landscapes of Strathearn and the Southern Scottish Highlands. A traditional façade gives little indication of the style and elegance inside this long-established hotel located in the village centre. The old coaching inn dates from the 18th century and was tastefully refurbished by the Milsom family in 1996 in a plush modern country-house style involving opulent fabrics, polished wooden floors, antiques and welcoming log fires. Public areas include a bar and library, and bedrooms are tastefully appointed and furnished. The man at the stoves is chef-patron David Milsom who brings a sure touch to culinary proceedings, whether you're eating in the main restaurant, clubby lounge bar or walled garden. Expect classic combinations given a modern spin, along the lines of pan-fried venison steak with stilton, roast root vegetables, garlic mash and redcurrant jus, or Scottish hake wrapped in Parma ham served with braised cabbage and bacon, tomato butter sauce and new potatoes. Finish with Seville marmalade pudding with Grand Marnier ice cream, then retire to the bar to set about the 100-strong array of malt whiskies.

Rooms 13 (2 annexe) **Facilities** STV Fishing Shooting arranged New Year Wi-fi **Conf** Class 10 Board 20 Thtr 20 **Parking** 22 **Notes** LB Closed 25-26 Dec

Times 12-2/6.30-9 Closed Xmas

CRIEFF   Map 3 NN82

Merlindale

★★★★ BED AND BREAKFAST

Perth Rd PH7 3EQ
☎ **01764 655205** 📠 **01764 655205**
e-mail: merlin.dale@virgin.net
web: www.merlindale.co.uk
dir: On A85, 350yds from E end of High St

Situated in a quiet residential area within walking distance of the town centre, this delightful detached house stands in well-tended grounds and offers a warm welcome. The pretty bedrooms are comfortably furnished and well equipped. There is a spacious lounge, an impressive library, and an elegant dining room where delicious evening meals and traditional breakfasts are served.

Rooms 3 en suite (1 fmly) S £50-£65; D £75-£90* **Facilities** STV FTV TVL tea/coffee Dinner available Cen ht Wi-fi **Parking** 3 **Notes** LB ⊗ Closed 9 Dec-10 Feb

FORTINGALL   Map 2 NN74

Fortingall

★★★★ 78% SMALL HOTEL

🍴🍴 Modern Scottish

Modern Scottish cooking in an Arts and Crafts village

☎ 01887 830367 & 830368 📠 01887 830367
PH15 2NQ
e-mail: hotel@fortingallhotel.com or enquiries@fortingall.com
dir: B846 from Aberfeldy for 6m, left signed Fortingall for 3m. Hotel in village centre

The imposing white house is master of all it surveys in the historic Arts and Crafts village of the same name, on the edge of Loch Tay. It lies at the foot of wooded hills in the heart of Glen Lyon, and with sweeping views down the valley, it's certainly a prime location, and one that is enhanced by the homely but polished approach of the staff. All the bedrooms are very well equipped and have an extensive range of thoughtful extras. The comfortable lounge, with its log fire, is ideal for pre-dinner drinks, and the small bar is full of character. Paintings of country scenes, including a flock of sheep above the mantelpiece, adorn the dining room, where the menus try out a soothing version of modern Scottish cookery, with seafood a strong suit. A fricassée of shellfish in a bisque with saffron potatoes is a fortifying

continued

FORTINGALL CONTINUED

opener to a meal that might proceed with lemon sole and asparagus in caper beurre noisette, or seared pork loin and slow-cooked belly with coco beans, chorizo and pea purée in a thyme jus. Go exotic for a dessert such as pistachio and olive oil cake garnished with pineapple, coconut sorbet, rum and mango foam.

Rooms 10 (1 fmly) **Facilities** STV Fishing Stalking ♫ Xmas New Year Wi-fi **Conf** Board 16 Thtr 30 **Parking** 20 **Notes** Civ Wed 30

Chef Darin Campbell **Owner** Iain & Janet Wotherspoon **Times** 12-2/6.30-9 **Prices** Food prices not confirmed for 2012. Please telephone for details **Wines** 42 bottles over £20, 30 bottles under £20, 10 by glass **Notes** Sunday L, Vegetarian available **Seats** 30, Pr/dining room 30 **Children** Portions, Menu

GLENDEVON
Map 3 NN90

An Lochan Tormaukin Country Inn and Restaurant

FK14 7JY ☎ 01259 781252   📠 01259 781526
e-mail: info@anlochan.co.uk
dir: M90 junct 6 onto A977 to Kincardine, follow signs to Stirling. Exit at Yelts of Muckhard onto A823/Crieff

This attractive whitewashed building was built in 1720 as a drovers' inn, at a time when Glendevon was frequented by cattlemen making their way from the Tryst of Crieff to the market place at Falkirk, the name Tormaukin is Gaelic for 'hill of the mountain hare', which reflects its serene, romantic location in the midst of the Ochil Hills. Sympathetically refurbished throughout, it still bristles with real Scottish character and charm. Original features like stone walls, exposed beams and blazing winter fires in the cosy public rooms ensure a warm and welcoming atmosphere.

Open all day all wk ◀ Bitter & Twisted, Thrappledouser Ö Aspall. **Facilities** Children welcome Dogs allowed Garden Parking

GLENFARG
Map 3 NO11

The Famous Bein Inn

 INN

 Modern British

Traditional inn offering good Scottish food

PH2 9PY
☎ 01577 830216   📠 01577 830211
e-mail: enquiries@beininn.com
web: www.beininn.com
dir: From S: M90 junct 8, A91 towards Cupar. Left onto B996 to Bein Inn. From N: M90 junct 9, A912 towards Gateside

Standing by the river in the glorious Glen of Farg, this former grand Georgian manor house and old drovers' inn is owned by a local farming family, well known for the quality of their beef. Just a few minutes drive the M90 (J9) south of Perth, but a world away from the hubbub, it offers a hearty Scottish welcome, a traditional interior and has developed a strong local following for its fuss-free Scottish cuisine. Whether you choose to eat in the bistro or the Balvaird restaurant, top-class local and seasonal produce is the order of the day. Unpretentious dishes such as black pudding tempura with poached egg, smoked ham hock and pearl barley broth get the ball rolling, while mains may deliver rack of lamb with creamed cabbage and bacon and red wine jus. To finish, try the sticky toffee pudding with rich toffee sauce. Short breaks for golf, fishing and shooting are offered.

Rooms 7 en suite 4 annexe en suite (4 fmly) (4 GF) **Facilities** tea/coffee Dinner available Direct Dial Cen ht Wi-fi **Conf** Max 32 Thtr 32 Class 25 Board 25 **Parking** 26 **Notes** Closed 25 Dec

Chef Jian Bin Yo **Owner** John & Alan MacGregor **Times** 12-9 Closed 25 Dec **Prices** Food prices not confirmed for 2012. Please telephone for details **Wines** 8 bottles over £20, 14 bottles under £20, 5 by glass **Notes** Sunday L, Vegetarian available **Seats** 65 **Children** Portions, Menu

GLENEAGLES

See AUCHTERARDER

GLENSHEE (SPITTAL OF)
Map 5 NO17

Dalmunzie Castle

★★★ 80% COUNTRY HOUSE HOTEL

◉◉ Traditional British ░ NOTABLE WINE LIST

Avant-garde cooking in a majestic piece of Scots baronial pastiche

☎ 01250 885224   📠 01250 885225
PH10 7QG
e-mail: reservations@dalmunzie.com
web: www.dalmunzie.com
dir: On A93 at Spittal of Glenshee, follow signs to hotel

Dating back only to the 1920s, Dalmunzie is a storybook piece of freebooting Scots baronial, all pitched roofs and conical turrets, sitting in an estate of a mere 6,500 acres, and handy for the Glenshee ski slopes. The Edwardian-style bedrooms, including spacious tower rooms and impressive four-poster rooms, are furnished with antique pieces. The drawing room enjoys panoramic views over the lawns, and golf and tennis are on hand, with hiking and biking encouraged as ways of enjoying the magisterial setting, while the dining room, which overlooks the front lawn, is kitted out with well-spaced tables in the traditional manner. The kitchen is in Katie Cleary's capable and inventive hands, from whence flow daily-changing menus with plenty of modern allure. The four-course deal may proceed from praline-crusted breast of wood pigeon with pain perdu, sweet potato crumble and morello cherry jus, through a sorbet refresher, to a main course such as salmon with vegetable 'spaghetti' and beetroot salsa in minted hollandaise, or venison loin with a haggis samosa and clapshot in red wine jus. Crème brûlée is no mere eggs-cream-and-sugar affair but is flavoured with coffee and served with hazelnut sablé, chocolate parfait and espresso foam.

Rooms 17 (2 fmly) **D** £190-£290 (incl. bkfst & dinner)* **Facilities** FTV ⚓ 9 ☘ Fishing 🚣 Clay pigeon shooting Estate tours Grouse shooting Hiking Mountain bikes Stalking New Year Wi-fi **Conf** Class 20 Board 20 Thtr 20 **Services** Lift **Parking** 43 **Notes** ⊗ Closed 20-28 Dec RS Nov-Jan Civ Wed 70

Chef Katie Cleary **Owner** Scott & Brianna Poole **Times** 12-2.30/7-9 Closed 1-28 Dec **Prices** Fixed L 2 course fr £13, Fixed D 4 course fr £45, Service included **Wines** 45 bottles over £20, 17 bottles under £20, 4 by glass **Notes** Vegetarian available, Dress restrictions, Smart casual, Jacket & tie preferred **Seats** 40, Pr/dining room 18 **Children** Portions

---

KENMORE Map 3 NN74

Kenmore Hotel

★★★ 78% HOTEL

◉ Traditional Scottish

Scottish cooking in an historic period inn on the River Tay

☎ 01887 830205 📄 01887 830262
The Square PH15 2NU
e-mail: reception@kenmorehotel.co.uk
web: www.kenmorehotel.com
dir: Off A9 at Ballinluig onto A827, through Aberfeldy to Kenmore, hotel in village centre

The Kenmore Hotel dates back to 1572 and is rightly proud of its history as Scotland's oldest inn. Bedrooms are tastefully decorated, and the choice of bars includes one with open fires. Legend has it that Robert Burns composed a poem on the bridge overlooking the Tay, which he then wrote on the Kenmore's chimney, where it remains to this day. If you're not in the area to write poetry, there's plenty more to do - salmon fishing on the River Tay, water sports on Loch Tay, walking, cycling or perhaps a round of golf should sort you out. The Taymouth conservatory-style restaurant enjoys impressive views over the river as it flows under the old arched bridge, courtesy of full-length windows. Simply laid tables need little adornment and the food is equally straightforward Scottish fare with substantial local flavours shining through. Kick off with Cullen skink, then move on to seared collops of Highland venison with sweet pickled red cabbage and redcurrant and bramble jus.

Rooms 40 (13 annexe) (4 fmly) (7 GF) **S** £69.50-£79.50; **D** £109-£129 (incl. bkfst)* **Facilities** STV Salmon fishing on River Tay Xmas New Year Wi-fi **Conf** Class 60 Board 50 Thtr 80 **Services** Lift **Parking** 40 **Notes** LB Civ Wed 150

Times 12-6/6-9.30

KILLIECRANKIE Map 5 NN96

Killiecrankie House Hotel

★★★ 86% SMALL HOTEL

◉◉ Modern British **V** 🍴

Satisfying country-house cooking in tranquil Perthshire

☎ 01796 473220 📄 01796 472451
PH16 5LG
e-mail: enquiries@killiecrankiehotel.co.uk
web: www.killiecrankiehotel.co.uk
dir: Exit A9 at Killiecrankie onto B8079. Hotel 3m on right

Overlooking the River Garry at the gateway to the Pass of Killiecrankie, this relaxed small-scale country hotel is run with a sense of fun that makes you feel immediately welcome. Built for a local church minister in 1840, the snow-white house sits in delightful landscaped gardens that make for a great pre-dinner stroll. Public areas include a wood-panelled bar and a cosy sitting room with original artwork and a blazing fire in colder months. Each of the bedrooms is individually decorated, well equipped and have wonderful countryside views. In the romantic, candlelit, tartan-splashed dining room, enthusiastic young staff ensure everything ticks along at the right pace, while the kitchen draws its supplies from local farmers, sea lochs and its own kitchen garden to construct menus of uncomplicated Franco-Scottish ideas. Sautéed wild mushrooms and smoked venison on olive oil toast is a deeply-flavoured, earthy opener, ahead of a well-balanced main course involving grilled sea bream fillets, Pink Fir Apple potato salad, saffron vegetable tartlet and a warm tomato coulis. Warm walnut and honey flan with vanilla ice cream wraps things up with aplomb. Killiecrankie has a well-earned reputation for wine, with a recommended bottle for each dish. Lighter lunchtime meals may be taken in the conservatory.

Rooms 10 (2 GF) **Facilities** FTV 🚣 Xmas New Year Wi-fi **Parking** 20 **Notes** Closed 3 Jan-12 Mar

Chef Mark Easton **Owner** Henrietta Fergusson **Times** 6.30-8.30 Closed Jan/Feb, L all week **Prices** Fixed D 4 course £38-£40, Service optional, Groups min 10 service 10% **Wines** 72 bottles over £20, 10 bottles under £20, 7 by glass **Notes** Pre-theatre menu from 6.15pm Mon-Sat, Sunday L, Vegetarian menu, Dress restrictions, No shorts **Seats** 30, Pr/dining room 12 **Children** Portions, Menu **Parking** 20

KINCLAVEN · Map 3 NO13

Ballathie House Hotel

★★★★ 78% COUNTRY HOUSE HOTEL

◉◉ Modern Scottish V

Modern country-house cooking at the threshold of the Highlands

☎ 01250 883268 ≣ 01250 883396
PH1 4QN
e-mail: email@ballathiehousehotel.com
web: www.ballathiehousehotel.com
dir: From A9, 2m N of Perth, take B9099 through Stanley, follow signs. Or from A93 at Beech Hedge follow signs for hotel, 2.5m

A Scots baronial house on the threshold of the Highlands, Ballathie has always been a resort for the sportingly inclined. The on-site golfing and cricket may have been consigned to a departed era, but it is still an enviable spot for anglers. Bedrooms range from well-proportioned master rooms to modern standard rooms, and many boast antique furniture and art deco bathrooms, or ask for one of the Riverside Rooms, set in a purpose-built development right on the banks of the river, complete with balconies and terraces. In the elegant buttercup-hued restaurant, the cooking uses materials from the surrounding estate and the region at large for dishes that are squarely in the modern British country-house manner. A grilled red mullet fillet is turned out on marinated vegetable salad with a citrus dressing and saffron aïoli, as a precursor to roast crown of partridge with salsify, Savoy cabbage and pear purée, or Gressingham duck breast and confit leg with macerated plum and hazelnuts in red wine jus. Desserts pursue gentle comfort in the style of mango parfait or chocolate marquise with blueberry compôte and passionfruit syrup.

.**Rooms** 41 (16 annexe) (2 fmly) (10 GF) **S** £65-£130; **D** £130-£290 (incl. bkfst)* **Facilities** FTV Putt green Fishing ⛵ Xmas New Year Wi-fi **Conf** Class 20 Board 30 Thtr 50 **Services** Lift **Parking** 50 **Notes** Civ Wed 90

Chef Andrew Wilkie **Owner** Ballathie House Hotel Ltd **Times** 12.30-2/7-9 **Prices** Fixed L 2 course fr £19.50, Fixed D 3 course fr £45, Service optional **Wines** 180 bottles over £20, 4 bottles under £20, 6 by glass **Notes** Sunday L, Vegetarian menu, Dress restrictions, Jacket & tie preferred, No jeans/T-shirts **Seats** 70, Pr/dining room 32 **Children** Portions

KINLOCH RANNOCH · Map 5 NN65

Dunalastair Hotel

★★★ 75% HOTEL

◉ Modern British

Traditional Scottish hotel with confidently prepared food

☎ 01882 632323 & 632218 ≣ 01882 632371
PH16 5PW
e-mail: info@dunalastair.co.uk
dir: A9 to Pitlochry, on N side take B8019 to Tummel Bridge then A846 to Kinloch Rannoch

Dunalastair is a hotel that trumpets its Highland heritage loud and proud. Dating from 1770, the venerable old house has done service as barracks for Jacobite soldiers as well as a staging post in the days of horse-drawn transport. Surrounded by unspoilt and beautiful countryside, this family-owned hotel offers a warm and friendly welcome and great hospitality. Once inside there's no doubting that you have left England behind and are north of the border: the restaurant is a classic Highland setting in the baronial vein, all oak panelling, stag's-antler chandeliers and tartan carpets setting the ambience to perfection for the superb Scottish ingredients that supply the backbone of the kitchen's contemporary reworkings of comforting country-house classics. You might start with the iconic haggis, neeps and tatties jazzed up with a whisky and Arran mustard sauce, and move on to roast loin of venison with fondant potato, balsamic shallots and raspberry jus. Stick with the Scottish theme to the end: traditional cranachan with fresh raspberries and shortbread.

Rooms 28 (4 fmly) (9 GF) **Facilities** Fishing 4x4 safaris Rafting Clay pigeon shooting Bike hire Archery Xmas New Year **Conf** Class 35 Board 30 Thtr 60 **Parking** 33 **Notes** Civ Wed 70

Times 12-2.30/6.30-9

Macdonald Loch Rannoch Hotel

★★★ 75% HOTEL

☎ 0844 879 9059 & 01882 632201 ≣ 01882 632203
PH16 5PS
e-mail: loch_rannoch@macdonald-hotels.co.uk
web: www.macdonald-hotels.co.uk
dir: Off A9 onto B847 Calvine. Follow signs to Kinloch Rannoch, hotel 1m from village

Set deep in the countryside with elevated views across Loch Rannoch, this hotel is built around a 19th-century hunting lodge and provides a great base for exploring this beautiful area. The superior bedrooms have views over the loch. There is a choice of eating options - The Ptarmigan Restaurant and the Schiehallan Bar for informal eating. The hotel provides both indoor and outdoor activities.

Rooms 48 (25 fmly) **Facilities** FTV ⊗ Fishing Gym Xmas
New Year Wi-fi **Conf** Class 80 Board 50 Thtr 160
Del from £95 to £130 **Services** Lift **Parking** 52
Notes Civ Wed 130

KINNESSWOOD · Map 3 NO10

Lomond Country Inn ▾

KY13 9HN ☎ **01592 840253** 📠 **01592 840693**
e-mail: enquires@lomondinn.co.uk
dir: M90 junct 5, follow signs for Glenrothes then
Scotlandwell. Kinnesswood next village

Gliders from Scotland's oldest club swoop above this
characterful small hotel, benefiting from the updraught
created by the spectacular Lomond Hills below which the inn
nestles. Take advantage of the capacious terrace for views
across nearby Loch Leven to the shapely summits of the
Ochill Hills, a glorious summer sunset panorama. Under new
ownership since late 2010, the inn continues to champion
Scottish real ales, with beers from Perth's Inveralmond
brewery going down well in the friendly, log fire warmed
village bar. Dine with a view in the homely restaurant, where
large windows make full use of the panorama to the loch;
meals are exceptional value and offer a choice of good,
pubby food like pies and curries with local favourites such
as game stew, enhanced by a daily-changing specials
board. This is an ideal stop-off point for visitors following
the local heritage trail or exploring the Kingdom of Fife.

Open all day all wk 7am-1am **Bar Meals** L served all wk
7am-9pm D served all wk 5-9 booking required Av main
course £5 food served all day **Restaurant** L served all wk
7am-9pm D served all wk 5-9 booking required food served
all day ⊕ FREE HOUSE ◀ Deuchars IPA, Calders Cream,
Tetley's, Orkney Dark Island, Ossian Lia Fail. ▾ 12
Facilities Children welcome Children's menu Children's
portions Play area Family room Dogs allowed Garden Parking
Wi-fi

KINROSS · Map 3 NO10

The Green Hotel Golf & Leisure Resort

★★★★ 73% HOTEL

◉ Modern European

Regional produce in a Perthshire golfing hotel

☎ 01577 863467 📠 01577 863180
2 The Muirs KY13 8AS
e-mail: reservations@green-hotel.com
web: www.green-hotel.com
dir: M90 junct 6, follow Kinross signs onto A922 for hotel

The long-established, white-fronted hotel specialises in
keeping golfers occupied - there are two parkland courses to
go at - and offers a range of other comforts too on the
shores of Loch Leven. Public areas include a choice of bars

and a well-stocked gift shop. The comfortable, well-
equipped bedrooms, most of which are generously
proportioned, boast attractive colour schemes and smart
modern furnishings. The cooking in Basil's Grill Room uses
some good regional produce such as guinea fowl, which
might come in a black truffle sauce, or new season's lamb
with a garlic and herb boudin. Spring pea velouté in October
seems to be yearning for the southern hemisphere, while
duck confit terrine wrapped in Parma ham, served warm
with mango salsa, is a typical starter.

Rooms 46 (3 fmly) (14 GF) **S** £62-£92; **D** £72-£132 (incl.
bkfst)* **Facilities** STV ⊗ supervised ⌁ 36 ♨ Putt green
Fishing ⌁ Gym Petanque Curling (Sep-Apr) Cycling
Shooting ♫ Xmas New Year Wi-fi **Conf** Class 75 Board 60
Thtr 130 **Parking** 60 **Notes** LB Civ Wed 100

Chef James Downes **Owner** Sir David Montgomery
Times 8.30-9.30 Closed L Mon-Sat **Prices** Fixed D 3 course
£22-£38, Starter £4.50-£7.50, Main £15-£22, Dessert £6-
£8.50, Service optional, Groups min 8 service 8% **Wines** 40
bottles over £20, 14 bottles under £20, 6 by glass
Notes Sunday L, Vegetarian available, Dress restrictions,
Smart casual **Seats** 90, Pr/dining room 22 **Children** Portions

The Windlestrae Hotel & Leisure Centre

★★★ Ⓐ HOTEL

☎ 01577 863217 📠 01577 864733
The Muirs KY13 8AS
e-mail: reservations@windlestraehotel.com
web: www.windlestraehotel.com
dir: M90 junct 6 into Kinross, left at 2nd mini rdbt. Hotel
400yds on right

Rooms 45 (13 GF) **S** £50-£110; **D** £60-£130 (incl. bkfst)
Facilities STV ⊗ supervised ⌁ 36 ♨ Gym Beautician Steam
room Toning tables Xmas New Year Wi-fi **Conf** Class 100
Board 80 Thtr 250 Del from £105 to £160 **Parking** 80
Notes LB Civ Wed 100

MEIKLEOUR · Map 3 NO13

Meikleour Hotel

PH2 6EB ☎ **01250 883206**
e-mail: visitus@meikleourhotel.co.uk
dir: From A93 (between Perth & Blairgowrie) take A984 into
village centre

In the shadow of the famously vast Beech Hedge of
Meikleour, this attractive old creeper-clad, gabled coach and
posting house ticks all the boxes for country sports
enthusiasts (with fishing on the local River Tay and shoots
nearby), whilst ale fans will revel in the house beer, brewed
at the nearby Inveralmond brewery. Add top-notch Scottish
provender (Arbroath smokies, local estate venison) to the
mix; it's little wonder that visitors touring the nearby Angus
Glens or skiing at Glenshee are amongst the dedicated
aficionados of this welcoming inn.

MEIKLEOUR CONTINUED

Open all wk 11-3 6-11 Closed: 25-30 Dec **Bar Meals** L
served all wk 12.15-2.30 booking required D served all wk
6.30-9 booking required Av main course £12 **Restaurant** L
served all wk 12.15-2.30 booking required D served all wk
6.30-9 booking required Av 3 course à la carte fr £23
⊕ FREE HOUSE ◄ Lure of Meikleour. **Facilities** Children
welcome Children's menu Children's portions Dogs allowed
Garden Beer festival Parking Wi-fi

| MUTHILL | Map 3 NN81 |

Barley Bree Restaurant with Rooms

★★★★ RESTAURANT WITH ROOMS

◉◉ Modern Scottish

Locally-sourced food in friendly contemporary restaurant

6 Willoughby St PH5 2AB
☎ **01764 681451** 📄 **01764 910055**
e-mail: info@barleybree.com
dir: A9 onto A822 in centre of Muthill

Originally an 18th-century coaching inn, Barley Bree is now
an attractive modern restaurant with rooms on the fringes of
the Perthshire Highlands. Situated in the heart of this small
village, genuine hospitality and quality food are obvious
attractions. The property has been transformed by the
current owners, and the stylish bedrooms are appointed to a
very high standard. In the dining room, well-spaced bare
wooden tables sit on vintage floorboards beneath an oak-
beamed roof and walls enlivened by local artists' work
warmed in the colder months by a wood-burning stove in a
huge, open brickwork hearth. The auld alliance is alive and
well in the kitchen, where a French chef-patron injects a
distinctly Gallic accent to the modern Scottish output.
Materials are well sourced, reaching the plate in the form,
perhaps, of seared wood pigeon breast with beetroot and
celery, followed by featherblade of beef with horseradish
mash and red wine jus. Finish with the Norman delights of
apple tarte Tatin with Calvados ice cream.

Rooms 6 en suite (1 fmly) S £60-£70; D £100-£150*
Facilities FTV tea/coffee Dinner available Cen ht Wi-fi
Parking 10 **Notes** LB ⊗ Closed 2wks Autumn/Jan RS Mon &
Tue Restaurant closed to public No coaches

Chef Fabrice Bouteloup **Owner** Fabrice & Alison Bouteloup
Times 12-2/6-9 Closed mid Feb-early Mar, 2 wks Oct, Xmas,
Mon-Tue **Prices** Starter £5-£10.50, Main £16.50-£22,
Dessert £5-£7.50, Service included **Wines** 53 bottles over
£20, 19 bottles under £20, 10 by glass **Notes** Sun 12-7.30,
Sunday L, Vegetarian available **Seats** 35 **Children** Portions,
Menu

| PERTH | Map 3 NO12 |

Murrayshall House Hotel & Golf Course

★★★★ 76% HOTEL

◉◉ Modern British

Polished cooking amid the rolling Lowland acres

☎ 01738 551171 📄 01738 552595
New Scone PH2 7PH
e-mail: info@murrayshall.co.uk
web: www.murrayshall.co.uk
dir: From Perth take A94 (Coupar Angus), 1m from Perth,
right to Murrayshall just before New Scone

The imposing country house stands in a lushly wooded 350-
acre estate, including two golf courses, one of which is of
championship standard. Bedrooms come in two distinct
styles: modern suites in a purpose-built building contrast
with more classic rooms in the main building. Perth is
distantly visible across the acres, so grab a window table, if
you can, in the elegantly furnished dining room. Murrayshall
isn't all about golf,however, as its highly polished, modern
European menus soon demonstrate. Slow-cooked short ribs
with truffle-scented celeriac and horseradish risotto
provides a memorable way of starting out, with fine
Lowlands produce adding allure to the principal dishes.
Pheasant breast poached in cider with the shredded leg-
meat, bacon and onions, or lamb no fewer than four ways
(cannon, neck, spare rib, breast) in mint sauce with garlic
mash, are among the possibilities. Fish might be halibut,
served on the bone with salt-cod dumplings and Puy lentils.
Meals conclude with a Franco-Scottish cheeseboard, or
something like blueberry mousse sablé.

Rooms 41 (14 annexe) (17 fmly) (5 GF) **S** £77-£100;
D £120-£150 (incl. bkfst)* **Facilities** STV ♨ 36 ⛳ Putt green
Driving range New Year Wi-fi **Conf** Class 60 Board 30
Thtr 150 Del from £150 to £160* **Parking** 120 **Notes** LB
Civ Wed 130

Chef Craig Jackson **Owner** Old Scone Ltd **Times** 12-2.30,
7-9.45 Closed 26 Dec, L Sat **Prices** Fixed D 3 course fr £28,
Service optional **Wines** 30 bottles over £20, 20 bottles under
£20, 8 by glass **Notes** Sunday L, Vegetarian available
Seats 55, Pr/dining room 40 **Children** Portions, Menu

Parklands Hotel

★★★★ 73% SMALL HOTEL

◉◉ Modern British

Creative, technically adept cooking in a smart setting

☎ 01738 622451 📄 01738 622046
2 St Leonards Bank PH2 8EB
e-mail: info@theparklandshotel.com
web: www.theparklandshotel.com
dir: M90 junct 10, in 1m left at lights at end of park area, hotel on left

Previously the residence of the Lord Provost, the Parklands Hotel is a fine Victorian building with extensive views over South Inch Park to Kinnoull Hill. The enthusiastic proprietors continue to invest heavily in the business and the bedrooms have a smart contemporary feel. The smart Acanthus Restaurant is its fine-dining option, an uncluttered space with leather high-backed chairs at linen-clothed tables on herrringbone parquet floors - all very tasteful with nothing to distract from the food. The kitchen takes a creative modern approach to its output. Sound technical skills are evident in starters such as scallops and pork with chilli, caramel and orange reduction, while mains could deliver wild duck with braised Puy lentils, artichoke purée and port jus. Chocolate assiette - tart, brownie, mousse - makes an indulgent finale.

Rooms 15 (3 fmly) (4 GF) **S** £92.50-£132.50;
D £112.50-£162.50 (incl. bkfst)* **Facilities** STV Wi-fi
Conf Class 18 Board 20 Thtr 24 Del from £124.50 to £154.50* **Parking** 30 **Notes** LB Closed 26 Dec-7 Jan Civ Wed 40

Chef Graeme Pallister **Owner** Scott & Penny Edwards
Times 7-9 Closed 26 Dec-7 Jan, Tue-Wed, L all week
Prices Fixed D 4 course £35, Service optional, Groups min 8 service 10% **Wines** 40 bottles over £20, 55 bottles under £20, 6 by glass **Notes** Vegetarian available, Dress restrictions, Smart casual, no shorts or jeans **Seats** 36, Pr/dining room 22 **Children** Portions, Menu

The New County Hotel

★★★ 77% HOTEL

◉◉ Modern British 🖐

Modish cooking in city-centre boutique hotel

☎ 01738 623355 📄 01738 628969
22-30 County Place PH2 8EE
e-mail: enquiries@newcountyhotel.com
web: www.newcountyhotel.com
web: www.opusone-restaurant.co.uk
dir: A9 junct 11 Perth. Follow signs for town centre. Hotel on right after library

This is a smart boutique-style hotel in the heart of the beautiful garden city of Perth. The bedrooms have a modern and stylish appearance and public areas include a popular bar and contemporary lounge area. The restaurant, Opus One, continues to earn plaudits for its confident modern cooking. The town centre location, next to the Bell Library, pulls in the business crowd for leisurely lunches, while Perthshire's culture vultures turn up for intimate get-togethers when in town for theatre, concert and gallery visits. The hotel goes for a clean-lined minimal modern look throughout, and while there's a cool, cosmopolitan vibe and crowd-pleasing fare in Café 22, and a cheerful, pubby feel to the bar-bistro, it is in the Opus One restaurant that the kitchen pulls out all the stops. Local produce is name-checked on an appealing menu of bang up-to-date ideas, kicking off perhaps with a brandade of salted Shetland pollock, teamed with a poached duck egg, chorizo and white onion velouté, followed by a fashionable treatment of lamb that sees roast loin, braised shoulder and sweetbreads served with haricots blancs and root vegetables.

Rooms 23 (4 fmly) **S** £60-£75; **D** £70-£140 (incl. bkfst)*
Facilities New Year Wi-fi **Conf** Class 80 Board 24 Thtr 120
Del from £130 to £150* **Parking** 10 **Notes** ⊗

Chef Romuald Denesle **Owner** Mr Owen Boyle, Mrs Sarah Boyle **Times** 12-2/6.30-9 Closed Sun-Mon **Prices** Starter £4.20-£7.75, Main £10.45-£22.45, Dessert £4.65-£6.75, Service optional **Wines** 50 bottles over £20, 14 bottles under £20, 10 by glass **Notes** Early bird menu available, Vegetarian available **Seats** 48 **Children** Portions

Best Western Queens Hotel

★★★ 75% HOTEL

☎ 01738 442222 📄 01738 638496
Leonard St PH2 8HB
e-mail: enquiry@queensperth.co.uk
dir: From M90 follow to 2nd lights, turn left. Hotel on right, opposite railway station

This popular hotel benefits from a central location close to both the bus and rail stations. Bedrooms vary in size and style with top floor rooms offering extra space and excellent views of the town. Public rooms include a smart leisure centre and versatile conference space. A range of meals is served in both the bar and restaurant.

Rooms 50 (4 fmly) **Facilities** STV FTV 🏊 Gym Steam room Xmas New Year Wi-fi **Conf** Class 70 Board 50 Thtr 200
Services Lift **Parking** 50 **Notes** ⊗ Civ Wed 220

Drumond Castle Gardens, Crieff, Perthshire

PERTH CONTINUED

Salutation

★★★ 70% HOTEL

☎ 01738 630066 📄 01738 633598
South St PH2 8PH
e-mail: salessalutation@strathmorehotels.com
dir: At end of South St on right before River Tay

Situated in heart of Perth, the Salutation is reputed to be one of the oldest hotels in Scotland and has been welcoming guests through its doors since 1699. It offers traditional hospitality with all the modern comforts. Bedrooms vary in size and are thoughtfully equipped. An extensive menu is available in the Adam Restaurant with its impressive barrel vaulted ceiling and original features.

Rooms 84 (5 fmly) **Facilities** 🎵 Xmas New Year Wi-fi
Conf Class 180 Board 60 Thtr 300 **Services** Lift
Notes Civ Wed 100

Holiday Inn Express Perth

BUDGET HOTEL

☎ 01738 636666 📄 01738 633363
200 Dunkeld Rd, Inveralmond PH1 3AQ
e-mail: info@hiexpressperth.co.uk
web: www.hiexpressperth.co.uk
dir: Off A9 (Inverness to Stirling road) at Inveralmond rdbt onto A912 signed Perth. Right at 1st rdbt, follow signs for hotel

A modern hotel ideal for families and business travellers. Fresh and uncomplicated, the spacious rooms include Sky TV, power shower and tea and coffee-making facilities. Continental buffet breakfast is included in the room rate; other meals may be taken at the nearby family pub or restaurant.

Rooms 81 (43 fmly) (19 GF) (8 smoking) **Conf** Class 15 Board 16 Thtr 30

Cherrybank Guesthouse

★★★★ 🏠 GUEST ACCOMMODATION

217-219 Glasgow Rd PH2 0NB
☎ 01738 451982 📄 01738 561336
e-mail: m.r.cherrybank@blueyonder.co.uk
dir: 1m SW of town centre on A93

Convenient for the town and major roads, Cherrybank has been extended and carefully refurbished to offer well equipped and beautifully presented bedrooms, one of which is on the ground floor. The delightful lounge is ideal for relaxation, while delicious breakfasts are served at individual tables in the bright airy dining room. Margaret and Robert Miller were finalists in this year's Friendliest Landlady of the Year award (2011-12).

Rooms 5 rms (4 en suite) (1 pri facs) (2 fmly) (1 GF)
Facilities tea/coffee Cen ht Wi-fi **Parking** 4 **Notes** ⊗

The Anglers Restaurant with Rooms

★★★ INN

Main Rd, Guildtown PH2 6BS
☎ 01821 640329
e-mail: info@theanglersinn.co.uk
dir: 6m N of Perth on A93

This charming country inn enjoys a peaceful rural setting and yet is only a short drive from Perth city centre and is popular with fishing and shooting parties along with race goers. The inn has been tastefully refurbished and the accommodation consists of en suite bedrooms that vary in size, each equipped with flat-screen TV. The restaurant offers local produce, and a daily changing blackboard. Comfortable leather chairs and a log fire induce a relaxed and homely atmosphere, ideal surroundings in which to sample one of the Inveralmond Brewery ales on offer at the bar. Expect food prepared to an award-winning standard: typical choices for a three-course dinner from the carte could include starters of potted Morecambe brown shrimps and Skye prawns, or fried herb and tomato risotto cake. Main courses could comprise roast herb marinated rump of lamb with haggis hack, or free-range chicken breast stuffed with black pudding. Banana and rum crème brûlée or sticky toffee pudding with butterscotch sauce are typical of the desserts.

Rooms 6 en suite (1 fmly) S £40-£75; D £100-£150
Facilities FTV TVL tea/coffee Dinner available Cen ht Wi-fi 🎣 Pool table **Parking** 40 **Notes** LB No Children

Open 11-3 5.30-mdnt Closed: Mon **Bar Meals** L served all wk 12.15-2.30 D served all wk 6.15-9 **Restaurant** L served all wk 12.15-2.30 booking required D served all wk 6.15-9 booking required ⊕ FREE HOUSE ◀ Ossian, LiaFail.
Facilities Children welcome Children's menu Children's portions Dogs allowed Garden

Clunie

★★★★ GUEST HOUSE

12 Pitcullen Crescent PH2 7HT
☎ 01738 623625 📄 01738 623238
e-mail: ann@clunieguesthouse.co.uk
dir: On A94 on E side of river

Lying on the north east side of town, this family-run guest house offers a friendly welcome. The comfortable bedrooms, which vary in size, are attractively decorated and well equipped. Breakfast is served at individual tables in the elegant ground-floor dining room.

Rooms 7 en suite (1 fmly) S £30-£40; D £60-£70* **Facilities** tea/coffee Cen ht Wi-fi **Parking** 8 **Notes** LB ⊗

Ballabeg Guest House

 ★★★ BED AND BREAKFAST

14 Keir St PH2 7HJ
☎ **01738 620434**
e-mail: ballabeg@btopenworld.com
dir: NE of city centre, off A94

Well situated for the town centre and benefiting from off-road parking, this property offers modern, comfortable bedrooms of a good overall size with a number of extras provided as standard. Well-cooked breakfasts with warm and genuine hospitality ensure a pleasant stay. All major credit cards are accepted.

Rooms 4 rms (3 en suite) (1 pri facs) D £57-£60*
Facilities FTV tea/coffee Cen ht **Parking** 4 **Notes** ⊗ No Children 16yrs Closed 5 Dec-Jan

Deans@Let's Eat

 Modern Scottish

Skilled modern Scottish cooking in smart setting

☎ 01738 643377
77-79 Kinnoull St PH1 5EZ
e-mail: deans@letseatperth.co.uk
web: www.letseatperth.co.uk
dir: On corner of Kinnoull St & Atholl St, close to North Inch & cinema

All the ingredients are still working together at this welcoming, unpretentious restaurant in a handy location near Perth centre. Since husband-and-wife-team Willie and Margo Deans took over the reins in 2005, the bottle-green corner frontage has become a fixture for local gastronomes. Inside is a warm setting of burgundy and terracotta with linen-clad tables, run with affable professionalism by the front-of-house team. After a career in Scotland's pedigree kitchens, Willie Deans knows where to lay his hands on a wealth of excellent Scottish produce as the backbone of his creative modern repertoire. Seared scallops get an exotic outing with harissa-braised lentils, coconut, Thai green curry sauce, and cauliflower mayonnaise, while mains could unite loin of lamb with glazed root vegetables, Stornoway black pudding, caramelised turnip purée, thyme sauce, and mushroom and potato pavé. Desserts are a strong suit - perhaps gingerbread pudding with rum and raisin ice cream and toffee butter.

Chef Willie Deans **Owner** Mr & Mrs W Deans
Times 12-2.30/6.30-10 Closed Sun-Mon **Prices** Fixed L 2 course fr £13.95, Fixed D 3 course fr £24.95, Starter £4.75-£9.50, Main £9.50-£25.50, Dessert £6, Service optional **Wines** 40 bottles over £20, 23 bottles under £20, 8 by glass **Notes** Vegetarian available, Dress restrictions, Smart casual **Seats** 70 **Children** Portions **Parking** Multi-storey car park (100 yds)

The North Port Restaurant

◉ British, International

Creative modern dishes in relaxed and intimate setting

☎ 01738 580867
8 North Port PH1 5LU
e-mail: thenorthport@mail.com
dir: In town centre behind concert hall & museum

The robust 18th-century stone building that is home to North Port sits in the historic heart of Perth just back from the River Tay, and handy for the town's concert hall and museums. There is much to like about the interior, which has the intimacy of an upmarket cabin with its wooden floors, ornately coffered darkwood ceiling and unclothed tables. Diligent sourcing of fine Scottish produce is firmly on the agenda of a kitchen that deals in imaginative modern British dishes, with blackboard specials to bolster a well-thought-out carte. Dinner kicks of with a simple but effective woodland mushroom crumble with parsnip crisps, ahead of a robust seared pork fillet teamed with black pudding, gratin potatoes and Calvados gravy. To finish, spiced oranges and caramel sauce are a perfect foil to a creamy vanilla cheesecake. Top value is on offer in the pre-theatre dinner menu.

Chef Kevin Joubert, Laurent Ladeveze **Owner** Kevin Joubert, Aleksandra Trzcinska **Times** 12-2.30/5-9 Closed 1st wk Jan, Mon, D Sun **Prices** Fixed L 2 course £7.95-£21, Fixed D 3 course fr £16.95, Starter £3.95-£7.95, Main £9.95-£21.95, Dessert £4.75-£6.95, Service optional **Wines** 3 bottles over £20, 16 bottles under £20, 6 by glass **Notes** Pre-theatre menu daily 5-7pm, Sunday L, Vegetarian available **Seats** 55, Pr/dining room 22 **Children** Portions, Menu **Parking** On street, car park Kinnoull St

63 Tay Street

◉◉ Modern Scottish **V** NOTABLE WINE LIST

Local, honest cooking by the River Tay

☎ 01738 441451
63 Tay St PH2 8NN
e-mail: info@63taystreet.com
dir: In town centre, on river

This modish contemporary restaurant in the historic riverside heart of Perth has a loyal local fan base. Views of the Tay make it a well-supported lunch spot, while dinner is a rather more sophisticated, formal affair, ably orchestrated by skillful waiting staff; the high-ceilinged dining room is a setting of understated neutral elegance enlivened by a changing cast of artwork on the walls. Chef-patron Graeme Pallister is a local, whose modern Scottish cooking brims with imaginative flair and plenty of Perthshire's peerless produce. Sea-fresh Mull scallops are a perfectly executed starter, partnered with lentils and ham, and a chilli galette;

continued

then comes local lamb, braised and served together with roasted loin, parmesan dauphine and Madeira-braised vegetables. To finish, chocolate soufflé comes with aniseed ice cream and bittersweet custard.

Chef Graeme Pallister **Owner** Scott & Penny Edwards, Graeme Pallister **Times** 12-2/6.30-9 Closed Xmas, New Year, 1st wk Jul, Sun-Mon **Prices** Fixed L 3 course £22-£24, Service optional, Groups min 8 service 10% **Wines** 248 bottles over £20, 6 by glass **Notes** Fixed D 5 course £35-£39, Vegetarian menu **Seats** 38 **Children** Portions **Parking** On street

PITLOCHRY	Map 5 NN95

See also **Kinloch Rannoch**

Knockendarroch House Hotel

★★★★ 74% SMALL HOTEL

◉ Modern Scottish

Intimate country house with good food

☎ 01796 473473 📄 01796 474056
Higher Oakfield PH16 5HT
e-mail: bookings@knockendarroch.co.uk
dir: Just off the A9

Knockendarroch's steepled rooftop soars skywards from its perch high on a thickly-wooded hillside - it feels cut off from the world, yet lies just a short stroll from the centre of Pitlochry. With just a dozen individually styled and very well appointed guest rooms, it is an intimate country house that delivers superb service, a cosseting upmarket interior, and accomplished cooking - a formula that has guests returning again and again. Superb Scottish produce underpins a menu of updated country-house classics, kicking off with seared Pentland Firth scallops partnered imaginatively with pesto risotto and parmesan crisp. Next up, Isle of Gigha halibut is teamed with saffron potatoes, stir-fried vegetables and a fresh mussel and herb broth, and it all ends just as you hope it might, with steamed marmalade pudding, vanilla crème anglaise and home-made Drambuie ice cream.

Rooms 12 (1 GF) **D** £138-£198 (incl. bkfst & dinner)*
Facilities FTV Wi-fi **Parking** 12 **Notes** LB No children 10yrs Closed Dec-Jan

Times D only (pre-theatre D fr 5.30 during season)

Green Park

★★★ 87% COUNTRY HOUSE HOTEL

◉ British

Lochside country-house hotel with charming fine-dining restaurant

☎ 01796 473248 📄 01796 473520
Clunie Bridge Rd PH16 5JY
e-mail: bookings@thegreenpark.co.uk
web: www.thegreenpark.co.uk
dir: Exit A9 at Pitlochry, follow signs 0.25m through town

With superlative views over Loch Faskally, the long-established family-run Green Park is a big hit with those touring Perthshire and the Southern Highlands. Guests return year after year to enjoy the thoughtfully designed bedrooms, many of which, including those in the splendid wing, enjoy these views. The restaurant is an important feature here, after all sightseeing does wonders for the appetite, and it fits in with the comfortable, traditional country-house hotel perfectly. Simply laid tables in a tranquil room of dark reds and browns are the place to tuck into some classic French cooking, where local Scottish ingredients, particularly seafood and game, steal the show. Salmon, sole and pistachio nut terrine, perhaps, served with croûtons and a sweet dill sauce, before main-course roast breast of pheasant filled with haggis, Savoy cabbage and a whisky consommé. Warm marmalade pudding and a Drambuie crème anglaise ends things on a comforting note.

Rooms 51 (3 fmly) (16 GF) **S** £66-£103; **D** £132-£206 (incl. bkfst & dinner)* **Facilities** FTV Putt green New Year Wi-fi **Services** Lift **Parking** 51 **Notes** LB

Chef Chris Tamblin **Owner** Green Park Ltd
Times 12-2/6.30-8.30 **Prices** Fixed D 3 course £21, Service optional **Wines** 10 bottles over £20, 65 bottles under £20, 8 by glass **Notes** Pre-theatre menu available from 5.45, Sunday L, Vegetarian available, Dress restrictions, Reasonably smart dress **Seats** 100 **Children** Portions, Menu

Dundarach

★★★ 77% HOTEL

☎ 01796 472862 📄 01796 473024
Perth Rd PH16 5DJ
e-mail: inbox@dundarach.co.uk
web: www.dundarach.co.uk
dir: S of town centre on main road

This welcoming, family-run hotel stands in mature grounds at the south end of town. Bedrooms come in a variety of styles, including a block of large purpose-built rooms that will appeal to business guests. Well-proportioned public areas feature inviting lounges and a conservatory restaurant giving fine views of the Tummel Valley.

Rooms 39 (19 annexe) (7 fmly) (12 GF) **Facilities** Wi-fi **Conf** Class 40 Board 40 Thtr 60 **Parking** 39 **Notes** ⊗ Closed Jan RS Dec-early Feb

Moulin Hotel

★★★ 75% HOTEL

☎ 01796 472196 📄 01796 474098
11-13 Kirkmichael Rd, Moulin PH16 5EW
e-mail: enquiries@moulinhotel.co.uk
web: www.moulinhotel.co.uk
dir: Off A9 take A924 signed Braemar into town centre. Hotel 0.75m from Pitlochry

Built in 1695 at the foot of Ben Vrackie on an old drovers' road, this great all-round inn is popular as a walking and touring base. Locals are drawn to the bar for the excellent home-brewed beers, with Ale of Atholl, Braveheart, Moulin Light, and Old Remedial served on handpump. The interior boasts beautiful stone walls and lots of cosy niches, with blazing log fires in winter; while the courtyard garden is lovely in summer, and bedrooms are well equipped. Menus offer the opportunity to try something local such as mince and tatties; Skye mussels; venison pan-fried in Braveheart beer; and Vrackie Grostel – sautéed potatoes with smoked bacon topped with a fried egg. You might then round off your meal with Highland honey sponge and custard, or raspberry crumble. A specials board broadens the choice further. Over 20 wines by the glass and more than 30 malt whiskies are available.

Rooms 15 (3 fmly) **S** £45-£77; **D** £60-£92 (incl. bkfst) **Facilities** FTV New Year Wi-fi **Conf** Class 12 Board 10 Thtr 15 Del from £95 to £110 **Parking** 30 **Notes** LB ⊗

Open all day all wk 11-11 (Fri-Sat 11am-11.45pm Sun noon-11) **Bar Meals** L served all wk 12-9.30 D served all wk 12-9.30 food served all day **Restaurant** D served all wk 6-9 booking required 🍺 FREE HOUSE 🍺 Moulin Braveheart, Old Remedial, Ale of Atholl, Moulin Light, Belhaven Best. 🍷 25 **Facilities** Children welcome Children's menu Children's portions Dogs allowed Garden

Craigroyston House

★★★★ GUEST HOUSE

2 Lower Oakfield PH16 5HQ
☎ 01796 472053 📄 01796 472053
e-mail: reservations@craigroyston.co.uk
web: www.craigroyston.co.uk
dir: In town centre near information centre car park

The Maxwell family delight in welcoming guests to their home, an impressive detached Victorian villa set in a colourful garden. The bedrooms have pretty colour schemes and are comfortably furnished in period style. There is an inviting sitting room, complete with deep sofas for those wishing to relax and enjoy the peaceful atmosphere. Scottish breakfasts are served at individual tables in the attractive dining room.

Rooms 8 en suite (1 fmly) (1 GF) D £70-£95 **Facilities** FTV tea/coffee Cen ht Wi-fi **Parking** 9 **Notes** LB ⊗ 🐾

Wellwood House

★★★★ GUEST HOUSE

13 West Moulin Rd PH16 5EA
☎ 01796 474288 📄 01796 474299
e-mail: wellwoodhouse@aol.com
web: www.wellwoodhouse.com
dir: In town centre opp town hall

Set in lovely grounds on an elevated position overlooking the town, Wellwood House has stunning views of the Vale of Atholl and the surrounding countryside. The comfortably proportioned bedrooms are attractively decorated and well equipped. The elegant lounge has an honesty bar and a fire on cooler evenings, and the spacious dining room is the setting for hearty breakfasts served at individual tables.

Rooms 10 rms (8 en suite) (2 pri facs) (1 fmly) (1 GF) S £45-£55; D £66-£80* **Facilities** FTV TVL tea/coffee Cen ht Licensed Wi-fi **Parking** 20 **Notes** ⊗ Closed 10 Nov-14 Feb

ST FILLANS
Map 2 NN62

The Four Seasons Hotel

★★★ 83% HOTEL

◉◉ Modern British **V**

Wonderful lochside location and creative cooking

☎ 01764 685333 📠 01764 685444
Loch Earn PH6 2NF
e-mail: info@thefourseasonshotel.co.uk
web: www.thefourseasonshotel.co.uk
dir: On A85, towards W of village

The manager of local limekilns who built this property in the early 19th century couldn't have chosen a better setting: it's on the bank of Loch Earn, with dramatic views to the south-west. It's a stylish place, with lots of highly polished wooden floors, open fires and unusual oriental-style tables, while the Meall Reamhar restaurant has modern furniture, lots of artwork and breathtaking loch views. The kitchen draws on ideas from various cuisines to produce menus that hold much of interest, from seared scallops on cauliflower velouté with Indian-spiced Puy lentils and spinach, to a main course of pavé of halibut with lemon and herb rice and citrus butter sauce. Techniques are sound, and pairings are successful, as in venison carpaccio with kumquat and lime dressing, then chicken breast in a shellfish nage with herb mousseline and truffled fondant potato.

Rooms 18 (6 annexe) (7 fmly) **S** £54-£108; **D** £108-£166 (incl. bkfst) **Facilities** FTV Xmas New Year Wi-fi **Conf** Class 45 Board 38 Thtr 95 **Parking** 40 **Notes** LB Closed 2 Jan-mid Feb RS Nov, Dec, Mar Civ Wed 80

Chef Mathew Martin **Owner** Andrew Low
Times 12-2.30/6-9.30 Closed Jan-Feb & some wkdays Mar, Nov & Dec **Prices** Fixed L 3 course £12.50-£17.50, Fixed D 2 course £28-£36.90, Fixed D 4 course £38-£46.90, Service optional **Wines** 71 bottles over £20, 29 bottles under £20, 8 by glass **Notes** Sunday L, Vegetarian menu, Dress restrictions, No jeans or trainers **Seats** 40, Pr/dining room 20 **Children** Portions, Menu

Achray House Hotel

★★★ 77% HOTEL

◉ Modern British ✋

Modern Scottish cooking in an idyllic location

☎ 0845 557 0774
PH6 2NF
e-mail: info@achrayhouse.com
dir: End of M9 onto A9. At Greenloaning take B822. Through Braco, left onto B827 to Comrie. Left onto A85 to St Fillans

The story goes that Queen Victoria commented favourably on the location of Achray House as she passed on her way to Balmoral, and it's easy to see what caught her eye: the family-run hotel has wonderful views of Loch Earn and the mountains beyond. If you are lucky you might spy an osprey doing a spot of fishing in the water. The well equipped bedrooms come in various sizes and include a suite with a lounge area; most rooms have loch views. The conservatory dining room also gets the great vista and is the setting for some ambitious modern Scottish cooking. Filo pastry parcels of haggis with an Irn Bru chilli jam might precede roasted monkfish with an orange and coriander beurre blanc, roasted beetroot and saffron potatoes.

Rooms 8 (3 GF) **S** £60-£80; **D** £80-£150 (incl. bkfst)
Facilities Xmas New Year Wi-fi **Conf** Class 20 Board 20 Thtr 20 **Parking** 30 **Notes** LB Closed Jan-2 Feb Civ Wed 50

Chef Cristopher Mamelin **Owner** Alan & Jane Gibson
Times 12-2.30/6-8.30 Closed 3-31 Jan, L Mon-Wed in low season **Prices** Fixed D 3 course £27, Service optional **Wines** 18 bottles over £20, 14 bottles under £20, 9 by glass **Notes** Game tasting menu in season & whisky tasting menu 5 course, Sunday L, Vegetarian available **Seats** 44, Pr/dining room 12 **Children** Portions, Menu

RENFREWSHIRE

GLASGOW AIRPORT
Map 2 NS46

Holiday Inn Glasgow Airport

★★★ 79% HOTEL

☎ 0871 942 9031 & 0141 887 1266 📠 0141 887 3738
Abbotsinch PA3 2TR
e-mail: operations-glasgow@ihg.com
web: www.holidayinn.co.uk
dir: From E: M8 junct 28, follow hotel signs. From W: M8 junct 29, airport slip road to hotel

Located within the airport grounds and within walking distance of the terminal. Bedrooms are well appointed and cater for the needs of the modern traveller. The open-plan public areas are relaxing as is the restaurant which offers a carvary and a carte menu. Wi-fi is available in the public areas with LAN in all bedrooms.

Rooms 300 (6 fmly) (54 smoking) **D** £51-£149*
Facilities STV FTV Wi-fi **Conf** Class 150 Board 75 Thtr 300 Del from £89 to £199* **Services** Lift Air con **Parking** 56 **Notes** LB Civ Wed 250

Holiday Inn Express Glasgow Airport

BUDGET HOTEL

☎ 0141 842 1100 📠 0141 842 1122
St Andrews Dr PA3 2TJ
e-mail: info@expressglasgowairport.co.uk
web: www.expressglasgowairport.co.uk
dir: M8 junct 28, at 1st rdbt turn right, hotel on right

A modern hotel ideal for families and business travellers. Fresh and uncomplicated, the spacious rooms include Sky TV, power shower and tea and coffee-making facilities. Continental buffet breakfast is included in the room rate; other meals may be taken at the nearby family pub or restaurant.

Rooms 143 (65 fmly) (11 GF) **S** £39-£89; **D** £39-£89 (incl. bkfst)* **Conf** Class 20 Board 30 Thtr 70

Premier Inn Glasgow Airport

BUDGET HOTEL

☎ 0871 527 8434 📠 0871 527 8435
Whitecart Rd, Glasgow Airport PA3 2TH
web: www.premierinn.com
dir: M8 junct 28, follow airport signs for Long Stay & Car Park 3 (Premier Inn signed). At 1st rdbt right into St Andrews Drive. At next rdbt right into Whitecart Rd. Under motorway. Left at garage. Hotel on right

High quality, budget accommodation ideal for both families and business travellers. Spacious, en suite bedrooms feature tea and coffee-making facilities, and Freeview TV in most hotels. Internet access and Wi-fi are available for a small fee. The adjacent family restaurant features a wide and varied menu.

Rooms 104 **D** £54-£58*

Premier Inn Glasgow (Paisley)

BUDGET HOTEL

☎ 0871 527 8432 📠 0871 527 8433
Phoenix Retail Park PA1 2BH
web: www.premierinn.com
dir: M8 junct 28a, A737 signed Irvine, take 1st exit signed Linwood, left at 1st rdbt to Phoenix Park

Rooms 40 **D** £54-£58*

HOWWOOD　　　Map 2 NS36

Bowfield Hotel & Country Club

★★★ 80% HOTEL

◉ Traditional British

Converted mill offering modern bistro cooking

☎ 01505 705225 📠 01505 705230
PA9 1DZ
e-mail: enquiries@bowfieldhotel.co.uk
web: www.bowfieldhotel.co.uk
dir: M8 junct 28a/29, A737 for 6m, left onto B787, right in 2m, 1m to hotel

The Bowfield Hotel and Country Club is a former textile mill and sits in a quiet spot, surrounded by landscaped grounds, yet it's not that far from Glasgow airport. Bedrooms are housed in a separate wing and offer good modern comforts and facilities. The restaurant is all quiet intimacy beneath its low wooden ceiling, with Scottish landscape prints on walls of whitewashed brick. The kitchen serves up food in the modern bistro idiom, bolstered by internationally inspired tapas-style dishes, burgers and steaks. Simple mains might see home-made steak and ale pie sitting alongside a hotpot of shoulder and best end of lamb with minted peas, shallots and pancetta, and to finish there could be a retro knickerbocker glory or Scottish cheese with home-made chutney and biscuits.

Rooms 23 (3 fmly) (7 GF) **Facilities Spa** FTV ⟲ supervised ♨ 18 Gym Squash Children's soft play area Aerobics studio Health & beauty Xmas New Year Wi-fi **Conf** Class 60 Board 40 Thtr 100 **Parking** 120 **Notes** ⊗ Civ Wed 80

Chef Ronnie McAdam **Owner** Bowfield Hotel & Country Club Ltd **Times** 6.30-9 **Prices** Food prices not confirmed for 2012. Please telephone for details **Wines** 8 bottles over £20, 21 bottles under £20, 7 by glass **Notes** Sunday L, Vegetarian available, Dress restrictions, Smart casual **Seats** 40, Pr/dining room 20 **Children** Portions, Menu

HOUSTON　　　Map 2 NS46

Fox & Hounds ⬤

South St PA6 7EN ☎ 01505 612448 & 612991
📠 01505 614133
e-mail: jonathon.wengel@btconnect.com
web: www.foxandhoundshouston.co.uk
dir: A737, W from Glasgow. Take Johnstone Bridge off Weir exit, follow signs for Houston. Pub in village centre

At the heart of the attractive village of Houston, this welcoming old coaching inn pulls in the plaudits for the beers which flow from the micro-brewery here; beer festivals in May and August add spice. One fan is singer Neil Diamond, who treated his chords to glasses of Peter's Well

continued

HOUSTON CONTINUED

bitter whilst staying locally in 2011, and indulged in fare from the homely menu, which mixes pub favourites with some inspired dishes; haggis with bashed neeps, champ and whisky cream or baked aubergine pie amongst them. A list of around 150 whiskies, including some rare ones, is the icing on the cake here.

Open all day all wk 11am-mdnt (Fri-Sat 11am-1am Sun from 12.30) **Bar Meals** Av main course £9 food served all day **Restaurant** Fixed menu price fr £20 Av 3 course à la carte fr £22 food served all day ⊕ FREE HOUSE ◀ Killelan, Warlock Stout, Texas, Jock Frost, Peter's Well. ♟ 10 **Facilities** Children welcome Children's menu Children's portions Dogs allowed Garden Beer festival Parking

LANGBANK   Map 2 NS37

Best Western Gleddoch House

★★★★ 73% HOTEL

☎ 01475 540711 🗐 01475 540201
PA14 6YE
e-mail: reservations.gleddochhouse@ohiml.com
web: www.oxfordhotelsandinns.com
dir: M8 to Greenock, onto A8, left at rdbt onto A789, follow for 0.5m, turn right, 2nd on left

This hotel is set in spacious, landscaped grounds high above the River Clyde with fine views. The period house is appointed to a very high standard. The modern extension is impressive and offers spacious and very comfortable bedrooms. Warm hospitality and attentive service are noteworthy along with the hotel's parkland golf course and leisure club.

Rooms 70 (22 fmly) (17 GF) **Facilities** Spa FTV 🐾 ⚷ 18 Putt green Gym Steam room Sauna Xmas New Year Wi-fi **Conf** Class 70 Board 40 Thtr 150 **Parking** 150 **Notes** Civ Wed 120

RENFREW

For hotels see Glasgow Airport

EAST RENFREWSHIRE

UPLAWMOOR   Map 2 NS45

Uplawmoor Hotel

★★★ 81% HOTEL

◉ Modern Scottish 🐾

Modern Scottish cooking in a converted barn restaurant

☎ 01505 850565 🗐 01505 850689
Neilston Rd G78 4AF
e-mail: info@uplawmoor.co.uk
web: www.uplawmoor.co.uk
dir: M77 junct 2, A736 signed Barrhead & Irvine. Hotel 4m beyond Barrhead

Uplawmoor dates from the 1750s, when it was a coaching inn for travellers from Glasgow to the coast. The modern bedrooms are comfortable and well equipped, while the beamed restaurant, in a converted barn, is where to head to for some modern Scottish cooking. Haggis, neeps and tatties are de rigueur, here served as a starter alongside Cullen skink or seared scallops with Stornoway black pudding and bacon. Game appears in season, say pheasant roasted with lemon and rosemary, local farms are the source of meat - perhaps saddle of lamb stuffed with sage and redcurrants in a red wine jus - and among fish main courses might be seared fillet of salmon given an Eastern treatment with the flavours of ginger, chilli and lime. Puddings tend to stay within the confines of sherry trifle or cheesecake.

Rooms 14 (1 fmly) (2 smoking) **S** £60-£70; **D** £85-£95 (incl. bkfst)* **Facilities** STV Wi-fi **Conf** Class 12 Board 20 Thtr 40 Del from £85 to £105* **Parking** 40 **Notes** LB ⊗ Closed 26 Dec & 1 Jan

Chef Paul Brady **Owner** Stuart & Emma Peacock **Times** 12-3/6-9.30 Closed 26 Dec, 1 Jan, L Mon-Sat **Prices** Fixed L 2 course £15.50, Fixed D 3 course £19.50-£25, Starter £4.25-£8.95, Main £9.95-£23.95, Dessert £4.75-£5.95, Service optional **Wines** 5 bottles over £20, 15 bottles under £20, 8 by glass **Notes** Early evening menu available 5.30-7pm Sun-Fri, Sunday L, Vegetarian available, Dress restrictions, Smart casual **Seats** 30 **Children** Portions, Menu

SCOTTISH BORDERS

ALLANTON — Map 3 NT85

Allanton Inn ⚐

TD11 3JZ ☎ **01890 818260**
e-mail: info@allantoninn.co.uk
dir: From A1 at Berwick take A6105 for Chirnside (5m). At Chirnside Inn take Coldstream Rd for 1m to Allanton

A perfect base to explore the Borders, this family-run 18th-century coaching inn has built up a formidable reputation for its local ales and excellent food. A large lawned area with fruit trees overlooking open countryside is an ideal spot to sup on a pint of Bitter & Twisted or tuck into locally-sourced dishes such as house cured and smoked pork fillet, or Peelham Farm rack of lamb with rosemary and garlic butter. Barbecues are held in the summer.

Open all day all wk 11am-11pm Closed: 2 wks Feb (dates vary) **Bar Meals** L served Mon-Sun 12-3 D served Mon-Sun 6-9 booking required Av main course £10 **Restaurant** L served Mon-Sun 12-3 D served Mon-Sun 6-9 booking required Av 3 course à la carte fr £23 ⊕ FREE HOUSE ◀ Ossian, Trade Winds, Pentland IPA, Game Bird, Bitter & Twisted, Piper's Gold. ⚐ 10 **Facilities** Children welcome Children's menu Children's portions Dogs allowed Garden Wi-fi

BROUGHTON — Map 3 NT13

The Glenholm Centre

★★★ ⌂ GUEST ACCOMMODATION

ML12 6JF
☎ **01899 830408**
e-mail: info@glenholm.co.uk
dir: 1m S of Broughton. Off A701 to Glenholm

Surrounded by peaceful farmland, this former schoolhouse has a distinct African theme. The home-cooked meals and baking have received much praise and are served in the spacious lounge-dining room. The bright airy bedrooms are thoughtfully equipped, and the service is friendly and attentive. Computer courses are available.

Rooms 3 en suite 1 annexe en suite (1 fmly) (2 GF) S £39-£42; D £64 **Facilities** TVL tea/coffee Dinner available Cen ht Licensed Wi-fi ⌂ **Conf** Max 24 Thtr 24 Class 24 Board 24 **Parking** 14 **Notes** LB Closed 20 Dec-1 Feb

EDDLESTON — Map 3 NT24

The Horseshoe Inn

★★★★ RESTAURANT WITH ROOMS

Rosettes not confirmed at time of going to press

French ◀ NOTABLE WINE LIST

Refined French cuisine in the Scottish Borders

EH45 8QP
☎ **01721 730225** 📠 **01721 730268**
e-mail: reservations@horseshoeinn.co.uk
web: www.horseshoeinn.co.uk
dir: A703, 5m N of Peebles

Set amid the glorious landscape of the Scottish Borders near Peebles, the only remaining aspect of the erstwhile run-down village boozer is its name. The owners pulled the place up by its bootstraps with a top-to-toe refurbishment back in 2005, since when the classy restaurant with rooms has established itself as a foodie destination to be reckoned with. The focus of its culinary efforts is the restaurant, a plushly-classical pillared dining room with flourishes of flamboyance in its lush fabrics, coffee, claret and gold colour scheme, and ornate gilt-framed mirrors that wouldn't look out of place in Louis XIV's boudoir. As we went to press a new chef arrived here. The menu will remain as it is for now, developing further as he settles in, making the most of a larder bursting with superb Scottish ingredients. Flavours come together in dishes that thrill with a vibrant creativity, although simple menu descriptions give little away. Proceedings might begin delicately with carpaccio of smoked scallops teamed with spiced mango and 'exotic' sauce, or crab and avocado with crustacean jelly, Jerusalem artichoke and lobster bonbon, then crank up the flavours into the more full-throttle territory of lamb loin and sweetbreads with gingerbread, beetroot, Comté cheese, gnocchi and vanilla jus. Fabulous artisan cheeses served with honeycomb, quince purée and oatcakes are the alternative to sweet-toothed endings such as mandarin soufflé with champagne sorbet.

Rooms 8 en suite (1 fmly) (6 GF) **Facilities** FTV tea/coffee Dinner available Direct Dial Cen ht Wi-fi Fishing **Parking** 20 **Notes** LB Closed 25 Dec & Mon & 2wks Jan RS Sun eve Rest closed, bistro open

continued

EDDLESTON CONTINUED

Chef Riad Peerbux, Andrei Carafa **Owner** Border Steelwork Structures Ltd **Times** 12-2.30/7-9 **Prices** Fixed L 3 course £19.50, Starter £11-£13.50, Main £16.50-£24, Dessert £8-£17.50, Service optional, Groups min 8 service 10% **Wines** 100 bottles over £20, 12 bottles under £20, 12 by glass **Notes** Tasting menu available, Sunday L, Vegetarian available, Dress restrictions, Smart casual **Seats** 40 **Children** Menu

ETTRICK	Map 3 NT21

Tushielaw Inn

TD7 5HT ☎ 01750 62205 📄 01750 62205
e-mail: robin@tushielaw-inn.co.uk
dir: At junct of B709 & B711(W of Hawick)

An 18th-century former toll house and drovers' halt on the banks of Ettrick Water, making a good base for touring the Borders, trout fishing (salmon fishing can be arranged), wildlife and bird watching, and those tackling the Southern Upland Way. An extensive menu is always available with daily-changing specials. Fresh produce is used according to season, with local lamb and Aberdeen Angus beef regular specialities. Local haggis smothered in melted Lockerbie Cheddar and steak and ale pie are popular choices.

Open all wk 🍺 FREE HOUSE **Facilities** Children welcome Dogs allowed Parking

GALASHIELS	Map 3 NT43

Kingsknowes

★★★ 77% HOTEL

☎ 01896 758375 📄 01896 750377
Selkirk Rd TD1 3HY
e-mail: enq@kingsknowes.co.uk
web: www.kingsknowes.co.uk
dir: Off A7 at Galashiels/Selkirk rdbt

In over three acres of grounds on the banks of the Tweed, a splendid baronial mansion built in 1869 for a textile magnate. There are lovely views of the Eildon Hills and Abbotsford House, Sir Walter Scott's ancestral home. It boasts elegant public areas and spacious bedrooms, some with excellent views. Meals are served in two restaurants and the Courtyard Bar, where fresh local or regional produce is used as much as possible. The impressive glass conservatory is the ideal place to enjoy a drink.

Rooms 12 (2 fmly) **Facilities** Wi-fi **Conf** Class 40 Board 30 Thtr 60 **Parking** 65 **Notes** Civ Wed 75

Open all day all wk Mon-Wed noon-11 (Thu-Sat noon-1pm Sun noon-11) 🍺 FREE HOUSE 🍺 McEwans 70/-, John Smith's. **Facilities** Children welcome Children's menu Play area Dogs allowed Garden

Over Langshaw (NT524400)

★★★ FARMHOUSE

Langshaw TD1 2PE
☎ 01896 860244 📄 01896 860668 Mrs S Bergius
e-mail: overlangshaw@btconnect.com
dir: 3m N of Galashiels. A7 N from Galashiels, 1m right signed Langshaw, right at T-junct into Langshaw, left signed Earlston, Over Langshaw 1m, signed

There are fine panoramic views from this organic hillside farm which offers two comfortable and spacious bedrooms. Hearty breakfasts are provided at individual tables in the lounge and a friendly welcome is guaranteed.

Rooms 2 en suite (1 fmly) (1 GF) D £65-£75* **Facilities** TVL tea/coffee Cen ht Wi-fi **Parking** 4 **Notes** 🐾 500 acres dairy/sheep/organic

HAWICK	Map 3 NT51

Mansfield House Hotel

★★★ 81% HOTEL

☎ 01450 360400 📄 01450 372007
Weensland Rd TD9 8LB
e-mail: reception@themansfieldhousehotel.co.uk
dir: A7 to Hawick onto A698 (Weensland Rd). Hotel 1.2km on right

Set in its own mature grounds at the top of a hill with spectacular views over Hawick, this hotel has undergone a complete refurbishment. The bedrooms, located on the basement level and the first floor, differ in size and include the fantastic Tower Room accessed via a steep, narrow staircase - but the climb is well worth the effort! Public areas are welcoming and the style is in keeping with the age of the building. The restaurant proudly uses local, quality ingredients for the menus.

Rooms 16 (2 fmly) **S** £70-£75; **D** £100-£110 (incl. bkfst)* **Facilities** FTV Xmas New Year Wi-fi **Conf** Class 160 Board 60 Thtr 160 Del from £95 to £105* **Parking** 25 **Notes** LB ⊗ Civ Wed 120

INNERLEITHEN	Map 3 NT33

Traquair Arms Hotel

Traquair Rd EH44 6PD ☎ 01896 830229
e-mail: info@traquairarmshotel.co.uk
dir: From A72 (Peebles to Galashiels road) take B709 for St Mary's Loch & Traquair

Amidst the heather-covered hills of the Scottish Borders stands this imposing pub, hotel and tranquil beer garden. It's one of only two places where you can drink Traquair Bear ale, brewed a stone's throw away at Traquair House. Scottish and Italian food includes roast haunch of Tweed Valley venison; local Borders lamb; tiger prawns with spaghetti, white wine and flat leaf parsley; and Italian sausage with borlotti beans, cherry tomatoes, toasted focaccia and salad. There are downhill and cross country mountain bike trails right on the doorstep.

Open all day all wk Closed: 25 Dec **Bar Meals** L served Mon-Fri 12-2.30, Sat-Sun all day D served Mon-Fri 5-9, Sat-Sun all day Av main course £9-£12 **Restaurant** L served Mon-Fri 12-2.30, Sat-Sun all day booking required D served Mon-Fri 5-9, Sat-Sun all day booking required ⊕ FREE HOUSE ◄ Deuchars IPA, Timothy Taylor Landlord, Traquair Bear Ale. **Facilities** Children welcome Children's menu Children's portions Dogs allowed Garden Parking Wi-fi

---

JEDBURGH — Map 3 NT62

Ferniehirst Mill Lodge

★★ GUEST HOUSE

TD8 6PQ
☎ 01835 863279
e-mail: ferniehirstmill@aol.com
web: www.ferniehirstmill.co.uk
dir: 2.5m S of Jedburgh on A68, onto private track to end

Reached by a narrow farm track and a rustic wooden bridge, this chalet-style house has a secluded setting by the River Jed. Bedrooms are small and functional and there is a comfortable lounge in which to relax. Home-cooked dinners are available by arrangement, and hearty breakfasts are served in the cosy dining room.

Rooms 7 en suite (1 GF) S £30; D £60 **Facilities** TVL tea/coffee Dinner available Cen ht Fishing Riding **Parking** 10

KELSO — Map 3 NT73

The Roxburghe Hotel & Golf Course

★★★★ 77% COUNTRY HOUSE HOTEL

◉ Modern, French ◐

A stately setting for modern Scottish cooking

☎ 01573 450331 📠 01573 450611
Heiton TD5 8JZ
e-mail: hotel@roxburghe.net
web: www.roxburghe.net
dir: From A68 Jedburgh take A698 to Heiton, 3m SW of Kelso

Built as a country home for the Dukes of Roxburghe, the hotel is a solid-looking turreted mansion in 500 acres of parkland. Within are all the trappings of a stately home - high ceilings, open fires and antiques - and there's a genuine country-house atmosphere.The elegant bedrooms are individually designed, some by the Duchess herself, and include superior rooms, some with four posters and log fires. Drinks in the library could precede dinner in the claret and green dining room, where formal service is the thing. The kitchen makes the most of Scotland's natural larder, roasting seasonal grouse and serving it with mushroom ravioli and cabbage mixed with bacon. Another possibility might be herb-crusted cod with shrimp risotto perked up by coconut foam, and before that could be West Coast mussels steamed with fennel and ginger, or honey-glazed duck breast with chorizo and loganberry sauce. Fruit is put to good seasonal use in puddings too: perhaps peach parfait with blood orange curd and nectarine sorbet.

Rooms 22 (6 annexe) (3 fmly) (3 GF) **Facilities** Spa STV ♨ 18 Putt green Fishing ◄ Clay shooting Health & beauty salon Mountain bike hire Falconry Archery Xmas New Year Wi-fi **Conf** Class 20 Board 20 Thtr 50 **Parking** 150 **Notes** Civ Wed 60

Chef Ross Miller **Owner** Duke of Roxburghe **Times** 12-2/7-9.45 **Prices** Fixed L 3 course £19.95, Starter £11.95-£17.50, Main £19.95-£27.50, Dessert £9.95-£14.50, Service optional **Wines** 80 bottles over £20, 8 bottles under £20, 10 by glass **Notes** Sunday L, Vegetarian available, Dress restrictions, No jeans, trainers or T-shirts **Seats** 40, Pr/dining room 18 **Children** Portions, Menu

Ednam House

★★★ 80% HOTEL

☎ 01573 224168 📠 01573 226319
Bridge St TD5 7HT
e-mail: contact@ednamhouse.com
web: www.ednamhouse.com
dir: From S: A1 to Berwick, A698 or A7 to Hawick, A698 to Kelso. From N: A68 to Carfraefmill, A6089 to Kelso

Overlooking a wide expanse of the River Tweed, this fine Georgian mansion has been under the Brooks family ownership for over 75 years. Accommodation styles range from standard to grand, plus The Orangerie, situated in the grounds, that has been converted into a gracious two-bedroom apartment. Public areas include a choice of lounges and an elegant dining room that has views over the gardens.

Rooms 32 (2 annexe) (4 fmly) (3 GF) **Facilities** FTV ◄ Free access to Abbey Fitness Centre Wi-fi **Conf** Board 200 Thtr 250 **Parking** 60 **Notes** Closed 22 Dec-6 Jan Civ Wed 100

Cobbles Inn

 British, Pacific Rim

Eclectic cuisine in cordial pubby setting

☎ 01573 223548
7 Bowmont St TD5 7JH
e-mail: info@thecobblesinn.co.uk
dir: A6089 from Edinburgh, turn right at rdbt into Bowmont Rd. Restaurant in 0.3m

The Cobbles is a whitewashed 19th-century coach house just off Kelso's pretty cobbled square. It is a proper pub with a crackling log fire to welcome visitors into its cosy beamed bar, where a buzzy, convivial vibe holds sway, and there's always plenty to keep you entertained - well-kept real ales, (including thier own ales from the local Tempest Brewing Co) quizzes, live folk music, and food that strikes a contemporary note. The kitchen has no allegiance to any particular culinary style, taking its inspiration from an eclectic mix of global styles that sees smoked salmon and prawn fishcakes served with a soft poached egg and spiced avocado purée, ahead of pan-roasted breast and rolled confit leg of Gressingham duck with ginger shallots, dauphinoise potatoes and plum sauce. To finish, vanilla crème brûlée is partnered with delicious filo pastry parcels of date and pistachio.

Chef Gavin Meiklejohn **Owner** Annika & Gavin Meiklejohn **Times** 12 Closed Mon **Prices** Fixed D 3 course £24.95-£29.95, Starter £4-£5.95, Main £9.95-£20.95, Dessert £4.95-£6.95, Service optional, Groups min 10 service 10% **Wines** 7 by glass **Notes** Sunday L **Seats** 35, Pr/dining room 40 **Children** Portions, Menu **Parking** Behind restaurant

Open 11.30-3 5-late (Sat-Sun & summer all day) Closed: 2wks Jan, Mon in autumn/winter **Bar Meals** L served Tue-Sun 12-2 D served Tue-Sun 5-9 Av main course £10.95 **Restaurant** L served Tue-Sun 12-2 Av 3 course à la carte fr £24.95 ⊕ FREE HOUSE ◀ Tempest Brewing Co ♻ Thistly Cross. **Facilities** Children welcome Children's menu

KIRK YETHOLM   Map 3 NT82

The Border Hotel ♇

The Green TD5 8PQ ☎ **01573 420237**
e-mail: borderhotel@aol.com
dir: From A698 in Kelso take B6352 for 7m to Kirk Yetholm

Just a mile from the border between Scotland and England, this 18th-century former coaching inn stands at the end of the famous Pennine Way long-distance walking trail. Naturally, this updated inn is the first port of call for weary walkers, who can expect a warm and friendly welcome in the character bar. Cracking pints of Pennine Way Bitter or Orkney Raven Ale will slake parched throats and the traditional British menu, which features local game and

farm meats, will satisfy healthy appetites. Follow Cullen skink with marinated Border lamb, peppered saddle of local venison, or Eyemouth haddock and chips, leaving room for a hearty pudding.

Open all day all wk Closed: 25 Dec **Bar Meals** L served all wk 12-2 booking required D served all wk 6-8.45 booking required Av main course £9.95 **Restaurant** L served all wk 12-2 booking required D served all wk 6-8.45 booking required ⊕ FREE HOUSE ◀ Pennine Way Bitter, Game Bird-Border Brewery, Raven Ale Orkney Brewery ♻ Westons Old Rosie. ♇ 10 **Facilities** Children welcome Children's menu Children's portions Play area Dogs allowed Garden Parking Wi-fi

LAUDER   Map 3 NT54

Lauderdale

★★★ 70% HOTEL

☎ 01578 722231 ▤ 01578 718642
1 Edinburgh Rd TD2 6TW
e-mail: enquiries@lauderdalehotel.co.uk
web: www.lauderdalehotel.co.uk
dir: On A68 from S, through Lauder centre, hotel on right. From Edinburgh, hotel on left at 1st bend after passing Lauder sign

Lying on the north side of the village with spacious gardens to the side and rear, this friendly hotel is ideally placed for those who don't want to stay in Edinburgh itself. The refurbished bedrooms and bathrooms are well equipped and well appointed. A good range of meals is served in both the bar and the restaurant.

Rooms 10 (1 fmly) **S** £55-£60; **D** £85-£90 (incl. bkfst)* **Facilities** STV FTV ♫ Xmas New Year Wi-fi **Conf** Class 200 Board 100 Thtr 200 Del from £150 to £160 **Parking** 200 **Notes** Civ Wed 180

The Black Bull

★★★★ INN

Market Place TD2 6SR
☎ 01578 722208 ▤ 01578 722419
e-mail: enquiries@blackbull-lauder.com
dir: On A68 in village centre

In the heart of the Scottish Borders, on the edge of the Lammermuir Hills, this whitewashed, three-storey coaching inn dates from 1750. The lovely bedrooms are furnished in period character and thoughtfully equipped with modern amenities. After a day of walking in the hills, visiting Thirlestane Castle, playing golf or checking out the Princes Street bargains in nearby Edinburgh, enjoy a gastro-pub-style lunch in the relaxed Harness Room bar or the more formal lounge bar. A light lunch menu of snacks and sandwiches is served from midday, while a typical supper menu might lead you to begin with Cullen skink or terrine of pheasant, hare and mallard. Follow with Border beef, Guinness and mushroom pie or something from the grill might appeal. To finish, there is brioche bread and butter pudding; or a selection of Scottish cheeses - Cooleeney, Gubbeens and Dunsyre Blue - with oatcakes.

Rooms 8 en suite (2 fmly) **Facilities** FTV tea/coffee Dinner available Direct Dial Cen ht Wi-fi **Parking** 8

Open all day all wk **Bar Meals** L served Mon-Fri 12-2.30, Sat-Sun 12-9 booking required D served Mon-Thu 5-9, Fri-Sun 12-9 **Restaurant** L served Mon-Fri 12-2.30, Sat-Sun 12-9 D served Mon-Thu 5-9, Fri-Sun 12-9 ⊕ BLACKBULL HOTEL (LAUDER) LTD ◀ Guinness, Landlord, Tetley, Deuchars IPA, Old Speckled Hen, Marstons Pedigree Ŏ Olde English. ☙ 27 **Facilities** Children welcome Children's menu Children's portions Dogs allowed

16 Market Place

★★★ Ⓐ BED AND BREAKFAST

16 Market Place TD2 6SR
☎ 01578 718776 & 07725 472543
e-mail: wendymcv@talktalk.net
dir: In centre of Lauder, opp Black Bull

Rooms 2 en suite S £25-£30; D £60-£70* **Facilities** FTV tea/coffee Cen ht Wi-fi Golf 9 **Parking** 1 **Notes** Closed Xmas ⊗

The Plough Hotel

Main St TD12 4JN ☎ 01890 840252 📄 01890 840252
e-mail: theplough@leitholm.wanadoo.co.uk
web: www.bordersteakhouse.com
dir: 5m N of Coldstream on A697. Take B6461, Leitholm in 1m

Set in a small village in rich farming country south of the Lammermuir Hills, this compact old coaching inn specialises in Aberdeen Angus steaks. The beef is sourced by the local butcher from the foremost livestock market in the Borders and well aged before preparation. The wide ranging menu also features chicken and haggis stack in Drambuie sauce; hand-pulled beers draw in the locals, whilst the beer garden is a tranquil retreat.

Open all day all wk Mon-Tue 4-12 Wed-Thu & Sun noon-mdnt Fri-Sat noon-1am **Bar Meals** L served Sun 12-4 D served Tue-Sun 6-9 **Restaurant** L served Sun 12-4 D served Tue-Sun 6-9 ⊕ FREE HOUSE ◀ Guinness, Real Ale. **Facilities** Children welcome Dogs allowed Garden Parking

Burt's

★★★ 78% HOTEL

◉◉ Modern Scottish

Friendly, family-run Borders hotel with modern Scottish menu

☎ 01896 822285 📄 01896 822870
Market Square TD6 9PL
e-mail: enquiries@burtshotel.co.uk
web: www.burtshotel.co.uk
dir: A6091, 2m from A68 3m S of Earlston

Owned and run by the Henderson family for over 40 years, this imposing 18th-century former temperance hotel stands on the picturesque market square, just 200 yards from the River Tweed. A hunting, shooting and fishing theme extends through the traditionally decorated restaurant and the bustling bar, where you'll find winter log fires, Scottish ales, over 80 malt whiskies, and a classic bar menu. In the restaurant, daily set menus evolve with the seasons, with modern Scottish dishes prepared from quality locally-sourced produce, including Borders game and salmon from the Tweed. Start proceedings with a plate of Teviot Smokery smoked salmon, then follow with saddle of lamb wrapped in herb mousse with dauphinoise and roast garlic jus, leaving room for an indulgent assiette of chocolate desserts - chocolate and mocha tart, orange chocolate mousse, white chocolate soufflé and chocolate ice cream. The smart bedrooms have been individually styled and include Wi-fi.

Rooms 20 S £72-£90; D £133-£140 (incl. bkfst)*
Facilities STV FTV Salmon fishing Shooting New Year Wi-fi
Conf Class 20 Board 20 Thtr 38 Del from £100 to £120*
Parking 40 **Notes** LB Closed 24-26 Dec & 2-3 Jan

Chef Trevor Williams **Owner** The Henderson family
Times 12-2/7-9 Closed 26 Dec, 3-8 Jan **Prices** Fixed L 2 course £22-£27.50, Fixed D 3 course £29.50-£36, Service optional **Wines** 40 bottles over £20, 18 bottles under £20, 8 by glass **Notes** Sunday L, Vegetarian available, Dress restrictions, Jacket & tie preferred **Seats** 50, Pr/dining room 25 **Children** Portions

MELROSE CONTINUED

Fauhope House

★★★★★ 🔒 GUEST HOUSE

Gattonside TD6 9LU
☎ 01896 823184 📄 01896 823184
e-mail: info@fauhopehouse.com
dir: 0.7m N of Melrose over River Tweed. N off B6360 at
Gattonside 30mph sign (E) up long driveway

It's hard to imagine a more complete experience than a stay
at Fauhope, set high on a hillside on the north-east edge of
the village. Hospitality is first class, breakfasts are
excellent, and the delightful country house has a splendid
interior. Bedrooms are luxurious, each individual and
superbly equipped. Public areas are elegantly decorated and
furnished, and enhanced by beautiful floral arrangements;
the dining room is particularly stunning.

Rooms 3 en suite **Facilities** tea/coffee Dinner available
Cen ht 🐎 Riding **Parking** 10 **Notes** LB ⊗

NEWCASTLETON   Map 3 NY48

Liddesdale

★★★★ INN

Douglas Sq TD9 0QD
☎ 01387 375255 📄 01387 752577
e-mail: reception@theliddesdalehotel.co.uk

Liddesdale is located in the peaceful 17th-century village of
Newcastleton overlooking the village square. There are well-
appointed bedrooms and bathrooms, and the public areas
offer various locations in which to dine. The welcoming
public bar is well used by locals and residents alike. Relaxed
and informal menus use the best local produce available.
The welcome addition of the beer garden this year shows
very good results.

Rooms 6 en suite (2 fmly) S £45; D £80* **Facilities** STV FTV
TVL tea/coffee Dinner available Direct Dial Cen ht Wi-fi 🐎
Golf 9 Fishing **Conf** Max 60 Thtr 40 Class 40 Board 40
Notes LB ⊗

PEEBLES   Map 3 NT24

Cringletie House

★★★★ COUNTRY HOUSE HOTEL

◉◉ ◉ Modern British **V**

Skilful cooking in a splendid dining room

☎ 01721 725750 📄 01721 725751
Edinburgh Rd EH45 8PL
e-mail: enquiries@cringletie.com
web: www.cringletie.com
dir: 2m N on A703

Cringletie is a perfect example of the work of 19th-century
architect David Bryce, who mastered the Scottish baronial
style. It's a magnificent building, turreted, in 28 acres of
grounds that include a kitchen garden that provides the
kitchen with vegetables, fruit and herbs. The first-floor
restaurant, under a spectacular painted ceiling, has an
appealing modern menu with a handful of choices at each
course. The kitchen draws on organic meat, wild seafood
and top-quality supplies and treats them with conviction,
turning out starters along the lines of honey-glazed duck
breast with crushed parsnip, plums, and rosemary jus, and
main courses like seared red deer with braised red cabbage,
beetroot and pancetta jus. Dishes can be elaborate with
distinct contrasting flavours: crisp pork belly and pig's ear
with roast langoustines, soubise and fennel, say, then fillet
of turbot with crab, shallot purée, and tomato and basil
dressing. Puddings, on the other hand, can be a theme on a
single element: pineapple mousse, carpaccio, sorbet, jelly
and Piña Colada. The individually designed bedrooms have
grace and charm, and for the ultimate luxury there's the
Selkirk Suite.

Rooms 13 (2 GF) **S** £130-£230; **D** £160-£260 (incl. bkfst)*
Facilities FTV Putt green 🐎 Petanque Giant chess &
draughts In-room therapy treatments Xmas New Year Wi-fi
Conf Class 20 Board 24 Thtr 45 Del from £169 to £209*
Services Lift **Parking** 30 **Notes** LB Civ Wed 60

Chef Craig Gibb **Owner** Jacob & Johanna van Houdt
Times 12.30-2.30/6.30-9 **Prices** Fixed L 2 course £10-£15,
Fixed D 3 course £30-£37.50, Tasting menu £65-£95,
Service optional **Wines** 68 bottles over £20, 9 by glass
Notes Tasting menu with wine £95, Sunday L, Vegetarian
menu, Dress restrictions, Smart casual, no jeans or trainers
Seats 55, Pr/dining room 12 **Children** Portions, Menu

Macdonald Cardrona Hotel & Golf Course

★★★★ 77% HOTEL

◉ British

Uncomplicated modern cooking with ravishing border-country views

☎ 01896 833600 📄 01896 831166
Cardrona EH45 8NE
e-mail: general.cardrona@macdonald-hotels.co.uk
web: www.macdonald-hotels.co.uk/cardrona
dir: On A72 between Peebles & Innerleithen, 3m S of Peebles

The rolling hills of the Scottish Borders are a stunning backdrop for this modern, purpose-built hotel. While golf is foremost on the minds of many guests, the location on the River Tweed means fishing is equally on the agenda, not to mention biking and hiking in the rolling Borders hills, or pampering in the classy spa. Spacious bedrooms are traditional in style, equipped with a range of extras, and most enjoy fantastic countryside views. The hotel features some impressive leisure facilities, including an 18-hole golf course, 18-metre indoor pool and state-of-the-art gym. When it comes to dining, the food arrives with a splendid backdrop through huge picture windows in the second-floor Renwicks restaurant. The kitchen keeps faith with quality local and seasonal produce, offering straightforward modern dishes based on well-thought-out combinations, ranging from smoked haddock pannacotta with lemon and caper dressing, to main courses involving grilled fillet of cod with spring onion and pancetta crust, braised leeks and herb mash, or slow-roasted belly of pork with Stornoway black pudding and apple purée. Finish with pineapple tarte Tatin and passionfruit parfait.

Rooms 99 (24 fmly) (16 GF) **S** £95-£175; **D** £105-£185 (incl. bkfst)* **Facilities** Spa STV 🐛 ⚓ 18 Putt green Fishing Gym Sauna Steam room Xmas New Year Wi-fi **Conf** Class 120 Board 90 Thtr 250 Del from £110 to £150* **Services** Lift **Parking** 200 **Notes** LB Civ Wed 200

Chef Ivor Clark **Owner** Macdonald Hotels
Times 12-2.30/6.30-9.45 **Prices** Fixed L 2 course £30, Service optional **Wines** 54 bottles over £20, 6 bottles under £20, 18 by glass **Notes** Sunday L, Vegetarian available, Dress restrictions, Smart casual **Seats** 70, Pr/dining room 200 **Children** Portions, Menu

Tontine

★★★ 82% HOTEL

☎ 01721 720892 📄 01721 729732
High St EH45 8AJ
e-mail: info@tontinehotel.com
web: www.tontinehotel.com
dir: In town centre

Conveniently situated in the main street, this long-established hotel offers comfortable public rooms including the elegant Adam Restaurant and an inviting lounge and 'clubby' bar. Bedrooms, contained in the original house and the river-facing wing, offer a smart, classical style of accommodation. The lasting impression is of the excellent level of hospitality and guest care.

Rooms 36 (3 fmly) (10 smoking) **S** fr £55; **D** £85-£110 (incl. bkfst) **Facilities** STV FTV Xmas New Year Wi-fi **Conf** Class 24 Board 24 Thtr 40 **Parking** 24 **Notes** LB

ST BOSWELLS Map 3 NT53

Dryburgh Abbey Hotel

★★★★ 73% COUNTRY HOUSE HOTEL

◉◉ Modern British 🌱

Exciting modern Scottish cooking and superb river views

☎ 01835 822261 📄 01835 823945
TD6 0RQ
e-mail: enquiries@dryburgh.co.uk
web: www.dryburgh.co.uk
dir: B6356 signed Scott's View & Earlston. Through Clintmains, 1.8m to hotel

Adjacent to Dryburgh Abbey, Sir Walter Scott's final resting place, this Victorian baronial mansion turned country-house hotel lies in acres of estate parkland, and offers comfortable public areas and an array of bedrooms and suites, each still displaying original features.The first-floor Tweed restaurant has superb views over the eponymous river. There are large bay windows, impressively high ceilings with decorative cornicing and ornate chandeliers in the traditional-decorated dining room, where you can expect modern Scottish food of verve and vigour, showing acute technical skills and creativity. Game and seafood from the local larder

continued

ST BOSWELLS CONTINUED

figure strongly as do vegetables and herbs from the kitchen's garden. Typical first courses on the daily-changing menu include confit of wild brill with beetroot pearls, vanilla dressing, shallot purée and baby herbs, and among mains might be whole roast local partridge with parsnip purée, winter greens, roast baby onions and thyme jus. Yuzu meringue pie with a coconut sorbet, watermelon and pistachio makes for an equally inventive finale.

Rooms 38 (31 fmly) (8 GF) **Facilities** FTV 🚭 Putt green Fishing 🏊 Sauna Xmas New Year Wi-fi **Conf** Class 80 Board 60 Thtr 150 **Services** Lift **Parking** 70 **Notes** Civ Wed 120

Chef Peter Snelgar **Owner** Dryburgh Abbey Hotel Limited **Times** 12-2/7-9 Closed L Mon-Sat **Prices** Fixed L 2 course £31.90-£40, Fixed D 3 course £105, Service included **Wines** 52 bottles over £20, 28 bottles under £20, 11 by glass **Notes** Sunday L, Vegetarian available, Dress restrictions, No jeans or sportswear **Seats** 78, Pr/dining room 40 **Children** Portions, Menu

Buccleuch Arms Hotel ♥

The Green TD6 0EW ☎ 01835 822243 📠 **01835 823965** **e-mail:** info@buccleucharms.com **dir:** On A68, 10m N of Jedburgh. Hotel on village green

Dating from the 16th century, this smart and friendly country-house hotel was originally an inn for the fox-hunting aristocracy. Set beside the village cricket pitch, it's an attractive brick and stone building with an immaculate garden. Inside, a large and comfortable lounge is warmed by a log fire in winter, while the spacious enclosed garden comes into its own during the warmer months. The bar serves one real ale at a time, but turnover is high so locals keep coming back to find out what's on offer - the Stewart Brewery, Broughton Ales, and the Hadrian and Border Brewery are just three of the regular suppliers. Menus change seasonally, but the specials may well change twice daily to reflect the availability of ingredients from the Scottish Borders countryside. Typical dishes include pressed ham hock with caramelised onions and parsley; fillet of Eyemouth haddock in crispy beer batter with chips, garden peas and home-made tartare sauce; and slow-cooked lamb casserole with pearl barley and red cabbage. 2011 was the 175th year anniversary of the hotel.

Open all day all wk 7am-11pm Closed: 25 Dec **Bar Meals** L served all wk 12-2 D served all wk 6-9 Av main course £10 **Restaurant** D served all wk 6-9 booking required ⊕ FREE HOUSE ◀ McEwan's 70/-, Stewarts Ales, Atlas, Orkney, Northumberland, Broughton, Guest ales. ♥ 8 **Facilities** Children welcome Children's menu Children's portions Play area Dogs allowed Garden Parking

Best Western Philipburn Country House

★★★★ 🅰 COUNTRY HOUSE HOTEL

☎ 01750 20747 📠 01750 21690 **Linglie Rd TD7 5LS** **e-mail:** info@philipburnhousehotel.co.uk **dir:** From A7 follow signs for A72/A707 Peebles/Moffat. Hotel 1m from town centre

Rooms 12 (2 fmly) **S** £90-£140; **D** £100-£185 (incl. bkfst)* **Facilities** FTV 🏊 Xmas New Year Wi-fi **Conf** Class 12 Board 24 Thtr 40 **Parking** 52 **Notes** LB ⊗ Closed 6-15 Jan Civ Wed 85

The Wheatsheaf at Swinton ♥

Main St TD11 3JJ ☎ 01890 860257 📠 **01890 860688** **e-mail:** reception@wheatsheaf-swinton.co.uk **dir:** From Edinburgh A697 onto B6461. From East Lothian A1 onto B6461

In the past few years, the Wheatsheaf has built up an impressive reputation as a dining destination. Run by husband and wife team Chris and Jan Winson, this popular venue is tucked away in the picturesque village of Swinton. The Wheatsheaf's secret is to use carefully sourced local ingredients in imaginative combinations. In addition to wild mushrooms and organic vegetables, wild salmon, venison, partridge, pheasant, woodcock and duck are all likely menu contenders subject to seasonal availability. Lunchtime offers the likes of sautéed Paris brown mushrooms and bacon in a tarragon crêpe with a Mull Cheddar glaze; and open omelette of Dunsyre Blue cheese and confit cherry tomatoes. In the evening settle back, enjoy the friendly service, and tuck into plates of seared scallops with a lemon and chive butter sauce; and braised shank of Border lamb, gratin dauphinoise and creamed Savoy.

Open Mon-Fri 5-11 Sat noon-mdnt Sun noon-11 Closed: 24-26 Dec, Mon-Fri L **Bar Meals** L served Sat-Sun 12-2 D served Mon-Sat 6-9, Sun 6-8.30 **Restaurant** L served Sat-Sun 12-2 booking required D served Mon-Sat 6-9, Sun 6-8.30 booking required ⊕ FREE HOUSE ◀ Deuchars IPA, Belhaven Best, Guinness. ♥ 12 **Facilities** Children welcome Parking

Tibbie Shiels Inn

St Mary's Loch TD7 5LH ☎ 01750 42231 📠 **01750 42302** **dir:** From Moffat take A708. Inn 14m on right

This friendly waterside hostelry positioned between St Mary's Loch and the Loch of the Lowes, is named after the woman who first opened it in 1826. Isabella 'Tibbie' Shiels expanded the inn from a small cottage to a hostelry which could sleep around 35 people - many of them on the floor! Famous visitors during her time included Walter Scott, Thomas Carlyle and Robert Louis Stevenson. Tibbie Shiels herself is rumoured to keep watch over the bar, where the selection of over 50 malt whiskies helps sustain long periods of ghost watching. Food from the traditional pub menu can be enjoyed in either the bar or the dining room. The majority of the ingredients are local, including the famous hill-farmed lamb, game and even herbs grown in the garden. Sandwiches, salads, ploughman's, toasties, paninis, burgers and jackets are all on offer, while the straightforward carte may tempt with chicken liver pâté followed by steak and ale pie, five-bean chilli or Scottish wholetail scampi served with home-made tartare sauce. There are plenty of evening events throughout the year.

Open all day all wk 10am-mdnt **Bar Meals** food served all day **Restaurant** food served all day ⊕ FREE HOUSE ◀ Broughton Greenmantle Ale, Belhaven 80/- ♻ Stowford Press. **Facilities** Children welcome Children's menu Children's portions Play area Dogs allowed Garden Parking Wi-fi

STIRLING

ABERFOYLE   Map 2 NN50

Macdonald Forest Hills Hotel & Resort

★★★★ 76% HOTEL

◉ Modern British

Promising modern cooking in beautifully situated resort hotel

☎ 0844 879 9057 & 01877 389500 📄 01877 387307
Kinlochard FK8 3TL
e-mail: forest_hills@macdonald-hotels.co.uk
web: www.macdonald-hotels.co.uk/foresthills
dir: A84, A873, A81 to Aberfoyle onto B829

Situated in the heart of the Trossachs with wonderful views of Loch Ard, Forest Hills is a popular resort hotel offering a good range of indoor and outdoor sports facilities, including a spa complex. The traditionally styled restaurant is relaxed and informal and has good views of the surrounding gardens and local landscape. The promising young team embraces some modern flavour combinations as seen in a starter of Earl Grey-smoked guinea fowl with pink grapefruit and sorrel salad and chilli syrup. Follow with braised lamb shoulder with creamed caraway cabbage and rosemary jus, leaving room for satsuma crème brûlée with chocolate and hazelnut biscotti and satsuma compôte.

Rooms 49 (16 fmly) (12 GF) **Facilities** Spa STV FTV 🕹 ♨ Gym Children's club Snooker Watersports Quad biking Archery Clay pigeon shooting ♫ Xmas New Year Wi-fi **Conf** Class 60 Board 45 Thtr 150 **Services** Lift **Parking** 100 **Notes** ⊗ Civ Wed 100

Times 7pm-9.30pm

CALLANDER   Map 2 NN60

Roman Camp Country House

★★★ 88% COUNTRY HOUSE HOTEL

◉◉◉ Modern French V

Confident cooking in a luxurious historical setting

☎ 01877 330003 📄 01877 331533
FK17 8BG
e-mail: mail@romancamphotel.co.uk
web: www.romancamphotel.co.uk
dir: N on A84, left at east end of High Street. 300yds to hotel

Drive down the private road which leads to Roman Camp (so called because of the nearby Roman earthworks) and it's hard to believe you're just a few hundred yards from Callander's main high street. Set in the Loch Lomond and Trossachs National Park in the former estate of the Earl of Moray, this 17th-century hotel is an ideal base for exploring Scotland's major cities. It's also a peaceful and opulent place to get away from it all. From low ceilings and large open fires in the three public rooms to the two formal dining rooms, where oak-panelling sets off multi-textured fabrics and ornate plasterwork, this place exudes luxury. Tables are crisply laid and served by polite and informative staff. Great Scottish ingredients are skillfully cooked by a chef who clearly knows how to put flavours together and is not afraid to simplify dishes where necessary. Examples of the classical French cooking with modern Scottish twists included mi-cuit salmon with celeriac remoulade and beetoot jelly - every component executed with aplomb. A main course of breast of Goosnargh duckling with foie gras and confit leg spring roll and sesame dressing is top-notch stuff, while a wonderful passionfruit tart with coconut sorbet and pistachio oil rounds things off nicely. A considered global wine list caters for all pockets with some special bottles at the top end.

Rooms 15 (4 fmly) (7 GF) **S** £95-£100; **D** £150-£200 (incl. bkfst) **Facilities** STV FTV Fishing Xmas New Year Wi-fi **Conf** Class 60 Board 30 Thtr 120 Del from £200 to £250 **Parking** 80 **Notes** LB Civ Wed 150

Chef Ian McNaught **Owner** Eric Brown **Times** 12-2/7-9 **Prices** Fixed L 3 course £25-£29, Fixed D 4 course £49-£50, Starter £12-£20, Main £27-£35, Dessert £10-£14, Service optional **Wines** 185 bottles over £20, 15 bottles under £20, 16 by glass **Notes** Tasting menu 4 course dishes change daily, Sunday L, Vegetarian menu, Dress restrictions, Smart casual **Seats** 120, Pr/dining room 36 **Children** Portions

CALLANDER CONTINUED

Annfield Guest House

★★★★ GUEST HOUSE

18 North Church St FK17 8EG
☎ 01877 330204
e-mail: reservations@annfieldguesthouse.co.uk
dir: Off A84 Main St onto North Church St, at top on right

Situated within easy reach of the town centre, this welcoming guest house offers comfortable, good-value accommodation. The spacious bedrooms are attractively decorated and well equipped. An elegant first-floor lounge is ideal for relaxation, and hearty breakfasts are served at individual tables in the pretty dining room.

Rooms 7 rms (4 en suite) (2 pri facs) (1 fmly) S £40-£65; D £60-£70 **Facilities** FTV TVL tea/coffee Cen ht Wi-fi Golf 18 **Parking** 7 **Notes** LB ⊗ No Children 6yrs Closed Xmas RS Dec-Feb Maybe closed for 2 months over winter ⌨

Arden House

★★★★ GUEST ACCOMMODATION

Bracklinn Rd FK17 8EQ
☎ 01877 330235
e-mail: ardenhouse@onetel.com
dir: Off A84 Main St onto Bracklinn Rd, house 200yds on left

This impressive Victorian villa lies in beautiful mature grounds in a peaceful area of the town. It featured in the 1960s hit television series *Dr Finlay's Casebook* and is a friendly, welcoming house. The comfortable bedrooms are thoughtfully furnished and equipped. There is a stylish lounge in addition to the attractive breakfast room where delicious breakfasts are served at individual tables.

Rooms 6 en suite (2 GF) **Facilities** tea/coffee Cen ht Wi-fi ♪ **Parking** 10 **Notes** ⊗ No Children 14yrs Closed Nov-Mar

Callander Meadows

★★★★ RESTAURANT WITH ROOMS

◉ Modern British

Pleasingly straightforward modern cooking in an unpretentious restaurant with rooms

24 Main St FK17 8BB
☎ 01877 330181
e-mail: mail@callandermeadows.co.uk
web: www.callandermeadows.co.uk
dir: M9 junct 10 onto A84 to Callander, on main street just past A81 junct

The Parkes' appealing restaurant with rooms is a light-filled, unpretentious place, with bare-wood floors and undressed tables, crimson walls and fresh flowers. Both proprietors are chefs, and have cooked at the Gleneagles Hotel (see entry, Auchterarder), but the cooking here tacks to a more straightforward course than grand-hotel dining. Start with a salad of smoked duck, peppers and noodles dressed in soy, and go on to roast loin of Trossach venison with a potato cake, roasted roots and redcurrant jus. Fish could well be fried Trossach trout, served with creamed leeks and saffron butter. Desserts do everything that is expected of them in the indulgence department, with the likes of white chocolate and Baileys cheesecake.

Rooms 3 en suite **Facilities** STV tea/coffee Dinner available Cen ht Wi-fi **Parking** 4 **Notes** ⊗ RS Winter Restaurant open Thu-Sun only No coaches

Chef Nick & Susannah Parkes **Owner** Nick & Susannah Parkes **Times** 12-2.30/6-9 Closed 25-26 Dec, Tue-Wed **Prices** Fixed L 2 course fr £9.95, Starter £4.95-£7.95, Main £12.95-£28.50, Dessert £4.95-£8.95 **Wines** 15 bottles over £20, 17 bottles under £20, 8 by glass **Notes** Sunday L, Vegetarian available **Seats** 40, Pr/dining room 16 **Children** Portions **Parking** 4, 80 yds council car park

Lubnaig House

★★★★ 🅰 GUEST HOUSE

Leny Feus FK17 8AS
☎ 01877 330376
e-mail: info@lubnaighouse.co.uk
web: www.lubnaighouse.co.uk
dir: From town centre A84 W, right onto Leny Feus. Lubnaig House after Poppies Hotel

Rooms 6 en suite 2 annexe en suite (4 GF) S £45-£55; D £70-£80* **Facilities** FTV tea/coffee Cen ht Wi-fi **Parking** 10 **Notes** LB ⊗ No Children 7yrs Closed Nov-Apr

The Lade Inn 🍷

Kilmahog FK17 8HD ☎ **01877 330152**
e-mail: info@theladeinn.com
dir: From Stirling take A84 to Callander. 1m N of Callander, left at Kilmahog Woollen Mills onto A821 towards Aberfoyle. Pub immediately on left

Standing 200 yards back fro the River Teith in the heart of the Trossachs National Park, the stone built Lade Inn is part of the surrounding Leny Estate and was built as a tearoom in 1935. First licensed in the 1960s, the traditional bar is noted for its real ales – try a pint of Belhaven Best – and home-cooked food. Typical dishes include smoked venison with spiced fruit chutney, beer-battered haddock, and sticky toffee pudding. There's a superb beer garden with three ponds and Scottish folk music is played every Friday and Saturday. Don't miss the pub's real ale shop, which stocks over 130 Scottish bottled beers from 30 micro-breweries, and the week-long beer festival in late August.

Open all day all wk noon-11 (Fri-Sat noon-1am Sun

12.30-10.30) **Bar Meals** L served Mon-Fri 12-3, Sat 12-9, Sun 12.30-9 D served Mon-Fri 5-9, Sat 12-9, Sun 12.30-9 booking required Av main course £10 **Restaurant** L served Mon-Fri 12-3, Sat 12-9, Sun 12.30-9 D served Mon-Fri 5-9, Sat 12-9, Sun 12.30-9 booking required Fixed menu price fr £14.50 Av 3 course à la carte fr £14 ⊕ FREE HOUSE 🍺 Waylade, LadeBack, LadeOut, Belhaven Best, Tennent's ᶞ Thistly Cross. ♇ 9 **Facilities** Children welcome Children's menu Children's portions Play area Family room Dogs allowed Garden Beer festival Parking Wi-fi

---

CRIANLARICH   Map 2 NN32

The Crianlarich Hotel

★★★ 77% HOTEL

◉ Traditional British

Simple, accurate cooking in smartly refurbished hotel

☎ 01838 300272   🖨 01838 300329
FK20 8RW
e-mail: info@crianlarich-hotel.co.uk
web: www.crianlarich-hotel.co.uk
dir: At junct of A85 & A82

A handy jumping off point for exploring Loch Lomond and Glencoe, the whitewashed Crianlarich Hotel sits at a crossroads by the railway line in a village that marks the halfway point along the West Highland Way and basking in classic chocolate box Highland vistas. Inside, a tasteful refurbishment blends Victorian oak panelling and period features with a stylish contemporary look that makes for an appealing setting, both in the the pleasant, smartly appointed bedrooms and the Highland Lounge dining room. The kitchen maintains a balance between old favourites and staying in step with modern trends to keep the repertoire moving forward. Haggis and clapshot could come drizzled in whisky sauce for a thoroughly Scottish starter, while main courses could bring on venison casserole with suet dumplings and braised red cabbage, or roast rack of Argyll lamb with a rosemary crust served with Savoy cabbage and port wine jus.

Rooms 36 (1 fmly) **Facilities** FTV ♫ Xmas New Year Wi-fi **Conf** Class 60 Board 40 Thtr 100 **Services** Lift **Parking** 30 **Notes** LB

Times 7-9.30 Closed L all week, D Sun & Mon

DRYMEN   Map 2 NS48

Best Western Buchanan Arms Hotel & Spa

★★★ 79% HOTEL

☎ 01360 660588   🖨 01360 660943
23 Main St G63 0BQ
e-mail: info@buchananarms.co.uk

This former coaching inn has benefited from on-going investment and refurbishment. Located in the quiet conservation village of Drymen, the hotel provides a perfect base for touring this area, with Loch Lomond just a few miles away. There are well-appointed bedrooms and welcoming public areas. Good leisure facilities are an added benefit.

Rooms 52 (9 fmly) (3 GF) **S** £40-£120; **D** £60-£160 (incl. bkfst)* **Facilities** Spa FTV ⓡ supervised Gym Squash Xmas New Year Wi-fi **Conf** Class 140 Board 60 Thtr 250 Del from £109 to £159* **Parking** 120 **Notes** LB ⊗ Civ Wed 100

Winnock Hotel

★★★ 75% HOTEL

☎ 01360 660245   🖨 01360 660267
The Square G63 0BL
e-mail: info@winnockhotel.com
web: www.winnockhotel.com
dir: From S: M74 onto M8 junct 16b through Glasgow. Follow A809 to Aberfoyle

Occupying a prominent position overlooking the village green, this popular hotel offers well-equipped bedrooms of various sizes and styles. The public rooms include a bar, a lounge and an attractive formal dining room that serves dishes of good, locally sourced food.

Rooms 73 (18 fmly) (19 GF) **Facilities** FTV Xmas New Year Wi-fi **Conf** Class 60 Board 70 Thtr 140 **Parking** 60 **Notes** ⊗ Civ Wed 100

The Clachan Inn

2 Main St G63 0BG ☎ 01360 660824
e-mail: info@clachaninndrymen.co.uk
dir: Telephone for directions

Believed to be the oldest licensed pub in Scotland, this quaint, white-painted cottage sits in a small village on the West Highland Way, and was once owned by Rob Roy's sister. In the bar, guest ales are changed often and there is a warming log fire to keep things cosy. Locate the appealing lounge bar for freshly-made food using the best of local produce, where the specials menu changes daily.

Open all day all wk Closed: 25 Dec & 1 Jan ⊕ FREE HOUSE 🍺 Guinness. **Facilities** Children welcome Children's menu Children's portions Dogs allowed

FINTRY   Map 2 NS68

Culcreuch Castle Hotel & Estate

★★★ 79% HOTEL

☎ 01360 860555 & 860228   📠 01360 860556
Kippen Rd G63 0LW
e-mail: info@culcreuch.com
web: www.culcreuch.com
dir: On B822, 17m W of Stirling

Peacefully located in 1,600 acres of parkland, this ancient castle dates back to 1296. Tastefully restored accommodation is in a mixture of individually themed castle rooms, some with four-poster beds, and more modern courtyard rooms which are suitable for families. Period style public rooms include a bar, serving light meals, an elegant lounge and a wood-panelled dining room.

Rooms 14 (4 annexe) (4 fmly) (4 GF) **D** £102-£190 (incl. bkfst) **Facilities** STV FTV Fishing New Year Wi-fi
Conf Class 70 Board 30 Thtr 140 Del from £119 to £129 **Parking** 100 **Notes** LB ⊗ Closed 4-18 Jan & 25-26 Dec Civ Wed 110

KIPPEN   Map 2 NS69

Cross Keys Hotel ♟

Main St FK8 3DN ☎ **01786 870293**
e-mail: info@kippencrosskeys.co.uk
dir: 10m W of Stirling, 20m from Loch Lomond off A811

Now run by Debby and Brian, this cosy inn is over 300 years old and offers seasonally changing menus and a good pint of Harviestoun Bitter and Twisted. The pub's welcoming interior, warmed by three log fires, is perfect for resting your feet after walk on the nearby Burnside Wood nature trails, or you can sit in the garden when the weather permits. The menu takes in game, apricot and chicken terrine with Cross Keys chutney; pork belly and loin of pork, roast celeriac fondant, apple and thyme sauce; confit duck leg and venison sausage casserole, cannellini beans and rhubarb sauce. Lighter lunches are available at lunchtime. Dogs are welcome in the top bar.

Open all wk Mon-Thu noon-3 5-11, Fri noon-3 5-1am, Sat noon-1am, Sun noon-mdnt Closed: 1 Jan **Bar Meals** L served Mon-Fri 12-3, Sat 12-9, Sun 12-8 D served Mon-Fri 5-9, Sat 12-9, Sun 12-8 **Restaurant** L served Mon-Fri 12-3, Sat 12-9, Sun 12-8 D served Mon-Fri 5-9, Sat 12-9, Sun 12-8 ⊕ FREE HOUSE ◾ Belhaven Best, Harviestoun Bitter & Twisted, Guinness Ö Addlestones. ♟ 10 **Facilities** Children welcome Children's menu Children's portions Family room Dogs allowed Garden Parking Wi-fi

The Inn at Kippen ♟

Fore Rd FK8 3DT ☎ **01786 870500**   📠 **01786 871011**
e-mail: info@theinnatkippen.co.uk
dir: From Stirling take A811 to Loch Lomond. 1st left at Kippen station rdbt, 1st right onto Fore Rd. Inn on left

Located in a picturesque village at the foot of the Campsie Hills, this traditional whitewashed free house enjoys views across the Forth valley to the Highlands. The stylish bar is a relaxing place to sample the extensive range of cask ales and wines, as well as a superb selection of spirits that reflects the proprietor's long career in the Scotch whisky business. Two separate areas offer a choice of casual or more formal dining from a menu driven by seasonal, locally sourced ingredients. Traditional and contemporary dishes reveal British, European and Oriental influences. Start, perhaps, with a twice-baked Parmesan soufflé before moving on to steak pie with seasonal vegetables; Thai seafood broth with sea bass, mussels and king prawns; or butternut squash, sage and Parmesan risotto. Tempting desserts include treacle and stem ginger pudding with coconut ice cream. There's a pretty garden area for summer dining, and a heated smoking deck.

Open all day all wk Fri & Sat noon-11 noon-1am **Bar Meals** L served all wk 12-5 D served all wk 5-9 booking required Av main course £16 food served all day **Restaurant** L served Sat-Sun 12-5 booking required D served Fri-Sun 5-9 booking required Fixed menu price fr £14 Av 3 course à la carte fr £20 food served all day ⊕ FREE HOUSE ◾ Killians. ♟ 9 **Facilities** Children welcome Children's menu Children's portions Dogs allowed Garden Parking Wi-fi

LOCHEARNHEAD   Map 2 NN52

Mansewood Country House

★★★★ GUEST HOUSE

FK19 8NS
☎ **01567 830213**
e-mail: stay@mansewoodcountryhouse.co.uk
dir: A84 N to Lochearnhead, 1st building on left; A84 S to Lochearnhead

Mansewood Country House is a spacious former manse that dates back to the 18th century and lies in a well-tended garden to the south of the village. Bedrooms are well appointed and equipped and offer high standards of comfort. Refreshments can be enjoyed in the cosy bar or the elegant lounge, and meals prepared with flair are served in the attractive restaurant. There is also a log cabin where pets are allowed.

Rooms 6 en suite (1 GF) **Facilities** FTV TVL tea/coffee Dinner available Cen ht Licensed Wi-fi **Parking** 6 **Notes** LB ⊗ RS Nov-Mar Phone for advance bookings

Tigh Na Crich

★★★★ BED AND BREAKFAST

FK19 8PR

☎ 01567 830235

e-mail: johntippett2@aol.com

web: www.tighnacrich.co.uk

dir: At junct of A84 & A85, adjacent to village shop

Tich Na Crich is located in the heart of the small village of Lochearnhead, surrounded by mountains on three sides and Loch Earn on the fourth. Inside is very well presented accommodation with many thoughtful extras provided. The generous breakfast is served in the comfortable dining room on individual tables looking out to the front of the property.

Rooms 3 en suite (1 fmly) S £40-£45; D £60-£65
Facilities FTV tea/coffee Cen ht **Parking** 3 **Notes** ⊗

PORT OF MENTEITH   Map 2 NN50

The Lake of Menteith Hotel

★★★ 74% SMALL HOTEL

⊛⊛ Modern Scottish

Great views, good food and warm hospitality

☎ 01877 385258   🖷 01877 385671

FK8 3RA

e-mail: enquiries@lake-hotel.com

dir: M9 junct 10, A84. At Blairdrummond take A873. Left onto A81 to Port of Menteith. Left onto B8034, hotel 200yds on right

A converted 19th-century manse in a beautiful location - on the shores of the Lake of Menteith in the Trossachs National Park - just an hour's drive from either Glasgow or Edinburgh. The hotel has been stylishly refurbished and decorated in a fresh, airy New England style, and bedrooms offer great views over the lake or the countryside. Dining is a highlight, with two dining options on offer. There's the Port Bar, with outdoor seating for the summer months; and a conservatory restaurant with stunning loch views and a slightly nautical feel. You might not expect anything too ground-breaking here but the kitchen is not afraid to experiment with contemporary techniques. Well-constructed canapes will get you in the mood, and then you might begin with pan-seared Oban scallops with watermelon and aubergine: a hint of cumin and sweet tomato sauce works well and seared watermelon adds a twist to the dish. Perthshire lamb three ways might follow – the three ways being herb-crusted loin, sweetbreads and braised belly, accompanied by excellent black olive gnocchi. For dessert, try the dark chocolate veloute with chocolate sauce and tonka bean ice cream.

Rooms 17 (5 GF) **S** £60-£155; **D** £80-£195 (incl. bkfst)*
Facilities FTV Xmas New Year Wi-fi **Conf** Board 18 Thtr 30
Del from £120 to £150* **Parking** 50 **Notes** LB Civ Wed 50

Chef Graham Campbell

STIRLING   Map 3 NS79

Barceló Stirling Highland Hotel

★★★★ 75% HOTEL

☎ 01786 272727   🖷 01786 272829

Spittal St FK8 1DU

e-mail: stirling@barcelo-hotels.co.uk

web: www.barcelo-hotels.co.uk

dir: A84 into Stirling. Follow Stirling Castle signs to Albert Hall. Left, left again, follow Castle signs

Enjoying a location close to the castle and historic town, this atmospheric hotel was previously a high school. Public rooms have been converted from the original classrooms and retain many interesting features. Bedrooms are more modern in style and comfortably equipped. Scholars Restaurant serves traditional and international dishes, and the Headmaster's Study is the ideal venue for enjoying a drink.

Rooms 96 (4 fmly) **Facilities** Spa STV ⌦ supervised Gym Squash Steam room Dance studio Beauty therapist Xmas New Year Wi-fi **Conf** Class 80 Board 60 Thtr 100
Services Lift **Parking** 96 **Notes** Civ Wed 100

Holiday Inn Express - Stirling

BUDGET HOTEL

☎ 01786 449922   🖷 01786 449932

Springkerse Business Park FK7 7XH

e-mail: info@expressstirling.co.uk

web: www.hiexpress.com/stirling

dir: M9, M80 junct 9, A91, Stirling/St Andrews exit. 2.8m, at 4th rdbt, 2nd exit to sports stadium, 3rd exit to hotel

A modern hotel ideal for families and business travellers. Fresh and uncomplicated, the spacious rooms include Sky TV, power shower and tea and coffee-making facilities. Continental buffet breakfast is included in the room rate; other meals may be taken at the nearby family pub or restaurant.

Rooms 80 (36 fmly) **S** £59-£119; **D** £59-£129 (incl. bkfst)*
Conf Class 14 Board 18 Thtr 30

Premier Inn Stirling

BUDGET HOTEL

☎ 0871 527 9038 📄 0871 527 9039
Glasgow Rd, Whins of Milton FK7 8EX
web: www.premierinn.com
dir: On A872, 0.25m from M9/M80 junct 9

High quality, budget accommodation ideal for both families and business travellers. Spacious, en suite bedrooms feature tea and coffee-making facilities, and Freeview TV in most hotels. Internet access and Wi-fi are available for a small fee. The adjacent family restaurant features a wide and varied menu.

Rooms 60 **D** £59-£65*

Linden Guest House

★★★★ GUEST HOUSE

22 Linden Av FK7 7PQ
☎ 01786 448850 & 07974 116573 📄 01786 448850
e-mail: fay@lindenguesthouse.co.uk
web: www.lindenguesthouse.co.uk
dir: 0.5m SE of city centre off A9

Situated within walking distance of the town centre, this friendly guest house offers attractive and very well-equipped bedrooms, including a large family room that sleeps five comfortably. There is a bright dining room where delicious breakfasts are served at individual tables with quality Wedgwood crockery.

Rooms 4 en suite (2 fmly) (1 GF) S £40-£70; D £50-£80*
Facilities STV FTV tea/coffee Cen ht Wi-fi **Parking** 2
Notes LB

Strathblane Country House

★★★ 78% COUNTRY HOUSE HOTEL

☎ 01360 770491 📄 01360 770345
Milngavie Rd G63 9EH
e-mail: info@strathblanecountryhouse.co.uk
dir: On A81 (Milngavie Rd) S of Strathblane. Hotel 0.75m past Mugdock Country Park on right

Set in 10-acre grounds looking out on the beautiful Campsie Fells, this majestic property, built in 1874, offers a get-away-from-it-all experience, yet is just a 20-minute drive from Glasgow. Lunch and dinner are served in the relaxed Brasserie Restaurant, and guests can visit the falconry or just kick back and relax in front of the fire with a book and a dram of whisky. Weddings are especially well catered for.

Rooms 10 (3 fmly) **S** £65-£99; **D** £84-£180 (incl. bkfst)*
Facilities FTV Falconry 🎵 Xmas New Year Wi-fi
Conf Class 60 Board 60 Thtr 180 Del from £115 to £135
Parking 120 **Notes** LB ⊗ Civ Wed 180

Creagan House

★★★★★ 🏚 RESTAURANT WITH ROOMS

◉◉ French, Scottish 🍷 NOTABLE WINE LIST

17th-century Trossachs farmhouse with warm hospitality and good food

FK18 8ND
☎ 01877 384638 📄 01877 384319
e-mail: eatandstay@creaganhouse.co.uk
web: www.creaganhouse.co.uk
dir: 0.25m N of Strathyre on A84

Secreted away in Strathyre's sheltered valley at the head of Loch Lubnaig, this converted 17th-century farmhouse has life-affirming Highland views worth making the trip for. Husband-and-wife-team Gordon and Cherry Gunn have run their restaurant with rooms for the best part of a quarter of a century with warmth, enthusiasm and amiable good humour. Meals are served at burnished refectory tables in a baronial dining room with a vaulted ceiling and grand stone fireplace. Gordon mans the stoves with skill and confidence, sending out classically inspired French dishes with a firm sense of Scottish terroir; herbs and vegetables come from the garden and local small-holdings, while meat is all reared on Perthshire farms. Among starters might be roast monkfish in pancetta, served with Jerusalem artichoke purée, and orange and vermouth sauce, followed by Isle of Gigha halibut with warm pâté of scallop, langoustine and crab with shellfish sauce, or venison loin with mulled pear purée and green peppercorn sauce. A bar stocked with 50-odd malts should ensure a sound night's sleep.

Rooms 5 en suite (1 fmly) (1 GF) S £75-£95; D £130-£150
Facilities FTV tea/coffee Dinner available Cen ht Wi-fi
Conf Max 35 Thtr 35 Class 12 Board 35 **Parking** 16
Notes LB Closed 7-22 Nov, Xmas & 18 Jan-8 Mar RS Wed &
Thu Closed

Chef Gordon Gunn **Owner** Gordon & Cherry Gunn
Times 7.30-8.30 Closed 7-22 Nov, Xmas, 18 Jan-8 Mar,
Wed-Thu, L all week (ex parties) **Prices** Fixed D 3 course
£31.50-£36, Service optional **Wines** 48 bottles over £20, 19
bottles under £20, 8 by glass **Notes** Vegetarian available,
Dress restrictions, Smart casual **Seats** 15, Pr/dining room 6
Children Portions

Dunnottar Castle, overlooking the North Sea

Sligachan, Isle of Skye

SCOTTISH ISLANDS
ISLE OF ARRAN

BLACKWATERFOOT   Map 2 NR92

Best Western Kinloch

★★★ 80% HOTEL

☎ 01770 860444   📠 01770 860447
KA27 8ET
e-mail: reservations@kinlochhotel.eclipse.co.uk
web: www.bw-kinlochhotel.co.uk
dir: Ferry from Ardrossan to Brodick, follow signs for
Blackwaterfoot, hotel in village centre

Well known for providing an authentic island experience, this
long established stylish hotel is in an idyllic location. Smart
public areas include a choice of lounges, popular bars and
well-presented leisure facilities. Bedrooms vary in size and
style but most enjoy panoramic sea views and several family
suites offer excellent value. The spacious restaurant
provides a wide ranging menu, and in winter when the
restaurant is closed, the bar serves a choice of creative
dishes.

Rooms 37 (7 fmly) (7 GF) **Facilities** STV ⚲ Gym Squash
Beauty therapy 🎵 New Year Wi-fi **Conf** Class 20 Board 40
Thtr 120 **Services** Lift **Parking** 2 **Notes** Civ Wed 60

BRODICK   Map 2 NS03

Kilmichael Country House

★★★ COUNTRY HOUSE HOTEL

◉◉ Modern British ✿

Refined cooking in stylish country-house hotel

☎ 01770 302219   📠 01770 302068
Glen Cloy KA27 8BY
e-mail: enquiries@kilmichael.com
web: www.kilmichael.com
dir: From Brodick ferry terminal towards Lochranza for 1m.
Left at golf course, follow signs

Kilmichael is a stylish small-scale country-house hotel set
in four acres of gardens in a tranquil glen, yet a mere five
minutes drive from the Brodick ferry. The handsome, white-
painted house - reputed to be the oldest on the island - is
tastefully furnished with antiques, artworks and china, and
the delightful bedrooms are furnished in classical style;
some are in a pretty courtyard conversion. The dining room -
an airy space with a classic look of claret walls, plush
golden fabrics and gilt-framed mirrors - is the setting for
interesting modern menus built on first-class Scottish
produce, including fruit and vegetables and herbs from the
garden and estate, and eggs from their own chickens and
ducks. Dinners take the format of canapés, followed by a
starter such as smoked salmon and prawn cheesecake with

a salad of herbs and flowers, then sorbet - lemon and
lavender, say - before roast Gressingham duck breast
stuffed with wild rice, walnuts and raspberries. To finish,
perhaps lemon berry tart with gin and lemon honeycomb
jelly, and home-made Cassis ice cream.

Rooms 8 (3 annexe) (7 GF) **S** £78-£98; **D** £130-£163 (incl.
bkfst)* **Facilities** Wi-fi **Parking** 14 **Notes** LB No children
12yrs Closed Nov-Feb (ex for prior bookings)

Chef Antony Butterworth **Owner** G Botterill & A Butterworth
Times 7-8.30 Closed Nov-Mar, Tue, L all week **Prices** Fixed D
4 course £45, Service optional **Wines** 32 bottles over £20, 23
bottles under £20, 3 by glass **Notes** Vegetarian available,
Dress restrictions, Smart casual, no T-shirts or bare feet
Seats 18

Allandale

★★★★ GUEST HOUSE

KA27 8BJ
☎ 01770 302278
e-mail: info@allandalehouse.co.uk
dir: 500yds S of Brodick Pier, off A841 towards Lamlash, up
hill 2nd left at Corriegills sign

Under enthusiastic ownership, this comfortable guest house
is set in delightful gardens in beautiful countryside. Guests
can relax in the lounge with its attractive garden views.
Bedrooms vary in size and have pleasing colour schemes
and mixed modern furnishings, along with thoughtful
amenities. In a peaceful location, Allandale is convenient for
the CalMac ferry and Brodick centre.

Rooms 4 rms (3 en suite) (1 pri facs) 2 annexe en suite (3
fmly) (2 GF) **Facilities** FTV tea/coffee Cen ht **Parking** 6
Notes ⊗ Closed Nov-Feb

ISLE OF COLL

ARINAGOUR   Map 4 NM25

Coll Hotel

PA78 6SZ ☎ 01879 230334   📠 01879 230317
e-mail: info@collhotel.com
dir: Ferry from Oban. Hotel at head of Arinagour Bay, 1m
from Pier (collections by arrangement)

Being the only inn on the Isle of Coll, it's no surprise that the
bar of this award-winning hotel is the hub of the island
community. Come here to meet the locals, soak in the
atmosphere, and enjoy stunning views over the sea to Jura
and Mull. The most popular drinks are pints of Loch Fyne ale
and malt whiskies from the list, but there is a good wine
selection too. In the summer months the fabulous garden
acts as an extension to the bar or the Gannet restaurant;
watch the yachts coming and going while enjoying a glass of
Pimms. Fresh produce is landed and delivered from around

continued

ARINAGOUR CONTINUED

the island every day and features on the specials board. Famed for its seafood, you'll find it in dishes such as seared scallops in garlic and lemon butter, and a platter of Coll langoustines that can be served hot or cold, with seasonal salad or fried potatoes. Among the non-fish options, try the chicken topped with haggis in a whisky sauce.

Open all day all wk **Bar Meals** L served all wk 12-2 D served all wk 6-9 Av main course £12 **Restaurant** L served all wk 12-2 D served all wk 6-9 booking required Av 3 course à la carte fr £28 ⊕ FREE HOUSE ◖ Loch Fyne Ale, Pipers Gold, Guinness. **Facilities** Children welcome Children's menu Children's portions Play area Family room Garden Parking Wi-fi

ISLE OF HARRIS

SCARISTA (SGARASTA BHEAG)   Map 4 NG09

Scarista House

★★★★ RESTAURANT WITH ROOMS

◉◉ Modern Scottish

Modern Scottish cooking in a Georgian house with stunning sea views

HS3 3HX
☎ 01859 550238   ▤ 01859 550277
e-mail: timandpatricia@scaristahouse.com
dir: On A859, 15m S of Tarbert

A former manse, this Georgian house has stunning views over a three-mile-long white beach and the Atlantic. Inside are fresh flowers, antiques, open fires in the library and drawing room, lots of CDs - and no TV. Uncomplicated, skilful cooking techniques are applied to the island's best produce - seafood, lamb, beef and game - to let flavours shine, with some well-balanced and often intriguing combinations. The no-choice dinner menu could start with a well-balanced dish of chicken and chervil dumplings with a velouté of spinach, coconut and cumin and proceed to a simple main course of Harris Minch langoustines with garlic and herb butter, Dijon mayonnaise and crushed olive potatoes. Other occasions might see mixed seafood with langoustine butter followed by seared loin of lamb with dauphinoise potatoes and aubergine purée. A pudding - perhaps velvety pannacotta flavoured with eau de vie de framboise with raspberry compôte or chocolate roulade - precedes a choice of Scottish cheeses.

Rooms 3 en suite 2 annexe en suite (2 GF) **Facilities** tea/coffee Dinner available Direct Dial Cen ht **Parking** 12 **Notes** Closed Xmas, Jan & Feb No coaches Civ Wed 40

Times 7.30-8 Closed 25 Dec, Jan-Feb, L Mon-Sat

TARBERT (TAIRBEART)   Map 4 NB10

Hotel Hebrides

★★★★ 78% HOTEL

◉ Modern Scottish

Local produce and bags of invention

☎ 01859 502364
Pier Rd HS3 3DG
e-mail: stay@hotel-hebrides.com
web www.hotel-hebrides.com

dir: To Tarbert via ferry from Uig (Isle of Skye); or ferry from Ullapool to Stornaway, A859 to Tarbert; or by plane to Stornaway from Glasgow, Edinburgh or Inverness

A modern and intimate hotel and restaurant hard by the Tarbert ferry terminal, the views across the pier and out to sea, with the hills of Harris in the opposite direction, mean there's really no need for an overly elaborate interior. The bedrooms are stylishly designed and include Wi-fi, high speed internet access and flat-screen TVs; the deluxe rooms have iPod docking stations and some rooms have loch and harbour views. A complimentary bus service is provided to the theatre in the summer months. In the restaurant, white walls, simple plants, bare-wood tables and bench seating are just the job. A passionate kitchen team is confident enough to experiment with different flavours on the Scottish menu, which makes good use of the abundance of game and seafood on the doorstep. So step into the Pierhouse Restaurant and tuck into Ryefield goats' cheese with poached pear, sticky gingerbread, white truffle, honey and port reduction, followed by local hand-dived roast scallops with cauliflower purée and beignet, crispy bacon, curry oil, and finish with a well conceived chocolate collection for dessert. The Mote Lounge bar is popular for drinks by the roaring fire.

Rooms 21

ISLE OF ISLAY

PORT ASKAIG   Map 2 NR46

Port Askaig

★★ 63% SMALL HOTEL

☎ 01496 840245   📠 01496 840295
PA46 7RD
e-mail: hotel@portaskaig.co.uk
web: www.portaskaig.co.uk
dir: At ferry terminal

The building of this endearing family-run hotel dates back to the 18th-century. The lounge provides fine views over the Sound of Islay to Jura, and there is a choice of bars that are popular with locals. Traditional dinners are served in the bright restaurant and a full range of bar snacks and meals is also available. The bedrooms are smart and comfortable.

Rooms 8 (1 fmly) (8 GF) **Parking** 21

PORT CHARLOTTE   Map 2 NR25

The Port Charlotte Hotel 🍷

Main St PA48 7TU ☎ **01496 850360**   📠 **01496 850361**
e-mail: info@portcharlottehotel.co.uk
dir: From Port Askaig take A846 towards Bowmore. Right onto A847, through Blackrock. Take unclassified road to Port Charlotte

On the west shore of Loch Indaal is the attractive conservation village of Port Charlotte, whose pretty whitewashed stone buildings include this completely restored hotel. A large comfortable conservatory opens out into the beer garden, which overlooks the sea. Warmed by open fires, the lounge and public bar are convivial gathering points for lovers of Scottish art displayed on the walls and the traditional music sometimes played here. Islay ales and whiskies make great aperitifs before tucking in to beef, lamb or game from local farms and estates; or scallops, lobster and crab landed by the Islay fishing fleet.

Open all day all wk **Closed:** 24-26 Dec **Bar Meals** L served all wk 12-2 D served all wk 6-9 Av main course £11.95 **Restaurant** D served all wk 6-9 Av 3 course à la carte fr £32 🌐 FREE HOUSE 🍺 Islay Ales. **Facilities** Children welcome Children's menu Children's portions Play area Family room Dogs allowed Garden Parking Wi-fi

ISLE OF MULL

TOBERMORY   Map 4 NM55

Highland Cottage

★★★ SMALL HOTEL

◉◉ Modern Scottish, International 🕯

Hospitable island hotel with locally-sourced cooking

☎ 01688 302030
Breadalbane St PA75 6PD
e-mail: davidandjo@highlandcottage.co.uk
web: www.highlandcottage.co.uk
dir: A848 Craignure/Fishnish ferry terminal, pass Tobermory signs, straight on at mini rdbt across narrow bridge, turn right. Hotel on right opposite fire station

You can't beat dining within sight of where the fish and seafood that you are eating is landed. In the case of David and Jo Currie's small-scale hotel and restaurant, this means the Mull waterfront, which lies just a few minutes' stroll from the dining room. It is a homely, welcoming place decorated with heaps of interesting art and objets, and the food fits the setting to a tee: unpretentious Scottish cooking from a chef who has the experience to leave the splendid ingredients to speak for themselves and not gild the lily. Fixed-price dinner menus cater to the needs of traditionalists without neglecting to engage those in search of modernity and invention; thus home-cured gravad lax with beetroot jelly and horseradish cream could start things off, while main course sees sea-fresh local scallops (hand-dived by 'George' in Tobermory Bay) sharing a plate with sticky pork belly and a deeply-flavoured cider sauce. For local meat fans, roast loin and braised shoulder of lamb with boulangère potatoes and black olive gravy should hit the spot. Wrap things up with a traditional cranachan. Bedrooms are individual; some have four-posters and all are comprehensively equipped to include TVs and music centres.

Rooms 6 (1 GF) **S** £110-£150; **D** £150-£185 (incl. bkfst)* **Facilities** FTV Wi-fi **Parking** 6 **Notes** LB No children 10yrs Closed Nov-Mar

Chef Josephine Currie **Owner** David & Josephine Currie **Times** 7-9 Closed Nov-Mar, L all week **Prices** Fixed D 4 course £49.50, Service included **Wines** 33 bottles over £20, 21 bottles under £20, 11 by glass **Notes** Vegetarian available, Dress restrictions, Smart casual **Seats** 24 **Children** Portions

TOBERMORY CONTINUED

Tobermory

★★ 80% HOTEL

◉ Modern Scottish ☺

Lovely harbourside setting and good food

☎ 01688 302091 🖨 01688 302254
53 Main St PA75 6NT
e-mail: tobhotel@tinyworld.co.uk
web: www.thetobermoryhotel.com
dir: On waterfront

The Tobermory Hotel is situated on the magically picturesque and tranquil Isle of Mull. From the pretty fisherman's cottages - now hotel and restaurant - you can gaze out onto the harbourside filled with colourful boats. It's a friendly, local operation and every effort is made to make you feel at ease. Bright and vibrant bedrooms come in a variety of sizes; all are cosy and comfortable. Cooking is simple and to the point and the kitchen aims to let the high quality local produce speak for itself. A typical menu could include Island mussels in garlic, dill and lemon sauce, roast rack of lamb with potato purée and port jus, and apple and cinnamon crumble with rum and raisin ice cream to finish.

Rooms 16 (2 fmly) (2 GF) **S** £38-£65; **D** £76-£128 (incl. bkfst)* **Facilities** FTV New Year Wi-fi **Conf** Class 26 Board 15 Thtr 26 **Notes** Closed Xmas

Chef Helen Swinbanks **Owner** Mr & Mrs I Stevens **Times** 6-9 Closed Xmas, Jan, L all week **Prices** Fixed D 3 course £25.50-£31.50, Service optional **Wines** 22 bottles over £20, 18 bottles under £20, 5 by glass **Notes** Vegetarian available **Seats** 30 **Children** Portions, Menu **Parking** On street

The Creel Restaurant with Rooms

★★★★ RESTAURANT WITH ROOMS

◉◉ British

Deserved reputation for first-class Orkney produce done right

Front Rd KW17 2SL
☎ **01856 831311**
e-mail: alan@thecreel.freeserve.co.uk
web: www.thecreel.co.uk
dir: A961 into village, establishment on seafront

When you run a restaurant in far-flung Orkney it's probably fair to say that you can't rely on passing trade, so it is a testament to the skill and dedication of husband-and-wife-team Alan and Joyce Craigie that they have built a reputation that has kept foodies turning up at their door

since 1985. The Creel sits in a serene seaside spot with views over the other-worldly seascapes that are a feature of the Orkneys, and is run with an unbuttoned vibe; the simple setting is decorated with local artwork and wooden seabird sculptures. Alan Craigie draws upon ingredients of spectacular purity - less-commonly seen fish species such as ling, wolf-fish, torsk and sea-witch turn up, while the North Ronaldsay sheep that goes into a neck of mutton Pithivier with pearl barley gravy will have been fed on seaweed. With such superb fish to hand, the modern cooking is weighted towards the piscine - perhaps seared diver-caught scallops and steamed plaice with red pepper and onion marmalade, or roasted hake fillet teamed with squid casserole and braised Puy lentils. Three bedrooms allow you to put up for the night and sample the island brewery's excellent ales, and malts from the Highland Park and Scapa distilleries. The stylish bedrooms are appointed to a high standard - most enjoy views over the bay - and breakfast is not to be missed, with local Orkney produce and freshly baked breads on the menu.

Rooms 3 en suite **S** £70-£80; **D** £110-£120* **Facilities** Dinner available Cen ht **Parking** 6 **Notes** ⊗ Closed mid Oct-Apr No coaches

Chef Alan Craigie **Owner** Alan & Joyce Craigie **Times** 7-8.30 Closed mid Oct-Apr, Mon-Tue, L all week **Prices** Fixed D 3 course fr £38, Service optional **Wines** 14 bottles over £20, 8 bottles under £20, 2 by glass **Notes** Vegetarian available **Seats** 20, Pr/dining room 12 **Children** Portions

Shetland

★★★ 73% HOTEL

☎ 01595 695515 🖨 01595 695828
Holmsgarth Rd ZE1 0PW
e-mail: reception@shetlandhotel.co.uk
dir: Opposite ferry terminal, on main road N from town centre

This purpose-built hotel, situated opposite the main ferry terminal, offers spacious and comfortable bedrooms on three floors. Two dining options are available - the informal Oasis bistro and Ninians Restaurant. Service is prompt and friendly.

Rooms 64 (4 fmly) **S** £89; **D** £120 (incl. bkfst)*
Facilities FTV Wi-fi **Conf** Class 75 Board 50 Thtr 300
Services Lift **Parking** 150 **Notes** ⊗

Glen Orchy House

★★★★ GUEST HOUSE

20 Knab Rd ZE1 0AX
☎ 01595 692031 📄 01595 692031
e-mail: glenorchy.house@virgin.net
dir: Next to coastguard station

This welcoming and well-presented house lies above the town with views over the Knab, and is within easy walking distance of the town centre. Bedrooms are modern in design and there is a choice of lounges with books and board games, one with an honesty bar. Substantial breakfasts are served, and the restaurant offers a delicious Thai menu.

Rooms 24 en suite (4 fmly) (4 GF) S £65; D £90*
Facilities STV FTV TVL tea/coffee Dinner available Cen ht Licensed Wi-fi **Parking** 10 **Notes** Closed 25-26 Dec & 1-2 Jan

ISLE OF SKYE

ARDVASAR   Map 4 NG60

Ardvasar Hotel

★★★ 74% SMALL HOTEL

☎ 01471 844223 📄 01471 844495
Sleat IV45 8RS
e-mail: richard@ardvasar-hotel.demon.co.uk
web: www.ardvasarhotel.com
dir: From ferry, 500mtrs, left signed Ardvasar

Beside the road towards the southern tip of Skye, sit out front to drink in the extraordinary views to the rocky foreshore, Sound of Sleat and the mountains of the Knoydart Peninsula, a ferry ride away via Mallaig. Once you've sipped your Skye-brewed beer or local malt, retire to the comfy lounge bar or dining room to indulge in some of Skye's most renowned seafood meals; the local boats may land salmon, crab, lobster or scallops. Estate venison and Aberdeen Angus beef extend the choice. Residents in the individually designed rooms can look to a fine Scottish breakfast to set another day in paradise going.

Rooms 10 (4 fmly) **Facilities** FTV 🎵 Xmas New Year Wi-fi **Conf** Board 24 Thtr 50 **Parking** 30 **Notes** LB

Open all day all wk 11am-mdnt (Sun noon-11pm) **Bar Meals** L served all wk 12-2.30 D served all wk 5.30-9
⊕ FREE HOUSE 🍺 IPA, Isle of Skye Red Cuillin.
Facilities Children welcome Children's menu Children's portions Dogs allowed Garden

BROADFORD   Map 4 NG62

Broadford Hotel

★★★★ 74% SMALL HOTEL

☎ 01471 822204 📄 01471 822414
IV49 9AB
e-mail: broadford@macleodhotels.co.uk
dir: From Skye Bridge take A87 towards Portree. Hotel at end of village on left

A stylish modern hotel, in the centre of this charming town, that has been appointed to a high standard and offers all the creature comforts. Many of the spacious bedrooms have wonderful sea views and all are attractively presented and very well equipped. Meals can be enjoyed in the fine-dining restaurant or more informal options are served in traditional bar.

Rooms 11 (1 fmly) **Facilities** STV Fishing 🎵 Xmas New Year Wi-fi **Conf** Class 80 Board 50 Thtr 150 **Parking** 20 **Notes** LB Civ Wed 100

CARBOST   Map 4 NG33

The Old Inn

IV47 8SR ☎ 01478 640205 📄 01478 640205
e-mail: enquiries@theoldinnskye.co.uk
web: www.theoldinnskye.co.uk
dir: From Skye Bridge follow A87 north. Take A863, then B8009 to inn

On the shores of Loch Harport and near the Talisker distillery, The Old Inn is a charming, 200-year-old island cottage and is very popular among the walking and climbing fraternity. Arrive early for a table on the waterside patio and savour the breathtaking views of the Cuillin Hills with a pint of Hebridean Ale in hand. Inside, open fires welcome winter visitors, and live music is a regular feature. With a great selection of real ales, the menu includes daily home-cooked specials, with numerous fresh fish dishes, including local prawns and oysters and mackerel from the loch.

Open all day all wk 11am-mdnt **Bar Meals** L served all wk 12-9.30 D served all wk food served all day **Restaurant** D served all wk food served all day ⊕ FREE HOUSE 🍺 Red Cuillin, Black Cuillin, Hebridean Ale, Cuillin Skye Ale, Pinnacle Ale. **Facilities** Children welcome Children's portions Family room Dogs allowed Garden Parking Wi-fi

Map 4 NG24

The Three Chimneys & the House Over-By

 Modern Scottish NOTABLE WINE LIST

Matchless produce immaculately cooked in a wild, romantic setting

☎ 01470 511258
IV55 8ZT
e-mail: eatandstay@threechimneys.co.uk
web: www.threechimneys.co.uk
dir: 5m W of Dunvegan take B884 signed Glendale. On left beside loch

The old crofter's cottage lies down a single track road on the shore of Loch Dunvegan amid the mystical beauty of the Isle of Skye's landscapes - an elemental setting that places it high on the wish list of many a foodie. That such special food is on offer in a wildly remote location seems an amazing feat to pull off, yet it is the peerless produce from the island that underpins the whole experience. Simplicity is the key to the low-beamed dining room, where bare-stone walls, head-grazing beams and homely fireplaces all contribute to an air of heart-warming domestic intimacy. Fixed-price menus change each day and are designed to celebrate the lamb, beef and venison reared on the island's hills, the herbs and vegetables grown in its crofts and gardens, and the pick of whatever is landed fresh that day from the sea; few places can boast such a sense of terroir. The food impresses with effortless craftsmanship and creativity, with chef Michael Smith delivering fine-tuned flavours in the modern Scottish idiom - everything is built on the ethos of treating superb raw materials with the respect they deserve. And 2011 saw the addition of a spanking new kitchen. A perfectly composed starter unites tartare of Armadale mackerel with cucumber and radish salad, apple and herring roe, for example. Next comes pot-roasted crown of partridge, cooked to perfect tenderness and teamed with tattie scones, choucroute of preserved leg, ceps and Savoy cabbage and elderberry sauce. To finish, the hot marmalade pudding with Drambuie custard is a fixture, but dark chocolate and amaretti delice with blueberries and crème fraîche delivers temptingly big flavours. The wine list is a fine piece of work, too, and does justice to the superb food. Bedrooms, in the House Over-By, are creative and thoughtfully equipped - all have spacious en suites and wonderful views across Loch Dunvegan. Breakfast is an impressive array of local fish, meats and cheeses, served with fresh home baking and home-made preserves, and the stylish lounge-breakfast area has the real wow factor.

Rooms 6 en suite (1Fmly) (6 GF) **Facilities** TV 6 STV FTV Tea/coffee Cen ht Direct dial Wi-fi **Parking** 8 **Notes** RS Sun & 31 Oct-Mar (no lunch) LB ✆

Chef Michael Smith **Owner** Eddie & Shirley Spear
Times 12.15-1.45/6.15-9.45 Closed 6-21 Jan, L Sun & Nov-Mar **Prices** Fixed L 2 course fr £27.50, Fixed D 4 course fr

£60, Tasting menu £85, Service optional, Groups min 8 service 10% **Wines** 180 bottles over £20 **Notes** Tasting menu 7 course, Vegetarian tasting menu on request, Vegetarian available, Dress restrictions, Smart casual preferred **Seats** 40, Pr/dining room 12 **Children** Portions

Map 4 NG35

Shorefield House

★★★★ 🏠 GUEST HOUSE

IV51 9PW
☎ 01470 582444
e-mail: stay@shorefield-house.com
dir: 12m from Portree & 8m from Dunvegan, off A850 into Edinbane, 1st on right

Shorefield stands in the village of Edinbane and looks out to Loch Greshornish. Bedrooms range from single to family, while one ground-floor room has easier access. All rooms are thoughtfully equipped and have CD players. Breakfast is an impressive choice and there is also a child-friendly garden.

Rooms 3 en suite (1 fmly) (2 GF) D £80-£97 **Facilities** STV FTV TVL tea/coffee Cen ht Wi-fi **Parking** 10 **Notes** LB ✆ Closed Xmas

Map 4 NG71

Duisdale House

★★★★ 81% SMALL HOTEL

 Modern 🖐

Modern Scottish cooking in remotest southern Skye

☎ 01471 833202 🖨 01471 833404
IV43 8QW
e-mail: info@duisdale.com
web: www.duisdale.com
dir: 7m S of Bradford on A851 towards Armadale. 7m N of Armadale ferry

Ensconced in the conservatory dining room, with views over the bleakly beautiful Sleat sound at the southern tip of Skye, you'll not readily find yourself hankering after urban bustle. If location is everything, the Duisdale would appear to have it licked. Each bedroom is individually designed and the superior rooms have four-poster beds. The eye-catching modern dining room with its red arched walls, high-backed designer chairs and views over the garden does hint at rarefied city style, and the menus reinforce that feeling of being in remote contact with the modern world, with offerings such as Skye scallops on courgette and saffron risotto with crisp ham and caper butter, saddle of lamb in herb and pine nut crust with potato gratin, garlic purée and spinach in a port-based jus, and dark chocolate fondant served with honeycomb, orange caramel and balsamic ice cream.

Rooms 18 (1 fmly) (1 GF) **S** £90-£180; **D** £170-£260 (incl. bkfst) **Facilities** STV Private yacht Outdoor hydropool Xmas New Year Wi-fi **Conf** Board 28 Thtr 50 Del from £167 to £230 **Parking** 30 **Notes** LB ⊗ Civ Wed 58

Chef George McCallum **Owner** K Gunn & A Gracie **Times** 12-2.30/6.30-9 **Prices** Fixed D 4 course £45, Service optional **Wines** 55 bottles over £20, 8 bottles under £20, 9 by glass **Notes** Vegetarian available, Dress restrictions, Smart casual **Seats** 50 **Children** Portions

Kinloch Lodge

★★★ COUNTRY HOUSE HOTEL

◉◉◉ French, Scottish **V** NOTABLE WINE LIST 🖐

The best of the Skye larder in Baronial splendour

☎ 01471 833214 & 833333   📠 01471 833277
IV43 8QY
e-mail: reservations@kinloch-lodge.co.uk
web: www.kinloch-lodge.co.uk
dir: 6m S of Broadford on A851, 10m N of Armadale on A851

The Highland pile at the foot of Kinloch Hill on the shore of Loch Na Dal amid the rugged landscapes of Sleat is home to food and cookery writer Claire Macdonald, or Lady Macdonald, since Kinloch Lodge is the 16th-century seat of her husband, the High Chief of Clan Donald. This, then, is a family home, but instead of prosaic family photos, oil paintings of generations of Macdonald lairds look down from the walls of the formal dining room where crisp white linen-clad tables are laid with posh plates and vintage silver cutlery. The whole house is well versed in the traditions of family hospitality: staff are helpful and affable, bedrooms and bathrooms are well appointed and comfortable, and public areas boast numerous open fires and relaxing areas to sit, while in the kitchen chef Marcello Tully stocks his larder with the pick of local, seasonal supplies. Well-balanced and creative modern Scottish dishes are presented with great flair, starting with perfectly-judged seared scallops with butternut squash risotto and crispy pancetta, before fillet of Mallaig cod with deep-fried red pepper gnocchi, roast cherry tomatoes, chargrilled vegetables and caper pesto. To finish, velvety avocado delice with dark chocolate ice cream and crème anglaise is a surprising yet intriguingly successsful combination. The wine list is well worth exploring. If you are inspired by all this, there is a

cookery school run by Claire MacDonald and a shop that sells her famous cookery books and produce.

Rooms 15 (8 annexe) (1 GF) **S** £240-£290; **D** £300-£420 (incl. bkfst & dinner)* **Facilities** STV FTV Fishing New Year Wi-fi **Conf** Class 20 Board 20 Thtr 20 **Parking** 40

Chef Marcello Tully **Owner** Lord & Lady Macdonald **Times** 12-2.30/6.30-9 Closed 1 wk Xmas **Prices** Fixed L 2 course £26.99, Fixed D 3 course £60, Service optional **Wines** 200 bottles over £20, 16 by glass **Notes** Tasting menu available, Sunday L, Vegetarian menu **Seats** 40, Pr/dining room 20 **Children** Portions

Toravaig House Hotel

★★★ 81% SMALL HOTEL

◉◉ Modern 🍃

Stylish haven of peace serving Skye's wonderful produce

☎ 01471 820200 & 833231   📠 01471 833231
Knock Bay IV44 8RE
e-mail: info@skyehotel.co.uk
web: www.skyehotel.co.uk
dir: From Skye Bridge, left at Broadford onto A851, hotel 11m on left. Or from ferry at Armadale take A851, hotel 6m on right

The elemental landscape of the Isle of Skye is all very well but you need the cosseting comforts of a chic boutique retreat, with stylish, well-equipped and beautifully decorated bedrooms, to soothe away the day's exertions after taking on nature in the raw. Seriously good food should ideally be part of the equation too, so Toravaig House ticks all the right boxes - a heavenly bolt-hole with dollops of contemporary style in an achingly beautiful setting overlooking the Sound of Sleat and the Knoydart Hills over on the mainland skyline. If your sea legs are up to it, go sailing on the hotel's own yacht, (available April to September) and you'll come to dinner in the Iona Restaurant ready to do full justice to the island's matchless produce that forms the bedrock of the highly-polished modern food. Dinner menus are well thought through and impress with their unshowy, well-balanced ideas - perhaps sea bass with scallop mousse and fennel and asparagus salad to start, while main course could bring local turbot with chicken wing, confit new potatoes, salsify, samphire and basil oil. Finish

continued

ISLEORNSAY CONTINUED

with lemon and tonka bean cheesecake with passionfruit jelly and gorseflower ice cream.

Rooms 9 **S** £75-£190; **D** £130-£230 (incl. bkfst)
Facilities STV Daily excursions (Apr-Sep) on hotel yacht Xmas New Year Wi-fi **Conf** Board 10 Thtr 15 Del from £100 to £200 **Parking** 15 **Notes** LB ⊗ Civ Wed 25

Chef Chris Braphay **Owner** Anne Gracie & Ken Gunn
Times 12.30-2.30/6.30-9.30 **Prices** Fixed D 4 course £48.50, Service optional **Wines** 48 bottles over £20, 20 bottles under £20, 6 by glass **Notes** Vegetarian available, Dress restrictions, Smart casual **Seats** 25 **Children** Portions

Hotel Eilean Iarmain

★★★ 78% SMALL HOTEL

◉◉ Traditional Scottish

Stunning views and accomplished Scottish cooking

☎ 01471 833332 📄 01471 833275
IV43 8QR
e-mail: hotel@eileaniarmain.co.uk
web: www.eileaniarmain.co.uk
dir: A851, A852, right to Isleornsay harbour

The waters of the Sound of Sleat are only a few yards from the door of this ninth-century former hunting lodge, and the view across to the Isle Ornsay lighthouse and the mainland hills beyond is rather special. Bedrooms are individual and retain a traditional style, and a stable block has been converted into four delightful suites. A seat by the window in the restaurant is a prize worth having. Mind you, you don't have to be sitting hard by the glass to appreciate the vista, nor, of course, to enjoy the beautifully presented modern Scottish cooking. Starting with a drink in the charmingly traditional lounge is never a bad idea, especially if the fire is lit. The bountiful produce from around these parts gets a good showing on the menu, but the cooking is far from parochial - this is confident, ambitious modern stuff. Hot-and-sour langoustine broth, for example, with broad beans and flavoured with coriander, chilli and lemongrass, shows a sure hand in the kitchen, and is full of fabulously plump langoustines. Next up, perhaps pan-seared rack of Highland lamb with black pudding mash, baby vegetables and pan juices, or herb-crusted halibut with king prawn tortellini and pearl barley broth.

Rooms 16 (10 annexe) (4 fmly) (3 GF) **S** £75-£145; **D** £110-£250 (incl. bkfst) **Facilities** FTV Fishing Shooting Exhibitions Whisky tasting 🎵 Xmas New Year Wi-fi **Conf** Class 10 Board 14 Thtr 25 Del from £150 to £195 **Parking** 20 **Notes** LB Civ Wed 30

Chef Marius Wilczynski **Owner** Lady Lucilla Noble
Times 12-2.30/6.30-8.45 **Prices** Fixed L 3 course £16-£22.50, Fixed D 3 course £38.50-£42.50, Service optional

Wines 60 bottles over £20, 10 bottles under £20, 6 by glass **Notes** Sunday L, Vegetarian available, Dress restrictions, Smart casual **Seats** 40, Pr/dining room 22 **Children** Portions, Menu

Cuillin Hills

★★★★ 77% HOTEL

◉◉ Traditional

Modern Scottish cooking in hotel with stunning views

☎ 01478 612003 📄 01478 613092
IV51 9QU
e-mail: info@cuillinhills-hotel-skye.co.uk
web: www.cuillinhills-hotel-skye.co.uk
dir: Right 0.25m N of Portree off A855. Follow hotel signs

Originally built as a hunting lodge for the Isle of Skye's then Lord Macdonald, this fabulous country-house hotel stands in 15 acres of mature grounds with magnificent views over Portree Bay, the Sound of Raasay and the cockscomb crags of the Cuillin Mountain range. Accommodation is provided in smart, well-equipped rooms that are generally spacious; some rooms are found in an adjacent building. When you call your restaurant 'The View' you had better come up with the scenic goods, and this split-level space does not disappoint, with a classic ivory and white interior hung with an ever-changing cast of works by local artists to entertain the eye, as well as nature's splendour outside the windows. The kitchen waves the Scottish flag for superb West Coast materials, which are brought together with European-accented influences - perhaps seared local scallops with cauliflower purée and bhaji and curried oil, followed by roast monkfish wrapped in pancetta and teamed with Parmentier potatoes and peperonata. Finish French-style with a citrus crème brûlée with vanilla shortbread.

Rooms 26 (7 annexe) (3 fmly) (8 GF) **Facilities** STV Xmas New Year Wi-fi **Conf** Class 60 Board 40 Thtr 100 **Parking** 56 **Notes** Civ Wed 45

Chef Chris Donaldson, John Geddes **Owner** Wickman Hotels **Times** 6.30-9 Closed L all week **Prices** Food prices not confirmed for 2012. Please telephone for details **Wines** 11 bottles under £20, 45 by glass **Notes** Sunday L, Vegetarian available **Seats** 40

Rosedale

★★★ 75% HOTEL

☎ 01478 613131 📠 01478 612531
Beaumont Crescent IV51 9DF
e-mail: rosedalehotelsky@aol.com
web: www.rosedalehotelskye.co.uk
dir: Follow directions to village centre & harbour

A trio of fishermen's cottages were knocked together in the 1960s to make this welcoming family-run hotel on the harbour front of the principal town on Skye. The atmosphere is wonderfully warm and friendly, and a labyrinth of stairs and corridors connects the comfortable lounges, bar and restaurant, which are set on different levels. Modern bedrooms offer a good range of amenities. A wealth of seabirds and marine mammals can often be spotted from the first-floor dining room, where well-executed traditional Scottish cooking, with seafood a notable strong point, is the order of the day.

Rooms 18 (1 fmly) (3 GF) **S** £40-£65; **D** £70-£150 (incl. bkfst)* **Facilities** Wi-fi **Parking** 2 **Notes** LB Closed Nov-mid Mar

SKEABOST BRIDGE   Map 4 NG44

Skeabost Country House

★★★ 75% COUNTRY HOUSE HOTEL

❀ Modern British **V**

Wide-ranging menus in a lochside hotel

☎ 01470 532202 & 08444 146572 📠 01470 532761
IV51 9NP
e-mail: manager.skeabost@ohiml.com
web: www.oxfordhotelsandinns.com
dir: From Skye Bridge on A87, through Portree towards Uig. Left onto A850, hotel on right

Its white walls contrasting vividly with the green of the hills, this luxury small hotel is right at the edge of Loch Snizort

and has wonderful views over the water. Originally built as a hunting lodge by the MacDonalds and steeped in history, Skeabost offers caring and helpful staff, charming day rooms and well appointed accommodation. The menus show a kitchen using fine native ingredients, and dinner, served in the panelled dining room overlooking the loch, could kick off with grilled haggis with asparagus tips, a poached egg and hollandaise, and go on to sirloin steak with the usual trimmings. Bolder combinations are successful too, judging by beetroot and goats' cheese tart served with pickled red cabbage, and sea bass baked with ginger, garlic and coriander accompanied by wild rice and tempura vegetables. Cranachan is a fitting way in which to finish.

Rooms 14 (5 GF) **Facilities** STV FTV ⅃ 9 Xmas New Year Wi-fi **Conf** Class 20 Board 20 Thtr 40 Del from £100 to £180* **Parking** 40 **Notes** LB Civ Wed 100

Owner Oxford Hotels & Inns **Times** 12-3/6-9.30
Prices Starter £4-£9, Main £12-£25, Dessert £4-£9, Service optional **Wines** 17 bottles over £20, 26 bottles under £20, 6 by glass **Notes** Tasting menu available, Sunday L, Vegetarian menu, Dress restrictions, Smart casual **Seats** 50, Pr/dining room 70 **Children** Portions, Menu

STAFFIN   Map 4 NG46

Flodigarry Country House

★★★ 78% COUNTRY HOUSE HOTEL

❀ Modern Scottish **V**

Good Scottish produce and majestic views

☎ 01470 552203 📠 01470 552301
IV51 9HZ
e-mail: info@flodigarry.co.uk
web: www.flodigarry.co.uk
dir: A855 from Portree, through Staffin to Flodigarry, hotel signed on right

Originally a Victorian hunting lodge, this charming place is located in woodlands on The Quiraing in north-east Skye, overlooking the sea towards the Torridon Mountains. The dramatic scenery is a real inspiration here, and the hotel serves up genuine Highland hospitality, breathtaking views and appealing Scottish food. You get the views from the restaurant (panoramic ones, over the sea towards the Torridon mountains) and there's bit of Scottish history for good measure - Flora MacDonald used to live here. Locally-caught seafood and shellfish figure large on the modern Scottish menu, which is a very good thing indeed given the location, but all ingredients are sourced with due diligence. Start with twice-baked crab soufflé or home-smoked Scottish salmon with celeriac remoulade, followed by grilled Skye langoustines or pan-roasted fillet of venison.

Rooms 18 (7 annexe) (3 fmly) (4 GF) **S** £80-£135; **D** £100-£210 (incl. bkfst)* **Facilities** FTV Xmas New Year

continued

Wi-fi **Parking** 40 **Notes** LB Closed Nov-15 Dec & Jan
Civ Wed 80

Chef John McLeish **Owner** Robin Collins
Times 12-2.30/7-9.30 Closed Nov & Jan, L Mon-Sat
Prices Starter £7.50-£17.50, Main £16-£35, Dessert £6.50-
£8.50, Service included **Wines** 29 bottles over £20, 8 bottles
under £20, 4 by glass **Notes** Sunday L, Vegetarian menu,
Dress restrictions, Smart casual **Seats** 30, Pr/dining room 24
Children Portions, Menu

The Glenview

⭐⭐⭐ RESTAURANT WITH ROOMS

◉ British, French 🍮

Traditionally based cooking in a homely hotel

Culnacnoc IV51 9JH
☎ 01470 562248
e-mail: enquiries@glenviewskye.co.uk
dir: 12m N of Portree on A855

The late-Victorian croft building near Staffin on the north-
east corner of Skye was once the Culnacnoc village shop.
Now a homely, white-fronted hotel, it offers individually
styled, comfortable bedrooms (front-facing rooms enjoy the
dramatic views) and, in the dining room, some simple,
traditionally based, but lightly modernised cooking based on
Highland and island ingredients, presented in the form of
daily-changing menus. You might start with artichoke soup
garnished with Sconser scallops and curry oil, and proceed
to Orbost beef with red onion sauce and mustard mash, or
cumin-scented rabbit with baby carrots, crispy polenta and
parsley dressing. Achmore crème fraîche and butterscotch
sauce are the accompaniments to a satisfying finisher of
baked chocolate mousse.

Rooms 5 en suite (1 GF) **Facilities** tea/coffee Dinner
available Wi-fi **Parking** 12 **Notes** ⊗ RS Sun & Mon closed

Chef Simon Wallwork **Owner** Kirsty Faulds **Times** 7-8.30
Closed Jan, Sun-Mon, L all week **Prices** Food prices not
confirmed for 2012. Please telephone for details **Wines** 10
bottles over £20, 10 bottles under £20, 4 by glass
Notes Vegetarian available **Seats** 22 **Children** Portions

Loch Bay Seafood Restaurant

◉ British Seafood 🍮

Straightforward seafood cookery by the bay

☎ 01470 592235
MacLeod Ter IV55 8GA
e-mail: reservations@lochbay-seafood-restaurant.co.uk
dir: 4m off A850 by B886

The lane fizzles out between a straggle of former fishermen's
cottages and the shore of the bay in north-west Skye. It feels
like the middle of absolutely nowhere, but the journey is
worth it for the views, the unruffled silence, and the dead
straight fish and seafood cookery of this homely little
restaurant. Look to the blackboard for the day's catch, and
expect hearty fish soup, crab and lobster risotto, monkfish
medallions in garlic butter, or halibut fillet in white wine
sauce. Lingering summer lunches are a particular pleasure,
and you'll be glad of a hot clootie dumpling to see you on
your way whatever the weather.

Chef David Wilkinson **Owner** David & Alison Wilkinson
Times 12-2/6-9 Closed Nov-Etr, Sun-Mon **Prices** Starter
£4.05-£10.40, Main £13-£22.55, Dessert £4.90-£5.70,
Service optional, Groups min 8 service 10% **Wines** 24
bottles over £20, 13 bottles under £20, 6 by glass
Notes Blackboard choices, child portions L, Vegetarian
available **Seats** 23 **Parking** 6

Stein Inn ☻

Macleod's Ter IV55 8GA ☎ 01470 592362
e-mail: angus.teresa@steininn.co.uk
dir: A87 from Portree. In 5m take A850 for 15m. Right onto
B886, 3m to T-junct. Turn left

The seas around Skye abound with fish while the land
supports sheep, wild venison and highland cattle. This inn,
the oldest on the island, offers fine food, and an impressive
selection of drinks: fine wines, real ales and no fewer than a
hundred malt whiskies. Highland meat, game and local
seafood feature strongly on the daily-changing menu, in
dishes such as Skye scallops in oatmeal, steak braised in
Skye ale, and Highland venison pie. Lunchtime bar food
includes local crab sandwiches, smoked salmon platter and
haggis toastie.

Open all day all wk 11am-mdnt Closed: 25 Dec, 1 Jan **Bar
Meals** L served all wk 12-4 D served all wk 6-9.30 Av main
course £8 **Restaurant** D served all wk 6-9.30 Av 3 course à
la carte fr £17.90 ⊕ FREE HOUSE ◗ Red Cuillin, Trade
Winds, Reeling Deck, Deuchars IPA, Dark Island. ☻ 9
Facilities Children welcome Children's menu Children's
portions Play area Family room Dogs allowed Garden Parking
Wi-fi

STRUAN   Map 4 NG33

Ullinish Country Lodge

★★★★★ 🛏 RESTAURANT WITH ROOMS

◉◉◉ Modern French **V** 🐾

Culinary paradise for foodies in an idyllic Skye setting

IV56 8FD

☎ 01470 572214 📠 01470 572341

e-mail: ullinish@theisleofskye.co.uk
web: www.theisleofskye.co.uk
dir: N on A863

Jaw-dropping views are just one of the attractions that bring visitors out to this far-flung corner of Scotland. Tucked away down an elusive track, the vista that greets you at Ullinish is truly memorable, embraced by three lochs and watched over by the Black Cuillins and MacLeod's Tables - it's hardly surprising that literary travellers Samuel Johnson and James Boswell chose to hole up in the 300-year-old farmhouse for a while in 1773, commenting that 'there is a plentiful garden in Ullinish'. Modern guests will find a comfortingly traditional interior that has survived the country-house vogue for boutique makeovers, and would not have upset the two companions; as you would expect, all bedrooms have amazing views, and come with half-tester beds; while in the dining room, wood-panels and a tartan carpet serve to remind you where you are. The island's excellent local larder ensures a sound basis for chef Craig Halliday's imaginative modern cooking; polished classical technique is deployed to great effect, pulling off full-on, sharply-defined flavours in sometimes off-the-wall combinations. A starter of pan-fried tuna Niçoise with 60-degree egg yolk, sautéed baby gem lettuce, black olive purée and anchovies delivers an array of dazzling flavours, while all the stops are pulled out for an ambitious, strikingly-presented main-course assemblage of pan-roasted sea bass with potato scales, shaved fennel salad, smoked horseradish and potato espuma, sweet-cured wild mushrooms, pressed tomato, and basil jelly. Dessert deploys plenty of cheffy technique with warm carrot cake topped with ginger beer foam and served with crème fraîche jelly, candied carrots and carrot sorbet.

Rooms 6 en suite S £90-£120; D £125-£165* **Facilities** tea/coffee Dinner available Cen ht **Parking** 8 **Notes** LB ⊗ No Children 16yrs Closed Jan & 1wk Nov No coaches

Chef Craig Halliday **Owner** Brian & Pam Howard
Times 7.30-8.30 Closed Jan, 1 wk Nov, L all week
Prices Fixed D 4 course £44.95, Service optional **Wines** 55 bottles over £20, 10 bottles under £20, 22 by glass
Notes Vegetarian menu, Dress restrictions, Smart casual, No T-shirts **Seats** 22

UIG   Map 4 NG36

Woodbine House

★★★ GUEST ACCOMMODATION

IV51 9XP

☎ 01470 542243 & 07904 267561

e-mail: contact@skyeactivities.co.uk
dir: From Portree into Uig Bay, pass Ferry Inn & right onto A855 Staffin Rd, house 300yds on right

Built in the late 19th century, Woodbine House occupies an elevated position overlooking Uig Bay and the surrounding countryside, and is well suited for walking and bird-watching enthusiasts. The ground-floor dining room has lovely sea views, as do the front-facing bedrooms.

Rooms 5 en suite (1 fmly) (1 GF) S £50-£64; D £64-£69*
Facilities FTV TVL tea/coffee Dinner available Cen Wi-fi Archery Mountain bike/sea kayak hire & boat trips **Parking** 4
Notes LB ⊗ RS Nov-Feb long stays or group bookings only

SOUTH UIST

LOCHBOISDALE   Map 4 NF71

The Polochar Inn

Polochar HS8 5TT ☎ 01878 700215 📠 01878 700768
e-mail: polocharinn@aol.com
dir: W from Lochboisdale, take B888. Hotel at end of road

By the water's edge in a beautiful location at the tip of South Uist, this mid-18th-century inn was once the change-house, where travellers caught the island's ferry. Sibling owners Morag MacKinnon and Margaret Campbell specialise in local seafood, meats and pastas, which are served in a dining room with outstanding views of the sea, the islands of Barra and Eriskay, and even dolphins playing. On summer Saturday nights the public bar echoes to live music.

Open all day all wk 11-11 (Fri-Sat 11am-1am Sun 12.30pm-1am) **Bar Meals** L served Mon-Sat 12.30-8.30, Sun 1-8.30 (winter all wk 12-2.30) D served Mon-Sat 12.30-8.30, Sun 1-8.30 (winter all wk 5-8.30) food served all day ⊕ FREE HOUSE ◧ Hebridean ales, Guest ales. **Facilities** Children welcome Children's menu Children's portions Family room Garden Parking Wi-fi

LOCATION INDEX

Contents

DINGWALL	133	GLENROTHES	109
DOLLAR	57	GLENSHEE (SPITTAL OF)	184
DORNOCH	133	GOLSPIE	141
DRUMNADROCHIT	134	GRANGEMOUTH	103
DRYMEN	209	GRANTOWN-ON-SPEY	141
DUMBARTON	74	GREENOCK	168
DUMFRIES	58	GRETNA SERVICE AREA	
DUNDEE	75	(A74(M))	61
DUNFERMLINE	107	GRETNA (WITH GRETNA GREEN)	60
DUNOON	38	GULLANE	173
EAST CALDER	174	HAMILTON	172
EAST KILBRIDE	171	HAWICK	200
EDDLESTON	199	HELENSBURGH	39
EDINBANE	220	HOUSTON	197
EDINBURGH	76	HOWWOOD	197
ELGIN	180	HUNTLY	27
ELIE	108	INNERLEITHEN	200
ERISKA	39	INVERGARRY	142
ETTRICK	200	INVERGORDON	143
EVANTON	134	INVERIE	143
FALKIRK	103	INVERKEILOR	33
FAULDHOUSE	175	INVERKEITHING	109
FINTRY	210	INVERNESS	144
FOCHABERS	181	INVERURIE	27
FORT AUGUSTUS	134	IRVINE	50
FORTINGALL	183	ISLE OF WHITHORN	61
FORTROSE	135	ISLEORNSAY	220
FORT WILLIAM	135	JEDBURGH	201
FOYERS	140	KELSO	201
GAIRLOCH	140	KENMORE	185
GALASHIELS	200	KILCHRENAN	40
GATEHEAD	48	KILDRUMMY	27
GATEHOUSE OF FLEET	60	KILFINAN	41
GIFFORD	173	KILLIECRANKIE	185
GLASGOW AIRPORT	196	KILMACOLM	168
GLASGOW	116	KILMARNOCK	49
GLENCOE	141	KINCARDINE	109
GLENDEVON	184	KINCLAVEN	186
GLENEAGLES	184	KINGUSSIE	152
GLENFARG	184	KINLOCH RANNOCH	186
GLENFINNAN	141	KINNESSWOOD	187

KINROSS	187	NEW GALLOWAY	67
KIPPEN	210	NEW LANARK	172
KIRKBEAN	62	NEWTONMORE	158
KIRKCALDY	110	NEWTON STEWART	67
KIRKCUDBRIGHT	62	NORTH BALLACHULISH	158
KIRK YETHOLM	202	NORTH BERWICK	173
KYLE OF LOCHALSH	153	OBAN	42
KYLESKU	153	OLDMELDRUM	30
LANARK	172	ONICH	158
LANGBANK	198	PEAT INN	111
LANGHOLM	62	PEEBLES	204
LARGS	50	PENICUIK	179
LAUDER	202	PERTH	188
LEITHOLM	203	PETERCULTER	23
LERWICK	218	PETERHEAD	30
LEUCHARS	110	PITLOCHRY	194
LINLITHGOW	175	PLOCKTON	160
LIVINGSTON	177	POLMONT	104
LOCHBOISDALE	225	POOLEWE	161
LOCHEARNHEAD	210	PORT APPIN	46
LOCHGILPHEAD	41	PORT ASKAIG	217
LOCHINVER	154	PORT CHARLOTTE	217
LOCKERBIE	64	PORT OF MENTEITH	211
LONGNIDDRY	173	PORTPATRICK	69
LUSS	41	PORTREE	222
LYBSTER	154	POWFOOT	69
MARKINCH	110	PRESTWICK	53
MARYCULTER	28	RATHO	102
MEIKLEOUR	187	RENFREW	198
MELROSE	203	RHU	47
MILNGAVIE	73	ROSLIN	179
MOFFAT	65	ROY BRIDGE	161
MONTROSE	33	ST ANDREWS	111
MOTHERWELL	170	ST BOSWELLS	205
MUIR OF ORD	154	ST FILLANS	196
MUTHILL	188	ST MARGARET'S HOPE	218
NAIRN	155	ST MONANS	116
NETHERLEY	28	SANDHEAD	69
NETHY BRIDGE	157	SANQUHAR	72
NEWBURGH	28	SCARISTA (SGARASTA BHEAG)	216
NEWCASTLETON	204	SCOURIE	161

SELKIRK	206	SWINTON	206
SHIEL BRIDGE	162	SYMINGTON	53
SHIELDAIG	162	TAIN	165
SKEABOST BRIDGE	223	TARBERT LOCH FYNE	47
SORN	49	TARBERT (TAIRBEART)	216
SOUTH BALLACHULISH	163	TAYVALLICH	48
SOUTH QUEENSFERRY	103	THORNHILL	72
SPEAN BRIDGE	163	THURSO	165
STAFFIN	223	TIBBIE SHIELS INN	206
STEIN	224	TOBERMORY	217
STEPPS	170	TOMATIN	166
STIRLING	211	TORRIDON	166
STONEHAVEN	31	TROON	53
STRACHUR	47	TURNBERRY	56
STRANRAER	72	UIG	225
STRATHAVEN	172	ULLAPOOL	167
STRATHBLANE	212	UPHALL	177
STRATHDON	32	UPLAWMOOR	198
STRATHPEFFER	164	WHITBURN	178
STRATHYRE	212	WHITEBRIDGE	167
STRONTIAN	164	WICK	167
STRUAN	225		

The Automobile Association would like to thank the following photographers, companies and picture libraries for their assistance in the preparation of this book.

Abbreviations for the picture credits are as follows: (t) top; (b) bottom; (l) left; (r) right; (c) centre; (AA) AA World Travel Library.

1 AA/D W Robertson; 3 AA/S Anderson; 7 The Gleneagles Hotel; 9 Photolibrary; 16 AA/J Smith; 21 AA/M Taylor; 29 AA/M Hamblin; 36/7 AA/S Whitehorne; 45 AA/J Carney; 55 AA/M Alexander; 63 AA/S Anderson; 70/1 AA/D Corrance; 81 AA/J Smith; 93 AA/K Paterson; 105 AA/R Weir; 117 AA/M Alexander; 136/7 AA/S Day; 147 AA/J Smith; 159 AA/J Henderson; 190/1 AA/S Whitehorne; 213 AA/R Weir; 214 AA; 238 AA/D Corrance.

Every effort has been made to trace the copyright holders, and we apologise in advance for any unintentional omissions or errors. We would be pleased to apply any corrections in any following edition of this publication.

Establishment Name Index

Linlithgow Palace, birthplace of Mary Queen of Scots

KEY TO ATLAS
AND COUNTY MAP

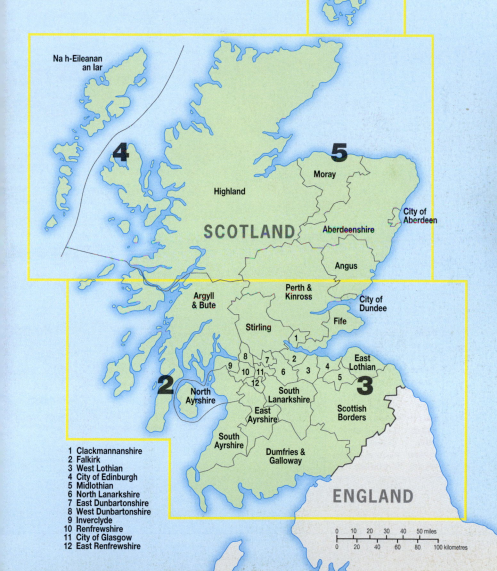

Shetland
Islands

6

Orkney
Islands

Na h-Eileanan
an Iar

4

Moray

5

Highland

City of
Aberdeen

SCOTLAND

Aberdeenshire

Angus

Perth &
Kinross

City of
Dundee

Argyll
& Bute

Fife

Stirling

1

8 7

2

East
Lothian

9

10 11

5

4

3

6

12

North
Ayrshire

2

South
Lanarkshire

Scottish
Borders

3

East
Ayrshire

South
Ayrshire

Dumfries &
Galloway

ENGLAND

1 Clackmannanshire
2 Falkirk
3 West Lothian
4 City of Edinburgh
5 Midlothian
6 North Lanarkshire
7 East Dunbartonshire
8 West Dunbartonshire
9 Inverclyde
10 Renfrewshire
11 City of Glasgow
12 East Renfrewshire

0	10	20	30	40	50 miles
0	20	40	60	80	100 kilometres

2

C EDIN	City of Edinburgh
C GLAS	City of Glasgow
CLACKS	Clackmannanshire
C DUND	City of Dundee
E DUNS	East Dunbartonshire
E RENS	East Renfrewshire
INVER	Inverclyde
MDLOTH	Midlothian
N LANS	North Lanarkshire
RENS	Renfrewshire
W DUNS	West Dunbartonshire
W LOTH	West Lothian

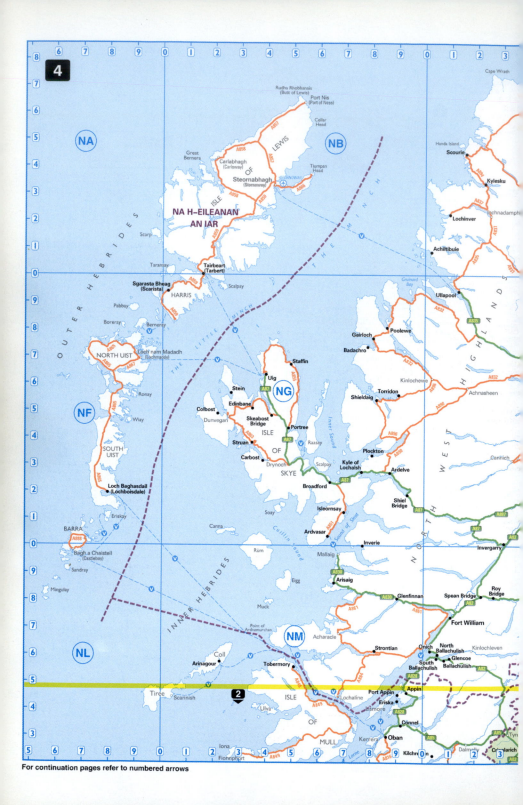

For continuation pages refer to numbered arrows

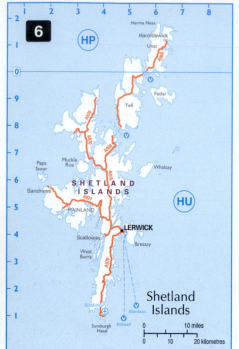

Bed & Breakfast Readers' Report Form

Please send this form to:–
Editor, The B&B Guide,
Lifestyle Guides,
AA Publishing,
Fanum House, FH13
Basingstoke RG21 4EA

or e-mail: lifestyleguides@theAA.com

Use this form to recommend any guest house, farmhouse or inn where you have stayed that is not already in the guide.

If you have any comments about your stay at an establishment listed in the Guide, please let us know, as feedback from readers helps to keep our Guide accurate and up to date. If you have a complaint during your stay, we recommend that you discuss the matter with the establishment.

Please note that the AA does not undertake to arbitrate between you and the establishment, to obtain compensation, or to engage in protracted correspondence.

Date

Your name (BLOCK CAPITALS)

Your address (BLOCK CAPITALS)

Post code

E-mail address

Name of establishment

Comments (Please include the name and address of the establishment)

(please attach a separate sheet if necessary)

Please tick here ☐ if you DO NOT wish to receive details of AA offers or products

PTO

Bed & Breakfast Readers' Report Form *continued*

Have you bought this guide before? ☐ YES ☐ NO

What other accommodation, restaurant, pub or food guides have you bought recently?

....

....

Why did you buy this guide? (tick all that apply)

Holiday ☐   Short break ☐   Business travel ☐   Special occasion ☐   Overnight stop ☐

Conference ☐   Other (please state)

How often do you stay in B&Bs? (tick one choice)

More than once a month ☐   Once a month ☐   Once in two to three months ☐

Once in six months ☐   Once a year ☐   Less than once a year ☐

Please answer these questions to help us make improvements to the guide.

Which of these factors is most important when choosing a B&B?

Price ☐   Location ☐   Awards/ratings ☐   Service ☐   Décor/surroundings ☐

Previous experience ☐   Recommendation ☐

Other (please state)

....

....

Do you read the editorial features in the guide?   ☐ YES ☐ NO

Do you use the location atlas?   ☐ YES ☐ NO

What elements of the guide do you find most useful when choosing somewhere to stay?

Description ☐   Photo ☐   Advertisement ☐   Star rating ☐

Can you suggest any improvements to the guide?

....

....

....

Thank you for completing and returning this form

Hotel Readers' Report Form

Please send this form to:–
Editor, The Hotel Guide,
Lifestyle Guides,
AA Publishing,
Fanum House, FH13
Basingstoke RG21 4EA

or e-mail: lifestyleguides@theAA.com

Please use this form to recommend any hotel where you have stayed, whether it is included in the guide or not currently listed. You can also help us to improve the guide by completing the short questionnaire on the reverse.

The AA does not undertake to arbitrate between guide readers and hotels, or to obtain compensation or engage in protracted correspondence.

Date:

Your name (block capitals)

Your address (block capitals)

....
....
....
....
....

e-mail address:

Name of hotel:

Comments ....
....
....
....
....
....
....

(please attach a separate sheet if necessary)

Please tick here if you DO NOT wish to receive details of AA offers or products ☐

PTO

Hotel Readers' Report Form *continued*

Have you bought this guide before? ☐ YES ☐ NO

Have you bought any other accommodation, restaurant, pub or food guides recently? If yes, which ones?

....

....

....

Why did you buy this guide? (tick all that apply)

holiday ☐   short break ☐   business travel ☐   special occasion ☐

overnight stop ☐   find a venue for an event e.g. conference ☐

other ....

How often do you stay in hotels? (tick one choice)

more than once a month ☐   once a month ☐   once in 2-3 months ☐

once in six months ☐   once a year ☐   less than once a year ☐

Please answer these questions to help us make improvements to the guide:

Which of these factors are most important when choosing a hotel?

price ☐   location ☐   awards/ratings ☐   service ☐

decor/surroundings previous experience recommendation ☐

other (please state) ....

Do you read the editorial features in the guide?   Yes ☐   No ☐

Do you use the location atlas?   Yes ☐   No ☐

What elements of the guide do you find most useful when choosing a place to stay?

description ☐   photo ☐   advertisement ☐   star rating ☐

Can you suggest any improvements to the guide?

....

....

....

....

Pub Readers' Report Form

Please send this form to:–
Editor, The Pub Guide,
Lifestyle Guides,
AA Publishing,
13th Floor, Fanum House,
Basingstoke RG21 4EA

or fax: 01256 491647
or e-mail: lifestyleguides@theAA.com

Please use this form to tell us about any pub or inn you have visited, whether it is in the guide or not currently listed. We are interested in the quality of food, the selection of beers and the overall ambience of the establishment.

Feedback from readers helps us to keep our guide accurate and up to date. However, if you have a complaint to make during a visit, we do recommend that you discuss the matter with the pub management there and then, so that they have a chance to put things right before your visit is spoilt.

Please note that the AA does not undertake to arbitrate between you and the pub management, or to obtain compensation or engage in protracted correspondence.

Date

Your name (BLOCK CAPITALS)

Your address (BLOCK CAPITALS)

Post code

E-mail address

Name of pub

Location

Comments

(please attach a separate sheet if necessary)

Please tick here ☐ if you DO NOT wish to receive details of AA offers or products

PTO

Pub Readers' Report Form *continued*

Have you bought this guide before?   YES ☐ NO ☐

Do you regularly use any other pub,
accommodation or food guides?   YES ☐ NO ☐

If YES, which ones?

_____

What do you find most useful about The AA Pub Guide?

_____

_____

_____

Do you read the editorial features in the guide?   YES ☐ NO ☐

Do you use the location atlas?   YES ☐ NO ☐

Is there any other information you would like to see added to this guide?

_____

_____

_____

What are your main reasons for visiting pubs (tick all that apply)
food ☐   business ☐   accommodation ☐   beer ☐
celebrations ☐   entertainment ☐   atmosphere ☐   leisure ☐
other

How often do you visit a pub for a meal?
more than once a week ☐   once a week ☐   once a fortnight ☐
once a month ☐   once in six months ☐

Restaurant Readers' Report Form

Please send this form to:–
Editor, The Restaurant Guide,
Lifestyle Guides,
AA Publishing,
13th Floor, Fanum House,
Basingstoke RG21 4EA

or e-mail: lifestyleguides@theAA.com

Please use this form to tell us about any restaurant you have visited, whether it is in the guide or not currently listed. Feedback from readers helps us to keep our guide accurate and up to date. Please note, however, that if you have a complaint to make during a visit, we strongly recommend that you discuss the matter with the restaurant management there and then, so that they have a chance to put things right before your visit is spoilt. The AA does not undertake to arbitrate between you and the restaurant management, or to obtain compensation or engage in correspondence.

Date

Your name (BLOCK CAPITALS)

Your address (BLOCK CAPITALS)

Post code

E-mail address

Restaurant name and address: (If you are recommending a new restaurant please enclose a menu or note the dishes that you ate.)

Comments

(please attach a separate sheet if necessary)

We may use information we hold about you to write, e-mail or telephone you about other products and services offered by us and our carefully selected partners, but we can assure you that we will not disclose it to third parties.

Please tick here ☐ if you DO NOT wish to receive details of other products or services from the AA.

PTO

Restaurant Readers' Report Form *continued*

Have you bought this guide before?   YES ☐   NO ☐

Please list any other similar guides that you use regularly

_____

_____

What do you find most useful about The AA Restaurant Guide?

_____

_____

Please answer these questions to help us make improvements to the guide

What are your main reasons for visiting restaurants (tick all that apply)

Business entertaining ☐   Business travel ☐   Trying famous restaurants ☐

Family celebrations ☐   Leisure travel ☐   Trying new food ☐

Enjoying not having to cook yourself ☐   To eat food you couldn't cook yourself ☐

Because I enjoy eating out regularly ☐

Other (please state)

How often do you visit a restaurant for lunch or dinner? (tick one choice)

Once a week ☐   Once a fortnight ☐   Once a month ☐   Less than once a month ☐

Do you use the location atlas ☐ YES ☐ NO?

Do you generally agree with the Rosette ratings at the restaurants you visit in the guide?

(If not please give examples)

_____

Who is your favourite chef?

_____

Which is your favourite restaurant?

_____

Which type of cuisine is your first choice e.g. French

_____

Which of these factors is most important when choosing a restaurant?

Price ☐   Service ☐   Location ☐   Type of food ☐

Awards/ratings ☐   Décor/surroundings ☐

Other (please state)

Which elements of the guide do you find most useful when choosing a restaurant?

Description ☐   Photo ☐   Rosette rating ☐   Price ☐

Other (please state)

Bed & Breakfast Readers' Report Form

Please send this form to:–
Editor, The B&B Guide,
Lifestyle Guides,
AA Publishing,
Fanum House, FH13
Basingstoke RG21 4EA

or e-mail: lifestyleguides@theAA.com

Use this form to recommend any guest house, farmhouse or inn where you have stayed that is not already in the guide.

If you have any comments about your stay at an establishment listed in the Guide, please let us know, as feedback from readers helps to keep our Guide accurate and up to date. If you have a complaint during your stay, we recommend that you discuss the matter with the establishment.

Please note that the AA does not undertake to arbitrate between you and the establishment, to obtain compensation, or to engage in protracted correspondence.

Date

Your name (BLOCK CAPITALS)

Your address (BLOCK CAPITALS)

Post code

E-mail address

Name of establishment

Comments (Please include the name and address of the establishment)

(please attach a separate sheet if necessary)

Please tick here ☐ if you DO NOT wish to receive details of AA offers or products

PTO

Bed & Breakfast Readers' Report Form *continued*

Have you bought this guide before? ☐ YES ☐ NO

What other accommodation, restaurant, pub or food guides have you bought recently?

....

....

Why did you buy this guide? (tick all that apply)

Holiday ☐   Short break ☐   Business travel ☐   Special occasion ☐   Overnight stop ☐

Conference ☐   Other (please state)

How often do you stay in B&Bs? (tick one choice)

More than once a month ☐   Once a month ☐   Once in two to three months ☐

Once in six months ☐   Once a year ☐   Less than once a year ☐

Please answer these questions to help us make improvements to the guide.

Which of these factors is most important when choosing a B&B?

Price ☐   Location ☐   Awards/ratings ☐   Service ☐   Décor/surroundings ☐

Previous experience ☐   Recommendation ☐

Other (please state)

....

....

Do you read the editorial features in the guide? ☐ YES ☐ NO

Do you use the location atlas?   ☐ YES ☐ NO

What elements of the guide do you find most useful when choosing somewhere to stay?

Description ☐   Photo ☐   Advertisement ☐   Star rating ☐

Can you suggest any improvements to the guide?

....

....

....

Thank you for completing and returning this form

Hotel Readers' Report Form

Please send this form to:–
Editor, The Hotel Guide,
Lifestyle Guides,
AA Publishing,
Fanum House, FH13
Basingstoke RG21 4EA

or e-mail: lifestyleguides@theAA.com

Please use this form to recommend any hotel where you have stayed, whether it is included in the guide or not currently listed. You can also help us to improve the guide by completing the short questionnaire on the reverse.

The AA does not undertake to arbitrate between guide readers and hotels, or to obtain compensation or engage in protracted correspondence.

Date:

Your name (block capitals)

Your address (block capitals)

....
....
....
....
....

e-mail address:

Name of hotel:

Comments ....
....
....
....
....
....
....

(please attach a separate sheet if necessary)

Please tick here if you DO NOT wish to receive details of AA offers or products ☐

PTO

Hotel Readers' Report Form *continued*

Have you bought this guide before? ☐ YES ☐ NO

Have you bought any other accommodation, restaurant, pub or food guides recently? If yes, which ones?

....

....

....

Why did you buy this guide? (tick all that apply)

holiday ☐   short break ☐   business travel ☐   special occasion ☐

overnight stop ☐   find a venue for an event e.g. conference ☐

other ....

How often do you stay in hotels? (tick one choice)

more than once a month ☐   once a month ☐   once in 2-3 months ☐

once in six months ☐   once a year ☐   less than once a year ☐

Please answer these questions to help us make improvements to the guide:

Which of these factors are most important when choosing a hotel?

price ☐   location ☐   awards/ratings ☐   service ☐

decor/surroundings previous experience recommendation ☐

other (please state) ....

Do you read the editorial features in the guide?   Yes ☐   No ☐

Do you use the location atlas?   Yes ☐   No ☐

What elements of the guide do you find most useful when choosing a place to stay?

description ☐   photo ☐   advertisement ☐   star rating ☐

Can you suggest any improvements to the guide?

....

....

....

....